RESEARCH IN THE SOCIAL SERVICES

RESEARCH IN THE SOCIAL SERVICES:

A FIVE-YEAR REVIEW

Henry S. Maas, Ph.D., Editor

Professor, School of Social Work
University of British Columbia
Vancouver, B.C., Canada

National Association of Social Workers, Inc.
2 Park Avenue, New York, New York 10016

164880

CONTENTS

INTRODUCTION

The purpose of this book is to update what we presented in the first volume of this series, *Five Fields of Social Service: Reviews of Research.*[1] The authors of chapters in the earlier book were not limited as to how far back into the relevant research literature they could go; their terminal dates were determined by the deadline set for a book initially planned for publication in 1965. With some slight variations, authors of the present chapters have reviewed research reports dating from late 1963 or 1964 to 1969. I hope a third publication will review another span of research from 1970 on.

Research germane to the problems of childhood dependency, family or neighborhood disorganization, and poverty and to the social welfare field's efforts to reduce or remedy such conditions is undertaken and reported under a wide array of auspices. Such research appears in the publications of many scientific disciplines and practicing professions. Jack Rothman's chapter on "Community Organization Practice" demonstrates vividly the broad spread of the literature on which serious students

---

[1] New York: National Association of Social Workers, 1966.

in a rapidly changing field of practice must draw for understanding. His chapter illustrates also the utility of a social work framework for organizing what is known and relevant.

In public welfare much research continues to be reported in highly abbreviated form and in relatively arcane or transient formats. Thus perhaps only a highly placed insider in a federal agency, close to both major funding sources and the return flow of mimeographed progress reports as well as to intramural studies, could provide the kind of comprehensive review Genevieve W. Carter gives in her "Public Welfare" chapter.

Research within child welfare is better established and its products are more readily accessible than in the newly expanding field of community organization and the more diffusely reported field of public welfare. In the past five years, however, child welfare research has had so full a harvest that Alfred Kadushin had to limit his "Child Welfare" chapter to American and British research on child placement— to studies of services and problems in adoption, foster home care, and institutional care.

Finally, research in family service and

7

neighborhood centers—reviewed by the same two authors, Scott Briar and William Schwartz, who wrote the earlier chapters for *Five Fields of Social Service*—has apparently decreased in the past few years. However, the range of journals and other research publications these authors had to examine remains far-flung.

Obviously, therefore, there is a need for periodic, comparative, and cumulative reviews of such substantively related but too often discrete studies. Mutually supportive or contradictory findings must be specified so that their implications for changes in welfare policies, programs, and practices can be implemented. No single unrepeated study can provide an adequate basis for large-scale rational action in the social services, for most studies are time or place specific and most of the conditions and processes being examined are both conceptually and operationally slippery. The need for critical reviews by specialists of the kinds who have contributed to this book seems clear. Their work performs a genuine public service.

But there are at least two deterrents to engagement in such service. The more obvious is the inordinate amount of work involved. To locate, read critically, distill, and organize for use the findings and formulations in the literature collated for the five reviews in this book have taken many months of time and effort that these authors might profitably have spent in other ways. Was their choice well made? For the second deterrent, hinted at in Briar's chapter, concerns the extent to which reviews of research contribute to indicated changes in the social welfare enterprise. For example, Briar's "Family Services" chapter in the earlier volume stated:

... much of the time ... spent on recording was devoted to the production of material primarily of use to supervisors for nonadministrative purposes.

These findings raise an important and interesting question. Why do supervisors need detailed case-recording? [P. 12.] The

research he reviewed raised similar questions about supervision, continuing as against short-term treatment, and other facets of family agency work, all offered in the cautious language of the researcher but clearly suggesting that family service workers might fruitfully modify some of their practices. Directions for new investments of effort lay in policy development in the family service field.

Five years later, one wonders to what extent that field has attended to the findings and implications of Briar's review. Aaron Rosenblatt, reporting an empirical study of "The Practitioner's Use and Evaluation of Research," concludes that "social workers need to make a long-range commitment to research" and "pay attention to research findings." [2] After a few decades of such continuing counsel from persons committed to research, the problem of research utilization calls for more than hortatory efforts.

In the present book, Kadushin's summaries of child welfare research indicate that there is little yield from the child placement worker's efforts to "match" the child and his caretakers or substitute family. Clinical efforts to assess "motivation" for parenting involve highly inferential and therefore unreliable judgments. For example, in "A Follow-up Study of Adopted Children," Lilian Ripple proposes: "Adoption practice in general calls for far too many assessments of far too much attitudinal and inferential material." [3] Kadushin's chapter in this volume cites this study and others confirming implications for changes in child welfare practice. But will child welfare agencies consider the evidence and reallocate hard-pressed staff time accordingly? Or will habitual practices continue to be pursued until less rational forces demand change?

The issue of research utilization is no-

---

[2] *Social Work*, Vol. 13, No. 1 (January 1968), p. 59.

[3] *Social Service Review*, Vol. 42, No. 4 (December 1968), p. 497.

where directly addressed in the five chapters of this book.[4] The authors' styles are essentially those of traditionally disciplined and careful weighers of evidence. They bend over backwards to avoid a premature thrust toward recommending a course of action. There is a tendency to call for further study. Some readers may find support for the proposition that research begets only more refined questions and methodologically more sophisticated research. But readers who as social agency staff members have been genuinely professional and critically questioning about their own efforts—and concerned about improving provisions and other services for their clients and potential clients—should find in the chapters of this book ample evidence to buttress some of their practice-derived propositions for change. The tentative language and questioning thoughtways of research can be translated into action formulations for the field by those whose cumulative experience in the social services indicates the need for specific kinds of change. Research may document—or contraindicate—formulations deriving from critical analyses of cumulative experience. Derived from both sources, the directions for change should be clear.

Beyond such bridging of current research modalities and service orientations, I hope that research reviewed from 1970 on for the third volume in this series will be able to include many summaries of studies demonstrating close liaison between research workers and practitioners in the processes of systematic inquiry—from the definition of the problem for study to the spelling out of conclusions and implications. Although details of the technology of research are likely to become increasingly incomprehensible to practitioners, the general purposes and processes of research seem to call for continuously shared involvement if findings are to effect indicated changes. The traditionally detached stance of investigators in other fields of inquiry is dysfunctional when this posture is extended to characterize relationships between researchers and consumers of (or should one say coproducers of?) research in the social services. Close linkage may be possible, however, only as we expand our conceptions of the purposes, perspectives, and processes of social work research.

New approaches to rational inquiry, promising better research utilization, are beginning to be considered. Warren describes a model of study that sets up "a special *ad hoc* action system to conduct the research and implement the findings." He continues:

A research project is a *social action episode* involving *task accomplishment* (including both the *research* and its *implementation*), in which a *consultant* enters into a relationship with a *client system*, out of which is set up a *project system*. Both of these systems undergo *planned and unplanned changes* as the tasks of research and implementation are attempted.[5]

Quoting Michael Brooks on the need for "evaluation procedure which not only accommodates but in fact facilitates the feedback process," Marris and Rein themselves propose studies providing "an imaginative serial analysis which can be rapidly communicated" in neighborhood action programs.[6] Their chapter on "Research"

---

[4] But *see* Chapter 4, "Utilization of Research: Principles and Guidelines," in Tony Tripodi, Phillip Fellin, and Henry J. Meyer, *The Assessment of Social Research: Guidelines for the Use of Research in Social Work and Social Science* (Itasca, Ill.: Peacock Publishers, 1969), pp. 94–130.

[5] Roland Warren, *Social Research Consultation: An Experiment in Health and Welfare Planning* (New York: Russell Sage Foundation, 1963), pp. 134–135. Brook nicely analyzes differences between Warren's assumptions about the researcher's role as an agent of change in a research consultantship and the "scholarly consultation" suggested by Hans L. Zetterberg in *Social Theory and Social Practice* (New York: Bedminster Press, 1962). Peter Brook, "An Inquiry in the Relationship between Research and Social Action" (Vancouver: School of Social Work, University of British Columbia, 1969). (Mimeographed.)

[6] Peter Marris and Martin Rein, *Dilemmas of Social Reform: Poverty and Community Action in the United States* (London, England: Routledge & Kegan Paul, 1967), pp. 201 and 206.

sharply illuminates the conflicting values of those who seek precise routes to knowledge and those who want to act quickly.[7] For studies in programs with well-articulated and long-range purposes, I have elsewhere discussed human science perspectives and research methods and responsibilities that may foster better communication between practitioners and research workers.[8] Enough "final reports" have been received unsympathetically or suffered subsequently a benign neglect for us intensively to reconsider prevailing research modalities. How can studies be undertaken (and cumulatively synthesized with related research) so that their results are more visibly influential in the fields of action and human need? There is no higher priority question for study by social work research methodologists.

Finally, I must comment on the general organization of this book, for it reflects on more than appears in print here. The five chapters are arranged alphabetically by title. This is an effort to bring some order —albeit an irrelevant one!—to a research publication about and addressed to a rather disorderly American social services scene. To say it is a changing scene might help to explain its disorderliness; such explanation, however, would be more comforting if there were some shared public and professional commitments to a tentative set of new designs. It is gratuitous to note, as the 1970s begin, that such are sorely needed.

Rational, public inquiry and debate about service organization and policy are rare in the United States today. Governmental White Papers and Royal Commission reports that in the United Kingdom and Commonwealth nations provide published bases for widespread discussion of contemplated social change—like the current Seebohm

Committee report on service delivery in England [9]—have no clear analogs in the United States. The disjunctive organization of American social services accurately reflects the disjunctive processes by which in large measure they have developed and become reorganized.

Thus a potpourri of services, agencies, and practices—child welfare, family services, casework, public welfare, community organization, the neighborhood center and group work—are designated in the titles demarcating the five chapters in this book. Since our intent is to communicate with social work colleagues whose concerns and efforts are identifiable and bounded, we have had no choice but to use, for the organization of this volume, existing service package labels. We do so reluctantly because there is little evidence that such divisions of the welfare enterprise are effectively and humanistically responsive to individuals' social welfare wants today.

In the next volume in this series I hope we shall find more evidence from studies that give guidance to service organization and social policy development. Less of such research will be focused on how things *were* and more of it on how they *might be* as proposals are examined through demonstration that has "utility for discovering new ways to do things." [10] We should in the next

---

[7] Ibid., pp. 191–207.

[8] *See* the section on "Social Research and Social Work," pp. 42–47, in Henry S. Maas, "Social Work, Knowledge and Social Responsibility," *Journal of Education for Social Work*, Vol. 4, No. 1 (Spring 1968), pp. 37–48.

[9] *Report of the Committee on Local Authority and Allied Personal Social Services*, presented to Parliament by the Secretary of State for the Home Department, the Secretary of State for Education and Science, the Minister of Housing and Local Government, and the Minister of Health, by Command of Her Majesty (London, England: Her Majesty's Stationery Office, July 1968).

[10] Edwin J. Thomas, "Field Experiments and Demonstrations," in Norman A. Polansky, ed., *Social Work Research* (Chicago: University of Chicago Press, 1960), p. 291. Since Thomas wrote this chapter there have been some second thoughts about demonstration projects. In many of the Office of Economic Opportunity programs evaluative study findings have seemed inconclusive, as several chapters in the present volume report. Moreover, relationships in the field between action programs and research teams have been problematic, as reports by Marris and Rein, op. cit., and others indicate. Still, the yield from Mobili-

decade have research reports from established centers for the study of family and child welfare policy—at the present time Martin Wolins is planning such a center at the University of California, Berkeley— and from regional research institutes in social welfare, of which Genevieve W. Carter heads one at the University of Southern California. Such organizations should provide a programmatic continuity for welfare research. They should diminish the proportion of ad hoc and disjunctive inquiries. They should be staffed with consultants who

help to convert findings into indicated reforms, thus improving the research delivery system.

Studies of policy and service organization problems should take cognizance in their designs of the continuous contributions research itself should make in the welfare enterprise. Units for ongoing evaluation and research feedback belong in every rationally evolving social service program. As such desiderata are realized, chapters comprising future volumes in this series can be written more cohesively and probably under quite different rubrics. These chapters will both reflect and provide further understanding for an increasingly responsible public's efforts to meet its emerging welfare wants.

HENRY S. MAAS

Vancouver, B.C., Canada
October 1970

---

zation For Youth, the forerunner of less well-funded OEO projects, has been considerable. For a thougtful appraisal of this demonstration project *see* Sidney E. Zimbalist's review ("Mobilization For Youth: The Search for a New Social Work" [Book Review Essay], *Social Work*, Vol. 15, No. 1 (January 1970), pp. 123–128) of Harold H. Weissman, ed., *The New Social Work* (4 vols; New York: Association Press, 1969).

CHILD WELFARE

By ALFRED KADUSHIN

This review covers fewer content areas but is more extensive geographically than the earlier review by Fanshel (24) in the first volume of this series of reviews of research in the social services. Because of space limitations services such as day care and homemaker service, which were included in Fanshel's review, are not discussed here. Coverage has been restricted to the full-time, out-of-home substitute care services—adoption, foster family care, and institutional child care. Where the earlier report covered child welfare research through 1964 published in the U.S.A. alone, an attempt has been made to include empirical research reports on these services published between 1964 and early 1969 in both the U.S.A. and England.[1]

The principal concern of this review, as was true of the earlier one, is the child in interaction with a social situation that necessitates his being cared for and protected by persons other than his natural parents. The focus is the child; the nature of the problem situations that bring him into care; the consequences and outcome of care; the agency and the workers who organize, arrange, and offer substitute care; and the substitute caretakers, both temporary and permanent.

Any restrictions on coverage are admittedly arbitrary. Even if all services—supportive, supplementary, and substitutive—generally contained under the rubric of child welfare were included, the limitations would still be arbitrary. The welfare of children includes much that goes beyond the boundaries of child welfare.

The deployment of social work personnel in child welfare supports the restrictions imposed by space considerations and offers another rationale for selection of content. The services selected for discussion—adoption, foster family care, and institutional child care—employ by far the great majority of child welfare social workers. This

[1] Since Fanshel's review of child welfare research appeared in 1966, three volumes of abstracts and annotated bibliographies of research in adoption (88), foster home care (20), and residential child care (21), by Rosemary Dinnage and M. L. Kellmer Pringle, have been published in England. They cover hundreds of studies through 1966.

is where the action is for most child welfare workers.

In 1967 a total of only 480 full-time professional social workers were employed in the day care programs of state and local public welfare agencies nationwide (112, Table 25, p. 32). Admittedly public welfare day care centers constitute only some 6 percent of licensed day care center facilities available (112, Table 13, p. 24); however, the likelihood is that only a limited number of the proprietary centers, which provide more than 50 percent of day care spaces available, would employ social workers. Ruderman notes in a study of day care in seven representative communities across the country that "only 7 percent of the day care centers have the regular services of a social worker" (95, p. 102). If Ruderman's estimate were applied to the 10,400 licensed day care centers throughout the country in 1967, an estimate of 700–1,000 full-time professional social workers employed in day care would be arrived at.

The most generous interpretation of statistics made available by the most recent nationwide survey of Homemaker–Home Health Aide Service indicates that there is a total of 775 social workers acting either as directors of homemaker services or as casework staff "responsible for the continuing plan for an individual or family receiving homemaker services" (5, Tables 4 and 5, pp. 210–211). By contrast, the most recent statistics available list 26,164 child welfare workers employed in public child welfare agency programs (12, Table 20, p. 27). Additional numbers are employed in voluntary agencies, but the figures on this are not available.

A survey of the number and content areas of articles relating to child welfare research published by social work and allied journals during the period January 1965 through June 1968 also supports the logic of the limitations set for this review. Of the 87 identified articles on child welfare published, over 40 percent were concerned with adoption and foster care and less than

15 percent were concerned with day care, homemaker service, and protective services together (72, p. 3). The child welfare research that has actually been conducted during the past five years reflects this difference in emphasis and concentration.

One additional note of explanation is necessary. Material selected for inclusion in this review has been restricted to empirical studies. This criterion was adhered to in Fanshel's review as well and is not intended to derogate practice wisdom or depreciate clinically derived knowledge. One can comfortably and wholeheartedly agree with Piaget's dictum that "an acute observation surpasses all statistics." However, practice tends to be fragmented, noncumulative, pragmatic, and idiosyncratic experience. The absence of controlled comparisons and the lack of procedure to establish the reliability and validity of inferences limit the accuracy of practice experience learning.

Research is not antithetical to clinical experience. It is a different approach to the same data but one that, like clinical experience, provides its own distinctively different advantages for the field. Research permits the "combined experience of many workers with many cases in a condensed and tested form" (81, p. 29). It provides a systematically summarized statement of the experience of many workers with many cases against which the worker can test his thinking in the clinical situation. Research provides the worker with a probability statement of the effects of variables the field has identified as relevant and significant to its work.

As such the decision to select for inclusion empirical research studies only is not a decision for better or worse content but for a different kind of experience. The clinician has the advantage of richness of perception; research offers greater reliability in judgment. The hope is that research results can permit the clinician to reduce the degree of uncertainty with which he operates in making inferences and decisions.

Adoption

The number of adoptions by persons un-related to the child continued to increase between 1960 and 1967, the latest year for which statistics were available at the time this report was prepared (1969). In 1960, 57,800 nonrelative adoptions were com-pleted; in 1967, 83,700 (111). Despite the continued increase in absolute numbers, the rate of increase seems to be leveling off. For the five-year period 1962–66 the average annual increase in completed non-relative adoptions was 6 percent; between 1966 and 1967 the rate of increase was 2.7 percent.

An increasingly larger proportion of non-relative adoptions is being handled by so-cial agencies. In 1960, 57 percent of all such adoptions were agency placements; in 1967 agencies were responsible for 74 per-cent.

The proportion of black children adopted by nonrelatives has remained fairly con-stant over the years, hovering around 9–10 percent. In 1960, 9 percent of nonrelative adopted children were black; in 1967 the figure was the same. This figure is of course slightly lower than the 11 percent of blacks in the total population.

Adoption of black children by relatives is somewhat higher than the nonrelative black adoption rate—13 percent of all rela-tive adoptions are of black children. Non-relative black adoptions appear to be higher in those jurisdictions where there is a higher proportion of independent adop-tions, indicating perhaps a tendency for blacks to adopt outside agency channels and/or the paucity of adoption services for blacks.

Children adopted by nonrelated couples are generally born out of wedlock. Over time there has been a gradual increase in the proportion of nonrelated adoptees who are illegitimate and a commensurate de-crease in the proportion of such children born in wedlock. In 1960, 77 percent of such children were illegitimate; in 1967, 87 percent were illegitimate.

The age at which children are placed for adoption continues to be somewhat older for agency placements as compared with independent placements. Twenty-three per-cent of all agency placements are made before the child is one month old; 73 per-cent of all independent placements are made during this period (111).

Policy Questions

The following are some of the policy prob-lems and issues currently of concern in adoptions:

1. What are the antecedents that bring children into adoption? Can these condi-tions be corrected so that fewer children become dependent?

2. What can be done to identify children for whom adoption is the best possible solution and who must therefore be made legally available for adoption as early as possible?

3. In the context of an unfavorable ratio of children to applicants, what can be done to recruit additional applicants for all adoptable children but especially for hard-to-place children—minority groups, older children, the handicapped?

4. What selection criteria are associated with successful adoptive outcome for all adopted children? for the special groups of adopted children? What selection cri-teria can be modified without risks?

5. What are the outcomes of adoptive experience for all adopted children and for special groups of adopted children? What are the psychosocial hazards of adoption for children?

6. What differentiates adoptive parent-hood and adoptive childhood from biologi-cal parenthood and nonadoptive childhood? What accommodative procedures help toward optimum adjustment to the unique-ness of the adoptive family situation?

7. What are the differences in selection criteria between long-term foster care and adoptive care? What effects does subsi-dizing adoptions have?

The research reviewed in the following

pages is related to only some of these questions and bears no relationship to others.

Application and Selection

No recent research has been conducted on the current applicant-to-child ratio. However, there is no reason to believe that there has been any change that would suggest revision of the conclusions of an earlier national study (44). The principal conclusion of that survey was that there had not been an "actual decline in applications to adopt between 1958–62 but rather a relative decline occasioned by the increasing numbers of children needing to be placed for adoption" (44, p. 386). The ratio in 1962 was estimated at 1.3 couples for every child available for adoption, near parity.[2]

Changes in the applicant-to-child ratio exert an unremitting pressure on adoption agency procedures. As a consequence the trend recently has been toward a liberalization of requirements and a greater flexibility in processing applications. Turitz (109) notes this in reporting on one hundred replies from member agencies to a request by the Child Welfare League of America for suggestions about revising the standards for adoption service. Eligibility requirements regarding infertility, age, income, housing, mothers' plans about working, and religious qualifications are all undergoing change in response to the need to attract a larger number of applicants. None of these items is regarded as an essential prerequisite for adequately fulfilling the parental role.

Bradley (10) obtained detailed statements

---

2 "The overall ration of applications to available children declined from 158 for each 100 available children in 1958 to 129 in 1962 and to 104 in 1967, with the ratio for voluntary agencies declining at a faster pace," according to a publication received following the completion of this chapter. Detailed figures on approved homes are found in this publication. Edwin Riday, *Supply and Demand in Adoption* (New York: Child Welfare League of America, 1969), p. 19.

from social workers from eight different agencies regarding their perception of 398 adoptive applicants. She checked workers' assessments with decisions made regarding acceptance and rejection of applicants to determine factors associated with selection of applicants. Factors having the highest association with acceptance "related to positive qualities of couple interaction in their marriage, flexible and outgoing characteristics of both husband's and wife's personalities, the couples' openness, their non-neurotic motivation for adoption, their adequate marital role performance and their acceptance of infertility" (10, p. 122).

However, another cluster of factors indicates that the agency was also likely to accept the application of a somewhat different group of parents who were perceived as suitable for accepting a child who deviated in some way—physically, emotionally, racially. "These tended to be marginal couples who were considered more suitable for marginal children" (10, p. 188). In other words two alternative but non-simultaneous routes led to a positive impression of couples as adoptive prospects, with the "better" couple seen as suitable for the "better" child and the marginal couple seen as more suitable for the marginal child (10, p. 189).

Bradley followed the natural history of the processing of the 398 applicants. The study process was completed with four or five interviews, indicating that the selection process is not a prolonged, elaborate procedure. She found also that only 26 percent of the applicants were rejected by the agencies. An additional 6 percent, regarded as poor prospects, might have been encouraged to withdraw, although they themselves made the decision to do so (10, p. 104). Despite the great concern with adoption of hard-to-place children or children with special needs, Bradley notes that two-thirds of the applicants requesting children over 5 were rejected and of the 200 children placed during the course of the study only 26 were black. While blacks were somewhat less likely to be rejected by the agency than white applicants (22 and 27 percent respectively), fewer blacks ultimately received a child because of the much greater tendency of black applicants to withdraw their applications even though they were regarded as good prospects by the agency (11 percent of whites and 27 percent of blacks withdrew) (10, p. 61). Interestingly the most highly professionalized agencies, having the largest number of staff members with master's degrees in social work, had the lowest percentage of rejection—12 percent—and the least professionalized agency, which had not a single MSW worker, had one of the highest percentages of rejection—43 percent (10, p. 110).

As was indicated earlier, adopters are using agency channels with increasing frequency. However, a sizable percentage of adoptions are still achieved independently of agencies. What distinguishes the agency applicant from the person who resorts to independent adoption channels? Little is known about differences between these two groups. A mail questionnaire study of couples who adopted through nonagency channels indicated that the requirement that children be placed with couples of similar religious background was a principal reason for the use of independent sources (7). In addition a sizable percentage of these couples had a history of divorce. The numbers involved in the study are small, so conclusions may be tenuous. However, the study points to the need for research on factors that explain the use of independent channels at a time when agencies are soliciting more applicants.

There is a persistent impression among adoption workers that adoption frequently results in subsequent pregnancy for the adopter. Earlier investigations tended to cast some doubt about the accuracy of such impressions; research studies relegate the idea to the mythology of the profession. Tyler carefully followed up 100 adopters who received a child through a private agency that kept detailed records of fertility status. Only 4 percent of the group "conceived within a time interval short enough [two years] to make a cause and effect relationship between adoption and pregnancy reasonable" (110, p. 589). As a therapeutic procedure for infertility, adoption appears relatively inefficient. Other studies support the conclusion that adoption per se does not lead to a higher likelihood of postadoption conception. However, for some small percentage of couples for whom clearly established organic factors are not involved, adoption is one of a wide variety of procedures that, by necessitating a change in the life situation of the adoptive couple, leads to a higher than expected rate of subsequent conception (43, 94).

Regarding the crucial need for adoptive parents, especially for hard-to-place children, recent research has provided evidence only of an easing of agency standards and a lowered applicant rejection rate in some highly professionalized agencies.

Postplacement Contact

Despite its importance, there is relatively little explicit research on the postplacement relationship. The most detailed study available is that by Gochros (34). Interview data were obtained from a group of 57 adoptive couples and their postplacement caseworkers about a year after the legal adoption. It was clear that there was a difference in perception of the purpose of the contact between placement and final adoption. Caseworkers saw the primary purpose as aiding the successful integration of the adoptive family; adoptive parents saw the contact as evaluative, to validate the agency's selection of them as adoptive parents. Few of the parents felt they received a clear, unambiguous statement of the purpose of the contact from their caseworkers.

This study of the postplacement contact reveals a principal concern of parents during the postplacement period, namely, that the child might be removed from their home. Paradoxically, despite the fact that the caseworker's orientation was geared toward helping, few thought that the contact was necessary for this purpose. Consequently it is not surprising that the median number of interviews per family during the course of the year was 3.83—less than one interview every four months. Forty-one percent of the adoptive parents felt that the interviews had "not been particularly helpful"; 19 percent felt that the visits had been of substantial help.

Parents reported help in two general areas: reassurance (such as reassurance that they were doing a good job, that their child was developing properly or that the agency would not take the child away) and problem solving (such as provision of child care and developmental information, legal procedural information or help with specific adoption problems such as how to tell their child about adoption). [34, p. 322]

Most helpful to most parents was reassurance from the worker that they were indeed doing a good job as parents.

Degree of helpfulness felt by the parent was positively related to the number of contacts, to the general level of adjustment of the parents, to the parents' readiness to use help, and to the clarity of the worker's interpretation of the purpose of the contact. There was no relationship between perceived helpfulness and age, experience, marital or parental status, or voluntary or public agency affiliation of the worker. Surprisingly there was no relationship between perceived helpfulness and whether the worker was the same for both adoptive study and postplacement visits.

An English follow-up study also found that the actual amount of supervision subsequent to placement was limited, 68 percent of the families having received fewer than three visits over a three-month period (35, Table 11, p. 86). Part of this was attributed by staff to the attitude of the adoptive family, who sought, once placement was effected, to divorce themselves as much as possible from the agency, thus reducing any sense of difference from biologically created families. Continuing contact reminded them of the fact that they had now, as during the selection process, to prove themselves fit parents—that the child was not theirs yet. Despite interpretation, adoptive parents did not see the supervisory period as help oriented but rather as a continuation of trial parenthood. Workers, while clearer about the fact that their principal role was to help effect the best mutual adjustment between parents and children, were not certain about how they could do this most effectively.

Although invited, none of the 59 non-relative adopters interviewed had returned to the agency for help—although they readily took the opportunity to discuss their problem with researchers.

Research that solicited responses of adoptive parents to postplacement contact shows only a limited number of the total group of parents interested in such contact. Involving adoptive parents in a process that differentiates them from the rest of the population of parents who do not get an agency along with their child poses a problem. In response to the specific question asked during an adoptive follow-up study of 160 families as to whether it was regarded as desirable for the agency to hold group meetings for adoptive parents, 70 percent of the white parents and 56 percent of the black parents said no (92, 93).

On 'Telling'

One of the recurrent problems uniquely encountered by the adoptive family is the necessity of sharing with the child the fact that he is adopted and helping him to understand and emotionally accept this. This proves to be a problem for adoptive parents as well as for children, since helping the adopted child accept his status requires prior acceptance by the parents of their status as adoptive parents.

Recent research around the "telling" process comes from some retrospective accounts of adopted children interviewed as adults. In one instance 16 adopted adults met in small groups over a period of six months to discuss their experience with having been adopted. They agreed that it was crucial for the parent to share with the child the fact that he was adopted, that integration of the meaning of adoption takes place only gradually and real understanding is not achieved until adolescence or even early adulthood, and that while it is necessary to reiterate the fact of adoption it should be referred to only on those occasions when the situation calls attention to adoptive status. These adopted adults pointed out that questions about biological parents should not be perceived as a threat to the relationship with the adoptive parents. Their own questions had been asked out of curiosity and "the majority of the group had no interest or desire in seeking out their biological parents" (37, p. 23). In general members of the group did not see themselves as different from others by virtue of the fact that they were adopted. They saw their adoptive parents as their "real" parents and identified with them. If the parents were comfortable about adoption and loved and accepted the child, these adults felt that the situation was not likely to be problematic.

A second study, done in Scotland, involved extensive interviews with 52 adults who had been adopted as children (70). The interviewees were referred to the researcher by local medical practitioners who were aware of the adoptive history of their patients.

Once again, in this group adoptees were clear that the child should be told about his adoptive status and they were curious about their origins. They wanted general factual information about their biological parents and were curious about them, but few seemed ready to seek them out—a procedure that is legally feasible in Scotland since adoption records are available to adopted children 17 years of age or older. Despite their curiosity they felt that they could not initiate discussion about their origins and that this information had to come from the adoptive parents on their own initiative. As adopted children they felt hesitant about taking responsibility for raising these questions out of fear of hurting, upsetting, or appearing disloyal to their adoptive parents. They saw their adoptive status as a fact that needed to be acknowledged but not overstressed. They saw their adoptive parents as their "real" parents even in those instances in which there was some estrangement in the relationship.

Despite their curiosity, neither group of respondents in the two studies cited wanted exhaustive information about their biological parents. Perhaps they were afraid of what they might find out. In any case they wanted and expected the adoptive parents to offer sufficient information for them to obtain some sense of their origins.

Another researcher in Great Britain conducted follow-up interviews with 59 adoptive parents two to five years after nonrelative adoptive placements. The problem of telling was discussed as one of the principal difficulties faced by the adoptive parents. There was general consensus about the desirability of telling if only, as was frequently the case, out of fear and anxiety that the child would inevitably find out from other sources. However, parents had difficulty in introducing the topic naturally and easily. They received little assistance from the children, who asked few questions —not, if the previously cited research is to be credited, out of a lack of curiosity, but out of a feeling that the parents should initiate the communication about this (35).

Parents were, as noted in other studies, not only ambivalent and uneasy about telling but also uncertain about the best procedure. Many were dubious about the story of the "chosen" child as a procedure of choice, since it was not congruent with the child's rejection by his biological parents. There was uncertainty too about what and how much to tell about the biological parents. Parents indicated they felt uneasy about telling the child since the knowledge of adoptive status might threaten his security; others defended against telling by suggesting the child did not seem interested and/or could not understand the meaning of adoption. Still others implied, although not directly, that telling would threaten the child's relationship to them. The children seemed to fear learning that they were neglected, they were not wanted for themselves, or they had contributed to the difficulty that resulted—the necessity for their adoptive placement.

The researchers point out that even though the social worker had made efforts to "prepare adopters to deal with telling confidently, realistically and positively" (35, p. 119), these parents still needed reassurance and advice in dealing with the problem. They had not, two to five years after adoption, accepted telling as first and foremost the parents' rather than the child's problem.

A principal anxiety over telling lies in the threat that the adoptive child may try to find and develop a relationship with his biological parents. Scottish laws provide an empirical test of the frequency with which adoptive children seek out their biological parents. McWhinnie notes:

At present, in Scotland it is possible for an adopted child on reaching the age of 17 to apply to Register House for information about his biological parents from the original birth certificate. I believe Register House receives approximately 30 such inquiries a year. [71, p. 12]

The Committee of Management of the British National Council for the Unmarried Mother and Her Child recommended, after studying whatever relevant data were available, that adopted persons should have the right of access to their original birth certificates. They note that the committee could find no evidence that the Scottish law that makes it possible for adopted persons aged 17 or over to see copies of the entries relating to themselves in the Registry of Births has caused any grave problems.

There seems little evidence from Scotland that many children have wished to follow up the information by making actual contact with their natural parents and this was usually when the adoption had been very unhappy. The knowledge of the name of the natural mother and where this is relevant the father, often appears sufficient to satisfy the adopted person's curiosity. That the knowledge can be made available as a right is said often to be sufficient to satisfy the needs of one adopted person. [102, pp. 30–31]

A significant section of the interview guide used in the Kornitzer study (63) concerned the process of telling and the adoptive parent's attitude toward it. The report of the results of this interview material is in impressionistic, descriptive terms. It must be noted, however, that the author is a perceptive, long-time student of adoption who is summarizing what has been learned as a result of conducting hundreds of systematic follow-up interviews. She notes that children are anxious to know about their background despite seeming indifference and that their loyalty to their adoptive parents is not threatened by the sharing of information. As a matter of fact, positive regard for and loyalty to the adoptive parent is enhanced through open and honest sharing of background material. It was also noted that desire for such knowledge was not tied to a desire to contact the biological parents. The motive for wanting to know lay most often in a desire on the part of the child to understand himself better and develop some feeling of identity through continuity with his past. A subgroup of 62 adult adoptees who provided information about their own adoptions indicated that few had attempted to locate their biological parents. When such contact was made there was little in the way of affection and/or respect in the relationship.

Follow-up Studies

Success in being selected as an adoptive parent may or may not be associated with high probability of success as an adoptive parent. The qualities necessary for winning an election may be different from the qualities necessary for effective discharge of the responsibilities of the office. Successful adoption outcome requires separate study from successful selection outcome.

Jaffee and Fanshel (47) designed a study to determine the factors relating to development and long-term adjustment of 100 children who had been adopted twenty to thirty years previously through four New York City adoption agencies. Interviews were conducted by experienced caseworkers with both adoptive parents independently and together and all interviews were tape-recorded. Parents filled out an attitudinal questionnaire at the end of the interview. The tape recordings were used to categorize the 100 families into three overall outcome groups—low problem, middle, and high problem—using judgments of adoptees' personal and social adjustment and the families' overall experience with the adoption as the basis for categorization.

Age at placement and number of re-placements prior to adoption were not related to outcome. Placement in homes where there were other children was associated with fewer problems in adjustment than placement in childless homes. Socioeconomic level showed a slight association with subsequent adjustment, but a stronger, although not definitive, relationship was demonstrated between child-rearing practice as reported by the parents and adoptees' adjustment.

The majority of the parents felt that their family had not encountered problems that could be directly attributable to the fact of adoption. However, telling had been cause for concern and adoptees who manifested marked curiosity about their biological parents tended to be among those showing more problems in adjustment. Moreover, one of the concepts guiding the interview was the idea of "entitlement"—whether or not the adoptive parents felt a sense of rightful possession of the child—and doubt and uncertainty about entitlement on the part of the parents was associated with more problems in adjustment on the part of the child.

Ripple conducted a follow-up study of adoptions completed by a voluntary agency (92, 93). This study was concerned with determining, in retrospect, which factors in the selection process were related to outcome. The study group was composed of 160 children, 40 of whom were black, placed for adoption before the age of 2 in families where there were no other children at the time of placement. The children were aged between 7 and 10 at the time of follow-up. Sources of data were agency records of the adoptive study and post-placement period, supplemented by additional records that became available when 108 of the 160 families reapplied for adoption of a second child. Follow-up data were derived from separate interviews with the adoptive mother and father and with the adopted child.

The criterion measure of outcome was a categorization of level of adjustment of the children made by the interviewers on the basis of interview material and observations of the child. Assessment was anchored to four key aspects of the child's functioning—successful completion of tasks of earlier developmental periods, development of relationships, acceptance of controls, and development of skills. Children were grouped, on the basis of interviewer assessment of functioning, into four levels of adjustment: (1) "within 'normal' range and showing no symptoms" (20 percent), (2) "within 'normal' range but showing some symptoms" (27 percent), (3) "some problems in adjustment" (29 percent), (4) "serious emotional or behavior problems" (24 percent).

The researchers note that "the criteria used for assessment of disturbance probably differed considerably from those used in the community at large" and that assessment of functioning was probably more rigorous than that generally applied. The criterion measure was not used to evaluate the "success" of adoptive outcome. It was for the purpose of dividing the study sample into several outcome groups that might be compared for the various predictive factors investigated.

Perhaps the greatest surprise is that no clear association was found between supposedly significant factors in the child's background and adjustment at follow-up. Factors studied included age at adoptive placement, number of preadoptive placements, apparent quality of care in placement, and the early behavior of the child himself. The only association with the child's background factors was the likelihood of more favorable outcome of children placed before 2 months of age, by contrast with the Jaffe-Fanshel study, which showed no age-related outcomes.

Similarly most of the economic and social factors regarding the adoptive couple showed no association with outcome. "Small but persistent differences in the white subsample showed higher education and economic status to be less favorable"—reflecting perhaps workers' inappropriately favorable evaluations of more articulate, sophisticated applicants (93, p. 486). Children placed with younger applicants in the white subsample were also more likely to be demonstrating poor adjustment at follow-up.

Feelings regarding childlessness, as far as these could be ascertained from review of the record, were not related to outcome. The proportion of children in the problem group at follow-up was just as high in those families in which both applicants were judged to have worked through these feelings to a substantial extent as in families in which such feelings were recognized but repressed or not worked through.

None of the evidence showed "matching" to be a favorable factor. It was difficult to study the relationship between certain other factors and outcome simply because, as a result of the selection process, there was little differentiation among adoptive parents with regard to these variables. Among such factors were "capacity for parenthood," "motivation for adoption," and "relationship to agency."

There was more substantial evidence to suggest that a child presenting problems during the immediate postplacement period was likely to manifest problems at follow-up and that there was a high association between parents' attitudes and behavior at follow-up and the child's adjustment. The latter finding does not necessarily indicate cause and effect, since the parental behavior may be in response to, rather than a cause of, the child's behavior. It is also of dubious value in sharpening selection study procedure, since the researchers found little relationship between the workers' assessment of parenting attitudes expressed in the adoptive study and parenting behavior as assessed by the interviewers at follow-up.

An accepting attitude by the parents toward telling and adherence to desirable procedures in telling was associated with positive adjustment.

One important finding gives emphasis to the limits of predictability of even the best study. Forty-two families (26 percent of the study group) had experienced some form of serious disruption, such as death, serious illness, separation, divorce, loss of business, or frequent moves. Children in 37 of these 42 families were in the two groups representing poorest adjustment. These children comprised 44 percent of the 85 children in the poorest adjustment groups. Most of these events were fortuitous and not even in the case of marital disruptions were the events predictable on the basis of data available during the adoptive study.

The major conclusion of the study is that prediction of outcome based on child or adoptive parent indicators is a difficult and dubious undertaking. Adoption practice in general has called for far too many assessments of far too much attitudinal and inferential material. Consequently it might be better to place greater effort on providing postadoption assistance with problem situations that arise, especially in the transitional period immediately following placement, since many adopters are experiencing parenthood for the first time. Other conclusions are already being implemented in changed adoption practice in the trend toward earlier adoptive placement and reduced emphasis on matching.

Another follow-up study of adoption, made by a Pennsylvania agency, involved 250 children in 200 families (64). All children in the study group were white, median age at adoptive placement was 7 months, and the median age at follow-up was 9½ years. Detailed agency records were reviewed to obtain background material on the adoptive children and parents. Follow-up interviews lasting some two to three hours were tape-recorded and included both father and mother. Interviewers completed ratings of family functioning and child's adjustment based on interview material and a 20 percent sample of the interviews were independently rerated, as a reliability check, on the basis of listening to the tapes.

The criterion outcome measure used in this study was a rating of family functioning as a unit at follow-up. The rating included an assessment of such factors as degree of family tension, presence of warmth and affection, and autonomy of family members. Families were sorted into four groups, from "superior" family functioning (children were happy, responsive, well adjusted; parents compatible and enthusiastic about the adopted child) to "low" family functioning (pathology in parent-child relationships, family faces serious problems). On such a four-point scale 39 families were rated as follows: 29 "superior" (14 percent), 98 "good" (49 percent), 53 "fair" (27 percent), 20 "low" (10 percent) (64, Section II, p. 24).

Once again, in this study of background factors and adoption outcome the surprising results, noted previously by Ripple and to some extent in the Jaffe-Fanshel study, were that

no child background factors were significantly related to outcome. Child characteristics such as: age at adoption, number of placements prior to adoption, psychological evaluation, rating of emotional deprivation, simply did not show enough relationship to outcome for statistical significance. . . .

. . . . .

It appears very much as though child background variables take on less and less import

as prognostic factors through the passage of time from placement to follow-up. [64, Section III, pp. 8, 14]

Wittenborn's earlier follow-up research had also failed to show any correlation between adoption outcome and information available on the child's background (116).

Variables relating to parents' activities and attitudes were much more significantly related to overall postadoption family functioning in the Pennsylvania study. If one thinks in terms of an index of adoption outcome based on weighted parent and child variables, the most heavily weighted items would be parental variables—especially satisfaction in adoptive role, acceptance of adoptive role, and warmth and affection toward the child. The study indicates also that many adoptive parents, about 40 percent, had difficulty communicating the fact of adoption and that success in this was, in a measure, related to general communication skills.

Kornitzer (63) interviewed adoptive parents in a follow-up study conducted in England. The adoptive mother was generally the respondent although some adoptive fathers were seen as well. The child was not interviewed. In some cases interview responses were written down during the course of the interview; in others this material was recorded later. All interviewing was done by the researcher-author and all codification and categorization of responses were apparently done by the same person. The research was conducted over a period of eleven years.

There are further methodological difficulties in that a heterogeneous group of adoptions were included in the study group —agency and nonagency, relative and nonrelative, de facto as well as legal. Although a total of 503 adoptive families were interviewed, the core of follow-up analysis is concerned with 233 children, all of whom were over 5 years of age at the time of the follow-up interview. These children were rated in terms of four levels of adoptive outcome: (1) success—"not just a happy adoption of a child but a happy family situation" (p. 13), (2) average—" quite successful in that they had no real or definite apparent problems and the relationship seemed to be straightforward and without anxiety, strain or signs of insecurity in the child who seemed to be developing 'normally' " (p. 14), (3) problems—"these were problems of a more or less serious nature —some were well in hand or likely to work themselves out" (p. 14), (4) bad or failed—"gross problems had developed . . . failure in parent-child relationships and/or termination of adoptive relationship" (p. 14).

The 233 adoptive children rated were categorized as success 41.2 percent, average 36.5 percent, problems 19.3 percent, bad or failed 3 percent. If the first two categories could be combined to cover a generally satisfactory adoptive outcome, it would include 77.7 percent of the children.

Private adoption agency placements totaled 85.6 percent satisfactory (47.4 percent success, 38.2 percent average) and public agency placements were almost exactly the same in terms of rated level achieved. However, the proportion of satisfactory independent placements was smaller: 41.6 percent rated success, 32.8 percent rated average, both categories totaling 74.4 percent. Age at time of placement was not related to outcome—a confirmation of findings in two previous studies. Kornitzer found that children adopted when age 3 or older were as successful as children placed when younger. Outcome in families that included "own" children were as successful as families with no "own" children. The author concluded that the data "do not suggest that there is, in general, greater risk in placing a child in a home where there are or may be 'own' children" (63, p. 176.)

In 56 instances the child studied had originally been placed as a foster child. The success rating of this subgroup was slightly higher than the success rating of the study group as a whole. The results "did not suggest that fostering was a bad way to begin an adoptive relationship" (63, p. 179). The most successful group of mothers were those who were in their 40s

at the time of adoption; the least successful were those in their 50s. Younger applicants, in their 20s, also had a poor outcome. "Lower business and professional" adoptive couples were apt to be less successful, an apparent agreement with Ripple's finding. Girls had a far larger proportion of negative adoptive outcomes than did boys. The author attributes this to the fact that both the girls and the adoptive parents are apt to be concerned with a possible repetition of the natural mother's out-of-wedlock pregnancy. This fear contaminates the relationship between the female adoptee and her parents. Finally, supporting earlier research findings regarding differential class use of adoptions, Kornitzer found that adoptions by relatives were more frequent among lower-class groups, while nonrelative adoptions were less characteristic of these groups.

Skeels (100) has continued his study of the effects of contrasting developmental experience by a follow-up into adulthood of two groups of children, one group that had adoptive home placements, the other a group that had remained in an orphanage. Both groups had initially been assessed as mentally retarded. When followed up twenty-one years later, the 11 children who had been placed in adoptive homes proved to have done demonstrably better in meeting life problems than had the institutionalized group. The difference between the socioeconomic status of the two groups was statistically significant. "Educational and occupational achievement and income for the 11 adopted subjects . . . compared favorably with the 1960 census figures for Iowa and for the U.S. in general" (100, p. 55).

Emotional Disturbance in Adopted Children

During the period under review there has been continuing concern with the question of the dangers to healthy emotional development that result from adoption. Research relevant to the problem has centered around two interrelated issues: (1) are adopted children more likely than other children to be emotionally disturbed and (2) in what ways if any are psychosocial problems of adopted children distinctively different?

The question of differential prevalence of emotional pathology in adopted children first requires accurate knowledge of the number of nonrelative adopted children in the population. Without such information it is difficult to know whether adopted children are referred for treatment in disproportionate numbers.

Reported adoption rates vary from one jurisdiction to another. Not only do rates vary among states because of differences in law and in reporting procedures, but the ratio of adopted to nonadopted clients in any one agency varies from year to year. Reece (91) demonstrates this in reviewing the statistics of the Langley Porter Neuropsychiatric Institute, where the percentage of adopted children ranged from 0 in 1956 to 4 percent in 1961.

Jonassohn (53) has cogently criticized the base rates used in studies evaluating the level of representation of adopted children in clinic populations, suggesting some of the difficulties in establishing an accurate base rate. In the absence of accurate base rate data and in the presence of so many variables that might determine differential use of clinical services, the more productive approach might be to turn aside from the question of possible overrepresentation of adopted children in psychiatric clinic facilities and study the adopted children who do appear for service. This in part has been the direction of some of the more recent research. While studying the question of overrepresentation, the researchers have also attempted to identify the distinctive aspect of the adopted child's pathology.

Reece (91) reviewed all cases on the Children's Service of the Langley Porter Neuropsychiatric Institute between January 1954 and December 1963. Of the 1,017 children treated, 30, or 2.9 percent, were nonrelative adoptees. The most frequent difficulty presented by the adopted children was aggressive, antisocial behavior.

Simon and Senturia (99) reviewed the admissions records of the department of psychiatry of a large metropolitan hospital over a three-year period. All adoptees in the sample were identified. At the same time information was obtained from the local courts and the state department of public welfare on adoptions in the community in order to calculate a base rate. The base rate proved to be similar to the estimated national figure, 1 percent of the population being nonrelative adoptees. The incidence of adopted children in the patient population was 5.5 percent, some five times larger than the expected rate. However, when the adult patients are included, the incidence of nonrelative adoptees falls to 2.6 percent. In actual numbers there were 35 nonrelative adopted patients among the 1,371 patients seen in the department during the period studied. The symptom picture of adoptees was clearly different from that of the general patient population. There were fewer neurotic patients among adoptees and a greater manifestation of personality disorders with antisocial behavior.

Kirk (60) obtained the cooperation of twenty-eight different agencies concerned with offering psychiatric casework and/or counseling service to children. The proportion of adopted children in the caseloads of these agencies varied widely from 2.5 to 33 percent, averaging 7.8 percent for the sample of 3,495 children. A check was made of the reliability of the records of the participating agencies and it was found that the proportion of adopted children reported by the agency was inversely related to reliability—"highest in those clinical units having the most unreliable records" (60, p. 296). Those clinics in the group that specialized in learning problems showed the greater proportion of adoptees among clients. The authors concluded that because of self-selection of clinic populations as well as because of doubts about the numbers of adopted children in the population it is hazardous to make any firm statements about overrepresentation of adoptees in clinic populations.

Menlove (75) compared 51 adopted children with an equal number of nonadopted clients at a children's psychiatric hospital. The two groups were matched in terms of age, sex, race, and socioeconomic background. Comparison of the two groups on the basis of nine different aggressive-type symptoms indicated that the adopted children manifested significantly more aggressive symptomatology. A breakdown of the adopted client group in terms of age at time of placement indicated that aggressive symptomatology was not related to this factor.

Offord (79) focused on the question of differences in presenting symptomatology between adopted and nonadopted children referred to the child psychiatry division of a general hospital. Twenty-five nonrelative adopted children referred to the clinic were matched in terms of some general variables with 25 nonadopted children. The mother's description of the child's behavior was categorized by a child psychiatrist as either a behavior disorder, neurotic disorder, or other. The psychiatrist was not aware of the background of the child categorized. Results indicated that the group of adopted children manifested significantly more behavioral problems than nonadopted children, and a comparison of the antisocial behavior of both groups resulted in the finding that the severity of the antisocial behavior of adopted children was likely to be greater than that of their nonadopted peers. Although numbers of children in each cell are quite small, the results suggested a relationship between age at adoptive placement and behavioral difficulties—a finding the author explains in terms of extent of maternal deprivation.

Jackson (45), in summarizing a review of the clinical records of 40 children treated at a child guidance clinic, also noted that the principal presenting symptom of the highest percentage of the group was aggressive acting-out behavior. Age at adoptive placement was not, however, related to symptomatology in this study.

Elonen (22), reporting on a longitudinal follow-up study of adopted children, found that neither the magnitude nor nature of disturbance distinguished adopted children from difficulties manifested by a "comparable non-adopted group living with their natural families who were also followed at the same time." School achievement was a frequently encountered problem. The report, however, suffers from serious gaps in the statistical material made available.

Schwartz (98) used personality tests to study differences in functioning between 25 boys placed for adoption before the age of 6 months by a social agency and 25 nonadopted peers matched on the basis of age, religion, socioeconomic status, sibling position, and verbal ability. At the time of the study all the children were about 9 years of age. Instruments used included Picture Q-Sort, Family Relations Test, a combination of the Thematic and Children's Apperception Tests, and figure drawings. Adoptive parents completed two self-administered questionnaires, the Semantic Differential and the Interpersonal Check Test. Results indicated that the adopted boys showed considerable uncertainty and anxiety concerning the permanence and reliability of object relations. They manifested constriction, overcontrol, and fearfulness in interpersonal relations, which contrasted with the spontaneity and vitality of emotional expression found among the control group. The adopted children tended to associate fear and anxiety with parental disapproval and tended to be inhibited in expressing even mildly aggressive feelings toward parental figures.

Kadushin (55) recapitulated the relevant studies available through 1966 and estimated that while nonrelative adoptees constituted some 1 percent of the population they represented about 4.3 percent of the psychiatric treatment clientele. However, despite this overrepresentation, some 98 percent of all adopted children are not likely to need psychiatric treatment (57). Adopted children seem to be overrepresented in psychiatric treatment populations at a statistically significant level. However, statistical significance does not, in this instance, appear to have practical significance. There is little difference in the percentage of children placed by agencies and seen in psychiatric facilities as compared with those patient adoptees placed through independent channels.

The available research fails to answer satisfactorily the question of overrepresentation of adopted children at psychiatric clinics. The ambiguity results primarily from demographic questions about baseline rates and from the lack of standardization of data regarding adoptions and clinical services. It is clear, however, that if such children are in fact overrepresented, the difference is not great. The research confirms the expectation that the great majority of adopted children can grow to adulthood with only the usual quota of human difficulties. However, research points with some consistency to the fact that if the adopted child does become emotionally disturbed he is likely to display aggressive symptoms characteristic of behavior disorders.

The theoretical explanations for the higher-than-expected prevalence of psychiatric disorders among nonrelative adopted children lies in the greater difficulty faced by such children in resolving identity problems and handling the rejection by their natural parents. They face the problem of "geneological bewilderment" since their biological antecedents are, to them, vague and uncertain. The existence of two sets of parents handicaps achievement of the task of fusing the intrapsychic "good" and "bad" parent images of infantile object relations. Parent-child interaction carries the burden of the parents' narcissistic wound at the knowledge of their infertility and of their anxiety about the shadowy biological background of the child. In addition every adopted child has faced discontinuity in mothering, separation from earlier caretakers, as he moved from some home into the adoptive home.

Sociologically the adoptive situation is problem filled. Adopted children usually become the first child of older parents. The average age of adoptive parents at placement is in the early 30s; most natural parents have their first child in their early 20s. The adopted child is also likely to be an only child. Adoption is an atypical procedure for achieving parenthood and the stress this minority group perception imposes on both parents and children makes for a psychiatric hazard.

Several researchers concerned with the distinctive pathology of adopted children referred for psychiatric treatment suggest that congenital factors may play a part, insofar as most nonrelative adoptees are illegitimate and the mother's tension and anxiety during pregnancy may adversely affect the fetus (75, p. 530). The pediatrics unit of a medical school hospital, in reviewing its records of children with minimal brain injury seen in their clinic, found that adopted children were disproportionately represented. A random sample of 1,000 records contributed 39 nonrelative adopted children. This 3.9 percent of adopted children was some three or four times the expected rate. The children exhibited hyperactivity, emotional volatility, and defects in self-control. A rigorous attempt to review the developmental record material in each case led to the conclusion that "indifferent prenatal medical care may have been crucial in determining brain injury" (59, p. 29).

Losbaugh (65) calls attention to a factor that had not previously received attention. She compared the electroencephalograph (EEG) findings of 75 adopted children with those of 75 nonadopted children matched for age and sex. There was a statistically significant difference in the extent of EEG abnormalities in the adopted group. She concludes that the data suggest "that adopted children as a group, due to various biosocial deprivations and insults, sustain a high percentage of neurologic damage. . ." (65, p. 4).

A higher risk of problem-causing congenital factors in children conceived as a result of incest is cited in a study by Adams (1). The data for the study derived from the work of the Department of Human Genetics at the University of Michigan, which offers consultation to child-placing agencies in the state, and involved comparison of children born of incestuous relationships with a control group matched for similar factors in the mother's background.

A comparison of the responses of adoptive parents of 10 schizophrenic children with responses of biological parents of schizophrenic children to a word association test indicated that the biological parents "gave significantly more unusual and deviant associations than did the adoptive parents . . ." (121, p. 503). The implication of the results as inferred by the researchers is that the adopted children's pathology had a constitutional component.

In summation, the relevant research suggests that there is a small but real risk of emotional disturbance in adopted children. If the risks of emotional disturbance run somewhat higher among adopted than among nonadopted children, it is still necessary to discover the rates for family-less children who remain unadopted. The practical question in child welfare is how much more or less disturbed the child is because he is adopted. The alternative for such a child is presumably long-term foster family or institutional care, and it is with children in such settings that the mental health of adopted children needs to be compared.

Hard-To-Place Children

There has been continuing concern with those children available for adoption but hard to place—older, handicapped, or of minority group or mixed parentage. Although during the 1950s there were a number of reports of adoption of foreign-born children, primarily from the Far East, recent concern with interracial adoption has centered on adoption by caucasian families of black, American Indian, or Mexican-American children.

CWLA and the U.S. Bureau of Indian Affairs are cooperating in a demonstration-research project that resulted in placement of 250 Indian children with caucasian families over a ten-year period, 1958–67. One hundred of these families are being visited periodically as part of an intensive longitudinal follow-up study. Preliminary analysis of Indian adoption project interviews currently available indicate the following:

1. Adoptive parents in the main did not especially seek out an Indian child but were rather content to accept one in an attempt to satisfy their basic quests for a child
2. While the adoptive parents were able to consider a child authentically different from themselves, they evidently set limits on the range of acceptable differences and very few would have considered the adoption of a Black child, even one who was quite light
3. The parents reflect a broad spectrum of political attitudes and are not predominantly liberals. Further their reported voting behavior closely approximated that of the general American voting Public in both the 1956 and the 1960 presidential elections
4. The first few years of the child's placement in the home may be generally characterized as representing a honeymoon period with few reports of even moderately serious developmental problems. [26]

Analysis of personality inventory responses of caucasian parents who adopted Indian children as compared with responses of a sample of parents who adopted caucasian children indicates that there was little essential difference between the two groups. There was no evidence that Indian adoption project families were motivated by the desire to foster racial integration. The child's ethnicity was clearly a secondary consideration. Adoption was primarily and principally in response to a desire for a child. This commitment to a child rather than to a political ideology is confirmed in other studies of motivation of adoptive parents crossing racial lines in adoptions. Regarding adoptive parents in the Indian project:

While far from being non-conformists they have a stubborn streak. They do have an independence of mind so that they do not appear to be easily led into accepting orientations which are socially alien to them. [It is not that they are indifferent to what their neighbors think,] it is rather that they would not allow themselves to be guided by such considerations. [27]

A follow-up interview study of 21 white families in Toronto who adopted black children was done at a time when most of the children were still of preschool age and had been in the home for an average of about three years. In two-thirds of the cases relatives had objected in some measure to the adoptive placements but opposition had diminished with time. Children seemed to be adjusting well, and admittedly the problem of racial identification by either the adoptee or the community had not as yet been fully encountered (2).

Researchers note that the worker's attitude is an important variable in transracial adoptions.

The attitude of the worker is very important in finding homes for the part-Black child. The families were sensitive to the attitudes of the social worker and were quick to react to what they interpreted as "prejudice" on the part of the worker. The social worker, too, must be flexibly undefensive about the child's racial background and feel that such a placement would be good and desirable. [105, p. 12]

An English demonstration-research project concerned with interracial adoptions noted in a preliminary report that some 46 percent of all nonwhite children adopted in England in 1966 were adopted by people who had first boarded them as foster children (90, p. 157). This compared with 13 percent of all white adoptees who achieved adoption through such a route. The report notes that initial placement for foster care may be a desirable procedure in the case of the hard-to-place child. It permits the parents to develop a commitment to the child without feeling an obligation to make him a full member of the family to begin with.

Recent studies confirm the findings of earlier reports recapitulating the results of special efforts to recruit adoptive parents for minority group and other hard-to-place children. The findings indicate that programs, whatever their success, have only a limited impact on the problem. Thus a report of activities of Toronto child welfare agencies that have offered leadership in transracial adoption indicates that at the start of a special project in October 1963, 141 nonwhite children were registered as needing adoptive homes (2). Over a three-year period 101 families, 78 percent of them white, adopted children. However, at the end of the project there were more nonwhite children in the care of the agencies than had been true at the start of the project (2, p. 36). The overall results tend to substantiate Billingsley and Giovannoni's conclusion that "the general interest in interracial adoption seems considerably out of proportion to its magnitude and its potential for meeting the needs. . . . of large numbers of Negro children in need of stable and permanent families . . ." (6, p. 71).

Transracial adoptions most frequently involve children of mixed racial background. Thus in a report of the placement of 115 nonwhite children in white homes over a twelve-year period, 107, or 92 percent, were part white (31).

Nonrelative adoption of black children by blacks is overall at a level that is closely proportional to the percentage of blacks in the population. The analysis by Herzog of the limited data available makes it additionally clear that if a ratio were computed that used as a baseline only those families whose income level permitted them to be available as potential adoptive applicants, black families would be seen to be adopting at a higher rate than white families (40, p. 17). The problem then is to increase an already high adoption rate among blacks in order to meet the needs of the disproportionately large number of black children available for adoption.

The procedure of choice for stimulating additional applications should most logically follow from the barriers to adoptive application that have been identified. Recent research confirms some of the findings of earlier studies cited by Fanshel in the earlier volume of this series. Fowler concluded from interviews with 287 black men and women that relatively "few economically secure childless Black couples appear to be interested in adopting eligible children at the present time. Seeking an emotionally secure place amid discriminating practices many of them had little energy left for the risks of parenthood" (29, p. 524). The research supports policy change efforts in the direction of subsidized adoptions. The Fowler study supports the conclusion of the earlier study by Deasy and Quinn (18) that lack of interest in adoption rather than lack of knowledge or hesitancy created by agency policies and procedures was the crucial factor limiting recruitment of black adoptive applicants.

Coulton concluded from an interview study with 15 middle-class black women that there "was a positive relationship between a sense of economic security and favorable attitude toward adoption" (16, p. 46). More-detailed interviews with 129 middle-class blacks in Hartford, Connecticut, in another study yielded complementary results. The study states that "overwhelmingly our informants attributed the existence of the problem [shortage of black adoptive homes] to the prevalence of low income, poor employment and inadequate housing among Blacks" (77, p. 48). Respondents seemed knowledgeable about adoption and favorably inclined toward adoption agencies, but only 3 of the 129 respondents were seriously interested.

Research attention has been devoted to other groups of hard-to-place children such as older children. Kadushin (56) did a follow-up study of 91 families who adopted children 5 years of age or older

at the time of placement. Intensive interviews with husband and wife were tape-recorded, transcribed, and independently analyzed by three professionally trained child welfare workers. In addition adoptive parents completed some projective-type questionnaires. The satisfactions and dissatisfactions in the adoptive experience with older children were reviewed in detail. The ratio between discrete satisfactions and dissatisfactions expressed by the parents and independently identified by at least two of the raters was used as a principal criterion for evaluating the success of the placements. Seventy-three percent of the placements were successful and 18 percent were rated unsuccessful. Using a second criterion of evaluation, a summarizing rating that was a composite of interviewer, reader, and parent rating of the total experience, yielded a somewhat higher level of success—78 percent successful, 13 percent unsuccessful. This outcome of the adoptive experience with older children is not significantly different from the outcome obtained in follow-up studies of placement of infants.

Welter (115) studied 72 children placed for adoption in the United States when five years of age or older. Thirty-six of the group were children born outside the United States and transferred to this country for adoption, many of them after a number of separations and re-placements. Some 85 percent of the children were judged to be showing "good" to "excellent" adaptation on follow-up (115, Table 40, p. 126). Supported also by evidence in research reviewed under "Follow-up Studies" earlier in this chapter, the finding from different samples is uniform: the child's age at placement, beyond the first two months, is unrelated to outcome.

Massarik's (74) follow-up study of 169 children who, when placed, presented some identifiable physical difficulty requiring other than routine treatment indicated the possibility of successful adoptive placement for such children. Assessment at follow-up was made on the basis of joint interviews with adoptive parents and "unstructured observation" of the children, almost all of whom were over 5. Forty-five of the group (27 percent) had difficulties categorized by a pediatrician as "severe," including cleft palate, hip dislocation, and congenital heart defect. Two judges independently rated the "research schedules" for a measure of "satisfaction and role fulfillment" for a subgroup of 71 children whose medical condition was not correctable. The results indicated that for most of the group family relationships were satisfying and fulfilling—36 percent rated "excellent," 41 percent rated "good," 23 percent rated "doubtful" (74, p. 102). Despite residual physical difficulties, the majority of the children were developing satisfactorily and were giving enjoyment to parents and peers. The findings support the results of other follow-up studies of hard-to-place children, indicating that such placements can be made with confidence in successful outcome. As Massarik notes, "perhaps workers have underestimated [adoptive applicants'] fundamental adaptive strengths and their potential for growth" (74, p. 134).

Massarik's study of the adoptive placement of physically handicapped children also demonstrates the fact that the hard-to-place child is channeled to the doubtful applicant. In this study couples with "atypical applicants' characteristics such as exceeding a maximum age, a marital history of prior divorce" were more likely to be asked to accept the more severely handicapped child. Follow-up ratings of adoptive outcome further demonstrated that the presence of such "atypical" factors in applicants' backgrounds had no relationship to the success of the adoption.

Summary of Research

The largest percentage of children available for adoption are illegitimate children of unmarried mothers. Normal white children are easily placed despite the fact that the ratio of applicants to available children has been sharply reduced. Blacks adopt almost in proportion to their percentage in the population, but more black children than white children ultimately fail to achieve adoption. Black couples who might adopt do not lack knowledge of adoption but rather lack interest in adopting. White couples who have accepted minority group children seem to be distinguished from the general group of adoptive parents in that they are apt to be inner directed and independent of community opinion.

Increasingly, nonrelative adoptions are taking place under agency auspices. Workers may vary in their evaluations of the acceptability of the same couple, but there is substantial agreement on criteria among groups of workers. Workers' conceptions of the acceptable couple include factors such as positive marital interaction and relationship, flexible and outgoing personality, nonneurotic motivation for adoption, and acceptance of their infertility. However, workers are ready to accept also couples who deviate in some ways from these criteria. To such couples they are ready to offer the hard-to-place child.

After placement, agency contacts are relatively infrequent before final adoption. Agency and clients perceive the purpose of the postplacement contact quite differently. Adoptive parents do not want postplacement contacts because of their fear that the child will be removed.

Adoptions are generally successful for 70–80 percent of the families, agency placements having a slightly higher rate of success than independent placements. Follow-up studies of the hard-to-place child indicate that success rates for these adoptions are equally high.

Children in good adoptive homes seem to demonstrate a capacity to reverse the consequences of earlier deprivations and traumas. Neither the child's family background nor his developmental background seems to include important variables in adoptive outcome. Findings on the child's age at placement are slightly contradictory, Ripple's study (92, 93) indicating that placement under age 2 months is significantly related to subsequent adjustment, but other recent research on outcome shows age as a nonsignificant variable.

Adoptive parents' age, income, education, socioeconomic status, and religion do not seem to be important variables affecting outcome. Matching of physical characteristics has no significant influence on outcome. The principal factors affecting outcome seem to be parent variables rather than child variables, and the significant parent variables relate to attitudes toward children and adoption ("entitlement"), child-rearing practices, and the marital situation. Research indicates that assessments of parents' motivation for adoption are of questionable significance as a predictor of successful adoptive parenting, as are attitudes toward infertility and the number and kind of other children in the home.

Adopted children are interested in knowing about their background although they are reticent about overtly indicating interest or initiating discussion of this. The most difficult aspect of the adoptive parent-child relationship revolves around the question of telling.

Adopted children are disproportionately represented in psychiatric facilities, but the majority do not seem to manifest emotional difficulties requiring treatment. If the adopted child becomes disturbed he is more likely to manifest aggressive acting-out behavior than neurotic behavior. There is much speculation regarding the psychodynamic explanation for these findings. There are some empirical data suggesting that adopted children born out of wedlock are responding to the greater risks of exposure to pathogenic environments during the prenatal period. There is little difference in the proportion of agency-placed children receiving psychiatric treatment as compared with independently placed children.

Community attitudes, responsive to "biological chauvinism," are still somewhat derogatory of the adoptive family. The adoptive family copes with its marginality either by acknowledging or rejecting its difference from other families. More adequate adjustment to adoption is supposedly related to acceptance of difference.

Practice Implications

1. The research suggests that criteria for valid assessment of adoptive applicants are difficult to formulate. Those criteria that have research support are likely to be difficult to measure in the interview situation since they relate to complex attitudes. Such attitudes undergo change in living interaction with the adopted child so that there is often little relationship between attitudes expressed in the adoption study and postplacement behavior manifested.

This argues for a deemphasis of selection procedures and supports the current tendency of some agencies to give greater attention to preparation for adoptive parenthood. The worker centers on being enabler, facilitator, and helper rather than evaluator and assessor.

2. It seems clear that telling is the most difficult problem for adoptive parents and children. Unfortunately the research does not indicate the best way to handle this in order to achieve most satisfactory outcome. It does support the agency contention that not telling involves considerable danger for healthy parent-child relationships and it does suggest that the agency explicitly make discussion of the problem of telling a matter for repeated worker-client contacts.

A child's failure to ask about his biological parents should not be interpreted as disinterest or indifference. Curiosity is presumed to be present; it is inhibited, however, and parents need to be encouraged to act on the presumption that it exists and to volunteer information.

Adoptive parents can be assured that adopted children have a "curiosity about the biological parents as people rather than a feeling for them as parents." They can be encouraged to share background information with the children without too great risk that this will result in efforts to seek out the biological parent. Workers feel more comfortable in sharing background information with the parents. Apparently blood is not thicker than the bond developed between adoptive parents and children.

3. Research on interracial adoption tends to indicate that applicants who are ready to participate in such adoptions are not necessarily neurotic but merely more independent of community opinion. Many such applicants act out of reasonably healthy motives, however strange such readiness to accept children of another race may appear to the worker.

It seems clear, however, that interracial adoptions are not likely to solve the problem of finding sufficient numbers of adoptive homes for minority group children. Research support for the fact that their economic situation makes some blacks hesitant about considering adoption should encourage action toward subsidization of adoption. During 1968–69 New York, California, and Minnesota passed legislation subsidizing adoption.

4. Research indicating the possibility that some percentage of illegitimate children are damaged in pregnancy is additional support for expansion of services to unmarried mothers.

5. The research tends to show that some percentage of hard-to-place children achieve successful adoption in the home in which they were initially placed on a long-term foster care basis. Long-term foster care is a quasi-adoptive situation; subsidized adoptions are a quasi-foster care situation. Sharp differentiation between foster home care and adoptive care becomes progressively more vague. It might be in the best interests of the hard-to-place child if practice explicitly utilized long-term foster care as a prelude to adoption. Foster parenting before adoption of hard-to-place children may help to develop the level of com-

mitment and acquaintance necessary to move the parents toward adoption. This might require selection of foster parents with adoption in mind as distinguished from the current tendency to perceive these two groups of substitute parents as distinctively different. Currently legislation is being suggested in some jurisdictions in support of such procedures. The legislation would give first preference in adoption to foster parents who have cared for the child for some minimum period of time if the child becomes legally available for adoption.

Foster Family Care

"As of March 1967 there were 132,700 licensed or approved foster family homes with an aggregate capacity of 283,400 children and 700 foster group homes having a capacity of 4,800 children" (112, p. 2). No count is available of additional independent, unlicensed foster family homes. The majority of the licensed foster family homes, 73 percent, were supervised by public agencies. Public foster care has been steadily increasing and voluntary agency foster care steadily decreasing. There has been a continuing trend for voluntary agencies to phase out their foster care program.

As of March 1967, 228,700 children were in foster family care under both public and voluntary agency auspices and an additional 2,500 children were in foster group homes (112, Table 17, p. 26). The rate per 1,000 of children in foster care has increased steadily each year, from 2.5 in 1933 to 3.2 in 1967. During the same period the rate for children in substitute care in institutions decreased from 3.4 to 1.1. The figures include only those children in substitute care for reasons of neglect, dependency, or emotional disturbance (112, p. 26). By 1975 it is estimated that 302,100 children will be living in foster homes, the anticipated rate then being 3.9 per 1,000 children (66, p. 13).

Policy Questions

Some of the principal policy questions that are or should be the concern of child welfare research include these:

1. What can be done to reduce the number of children coming into foster care?

2. What criteria help determine when a child should be removed from his own home? What criteria then determine the choice of substitute care facility?

3. What can be done to increase the number of desirable foster homes for the general group of children needing care and for special groups of children, i.e., minority group children, the emotionally disturbed, the mentally and physically handicapped?

4. What characteristics identify the "successful" foster home for the general group of children coming into care as well as the home that is successful with special groups of children? Once such homes have been recruited and selected, how can children be matched to them in order to reduce the replacement rate?

5. How can the time in care be reduced to a minimum? What factors are associated with prolongation of care and what arrangements are most productive and least damaging for the child needing long-term care?

6. What definition of the foster parent role contributes optimally to the best interests of the child and others involved in foster care services?

7. How can foster parents and foster children be helped to develop and accept a clearer perception of their roles in relation to each other, the natural parents, and the worker?

8. What are the processes of relationship and interaction in the foster home that promote normal development of the child? What actions should foster parents and workers take to ensure such development?

9. How can service delivery be made more effective and efficient so that most of the families in need are reached, with a staff that is adequate in both quantitative and qualitative terms?

The research reviewed in the following sections bears on some of these questions. Other questions have not yet become problems for systematic investigation.

Coming into Care and the Foster Care Career

A recent CWLA study (76) is concerned with the genesis of the foster care event. Seven cities throughout the country, differing in size, economic level, and available social welfare services, were selected for study. Information was obtained on all requests for foster care made to all sixty-nine child care agencies in the seven cities over a three-month period in 1966—a total of 1,448. Definition of foster care services in this study included not only foster family care but also adoptive and institutional care. Illegitimate children being placed for adoption and unmarried mothers seeking maternity home care were included, making the population of the study different in composition from the Jenkins study (51) cited later. If findings on the unmarried mother and illegitimate child are ignored, the kinds of problems brought to the agency are seen to be similar to those precipitating the need for service in other studies—parents who neglected, abused, or abandoned their children; parents who were incapable of caring for their children because of physical or mental illness, socioeconomic stress, including inadequate financial resources, or family breakdown resulting from death, desertion, separation, or divorce; children who presented an inordinate burden of care because they were emotionally disturbed, manifested socially deviant behavior, or were physically or mentally handicapped. In the Jenkins study (51), 24 percent of the mothers were either unaware of or opposed to the decision for placement; in this study 15 percent of the mothers were unaware and unaccepting of the agency's plans for the child.

As in other studies, the emotionally disturbed and physically handicapped children came from a wider range of socioeconomic backgrounds than was true for other groups and more frequently from white families of higher income levels. The majority of the families presenting other reasons for service were concentrated in the lowest socioeconomic groups living on marginal income. Only a limited number of the children, 24 percent, were living with both parents in an intact family.

Socioeconomic background was a variable associated not only with request but also disposition of request. For instance, emotionally disturbed children from families with higher income, education, and occupational status were more frequently placed in specialized institutions than in foster homes. The reverse was true for children from more deprived backgrounds manifesting the same difficulties.

Information was obtained from caseworkers with regard not only to actual disposition of the request but also the ideal disposition that might have been made if adequate resources had been available. In 34 percent of the cases some decision other than the ideal decision had to be implemented. In 36 percent, in which more adequate financial assistance was needed to maintain the child in his own home, this was not available. In the 46 percent for which homemaker service might have obviated the need for placement of the child, this was not available. In a more limited percentage of cases day care or family therapy was needed for an ideal decision but was not available. The ideal decision that could not be implemented because the requisite services were not available was most often maintenance of the child in his own home.

The adequacy of resources in any community is not linearly related to financial capacity of that community. This suggests that community attitudes toward the importance of meeting children's needs is a determinant of resource allocation. Moreover, requests for service seemed to be influenced by services available so that requests made do not accurately reflect actual community needs.

Schaffer (97) conducted a study in Scotland directed toward the same general question—antecedent factors that determined a child's coming into temporary foster care—but with a more delimited focus. He compared the precare experience of two groups of families matched for socioeconomic background and living in the same locality, but in every instance the event that precipitated the need for child care was the hospitalization of the mother for confinement. One group of 100 families did not need foster care for their children when the mother was hospitalized; a second group of 100 families placed their children in foster care during this period. Interviews were conducted with the mother while in the hospital after delivery to elicit the factors that resulted in these different decisions regarding child care. Additional information on family functioning was obtained from the local health visitor who had contact with the family.

The 100 families that neither sought nor needed foster care for their children were able, in each instance, to arrange alternate private care. In almost all cases this involved the enlistment of assistance from relatives, especially grandmothers, aunts, fathers, and older siblings. In less than 10 percent of the cases was homemaker service the resource of choice.

Families that applied for and needed foster care were distinguished from the first group not so much with regard to the availability and accessibility of surrogate mother resources within the family but rather in attitudes toward the use of such resources and in attitudes regarding priority given the needs of children as against the needs of adults in the family. Fathers in the group of families using foster care were less willing to assume the maternal role, which in turn reflected a general lack of involvement in child care; contact with relatives was less cordial so there was a hesitancy to ask them to help. Attitudes toward the children suggested a greater readiness to accept the more impersonal, formal channels of public care. Even though both groups of families were structurally intact and in contact with the extended family, the affectional, interpersonal family ties were weaker and more tenuous for the group of families that made use of foster care. Visiting was less frequent and there was less of a pattern of intrafamily mutual aid.

The group of families that kept the children at home gave the need to do this high priority when they faced the problem of role coverage with the mother's hospitalization. In the second group of families

this ordering of priorities is not seen—relatives were not approached for fear of owing a debt of gratitude toward them, grandmothers were not prepared to stay away from work and unemployed fathers preferred to see their children go into care rather than shoulder the responsibility of their supervision. [97, p. 84]

While the researchers regard these differences as the more important factors contributing to the difference in child care arrangements, it should be noted that the group of families using foster care had a significantly larger number of younger children who impose a greater burden of care. In addition, these families had suffered a significantly greater proportion of loss through death of maternal grandmothers, were somewhat more geographically distant from grandmothers, and were generally more predisposed to use agency service at every point of crisis.

Jenkins and Sauber (51) attempted to answer the same question for a more heterogeneous group of children who came into publicly supported foster care in New York City during a four-month period in 1963. During this period 891 children coming from 425 families were placed. Information on the family situation during the year prior to placement was obtained from interviews by experienced social workers with the parents or parental surrogates responsible for the care of the child during this period. Interviews were conducted immediately after placement. Most of the chil-

dren were placed in foster family care, but some limited groups of children included in the study were placed in group homes or institutions. All children experienced placement for the first time.

The single most frequent factor necessitating placement was the mother's illness —either physical illness, including confinement (29 percent), or mental illness (11 percent). In 17 percent of the cases the child's behavior necessitated removal from the home and in 10 percent of the cases the child was placed to protect him from the neglect and/or abuse of parents. There was a large catchall group resulting from a variety of family problems—divorce, death, abandonment, imprisonment—accounting for 33 percent of the placements.

But the precipitating event obtained its potency for requiring removal and placement of the children primarily because the ongoing family situation was, for most of the group, highly problem filled. Forty-one percent of the families were single-parent families, public assistance payments were the major source of support for 38 percent of the families, and 76 percent were members of minority groups. The living situation during the year preceding placement was, for a high proportion of the group, marginal and burdensome. These families are high risk and placement prone. The report notes:

The overall picture of the retrospective year shows marginal families without sufficient resources to sustain themselves in the community when additional pressures or problems are added to their preexisting burdens. [51, p. 61]

The fact that high percentages of children coming into care are referred by police (51, p. 73), even when the social agency already had contact with the family, suggests the need for twenty-four-hour child welfare intake as well as greater sensitivity on the part of social workers to the symptoms of family breakdown.

Only in the case of the 17 percent of the families for which placement resulted primarily from the disturbed behavior of the child were the children likely to be white, from an intact, adequately supported family. The child's behavior had exhausted the emotional resources of the family, other relatives were unwilling to undertake the burden of care of such a child, and the cost of private psychiatric treatment was beyond the family's capacity, as it is for most.

Following the precipitating event, placement occurred as a consequence of the kinds of factors highlighted by the Schaffer study (97)—the unwillingness or inability of other persons in the immediate family to care for the children. The level of commitment to care of the children within the immediate family group was such as to require substitute care. Furthermore, many of the families, especially in the physically incapacitated group, saw placement as a desirable resource through which children could be adequately cared for during an emergency.

Children coming into care because of physical illness of the mother were likely to remain in care for a limited period of time. Children placed because they manifested emotional problems were likely to remain in care the longest. Some 49 percent of the group moved out of placement within a three-month period and in these instances foster care performed its classical function —temporary care during an emergency. Moreover, the researchers thought that in 17 percent of the cases studied placement was avoidable if alternative available resources had been exploited by a family with the help of a social worker (51, p. 185).

Some recent studies of homemaker service as related to foster care confirm what is suggested in the studies cited, namely, that some children would not have needed to come into care if adequate alternative community resources had been available. A report of a special homemaker service to single-parent families notes the following:

[In 1967] the use of this service enabled 109 children to remain in their own homes during periods when parents were faced with illness or some other crises that would otherwise have propelled the children into placement in foster homes. [104, p. 75]

Brewster (11) describes the development of an extended range of child welfare services in one community, including homemaker, day care, and protective services. She notes that "while referrals have nearly doubled since the beginning of the program the placement of children in foster care has dropped sharply" (11, p. 150).

Maas (68) attempted to factor out the variables characterizing the child who is likely to remain in long-term foster care as contrasted with peers whose stay in foster care is of shorter duration. Population for the study was derived from the earlier nationwide study of foster care, *Children in Need of Parents* (69). The follow-up study, like the original, did not include any child in care for less than three months. The follow-up sample of 422 children included 101 children who left foster care in less than three years and the long-term group of 130 children who remained in care for ten years or longer. More than 75 percent of the children had remained in foster care for longer than three years and 31 percent for more than ten years—confirmation that for many children foster care is not temporary care. The factors that tended to differentiate the long-term cases (in care more than ten years) from short-term cases (less than three years) all point to multiple disadvantages. Long-term care children were likely to be from minority groups and/or from Catholic families at the lowest economic level whose parents, with whom they had a tenuous or marred relationship, maintained no contact with the agency. They were children who functioned intellectually at below-average levels and 20 percent of whom had some irremediable physical disability. Children on the caseloads of large city agencies faced an additional hazard for remaining in care since they seemed to lose their visibility to agency personnel.

Jenkins (49) also studied the placement career of children to determine the difference between children who returned home within a short period after placement and those retained in care for a longer time. She followed 891 children from 425 families for a period of two years following placement, relating duration of care to characteristics of the child, the family, and reasons for placement. She found in New York City, as did Maas in his nationwide study, that the longer a child is in placement the longer he is likely to remain. The curve for leaving care flattens appreciably with the passage of time.

In both the Jenkins and Maas studies, family composition was not related to length of time in care. But unlike Maas, Jenkins found that in New York both housing and income were related in an unexpected direction—families more adequately housed and with more adequate income had a larger percentage of children in the long-stay group. This apparently results from a compounding of these factors with the reason the child came into care. Children with behavioral disturbances were more likely than any other group to remain in care beyond two years. Since such children came from intact families with adequate incomes, Jenkins' results reflect this.

Foster Care Selection and the Foster Home

Some of Fanshel's (25) hypotheses, confirmed to a limited extent by his data, are empirically supported by Wakeford (113). These relate to the home-centered orientation of women highly motivated to foster children. Wakeford interviewed 66 British foster parents as well as a random sample of 148 parents whose names were obtained from the Register of Electors in the same area. All of the foster parents expressed desire to continue in the role while none of the 148 controls expressed any interest in fostering. The principal difference between the two groups lay in the fact that the foster mother highly evaluated the role of mother and homemaker and derived her principal satisfactions from such activity and conversely had little interest in activities outside the home. She derived her status and self-esteem from child care, and the presumed disadvantages of large families were advantages to such a woman.

Staged dramatic vignettes about foster care have been used experimentally as a procedure for recruitment (106). Attitudinal scales and postpresentation interviews were used to ascertain the impact of the productions on attitudes toward foster care. The study did not present results of effects on recruitment. However, the research established the fact that different groups in the community have strongly different attitudes toward the foster child, the foster parent role, and the foster care agency. It is suggested that agencies need to tailor their recruitment campaigns to the group in the community to which they are directed.

Exemplifying the tendency to view foster parents as colleagues is the attempt by one agency to involve them in the selection procedure. Applicants were given the names of active foster parents and asked to contact them to talk about foster family care (30). Over a three-month period in 1967 twenty such contacts were made. Comparison with application and selection statistics for the same three months during the previous year tended to show that the procedure did not make much difference in the number of interviews in the subsequent study, in the nature and focus of the initial interview, or in the percentages of acceptance or rejection. However, applicants seemed better prepared for the initial interview and appreciated the opportunity for exploration before being committed to a formal study. Foster parents felt more integrated with the agency and were reassured by the interest of others in foster care and by the opportunity to use their experience to help others.

Cautley (17), in a detailed study of 115 foster homes caring for latency-age children, also found that the foster parents came from large families and that they had fewer natural children than their own parents. The principal motivation of most of the foster parents was the satisfaction derived from having children in the home—there was a felt need for children. While foster mothers indicated that they were better known to the workers than were foster fathers and that they found the contact with the worker helpful, they were handicapped by having been given too little knowledge of the child prior to placement and by the high turnover rates of workers. About one-third of the mothers said there had been times when they did not know who their caseworker was.

An interesting research innovation used in this study was a Weekly Behavior Report Form. Every fourth week foster mothers wrote descriptions of the foster child's "most difficult behavior" and "most pleasing behavior" during the previous week and the foster parents' response to the behavior. Cooperation in the use of the forms was excellent. The foster families in the study group were selected because they were caring for white latency-age children who were evaluated as disturbed. Degree of disturbance was established through use of the Borgatta-Fanshel Child Behavior Characteristics Schedule (8). A significant relationship was found between the number of placements a child experiences and both his degree of disturbance and the social worker's rating of how difficult he is to have in a family group. Time in placement per se is not a significant variable, but risk of placement increases with time in placement. The child's confusion and conflict about his foster care status tend to diminish with time in placement.

A global success rating was established for each family. Success was defined as the extent to which the goals of the placement were being met as judged by the caseworker assigned to the family.

The image of the "successful" foster home which emerges out of the analysis from the point of view of the social workers is one of parents who are generally well suited to the foster child in their care, who in fact meet their child's specific needs, who are able to provide consistent discipline but who at the same time are sufficiently flexible in their expectations for the child's behavior and who are themselves persons who feel confident of their roles as parents. [17, p. 67]

Skill in handling the child's major problems accounted for the major part of the variance in the global success rating.

A factor analysis of discrete variables indicated that only a limited number of the variables identified for study were correlated with the global success rating, and even those correlations barely achieve significance. Few of the foster parent developmental history factors correlated with success except religious orientation of the foster mother's parents, which was negatively associated with success. This is probably related to another negatively related variable—"number of areas in which the foster parents are autocratic." Information provided by the foster father that his parents were "affectionate" toward him correlates positively with success. Parents with more children of their own and hence more experience in child-rearing were more successful, as were families in which foster parents "received encouragement from each other." Although the range of socioeconomic levels of these families was rather narrow, success was positively related to "general economic level of the family."

Solomon (101) focused on the capacity of foster parents to assist latency-age children in meeting two developmental tasks postulated by psychoanalytic theory as being significant for mastering this period —continued resolutions of the Oedipal struggle and solidification of the superego. Thirty-five foster families were studied, the source of the data being extended interviews with foster parents. While it was clear that physical care of the children was adequate in all families, in only one-third of the cases was the foster family aware of these two developmental tasks and actively engaged in helping the foster children achieve them. Some of the research suggests that failure stemmed from characterological defects in the foster parents. However, material by Cautley (17) and Fanshel (25) on child-rearing approaches of foster parents indicated that class and/or educational factors may be more significant in determining the way these parents implement the parental role.

Parker (81) attempted to develop and then validate a table predicting success in foster care. "Success" was defined as un-interrupted maintenance of the child in the same foster home over a period of five years; if the child was removed at any time before five years had elapsed the case was categorized as a "failure." Parker applied this outcome criteria to a series of 209 foster placements after eliminating those cases in which removal of the child seemed to be the result of purely situational or administrative factors. Preplacement information on the child, the natural parents, and the foster home was obtained from a careful review of agency records, and the relationship of such units of information to outcome criteria was analyzed. Fifty-two percent of the 209 cases were successful in that the child was maintained in the home over a five-year period. The factor most significantly related to failure in outcome was the presence in the foster home of a younger natural child of the foster parents. Older children coming into foster care and children with behavioral problems were more likely to fail. Children who had previous experiences as foster children and children who had been removed from their own homes at earlier ages were more likely to be successful. Child-rearing in an institution during infancy was not related to failure unless the institutional experience had been prolonged beyond two years. The number of previous moves was not related to failure.

Based on these general conclusions, a weighted predictive table was formulated. The author points out that only the concatenation of factors is predictive, not the discrete factors themselves. Changing any element in the predictive table changes the weighting. With this caveat Parker applied the table to another series of 108 cases, and while not as effectively discriminative as had been hoped, the table did predict many of the cases that did fail.

A Scottish study attempted a recapitulation of the functioning of 205 young adults who had spent most of their childhood in substitute care (28). Of the 205 subjects followed up for two years after they be-

came legally independent at age 18, 139 had been cared for during childhood in foster boarding homes. At age 20, the period of the last follow-up, 96 percent of the group were employed or in training and independently responsible for their own support. In every instance relations with foster parents were categorized as good (90 percent) or fair (10 percent) during care, but by age 20, 25 percent had lost contact with their foster parents. The delinquency rate was high, however, 17 percent having been convicted of some crime at some time before age 20. Assessment of performance needs to take into consideration not only difficulties in the interpersonal living situation encountered by the group but also limitations in potentialities—more than 50 percent of the group had tested IQ scores below 90 (28, p. 61).

The study is one of the few recent boarding home follow-up studies available, but it suffers from the fact that limited information is provided regarding such methodological matters as procedure for data collection, sources of data, and reliability checks utilized.

Reactions to Placement

Despite the considerable practice wisdom available in descriptive clinical reports, little empirical study has been made of the effects on children of the separation necessitated by moving into a foster home or the process of adaptation to the experience. Thomas (108) hypothesized that placement involves separation from and loss of relationship with persons who afforded the child gratification. Such loss initiates a process of grief and mourning through which the child does the work of removing cathexis from libidinal objects from which he is now separated so as to make psychic energy available for investment in new objects, namely, the foster parents. The process of mourning supposedly consists of a series of sequential steps, reflected in clearly identifiable behavior and appropriate accompanying affect—preprotest, protest, despair, detachment. Such a process of intrapsychic reorganization is a burden that makes more difficult the mastering of normal developmental tasks. Furthermore, since psychosocial development is facilitated by supportive object relationships, any loss of objects is likely to have adverse consequences for development. Children experiencing object loss and the necessary adaptation can therefore be expected to show failures in achievement of demands selected for examination in the research—doing chores, developing peer relationships, sharing with foster parents.

Basing her research on this framework, Thomas interviewed the foster parents of 35 children who had no previous placement but who had been in their current placement for at least nine months. All were normal white latency-age children. A heavy demand was made of respondents, who were asked to detail, retrospectively some nine to eighteen months later, the foster child's behavior and accompanying affect for four distinct periods: the first week in placement, one week to two months, two to eight months, and eight to nine months. The timing reflected the different phases of the mourning process.

The grief process was found to be sequential, although not as clear as had been hypothesized. Resolution of object loss was found to be associated with consensus about and clarity of future plans. Separation and object loss were less difficult for those children who had some clear idea about what would happen to them. Surprisingly, there was little difference in the process between those children who were visited rarely by their natural parents and those children who received frequent visits.

The inner life of the placed child is not readily available to exploration and explication. Clinical interviews are, of course, the principal procedure through which an attempt is made to free the child to communicate his private thoughts and feelings. But he can only share, if he is willing, those thoughts and feelings of which he is aware.

The Thematic Apperception Test (TAT) is designed to allow the child to reveal content not yet at the level of his explicit awareness. North (78) used the TAT with 12 school-age nonhandicapped foster children who had been placed at least twice and whose natural parents did not visit them regularly. The TAT responses of these children were compared with those of a matched control group of children. The foster children did show a significantly greater degree of need affiliation. However, death and departure themes, connoting anxiety over separation from and hostility toward parental figures, were not significantly different for the two groups, although differences were in the expected direction. There was only negligible difference in the mean incidence scores for the category of angry and fighting words, although a significant difference for the category of sad, crying words. In general the impression was of "children who are primarily yearning for affiliation and who are somewhat depressed" (78, p. 46).

A more family-focused orientation to separation experience in placement suggests that filial deprivation for parents is a process paralleling parental deprivation for children. As part of a larger study (50), some 430 parents were asked: "How did you feel the day your child was placed?" Reactions identified included sad, mad, glad feelings—sadness, anger, bitterness, relief, thankfulness, worry, nervousness, guilt, shame, emptiness. Eighty-eight percent of parents reported a feeling of sadness at the separation, followed, in frequency, by feelings of nervousness and worry. From 30 to 39 percent of the parents reported feelings of guilt and shame—fathers more frequently feeling shame, mothers more frequently feeling guilt. These feelings were directed against themselves. About half the parents reported feelings of anger and bitterness or thankfulness and relief. In most instances such feelings were directed toward the agency. Anger and bitterness were likely to be felt when separation resulted from neglect and/or abuse, thankfulness when the event precipitating separation was physical illness of the mother, and relief and guilt when separation was occasioned by the child's behavioral maladjustment. Guilt was more frequently expressed by mothers of children placed because of emotional disturbance than by mothers whose children were placed because of abandonment, neglect, or abuse.

Holman (42) obtained the responses of 20 foster children to questions designed to evaluate their knowledge of their foster care status. Although it is a limited study with doubtful outcome criteria, he found that those children who had a greater knowledge about why they were in foster care were likely to have less difficulty in care.

Long-term Foster Care Services

With the recognition that for a sizable percentage of children foster family care is not a temporary expedient, more explicit attention is being devoted to development of planned long-term placement. This involves acceptance by both agency and foster parents of a plan to maintain this child in this home indefinitely. It is a quasi-adoptive situation in which the foster parent is granted more autonomy than is the case in the usual foster care arrangement.

The explicit need for a resource such as planned long-term foster family care is documented in a study of the experience of a large voluntary adoption agency in New York that initiated such a program for minority group children (73). The agency accepted into the program "any child from birth to 3 years of age who could benefit from family life but whose parents could not provide a home and for whom adoptive homes were hard to find" (73, p. 167). At the end of a 3½-year period some 662 children had been placed in foster homes with the agency's considered plan that they remain there until fully grown. This group constituted more than half of the 1,211 children referred to the project, some of whom subsequently returned home or were adopted.

A study was made of the development of the children for whom long-term continuation in foster care was planned, and workers' evaluation indicated that in 97.4 percent of the cases overall development was either average or good. Judgments were made by the child's caseworker in terms of some anchoring statements developed by staff consensus and were based on the worker's knowledge of the child supplemented by medical, psychological, and school reports. A reliability check of workers' evaluations was made by the researchers in 10 percent of the cases. The researchers conclude that as far as can be ascertained after a limited period in long-term postcare, the development of the children seems to be satisfactory.

Almost 34 percent of the 261 children removed from the project through adoption were adopted by their foster parents. If this had not happened the project's adoption rate would have been just over 13 percent. As it was, the rate was 21.6 percent. Parents who had considered legal adoption but who were hesitant noted that the main barrier to adoption was financial.

The need of children for long-term foster care can be met by programs that offer the status of agency employee to foster parents. Pratt (86, 87) describes an experimental program in which foster mothers are hired as agency employees, living with their husbands and five foster children in houses in residential areas leased by the agency. The foster fathers continue their regular employment outside the home.

This demonstration program of "assembled families" involved 11 foster homes serving 54 children, all of whom are in long-term care. All of the children in the group were black, from severely deprived backgrounds, and all had been institutionalized for some period of time before foster group family placement. Their adjustment to the foster home was "generally satisfactory," but a detailed study of functioning based on interviews and psychological examination showed some 22 percent demonstrating "very poor" functioning after ten months in placement (38, Table I,

p. 13). Level of child functioning in these long-term placements was less satisfactory than in Madison's study cited earlier. However, the group in the Hampton study was older and subject to traumatizing insults over a longer period of time.

Payment was at the rate of about $5,400 a year (in 1963) and included vacations, sick leave, and time off each week. The relationship between the foster parents and the social worker was conceptualized as approximating that of supervisor and student social worker or case aide. Staff meetings of foster parents were scheduled regularly. They developed strong identification with the agency and they perceived their status as "working for Family and Child Services." "There was no evidence of incompatibility between the employee status and the parenting role" (87, p. 27). Nor was there any evidence that care of the children was adversely affected by the financial return offered.

The project suggests a tempering of social workers' optimism that offering foster parents employee status and more adequate remuneration will in itself resolve the problem of finding a sufficient number of adequate foster homes. Despite the offer of employee status and salary it took twenty-two months to attract and select the first seven couples. The report notes that "our hypothesis that it would attract many women who otherwise would of necessity be working outside the home was not substantiated" (87, p. 27). Employee status does enhance and support foster care functioning, and for some the financial supports make implementation of a desire to become a foster parent possible. But the desire to accept children for care is a prior and more fundamental consideration.

At the end of the five-year demonstration period 90 percent of the children selected remained in these homes on a long-term foster care basis and 90 percent of the foster parents continued in service. This substantiated the hypothesis of the demonstration that recruitment of foster parents on an employee status for long-term foster care was practical.

Service Delivery and Staffing

The past several years have witnessed growing concern with the service delivery system. There have been recurrent and increasingly vehement accusations of discriminatory client selection—that is, of "creaming" the client group through offering service not to those in the greatest need but to those with greatest competence in enacting the role of client. Added to chronic complaints of fragmentation, lack of coordination and overlap of services, physical and psychological distance between agencies and service populations, lack of responsiveness and administrative inflexibility of agencies, this has generated pressure for innovations in service delivery.

Purvine and Ryan (89) attempted an empirical test of some of the presumed deficiencies in service delivery. They studied the intake of the total child welfare agency network in a metropolitan community of 2 million people over a five-week period in 1964. All of the major child welfare agencies in the community—public and private, sectarian and nonsectarian—were included in the study.

The 686 "inquiries" received by the network of agencies during the study period were categorized in terms of three general problem groupings. The largest group was for foster family care service and for casework service resulting from parental difficulties—neglect, abuse, mental or physical illness. The second largest group was for adoption service for both the unmarried mother and the illegitimate child. The third group was for casework or substitute care service resulting from problems of child behavior or child incapacity.

"The study was not designed to identify need for service as differentiated from request for service, but there is some indication that the discrepancy between the two may be sizable" (89, p. 128). A recapitulation of the total number of illegitimate hospital births in the community during the study periods, added to the number of incompleted referrals to the agencies during this period, indicated that the need for service was much greater than is suggested by the count of actual inquiries made.

The unmarried mothers' group had the highest rate of acceptance for service—65 percent. Intake was rapid and the decision to accept was made by the intake worker. The largest problem group—request for service because of parental difficulties— was least likely to be accepted, only 29 percent of the inquiries eventuating in acceptance. A request for adoption service was much more likely to be accepted (63 percent accepted) than was a request for financial assistance (13 percent accepted).

There was almost no difference between white and nonwhite applicants in the overall acceptance rate, but acceptance of black applicants was more heavily concentrated in the public agency sector. Inquiries from applicants of higher occupational status were more likely to be accepted. Referrals by professionals were more likely to result in acceptance than either referrals from nonprofessionals or self-referrals. In general, then, the study supported many of the presumed deficiencies in service delivery.

The most significant recent innovation in service delivery came with the development of the neighborhood service center. This was designed to be an agency offering residents of a specific and limited geographic area centralized access to a wide range of services and programs. The neighborhood service centers are, as the name implies, concerned with child welfare as only one of a wide variety of problem situations for which service is offered. Consequently research on the service centers is child welfare research in only a limited sense.

The best research review of the centers is the one conducted by Perlman and Jones (84). This study reviewed the work of some seven agencies responsible for twenty-one centers. Data were obtained through visits, interviews with agency staff, and record reading. The study tends to support the contention that people in need will make greater use of services if these are located in their immediate neighborhood.

However, in dealing with the same problems previously encountered by traditional agencies, the neighborhood centers tended to resort to traditional alternatives.

Faced by demands which were beyond their resources, services tried to restrict their clientele rather than reach out to them, to limit the services provided to meet minimum legal and administrative requirements rather than to serve the needs of people. [84, p. 77]

Furthermore, "aspirations to provide a coherent, multi-sided service ran into the same problem of specialization and fragmentation" as units within the agency began to establish autonomous enclaves (84, p. 43).

The service centers not only attempted service delivery in a new way, they attempted to implement a changing emphasis in the kinds of services offered. There was less determined focus on psychological change procedures and more explicit concern with meeting the concrete needs of the client in an effort to reduce environmental stress. Strategies of advocacy, brokerage, and active mobilization of client power for social action supplemented direct work with the client.

A comprehensive program of multiple, integrated services offered by a center centrally located with respect to the population at risk meets only partially the criticism of traditional service delivery systems. To make service more psychologically accessible required, it was felt, some change in the nature of the personnel available to the client. As a consequence one component of the changed delivery system was the addition of indigenous nonprofessional staff. The change was multiply determined. Not only was social distance between helper and helped reduced, but the changes in staffing helped meet the persistent need for additional social service staff as well as providing "new careers" for the poor. The change in staffing received impetus from both the civil rights movement and the War on Poverty.

Child welfare agencies have for some

time employed nonprofessional personnel. These have generally been college-educated workers trained in areas other than social work. However, the agencies continue to face the problem of finding a sufficient number of professionals. With the growing realization and gradual acceptance of the fact that there will never be enough professionally trained child welfare workers, efforts have been made to develop new models in deployment of the professional staff persons available.

The trend has been in the direction of amplifying the impact and effectiveness of professionals by working through auxiliary staff with less extensive education. One procedure in implementing this approach is the team model. This involves having a group of three or four college graduates functioning under the direction of a graduate social worker who is the team leader. Responsibility for decision-making and treatment planning rests with the team leader, but these are implemented by team members under the leader's direction. A discussion of the rationale of the team model and suggestions for its implementation in foster care may be found in a CWLA pamphlet (13). (See also reports by Brieland [12] and Gil [33].)

Little research has been done on such programs. There are a few descriptive accounts (15, 114) which indicate that the model is feasible and achieves some of the intent. Interestingly enough both accounts note that the secretary, one of whom is assigned to each team, is instrumental in seeing that routine team responsibilities are carried out. The general feeling seems to be that the team model, especially when strengthened by the addition of competent secretarial-administrative assistance, holds promise for increasing the employment possibilities of non-MSWs in child welfare with assurance that service to the client will not suffer as a consequence.

Such a model may be an unnecessarily complex approach as against simply hiring nonprofessional workers for the job that needs to be done. This is a question raised by the only recent empirical study of the actual differential utilization of professional and nonprofessional staff in child welfare agencies. Jones (54) studied the actual job assignments and activities of nonprofessional workers in agencies offering a foster family care service. The study population consisted of twelve voluntary agencies employing a total of fifty-three nonprofessional workers. In each of the agencies at least 51 percent of the casework and supervisory staff were graduate social workers. This condition was imposed to ensure that the agency did have a choice in making task assignments. Information was obtained on the basis of structured interviews with administrators responsible for the foster family care program and with the supervisors of the nonprofessional workers.

Despite the general presumption that a differentiation is made between job activities of professional and nonprofessional workers, the researcher found that "during the time of the study 86 percent [of the nonprofessional workers] were assigned the same kinds of jobs as professional workers" (54, p. 315). Furthermore, there was

similarity rather than difference in both kind and degree of controls used in supervising professional and non-professional workers— agency policies were almost the same for professionals and non-professionals—and 96 percent of the non-professionals participated in inservice training that included professional workers. [54, p. 323]

Although the basis for evaluation is not detailed, the researcher concludes that the quality of the nonprofessionals' work was satisfactory.

Apparently, then, despite the supposed clear differentiation between professional and nonprofessional workers, once they are hired by an agency it is difficult to tell them apart in terms of job content, agency policy, in-service training, or supervisory procedure. Because this is a somewhat startling conclusion, at variance with what the social work profession thinks is and should be the case, it might be well to note that a similar, more rigorous study of professionals and nonprofessionals in a large psychiatric hospital concluded: "There was no apparent difference between MSW's and non-MSW's on the staff as to the kinds of activities in which they were involved" (4, p. 137).

Jones spells out a useful categorization of the kinds of activities that might be more productively assigned to nonprofessional workers. These include supportive services (escort activity, friendly visiting), administrative assistance (making appointments, routine reports, preliminary screening of foster parent applicants), and enriching services (tutoring, recreational activity with foster children). This is one of a number of attempts to detail the differences between the child welfare tasks that might legitimately be assigned to employees with different levels of training. However, unless it can be clearly established that professionals can more effectively and efficiently do the tasks denied to others, agencies will find it difficult to recruit and retain staff members to do the less interesting, less rewarding tasks.

Perhaps a practical approach to ameliorating the staff gap lies in reallocation of the child welfare workers' disposition of work time. A study in England of diary sheets of the daily work activities of thirteen child welfare workers indicated that in an average workweek of forty-seven hours, nineteen hours were spent with clients (48, p. 156).

Summary of Research

The child coming into foster home care comes, for the most part, from chronically deprived lower-class families facing crisis situations. While most of the children are white, minority group children are over-represented. A disproportionately large number of children come from single-parent homes.

The situation that most frequently brings children into short-term care is illness of the mother. Problems in parental role implementation owing to death, divorce, desertion, and inadequate income, which are manifested frequently in neglect and/or abuse, bring a sizable group of children into long-term care. A third cluster results from the child's disturbed behavior or physical or mental handicaps, another antecedent of long-term care. The children coming into care because of disturbed behavior or handicaps are more likely to come from a wider range of socioeconomic backgrounds than is true for the first two groups. Aside from the last group of children, foster home care is a service to the more socioeconomically deprived sectors of the population.

Whether or not a child comes into care is a function not only of the family's crisis situation and/or the child's behavior, but also of community attitudes and available family and child welfare services. The rate and nature of utilization of foster home care differ widely from one community to another. The greater the variety of child welfare resources the community provides, the more likely it is that the actual disposition of the request for placement approaches the most desirable disposition for the child. Placement is not always a last resort after all, for less radical alternatives than the child's removal from his family have often not been fully explored and exploited. Families differ, too, in the intrafamily resources they are ready and willing to bring to bear in order to prevent placement and in the relative priority given to the child's needs as against the needs of adults in the family.

For many children foster home care is not a temporary substitute care resource. Probably as many as 25 percent of all children placed run the risk of growing up in foster care as "orphans of the living," and the longer a child is in care, the longer he is likely to remain in care. While in care the child is likely to experience two or three re-placements. Children coming into care because they are manifesting disturbed behavior run a high risk of re-placement. Many children make an adequate adjustment to long-term foster care and studies of current functioning of children in such care, as well as follow-up studies of children who have grown up in such care, indicate that relatively normal psychosocial development is possible in this situation, although relatively high delinquency rates coupled with intellectual deficits of unstudied origins, have been found.

The research suggests that investigation of the child–foster home interactional configuration is more likely to be illuminating than a study of discrete variables associated with either the child or the foster home. Foster parents are not a homogeneous group: some obtain greater satisfaction from caring for younger children while others prefer older children; some are interested in short-term contact with the child, others in a quasi-adoptive relationship. When child and foster parent temperaments complement each other, this matching ensures greater probability of continuation in the home. Discrete child variables that were identified as associated with failure were prior experience of more than two years in an institution, lack of understanding of the meaning of foster care, older age at placement, and number of re-placements experienced. Effects of visits from parents were contradictory.

Foster parents are generally members of the blue-collar or semiskilled working class and beyond middle age. They come from large clannish families and the foster mother's interests revolve around homemaking and child care. The foster father derives satisfaction from contributing to the community and keeping his wife happy in her homemaking orientation. He is not a passive member of the household, but tends to be perceived as such by the social worker since he feels that child care and discussions of child care are not appropriately within his role. Given the somewhat limited educational background and rural, folk-oriented ideology of foster parents, there is apt to be a discrepancy in child care attitudes as expressed by foster parents and social workers.

Foster parents are becoming progressively harder to recruit; other foster parents may be useful in recruitment and orientation. Only a small percentage of those inquiring ultimately accept children in placement. Attrition is more a consequence of applicant withdrawal than of agency rejection.

Foster parents have difficulty in distinguishing the uniqueness of the foster parent role from the natural parent role. There is considerable confusion in the mind of the foster parent regarding the respective responsibilities toward the child of themselves, the agency, and the natural parents. The definitions of the foster parents' relationship to the agency, as perceived by them, and of their role vis-à-vis the social worker are highly ambiguous.

Motivation was not a crucial determinant of foster parents' competence, although some motivations, especially those deriving from the exploitation of fostering to meet neurotic needs, seem to be more likely to be associated with failure. However, the significance of motivation derives from the way it is expressed in the total foster family configuration.

Some discrete foster family variables associated with the greater likelihood of failure are lack of warmth toward and understanding of the child, autocratic family relationship, and natural children in the home of approximately the same age as the foster child. Some variables associated with success were economic well-being, child care experience of the foster mother, and a cooperative relationship between foster father and mother.

Foster care workers showed a clearly defined conception of the ideal foster parent, which tended to reflect middle-class values. Actual selection of foster parents frequently tended to violate the ideal conception since a limited applicant pool did not permit much selectivity. There is low reliability of assessment of the same foster home by two different workers. The more the foster parents' attitudes resembled the worker's, the greater the likelihood that the worker understood the parents.

Practice Implications

1. Two different relationships that appear substantiated by the research point to the same recommendation for action: (a) the relationship between time in care and the likelihood that a child will continue in care and (b) the relationship between number of re-placements and degree of disturbance likely to be manifested by the child. Both argue for maximum agency and worker efforts shortly after the child moves into placement. It is at this point in the placement career that the best efforts need to be concentrated. If there is any possibility that the child can be returned home, the chances of implementing that possibility decrease with the passage of time. If there is little possibility that the child can return home and long-term care is highly likely, success in the first placement will reduce the probability of problems during the history of placement. The most crucial of all placements is the first, and the most crucial of all times in the first placement is the early period.

2. For a long time there has been a concern about "telling" in adoption. There has been no concern with this in the foster situation, perhaps because most foster children are older when placed and are aware of what is going on while it is taking place. The research tends to show that greater knowledge and understanding of what prompted placement and what foster care means are associated with better adjustment to the situation. This suggests that child welfare workers be more explicitly concerned with sharing, either directly with the child or indirectly through the foster parents, what made it necessary for the child to come into care. In doing this, the workers themselves have to be clear as to why placement was necessary. Here, as with telling in adoption, the risk is run of incurring the child's hostility, devaluing the

natural parents in the child's mind, and enhancing the child's feeling of rejection or self-contempt. However, the consequences of lack of clarity on the part of the child regarding why he is where he is constitute a greater danger.

3. The research suggests the need for greater flexibility in the provision of services currently available. Hours of homemaker care and length of care need to be extended if the service is to be more useful in preventing placement. Requiring for homemaker service the availability of a parent in the home excludes from consideration for this service the large number of single-parent families facing placement decisions. Reserving some openings in day care centers on a rotating basis for children in risk of placement might help to maintain some children in the home.

4. Research identifies the single-parent family as a high-risk group for foster care. Practice might need to give greater support to measures designed to protect the single-parent family, such as special insurance programs, special housing, reserved day care facilities, and special subsidies.

5. The child in placement becomes progressively more "invisible" to agency staffs, especially if things are going well. The pressure of current decisions seems to take precedence over decisions already made and implemented with some degree of success. To retrieve for visibility children who may get lost in the file, periodic explicit review of plans for the child is necessary.

6. Research use of agency foster care records suggests that greater effort be made to record systematically the pattern of foster family performance with regard to the succession of children the family has fostered. Currently such performance tends to be recorded in the child's record, but there is no regular pattern of maintaining a record on the foster family as such. Such records would give workers a longitudinal view of the family's performance with various children and highlight, for decision-making, the foster family's greatest strengths.

7. There is limited research on the ef-

fects of identifying the foster parent as an agency employee and paying him a reasonable wage for work performed. While the research indicates that such an innovation may not greatly increase the number of foster homes available, it also shows that employee status and wage payments that enhance foster parent status are not antithetical to concerned good care of the children. Such provisions have the further salutary effect of more clearly defining reciprocal agency–foster care roles. Practice can therefore move with some assurance toward implementing this modification in foster parent status.

The shift to employee-colleague status involves a shift in perception of the foster parent so that he is seen as more capable of autonomous decision-making, of participating more actively in decision-making, and of sharing in the general responsibilities of the agency. Research reports on involvement of foster parents in recruitment, selection, and orientation of other foster parents point to a desirable extension of foster parent functions.

Change of status redefines what a foster parent is; a redefinition of who a foster parent is might also be needed. The definition might include friends and close relatives. Poor families are likely to have poor relatives and relatives may be unable, rather than unwilling, to assume the cost of care of additional children without assistance. Foster care payments to fathers would permit compensation for loss of earnings if the father were to stay at home to care for the child.

It is recognized that such redefinitions are more political questions than technical ones. Employee status, adequate wages for foster parents, and liberalization of the definition of the foster parent role are likely to require a substantial increase in the cost of the service. It might be noted that programs in New Orleans and Seattle paying substantial fees to foster parents are currently being studied by CWLA.

8. There is little question that more adequate resources such as day care and homemaker services available at the point of crisis would reduce the necessity of placement for some children. Research showing the discrepancy between the ideal and actual placement decisions resulting from the lack of availability of these resources testifies to this. There is also evidence that more adequate income maintenance allowances, more adequate housing, and more adequate medical services would enable the family to come to crisis situations with a greater possibility of maintaining the child in the home. If this is an old refrain for social workers—and it is likely to be a refrain repeated in the next volume of this series of reviews of the research—it is because implementation of these research findings is more a political than a technical problem.

9. Limited research indicates that nonprofessionals in child welfare agencies are performing the same functions as professionals, and—as far as can be ascertained—as satisfactorily. At least there is no evidence to the contrary. Agencies might with greater assurance hire nonprofessionals and, if they are still hesitant about giving them autonomy in doing the jobs professionals do, include them as members of a team led by professionals.

Research regarding the foster grandparent program (discussed in the following section on institutional care) suggests further that the field might explore, more courageously and imaginatively, the possibility of employing neighborhood people and/or mothers on public assistance as foster parents and case aides.

10. For children who are likely to remain in substitute care over a long period of time and who for one reason or another cannot be placed for adoption, long-term foster care is a viable alternative. Consequently more frequent efforts should be made to formalize such arrangements.

Institutional Child Care

In September 1965 there were some 3,763 residential institutions for children in the U.S.A. Institutions for dependent and neglected children comprised the largest single category—40 percent of all institutions for children. Dependent and neglected children constituted the largest single group of children receiving institutional care (80, p. 255). Residential facilities for mentally retarded children represented 19 percent of the institutions, correctional facilities for delinquents 17 percent, institutions for the physically handicapped 10 percent, facilities for emotionally disturbed children 8 percent, and maternity homes for unmarried mothers 6 percent (103, p. 1). Fifty-two percent of all institutions were under private voluntary auspices, the majority of these being sponsored by religious denominations; a third were public facilities; and some 15 percent were private proprietary operations.

It was noted earlier that this review was restricted to substitute care services. At this point it is necessary to make explicit another restriction relevant to the review of institutional child care as a substitute care service. There is a great variety of child care institutions, many of them highly specialized and serving the needs of special groups of children. These include institutions for delinquent, physically handicapped, and mentally deficient children. Research regarding the work of such institutions has not been included in this review. The content has been confined to institutions serving dependent and neglected children and to residential treatment centers. In 1966 some 72,000 children lived in institutions for the dependent and neglected. At the same time residential treatment centers cared for 7,100 emotionally disturbed children (80, Table 1, p. 253).

Policy Questions

The following are some of the policy problems relating to institutional child care:

1. What are the major aspects of children's institutions that differentiate them from one another?

2. What can be done to "deinstitutional-ize" institutions further—reducing the damaging effects of institutionalization and increasing individualization in the context of congregate child care?

3. What kinds of children need and can use what kinds of institutional placement most productively? What kinds of children are most likely to be harmed by institutional care and what specific aspects of institutional care are likely to have harmful consequences for such children? Specifically, what kinds of congregate care can be provided with salutary effects for children under 3 years of age?

4. What are the effects on the child and the family resulting from the child's entry into an institution and how can this transition be made most effectively?

5. What are the effects on the child and family of termination of institutional living and how can this transition be made most productive?

6. What are the effects on children and families of racial integration of institutions? What are the problems encountered and desirable solutions formulated?

7. How can the aims of the peer group and the institution be made more congruent and mutually supportive?

8. How can child care personnel turnover be reduced so as to provide greater continuity in child care? How can staff be effectively recruited? What kinds of training are needed and how should training be provided? What patterns of professional-nonprofessional staff relations are likely to be most productive in different kinds of child care institutions?

For some of these questions, recent research has added to child welfare's store of knowledge, modifying some of its overgeneralized assumptions.

Separation and/or Deprivation: Institutional Effects

All of the substitute care services have in common the fact that in every instance the child is separated from his parents. Separation may or may not impose a simultaneous burden of deprivation, but since some measure of maternal deprivation has often been a concomitant of separation, especially when institutionalization followed separation, this might be an appropriate point to recapitulate briefly the major deprivation-separation research published between 1965 and 1970.

In the chapter on child welfare in the first volume of this series Fanshel (24) noted the initial impact on child welfare practice of Bowlby's (9) review of the relevant research. Fanshel also summarized the subsequent, more critical assessment of this research, which tended to clarify the complexities of the separation-deprivation hypothesis.

Recent research tends to confirm the supposition that separation of young children from parents is a stressful experience (39). It is the loss of the specific relationship to the parents that seems to be the more significantly disturbing aspect of separation rather than the change from a familiar to an unfamilar environment, although this too contributes some component of stress. However, the age at which a differentiated object relationship to the parent is established, so that separation will be felt as trauma, is still a matter of doubt.

Recent research also supports the contention that institutional care presents a risk for development. Decarie (19) carefully tested object relations development of 90 children, 30 living in their own homes, 30 shortly after placement in adoptive homes, and 30 in an institution. The children were between 3 and 20 months of age at the time of testing. Level of object relations development was most advanced for the own home group, least advanced for the institutionalized group, as anticipated. Mental age was a variable of much greater significance than differences in environment in accounting for differences in levels of development. Given this fact and the fact that no attempt was made in selecting children for the study to control for possible differences in intellectual endowment, the author is cautious about attributing too much of the weight of his results to differences in the living situation. Nevertheless this highly sophisticated study, which is difficult to summarize, does support the contention that institutional living has adverse effects on object relations development.

Some of the focus in the discussions of separation-deprivation has shifted to the contribution the child makes to the caretaker-child interaction. Recent research supports the idea that while there is no question that separation is stressful, what the child makes of it depends in part on constitutional factors. There are wide constitutional variations in predispositions and temperament that have significant implications for the meaning the separation experience will have for the child (107). There is also clearer recognition of the fact that the child's interpersonal environment is partly what the child makes it—that different children "make" the same substitute caretaker more or less adequate in meeting the child's needs since different children evoke different reactions from the same person. The child in some measure determines his environment; it is not solely defined for him by the caretaker selected for him by the agency.

There is currently more evidence to support the assumption that for the child to live in his own home with his own parents does not automatically guarantee that his essential needs will be met. For example, the Head Start program, with its emphasis on the cognitive deficits incurred by children living in their own home when the stimulation offered in the home was limited, tends to emphasize this. Additional support comes from recent detailed studies of child life in multiproblem families (83). In short, substitute care and deprivation are not necessarily synonymous; own home and adequate care are not necessarily synonymous.

Recent research has called into more serious question the continuation hypothesis, which suggests the inevitable persistence of the effects of early stressful experience and predicts unfavorable adult prognosis from pathological child diagnosis. Heston and his colleagues (41) compared the psychosocial functioning of 47 adults who as infants lived in children's institutions for a mean period of two years and seven months with a group of 50 adults who as infants had no significant institutional experience. The latter group contained some adults who had less than three months of institutional experience. "Comparison was based on school, police, veterans, armed services and hospital records, among several others, plus a personal interview and [Minnesota Multiphasic Personality Inventory]" (41, p. 1110). Personal interviews were conducted with 72 of the 97 adults studied. The information available on each subject was evaluated independently by three psychiatrists, two of whom had no knowledge of the institutional background information. Evaluation of psychosocial functioning was made in terms of a Mental Health Sickness Rating Scale developed at the Menninger Foundation. The mean score attained on the scale was 73 for the group with institutional background and 72.7 for the group with no or minimal institutional experience. Such a score on the scale suggests normal, average, "everyday" adjustment. Researchers at Menninger who formulated the scale estimate that the bulk of the general population falls between 60 and 85 (67, p. 410).

MMPI responses of the two groups were indistinguishable and there were negligible differences in IQ scores. The authors concluded that "subjects cared for in foundling homes were no different as adults from the subjects who had had no, or only insignificant group care as children. . . . It appears that the human organism has the happy capacity of reversing the effects of childhood trauma of the type connoted by institutionalization" (41, p. 1109). Most of the institutionalized children were subsequently adopted or raised in foster care and the researchers note that "the factor most clearly related to the reversal of the effects of institutional care as seen in the subjects of this report is the corrective experience of family living . . ." (41, p. 1109).

Passingham compared groups of delinquents with each other in terms of intellectual development and level of emotional adjustment. One group of 50 delinquents had experienced separation from their parents and placement in a children's home for over a six-month period; a second group of 50 had not been separated from their parents and came from families "where there was no history of divorce, separation or death of parents, father was in regular employment, neither parent suffered from bad health and there was, as far as was known, little friction in the family" (82, p. 35). The specific hypothesis tested was that among delinquents "at roughly equal stages of their career those who had a history of separation from their parents and children's home experience would be found to be both more intellectually retarded and emotionally maladjusted than those from stable home backgrounds" (82, p. 34). Tests used included the Wechsler Intelligence Test, a word recognition test, a personality inventory, and a manifest anxiety scale.

There were no significant differences between the stable home background group and the children's home group except for the fact that the latter had a significantly higher incidence of enuresis. A comparison within the children's home group itself between children who had experienced "early admission, long stay, many moves" with those who had experienced "late admission, short stay, few moves" revealed no significant differences—although the comparison involved only a small number of children.

It is not suggested that separation and institutionalization do not make a difference. A careful reading of the details of the research reports makes clear that it does. However, the complexity of interaction among the many variables that feed into the outcome of separation and institutionalization make it doubtful that such experience will result in any particular kind of outcome—such as, for instance, the affectionless character. Because the group of children subjected to this experience tend to be heterogeneous in terms of their later behavior, statistical studies yield negative results. Different behaviors tend to cancel each other out.

As a consequence of these and additional studies, earlier pessimism based on assumptions about the inevitably lasting effects of early trauma has been mitigated. More detailed reviews of some of the research are provided by Bronfenbrenner (14), Kadushin (58), and Kohlberg (62). There is, conversely, more hope that providing a favorable opportunity for growth, through substitute care services, will enable the child to overcome a bad start. It might be well to indicate that some childhood disorders, notably severe antisocial, aggressive, acting-out behavior, are quite intractable and therefore likely to show greater continuity and persistence into adulthood.

The current assumption is that good substitute care can provide the child with most of what he needs and does get in a normal, healthy, well-functioning family of his own. The principal requisite to normal biopsychosocial development that is most difficult for substitute care to provide is continuity of a warm, intimate relationship with one mothering person or a mothering group (120). Adoptive care, especially when placement follows shortly after birth, is most successful in meeting this need; institutional care is likely to be the least capable of the substitute care services in this respect.

Child welfare thus seems currently more balanced in its assessment of separation as contrasted with the feelings of shock and guilt that followed Bowlby's report and that resulted in an overdetermined rejection of all kinds of institutional care. This balance has been achieved partly as a result of the research cited, partly as a consequence of the fact that many of the significant questions regarding separation and deprivation are still open to debate (e.g., identification of critical periods; explication of the different effects of maternal deprivation, discontinuity, and distortion; operational definitions of the intensity, variety, complexity, and sequence of stimulus-

depriving experiences and their effects on children), and partly because the service needs for a facility such as institutional care have pressed for a reconsideration of the differentiated use of institutions. Since the need for substitute care services, including institutions, is great, social work's responsibility is to offer the services and at the same time systematically to increase the positive potentialities associated with such services.

Few studies have attempted to examine the effects of institutionalization on adolescents, almost all of such studies being concerned with children. Jaffe (46) attempted to study this question with regard to a group of 72 Israeli adolescents, 10–15 years old, all of whom had been institutionalized for two years because of dependency and neglect. He compared this group with a comparable group of children awaiting institutional placement who might then be expected to "reflect needs and problems typical of dependent children on the threshold of institutional placement" (46, p. 65). Differences between the candidate group and the group that had already experienced institutionalization would then suggest the consequences of institutional living. Both groups were compared with a third—control—group of schoolchildren living at home. Various objective personality measures were used in the study, supplemented by interviews with social workers and teachers. In general the institutionalized children showed better test results than those awaiting placement but poorer results than the regular schoolchildren on most of the variables studied. These findings suggest that institutionalization aided rather than adversely affected overall adjustment, although there was a clear impression of a pervasive feeling of depersonalization on the part of the institutionalized group. Length of institutionalization was not generally related to adjustment.

Wolins' (117, 118) more wide-ranging research is essentially concerned with the fundamental question of the developmental consequences of group care as compared with care in a family setting. However, most of the subjects of the research were adolescents when studied. The group care settings studied were located in Poland, Austria, Yugoslavia, and Israel and varied in their degree of similarity to a familial model of child-rearing. The Austrian *Kinderdorf*, consisting of family unit cottages of nine children of both sexes and varying ages under the supervision of a resident "mother," most closely approximated the familial model. Least like the family were the kibbutz youth groups included for study, which consisted of forty boys and girls, young adolescents within a limited age range. The Yugoslav and Polish children's homes fell somewhere between these extremes. Whatever the nature of difference in living arrangements, however, all of the settings selected for study offered the child a group context for living.

In each instance the children in group care were compared with neighboring agemates living in their own homes with their own parents. Attributes selected for study were "functioning intelligence, maturity, and social integration." The Ravens Progressive Matrices Test was used as the basis for testing intellectual functioning. Psychosocial development was evaluated on the basis of eight cards of the Murray TAT. This was further supplemented by global clinical judgments made by clinical psychologists on the basis of all case record materials available on a child except clues to his location. Reliability of judgments was ensured by provisions for independent coding by more than one rater and by rerating after a lapse of time.

The study indicates that "children reared in five different types of group care programs appear to show little or no intellectual or psychosocial deficiencies when compared with controls from home environments" (118, p. 51). The overall conclusion is firmer with regard to intellectual functioning than with regard to psychosocial development. In general, however, the data adequately support the overall contention that group care of adolescents shows few negative consequences.

Since most of the children were tested as adolescents and since most were initially admitted to the group care program when older than 5, the study does not materially contribute to the debate regarding the effects of group care on infants and young children. Whatever limited data are available regarding the small sample of children who entered these group care facilities before the age of 5 and remained long enough to be included in the study tend to support the view that group care is not necessarily damaging. Thus Wolins notes that "children placed at an early age [prior to 6 years] and tested in adolescence tend to have essentially the same Ravens Progressive Matrices Test scores as do agemates who entered considerably later" (117, p. 8).

Child and Staff Behavior

Polsky (85) studied the residential treatment center from a social systems frame of reference. Three different senior boys' cottages were the context for research observation and the unit of observation was the event. An event was defined as a specific time-limited counselor-resident interaction around some functional situation. Observers were trained to use a schedule that consisted of three sections: (1) identifying data relating to the events recorded, (2) items describing the boys' behavior, and (3) staff behavioral response in the event. The items included in the schedule reflected the researchers' theoretical presuppositions regarding the functions of staff-resident interactions.

The four principal functions of child care in the cottages were identified as monitoring, guidance, support, and integration. Monitoring of the residents' behavior by the child care worker is an instrumental function concerned with meeting institutional demands. This relates to cottage housekeeping and maintaining the standards of the institutional community regarding, for example, language or dress, and the regulation of subsystems in the institution such as school, work, and appointments with therapists. Guidance is an instrumental function concerned with encouraging the development of autonomous goals on the part of the residents and of the cottage group. In discharging this function the child care worker is responsible for helping the group perceive, articulate, and implement those activities that are not in response to institutional imperatives but are in response to individual and group needs. Support, comforting, or nurturance is an expressive function related to meeting emotional needs of individual cottage residents. Integration is an expressive function focused primarily on harmonizing relations among residents and between residents and staff.

The schedules were used to record observations of events over a four-week period on weekdays in the afternoon and early evening in each of three different boys' cottages. A total of 54 boys (18 in each cottage) and 6 child care workers (2 in each cottage) were the subject population of the research. Analysis of the results indicated considerable uniformity among the cottages in the emphasis given the four different functions identified by the social systems theory.

Child care workers in all the cottages gave primary emphasis to the monitoring, custodial, or supervisory function. About half of all of the child care activity was devoted to discharging this function. Twenty-eight percent of the time was concerned with the support, comfort, nurturing function. Only 9 percent of the time was related to guidance and only 5 percent was spent on the integrative function. There were discrepancies between resident behavior and staff behavior. While about half of staff time was concerned with monitoring, only 16 percent of resident time was related to this, and, inversely, while residents were concerned with self-gratifying activity half of the time, staff were involved in the counterpart support, comfort, nurturing function only 19 percent of the time.

Although system maintenance requirements dictated the heavy emphasis on monitoring in all cottages, there was a variation in extent of emphasis among cottages in re-

sponse to the particular approach and predilection of the head child care worker in each cottage. In the cottage with the heaviest custodial emphasis 53 percent of the time was spent on monitoring; in the cottage with the lightest custodial emphasis 43 percent of the time was spent on monitoring. As the researchers indicate, one cottage is different from another, but not all that different.

The attempt to relate role configuration in each cottage to the way the child care staff ran each cottage is based on the presumption that pattern of emphasis given by child care staff to the four key functions affects the behavior of residents. The research tends to show that the cottage that has the least monitoring-custodial emphasis and the greatest emphasis on the integrative function also had more positive inter-peer relational roles. However, support for the conclusion is relatively weak and there is considerable overlap in the relational role configuration from cottage to cottage—an outcome that might have been anticipated from the fact that the child care workers were differentiated only on the basis of emphasis accorded the key functions rather than on being essentially dissimilar in approach.

The research is to be commended in its attempt to study systematically resident–child care staff interaction in a residential treatment center in accordance with some consistent explanatory theoretical framework. It demonstrates the strength of functional imperatives demanded by any social system if it is to operate with some stability and carry out assigned tasks effectively. In the face of this it suggests the effort that needs to be made to train staff to an explicit awareness of the operational mechanics of the social system of an institution and the deliberate effort that needs to be made to change interactional behavior to achieve alternative tasks that might be regarded as desirable. Such knowledge would be important, for instance, in moving from a custodial approach with emphasis on monitoring to an approach that seeks to enhance residents' autonomy and that consequently emphasizes the guidance function of child care staff. The research is strongest in giving a clear picture of resident-staff interaction derived from systematic observation. It tells less of the relation between the pattern of child care interaction used by staff and any kind of behavioral change in residents.

Finally, Polsky's study clarifies the institutional constraints on child care workers. While systemic requirements are mediated by child care staff members, each of whom has a different configurational approach to his job, unless the child care worker made a deliberate, conscious effort to meet these requirements in a novel way, the chances are that the operational constraints of the system would tend to reduce variations in approach among the different child care workers.

Klein, Kofsky, and Klein (61) attempted an objective, descriptive, naturalistic study of children's behavior in a residential treatment setting. As child care workers came off duty they were interviewed regarding a specific child's reaction to significant interpersonal situations encountered during the previous eight hours. Among the situations included for inquiry in the structured interview were those concerned with the child's reaction when the child care worker had to stop the child from doing something, when the child was forced to wait for something he wanted to do, when he needed to be reminded to do something he was supposed to have done, when he was attacked or teased by another boy. Interviews were tape-recorded and were conducted at three different points in time: one year after admission, five months later, and thirteen months later. These detailed observations were made on 6 boys aged 10–12.

While the children's behavior was not observed directly by the researchers, what the child care workers reported provided data for independent categorization by two judges who listened to the tape recording of child care workers' interview responses. Categorization of reported behavior was in terms of gradation between tendencies to dominate or submit and between love and

hate. Surprisingly the most frequently recorded category of behavior was affection-cooperation. The most significant shift in reported behavior was from verbal aggressive to passive aggressive. This suggests that the change involved not so much "a drop in hostility as a change in the way children expressed these feelings and related to other people" (61, p. 17). The change may come about as a consequence of the influence of therapists who, acting as socializing agents of the general culture, help the children not so much to change their basic feelings but rather to express these feelings in a more socially acceptable manner.

Child care workers and staff in contact with the children studied were also asked to rate their perception of the children's behavior in terms of the same variables used by the judges who had rated the ongoing reports of the children's behavior. While the most frequently reported behavior fell in the affection-cooperation category, the staff tended in their perceptions to exaggerate the frequency of aggressive behavior and to minimize friendly interactions.

Perhaps aggressive behavior was more visible because it was more problematic or the staff had a need to distance themselves by exaggerating the difference between these and other children or, having categorized these children as needing treatment, child care staff needed to perceive them as more pathological than was suggested by the more objective descriptions of the children's behavior.

Residential Treatment Follow-up

A study by Allerhand (3) at Bellefaire, a midwestern residential treatment center, carefully reviewed the institutional and postinstitutional experience of 50 middle-class boys, each of whom had been at Bellefaire for at least six months, the average length of stay being 3½ years. Boys selected for study were regarded as "satisfactorily representative" of the Bellefaire population. Tape-recorded follow-up interviews were conducted by a single interviewer with the boys, their families, and, when appropriate, with their postinstitutional therapist, between one to two years after leaving Bellefaire. At the point of follow-up all of the group were late adolescents. Lengthy past records, psychological tests, and staff reports by cottage child care workers, teachers, and caseworkers made up the available data covering the boys' experience at Bellefaire.

The record data and typescripts of the follow-up interview were read and rated by twelve "sophisticated social workers, experienced in case work," none of whom was on the Bellefaire staff. All judges received training in the use of the scales and judgments were made independently by each of two different judges for each item included in the study. Judgments were made of the boys' casework accessibility, casework experience, interpersonal relationship with peers and institutional adults, and role performance in the cottage and at school at three points in time—three months after admission to Bellefaire, fifteen months after admission, and at discharge. Judgments at follow-up were made in terms of intrapsychic balance and fulfillment in the family and in the community of such roles as son, student, employee, peer group member, and boyfriend.

An additional and significant item of judgment was an assessment of the level of support or stress inherent in the psychosituation in which each of the boys had to function after discharge. Evaluation of support or stress encountered resulted from a review of the interpersonal situation (relationship with family, peers, other adults), the living situation (home arrangements and responsibilities), and the cultural situation (school, work, leisure). The postdischarge living situation is viewed as an intervening variable between the institutional experience and adaptation at follow-up.

One of the more significant findings is confirmation of the fact that adaptation at point of discharge is not in itself indicative of adaptation at follow-up. Boys who were doing well at discharge in terms of their adaptation to the institutional situation and institutional roles were doing poorly at follow-up. Other boys who were evaluated as showing poor adaptation at discharge proved to be doing well at follow-up. The lack of congruence between the expectation at discharge and actual performance at follow-up was related to the level of stress or support provided by the living situation to which the boy returned. A high level of adaptation at discharge could subsequently be vitiated by a stressful postdischarge living situation. "It is the supportive or stressful nature of the post-institutional milieu that appears to be the critical factor in success, without regard to the within-institution career pattern" (3, p. 142).

Only at the extreme end of the continuum was the boys' adaptation at discharge impervious to the effects of stress or support from the postdischarge environment. For some, their capacity for adaptation had been so strengthened by the institutional experience that they could successfully cope with postdischarge stress; for others, who had been unable to respond even to the benign environment of the institution, no amount of postdischarge support seemed sufficient to enable them to adapt adequately. Postdischarge levels of adaptation were also a function of the extent to which recommendations of Bellefaire staff for aftercare living had been implemented.

The researchers raise a question about the transferability and generalizability of the institutional experience. Institutional living prepares for institutional living. But since the child ultimately needs to take his place and live in the community it is recommended that the institution afford the child an opportunity for more direct exposure to community demands.

Prior halfway experiences such as ability to leave the grounds for school or work during the stay in the institution made more certain the forecast that the boy would be able to make his way when he finally returned to the community. [3, p. 140]

Bellefaire provides a program of intensive casework contact as part of its therapautic procedure. Most of the boys in the study group were involved in such contact. The aims of the caseworkers varied from simple support and reeducation to insight-oriented personality change. In earlier periods of contact with the boys the aim of casework was closer to the support-reeducation end of the continuum; toward the termination of contact the aim in 51 percent of the cases was toward the personality modification end of the continuum.

Involvement in casework was directly and significantly related to successful adaptation to institutional roles and to peers and adults at the point of discharge. Children diagnosed as neurotic were most likely to make effective use of casework. There was an association, although not statistically significant, between productive use of the institutional casework program and "interpersonal role fulfillment" at follow-up. Interpersonal role fulfillment is concerned with relationship with family and peers. There was no relationship, however, between the institutional casework contact and such factors as school/work productivity, use of leisure time, self-attitudes, or impulse-control balance.

Of considerable interest to practitioners is the fact that "no particular impact in casework or role-fulfillment variables was noted when a change in caseworker occurred" (3, p. 140; 70). Length of stay in the institution was not significantly related to postinstitutional adaptation.

Of interest to researchers is the fact that caseworkers' evaluation and prognostication showed a more highly significant relationship with what actually happened to the child subsequently than did the "objective" measuring instruments used by the research staff in the study.

Service Delivery and Staffing

An imaginative departure in meeting the problem of staffing children's institutions was initiated with the foster grandparent program. Sponsored by the Office of Economic Opportunity, the program involved employment of elderly Americans with limited income to give care to institutionalized children. Foster grandparents were not assigned to cover the continuing responsibilities of the regular staff, but were intended to provide institutionalized children with a daily two-hour personal contact with a concerned, mature adult. Such contact was to involve social activities as well as help with personal care of the children. Foster grandparents come to the institution for four hours a day five days a week and divide their attention between two foster grandchildren to whom they are assigned.

Several studies have attempted to evaluate the consequences of providing institutionalized children with this kind of individualized contact. One study by Greenleigh Associates (23) reviewed the program as implemented in a variety of contexts—children's hospital wards and institutions for the retarded, the emotionally disturbed, the dependent and neglected. Based on "professional observation," "expert opinion," and record review, this sample study of 370 children showed 70 percent of them to have "improved in their social and emotional behavior or in health and physical condition" (23, p. 7). These were short-term effects. Children in the institution for emotionally disturbed children were least affected by the program.

A more rigorous study (96) of 60 children, infants to 6 years of age, in a home for the dependent and neglected confirms the positive effects of the program. Before-and-after measures using standardized tests, structured periodic observations, and regular interviews with staff indicated that the program had positive effects on social behavior, alertness, and motor and social development. Children manifested decreased fretfulness, impulsiveness, hyperactivity, and aggressiveness. They were more outgoing and more confident, showed improvement in social skills, and related better to peers and authority figures. The short-range effects that mitigate some of the negative effects of institutionalization resulted not only from time in contact between children and foster grandparents but also from intensity of contact—the depth of emotional involvement of children and oldsters in a special friendship relationship that was personalized and individualized. Johnstone (52) presents a descriptive account of a successful grandparent program with emotionally disturbed children needing temporary substitute group care.

Residential treatment continues to be an expensive resource.

In addition to providing a therapeutically sound environment and individually oriented psychotherapy the institution must fulfill all the functions of parents, school and family physician besides offering the cultural and recreational opportunities of a middle class suburb. All this has to be done with salaried personnel working around the week in shifts. [32, p. 5]

It is not surprising, then, that only a limited number of residential treatment centers are in operation and that each is able to take only a limited number of the many children diagnosed as requiring the services of such a facility.

In response to this situation Ganter and Polansky (32) formulated a research-demonstration project designed to enhance the accessibility to treatment of such children within the community. These children were referred for residential treatment because they could not make productive outpatient use of the community child guidance clinic service. Ganter and Polansky identified several factors indicative of a child's capacity to assume the role of client at a community clinic—the child's level of organizational unity, which related to the child's incorporation of controls and limits, and the child's capacity for self-observation —that is, his introspective objectivity. A group of 47 children were identified as requiring or likely to require residential treatment because they were not accessible to individualized outpatient treatment. Such children were then offered an intensive group experience: three-hour sessions twice a week over a six-month period. The purpose of the group experience was to develop the child's level of organizational unity, which

implies greater self-control, and capacity for self-observation. Since these factors were associated with accessibility to individual outpatient treatment, the group experience was designed to salvage the child for the child guidance clinic. Parents were also involved with the project in individual sessions with caseworkers and in weekly parents' group meetings.

Since the purpose of the project was to prepare the child for outpatient child guidance clinic treatment, the empirical test of the effectiveness of the demonstration-experiment was the percentage of such children who ultimately were assessed as accessible to outpatient treatment. Of the 47 children in the program, 39 completed the full six months of the group experience. Of these 39, a total of 31 remained in outpatient contact for at least three months, at which point their accessibility to treatment was assessed by their therapists. Accessibility to treatment was evaluated in terms of such factors as motivation to change, degree of trust in the therapist, freedom to communicate, and capacity for self-observation. Twenty-eight of the children were "regarded by their individual therapist, as high on accessibility to treatment" (32, p. 108). These children, some 60 percent of the group selected for study because they were initially likely applicants for residential treatment, now demonstrated a capacity to use outpatient treatment. Determination of whether the child ultimately benefited from the use of outpatient treatment was not within the scope of the project.

This demonstration project is an excellent example of the identification of some clearly specified attributes needing correction if a child is to use a service effectively and the design of a corrective procedure explicitly directed toward strengthening those characteristics identified as requiring change. All of the group activities and interactions were geared to helping the child develop a greater measure of self-control and/or increasing his capacity for self-observation. If change takes place as a result of experimental intervention there would then be some assurance of knowing what contributed to the change. And yet even in a carefully formulated design such as this there were such situation-specific factors as expectation and relationship, such as habituation to and familiarity of contact with certain therapeutic personnel, which might have contributed to change over and above the experimental procedures designed to enhance levels of "organizational unity" and capacity for self-observation.

Institutional child care staff turnover is high. A recent national study in England of staffing in over a thousand institutions representing some 64 percent of all children's institutions in the country noted that the "annual wastage of full time care staff for all children's homes was 31 percent. In view of the great importance of continuity for the care of children this is a very disturbing figure" (119, p. 69). Some of the reasons for staff turnover cited by the report are familiar—the lack of any clear career structure for child care personnel, social and professional isolation, inadequate free time, especially at a period when the workweek is in general being shortened, the lack of job status, community underestimation of the importance of the job, conflicts with professional personnel in the institutions, and lack of privacy.

Institutional Desegregation

While there are no empirical studies of the process of institutional desegregation and its effects there are a number of reports of such experience (36). These point to the fact that institutional board members need to be prepared and helped to accept such change. (A large percentage of institutions have voluntary, denominational auspices.) This may often involve changes in charters that restrict an institution to white children. Desegregation involves hiring more blacks in staff positions and in positions of more responsibility. The problem in desegregating an institution seems to lie least frequently with the children and

parents and most frequently with the surrounding community. Black children admitted to an institution may be attending neighborhood schools and using recreational facilities such as pools, parks, ice cream parlors, and movie theaters. An institution situated in a community that has not taken steps to desegregate will find it especially difficult to achieve desegregation itself. Involvement of community residents and leaders in the planning sometimes helps. Concerned parents and children in the institutions can be prepared for the change and encouraged to express and discuss any anxieties they feel about this. Preparation of the staff might involve having blacks and whites eat together and encouraging black staff members to bring their children to the institution on visits.

Summary of Research

As contrasted with adoption and foster care, relatively little empirical research has been done on the kinds of child care institution that are the concern of this review. There are studies showing deleterious consequences for younger children in institutions as compared with children raised in their own homes in terms of cognitive deficits, time sense, speech development, and capacity for relationship. The questions of matching of the two groups studied and unfair comparison of poor institutions versus good natural homes have been raised. Despite this there seems to be agreement that young children in institutional care run a risk. Recent research has found little support for the permanence of damage. Whether institutions might be organized productively for children under 3 is a question for further study.

Accessibility to treatment in the institution is related to freedom to communicate feelings. Relationships are established more readily with staff directly charged with care of the child. The social system of the peer group exists side by side with the formal institutional social system as established by the agency. Child care staff members tend to adjust to the inmate social system and become integrated with it, which both results from and further contributes to their alienation from the professional staff. There is considerable conflict between the child care and professional staffs. This is one of a number of factors contributing to high staff turnover and its most serious consequence—discontinuity in relationships children have established with institutional parent surrogates.

Child care staff members devote a major amount of their time to system maintenance monitoring. More positive cottage peer relationship is weakly associated with greater emphasis on integrative functions of child care staff. Positive effects for children in institutional care derive from personalized contact with auxiliary personnel such as in the OEO foster grandparent program. Such supplementary workers may be of special significance to children in institutions because of the high turnover of full-time child care staff.

Residential treatment centers care for a limited group of institutionalized children. Adjustment in the institution does not guarantee adjustment to postinstitutional living. The psychosituation to which the child returns is an important variable affecting follow-up outcome. Residential treatment centers are generally small and therefore accept only a small percentage of those referred to them. Most of the children accepted have manifested difficulty over a prolonged period and have generally previously been under treatment—unsuccessfully—in the community. Most of them are boys and come from families exhibiting multiple pathologies. Special efforts to prepare such children for more effective use of outpatient clinic facilities may permit some percentage of them to be maintained at home while under treatment.

Entrance into care at an early age and lack of contact with interested and concerned parents or other relatives is associated with poorer institutional adjustment.

Special individualized stimulation in the institutions is associated with more normal overall development.

Practice Implications

1. The research available suggests that we can cautiously relax our negative attitude toward the institution. The institution is merely one of a number of different ways in which children can be given care. For some children it is a satisfactory alternative. With proper safeguards for an adequate staff-child ratio, an enriched program, and provision for a therapeutic environment, the risks, even for young children, are not likely to be great. The rub, of course, is in ensuring the availability of the conditions necessary to reduce risk.

The difficulty in attracting and retaining an adequate number of competent people to staff the institution is something of which the field has been keenly aware for some time. Personnel is the key not only to adequacy of care, but also continuity of care. The largest component of the solution lies with the community in its willingness to allocate more resources to permit appropriate pay and work hours and subsidized education for child care workers. Social workers, in their turn, have to be willing to share with child care workers in institutions greater responsibility, autonomy, and equality on treatment teams. The team format, discussed in the section of this chapter on foster care, is congruent with the institutional setting and might be considered for implementation. Wider use of auxiliary personnel such as foster grandparents is indicated.

Stabilizing the staff situation will reduce one of the most distinctive hazards of institutional care—discontinuity in relationships. Suggestions have been made for structural innovations to achieve this end as well. One suggestion is to develop an "institution with satellites. It would consist of quite a number of group homes in the neighborhood of a central institution which would be an administrative and service facility" (120, p. 88). This would include, for example, clinics, an infirmary, schools, homemaking and babysitting personnel, and casework services. The group homes would be dwellings scattered around the neighborhood but belonging to the institution. Foster parents in charge of the group home would be agency employees paid a living wage. The idea suggests an adaptation of the childen's village, which has been quite successful in Europe but has not been tried extensively in the United States.

2. The European approach to separating the routine child care and cottage maintenance functions from the functions of socializers and educators might be profitably experimented with in the U.S.A. The child care institution is a natural setting for increased exploitation of "new careers" for the poor.

3. The research pointing to the factors that make a child accessible to the kinds of treatment available in institutions suggests that a sizable percentage of children are not equipped to make use of such treatment. When the child can use the treatment it is likely to be associated with favorable outcome on follow-up. But for children not capable of effectively using the treatment procedures available, consideration should perhaps be given to implementation of different approaches. There is little in the literature suggesting, for instance, that behavior modification approaches have been tried in the kinds of institutions with which this review is concerned.

4. The research indicates the desirability of reducing the emphasis on monitoring and increasing the emphasis on other child care functions such as support and integration. The constraints of systems maintenance needs may admittedly make such changes in emphasis difficult.

5. More active programs for children to experience community living while still in the institution is an important transitional procedure. Allerhand's research points to the need for this to be given more explicit consideration in practice. It also confirms the fact that implementation of explicit planning for postrelease living helps to ensure the greater probability of success at follow-up.

6. Continuity to maintain a sense of identification involves more than continuity in relationship with a caretaking person. It also involves continuity in experiences and procedures that are familar to a child. This suggests continued emphasis on an orientation already accepted by institutions. Visits in preparation for placement are designed to reduce discontinuity in the living experience, as does permitting the child to take into the institution toys and other objects to which he is greatly attached. Perhaps institutions may make facilities available so parents can stay at the institution for the child's first few days in care or over weekends.

Impressions of Child Welfare Research

Reviewing child welfare research over a period of time inevitably precipitates some general impressions. The research activity between 1965 and 1970 graphically reflects the effects of public support of such efforts. A sizable percentage of the research reviewed, especially those efforts more rigorously designed and with larger populations, were sponsored by the Research and Demonstration Grant Program of the U.S. Children's Bureau. Many of the more ambitious projects currently in process but not yet reported are supported by the same program, i.e., the Delaware Longitudinal Study of Adoptive Children and the Fanshel-Jenkins New York City Study of Foster Care. The modest federal government budget allocated to this program has paid substantial dividends in adding to the limited stockpile of child welfare research findings.

There is apparently no general theoretical system applicable to child welfare problems that holds the allegiance of any sizable group of researchers. Having lost our innocence about psychoanalytic theory, we have found nothing as systematic and comprehensive to take its place as a guide to research.

Perhaps this is to be expected. The phenomena with which different researchers are concerned are too diverse to expect that a single comprehensive theory would have explanatory power for all. Little theories are needed—theoryettes—that are sufficient unto these diverse phenomena. More often than not, however, no theoretical basis is offered for selection of the question to be researched, for the methodology with which it is researched, or for the explanation of the research results. Much of the research is thus an ad hoc enterprise rather than being related to efforts to confirm or invalidate some theoretical preconceptions.

The research available speaks with forked tongue. Often it is contradictory and noncumulative. When we begin to see a clear, unambiguous finding, the level of correlation is so modest that the clinician can apply it in the specific instance, which is the only ballpark the clinician plays in, with considerable hesitancy and misgiving. Even the low correlation levels achieved may appear to the clinician to be achieved under precious research conditions that are a simplification of the complex, fluid situation he faces. "Hard findings," then, are not all that hard. Even findings that have substantial statistical significance may have little practical significance. The understandable worker reaction is, "Research, who needs it?"

Part of this is inevitable. Research has traditionally been concerned with repetitive regularities, with probabilities, with the large group; the clinician is concerned with the idiosyncratic, individual instance. But the higher the probability estimate research can offer the clinician, the greater the certainty, the larger the reduction in the margin of error the clinician risks in applying the generalization in the specific instance.

To do this replication, not duplication, of research efforts is needed. When more than one researcher has devoted effort to the same question, it has been, for the most part, duplication—research on the same general question but with differently defined populations, differently defined criteria, differently defined variables, different instrumentation. Replication would keep the methodology constant and permit more cumulative findings.

But perhaps the area of greatest shortcoming is tied to the suggestions made earlier for practice. The writer pointed to the fact that the nexus of professional activity lies in the crucial decisions made regarding the substitute care story and that the context in which such decisions are implemented lies in the process of worker-client interaction. If the worker is going to move toward reducing effort devoted to selection and evaluation and increasing focus devoted to ensuring the success of the placement, research would have to move from current concentration on problems that relate to selection to concern with the process of what is done to help the child and his family live with each other in a mutually satisfying manner. More research attention needs to be given to the process of what the social worker actually does when he is doing child welfare social work.

How does the worker go about preparing the child and the substitute caretaker for placement? How does the worker modify harmful attitudes and behavior? What is done to help the child resolve conflicts in identification that come from "living in one family and loving in another"? What specific interventions make a home from which a child needed to be removed a safe place to which he can be returned?

And perhaps here research-demonstration efforts may productively include study of learning-behavioral modification approaches as applied to process in child welfare services. While this orientation threatens to become the dominant orientation in other clinical fields, it has been given little explicit attention in child welfare.

At various points in the substitute care story, significant decisions need to be made —to remove the child from his own home or to work to maintain the home for the child, to remove the child from one foster home and place him in another, to offer foster home care or institutional care, to remove the child from substitute care and return him to his home, to select or reject foster care and adoptive applicants, to close a foster home, to refer or accept for treatment, to see collaterals and determine what information would be most productive to obtain. One of the supposedly distinguishing aspects of professional activity is that decisions are made rationally in terms of knowledge of cause-and-effect relationships. If the child welfare worker is going to make crucial decisions in a professional, rational manner, then child welfare research will need to devote more effort to child welfare decisions as a product and decision-making as a process.

Computerization of decision-making has been suggested in view of human limitations in processing a large number of complex variables. An alternative suggestion has been made to establish a central diagnostic center for decision-making. Any alternative requires, however, that the field make available the knowledge on which computerized or central organizational decisions are made.

One more gap in research interest and efforts needs mentioning. If it is said that child welfare is concerned not only with services but also with social policy that affects children, it is necessary to include these considerations on the research agenda. Specifically, what would be the effects on substitute care programs of family allowances, a negative income tax, a guaranteed annual income, subsidized adoptions, adequate wages for foster parents, elective abortions, group care for children under 3, or the professionalization of the mother substitute role? Child welfare research should perhaps grow out of and be more directly related to social policy questions of this nature.

Ultimately the crucial distinction between the professional and lay person lies in the fact that the professional possesses greater valid, systematic knowledge, and skills derived from that knowledge, about some phenomena. Skills based on valid, systematic knowledge may not in themselves be sufficient to identify a profession, but they are essential prerequisites. All other criteria of a profession are secondary to this criterion. Whatever have been, are, and will be the deficiencies of child welfare research, it is difficult to see a viable alternative to this kind of activity in validating social work's claim as a profession.

But having made that brave statement, having sounded the trumpet once again, and hearing the fading echoes of repeated previous blasts, we find it difficult to evade a failure of nerve. Given the complexity of the human condition, given the changing nature of the problems we seek to understand even as we are seeking to understand them, given accident and happenstance and individual, group, and community uniqueness, it is not likely that even the best research will give us all the answers necessary. Some component of social work will always remain more art than science, yielding more to the intuitively responsive clinician than to the cognitively gifted scientist. Research may never be able to give us as much as we want. But research may be able to give us some increasingly modest increment of what we need.

REFERENCES

1. Adams, Morton S., Davidson, Ruth T., and Cornell, Phyllis. "Adoptive Risks of the Children of Incest—A Preliminary Report," *Child Welfare*, Vol. 46, No. 3 (March 1967), pp. 137–142.
2. *The Adoption of Negro Children—A Community Wide Approach.* Toronto, Canada: Social Planning Council of Metropolitan Toronto, July 1966.
3. Allerhand, Melvin, Weber, Ruth, and Haug, Marie. *Adaptation and Adaptability: The Bellefaire Follow-up Study.* New York: Child Welfare League of America, 1966.
4. Barker, Robert L., and Briggs, Thomas

L. *Differential Use of Social Work Manpower*. New York: National Association of Social Workers, 1968.

5. Bell, Grace. "Report of 1966 Survey—Homemaker–Home Health Aide Service in the United States," *Readings in Homemaker Service*. New York: National Council for Homemaker Services, 1969.

6. Billingsley, Andrew, and Giovannoni, Jeanne. "Research Perspectives on Interracial Adoptions," in Roger R. Miller, ed., *Race, Research, and Reason: Social Work Perspectives*. New York: National Association of Social Workers, 1969. Pp. 57–77.

7. Bluth, Howard. "Factors in the Decision to Adopt Independently," *Child Welfare*, Vol. 46, No. 9 (November 1967), pp. 504–513.

8. Borgatta, Edgar F., and Cautley, Patricia W. "Behavioral Characteristics of Children: Replication Studies with Foster Children," *Multivariate Behavioral Research*, Vol. 1 (October 1966), pp. 399–424.

9. Bowlby, John. *Maternal Care and Mental Health*, Monograph Series No. 21. Geneva, Switzerland: World Health Organization, 1951.

10. Bradley, Trudy. *An Exploration of Case Workers' Perceptions of Adoptive Applicants*. New York: Child Welfare League of America, 1966.

11. Brewster, Berta M. "Extending the Range of Child Welfare Services," *Children*, Vol. 12, No. 4 (July–August 1965), pp. 145–150.

12. Brieland, Donald. "Of Manpower, Models and Motivation," in Helen Fradkin, ed., *Use of Personnel in Child Welfare Agencies*. New York: Columbia University School of Social Work, 1967.

13. ———, Watson, Kenneth, Hovda, Philip, Fanshel, David, and Corey, John. *Differential Use of Manpower: A Team Model for Foster Care*. New York: Child Welfare League of America, 1968.

14. Bronfenbrenner, Urie. "Early Deprivation in Mammals and Man," in Grant Newton, ed., *Early Experience in Behavior*. Springfield, Ill.: Charles C Thomas, 1966.

15. Carey, John, Hickey, Paul, and Melican, Thomas. *Meeting the Manpower Crisis in Child Welfare*. National Conference on Social Welfare, May 1966. Mimeographed.

16. Caulton, George W. "Middle Class Negro Perspectives on Economic Security as Related to Attitudes toward Adoption," *Smith College Studies in Social Work*, Vol. 37, No. 1 (November 1966), pp. 45–46.

17. Cautley, Patricia. *Successful Foster Homes—An Exploratory Study of Their Characteristics*. Madison: Wisconsin Department of Public Welfare, 1966.

18. Deasy, Leila C., and Quinn, Olive W. "The Urban Negro and Adoption of Children," *Child Welfare*, Vol. 41, No. 9 (November 1962), pp. 400–407.

19. DeCarrie, T. G. *Intelligence and Affectivity in Early Childhood*. New York: International Universities Press, 1965.

20. Dinnage, Rosemary, and Pringle, M. L. Kellmer. *Foster Home Care—Facts and Fallacies*. London, England: Longmans, Green & Co., 1967.

21. ———, and Pringle, M. L. Kellmer. *Residential Child Care—Facts and Fallacies*. London, England: Longmans, Green & Co., 1967.

22. Elonen, Anna, and Schwartz, Edward. "A Longitudinal Study of Emotional, Social and Academic Functioning of Adopted Children," *Child Welfare*, Vol. 48, No. 2 (February 1969), pp. 72–78.

23. *An Evaluation of the Foster Grandparent Program*. New York: Greenleigh Associates, October 1966.

24. Fanshel, David. "Child Welfare," in Henry S. Maas, ed., *Five Fields of Social Service—Reviews of Research*. New York: National Association of Social Workers, 1966. Pp. 85–143.

25. ———. *Foster Parenthood—A Role Analysis*. Minneapolis: University of Minnesota Press, 1966.

26. ———. "The Indian Adoption Project: A Preliminary Report." Paper presented at the Mid-West Regional Conference, Child Welfare League of America, Omaha, Nebraska, May 1966. Mimeographed.

27. ———. "Progress Report—Adoption of American Indian Children by Caucasian Families—A Study in Cross Ethnic Adoption." New York: Child Welfare League of America, November 1966. Mimeographed.

28. Ferguson, Thomas. *Children in Care and After*. New York: Oxford University Press, 1966.

29. Fowler, Irving. "The Urban Middle Class Negro and Adoption: Two Series of Studies and Their Implications for Action," *Child Welfare*, Vol. 45, No. 9 (November 1966), pp. 522–524.

30. Gabrovic, Audrey. "Participation of Active Foster Parents in the Study of New

Applicants," *Child Welfare*, Vol. 48, No. 6 (June 1969), pp. 357–361.

31. Galley, Grace. "Interracial Adoptions," *Canadian Welfare*, Vol. 39, No. 6 (November–December 1963), pp. 248–250.

32. Ganter, Grace, Yeakel, Margaret, and Polansky, Norman. *Retrieval from Limbo—The Intermediary Group Treatment of Inaccessible Children.* New York: Child Welfare League of America, 1967.

33. Gil, David. "Social Work Teams—A Device for Increased Utilization of Available Professional Educated Social Welfare Personnel," *Child Welfare*, Vol. 44, No. 8 (October 1965), pp. 442–450.

34. Gochros, Harvey. "A Study of the Caseworker–Adoptive Parent Relationship in Postplacement Services," *Child Welfare*, Vol. 46, No. 6 (June 1967), pp. 317–325.

35. Goodacre, Iris. *Adoption Policy and Practice.* London, England: George Allen & Unwin, 1966.

36. Gula, Martin. *Quest for Equality*, Children's Bureau Publication 441. Washington, D.C.: U.S. Department of Health, Education & Welfare, 1966.

37. Hagen, Clayton, Nicholson, Barbara, Iverson, Evelyn, and Adelsman, Gayle. *The Adopted Adult Discusses Adoption as a Life Experience.* Minneapolis: Lutheran Social Service of Minnesota, 1968.

38. Hampton, Barbara. *Twenty-nine Children in Foster Care—A Study of Children in "Assembled Families."* Washington, D.C.: Family & Child Services, U.S. Department of Health, Education & Welfare, December 1968.

39. Heinicke, Christoph M., and Westheimer, Ilse. *Brief Separations.* New York: International Universities Press, 1967.

40. Herzog, Elizabeth, and Bernstein, Rose. "Why So Few Negro Adoptions?" *Children*, Vol. 12, No. 1 (January–February 1965), pp. 14–18.

41. Heston, L. L., Denny, D. D., and Pauley, I. B. "The Adult Adjustment of Persons Institutionalized as Children," *British Journal of Psychiatry*, Vol. 112 (1966), pp. 1103–1110.

42. Holman, Robert. "The Foster Child and Self-Knowledge," *Case Conference*, Vol. 12, No. 11 (March 1966), pp. 295–298.

43. Humphrey, Michael, and MacKenzie, Kim. "Infertility and Adoption Follow-up of 216 Couples Attending a Hospital Clinic," *British Journal of Preventive*

and *Social Medicine*, Vol. 21, No. 2 (April 1967), pp. 90–96.

44. Hylton, Lydia. "Trends in Adoption, 1958–1962," *Child Welfare*, Vol. 44, No. 7 (July 1965), pp. 377–386.

45. Jackson, Lydia. "Unsuccessful Adoptions: A Study of 40 Cases Who Attended a Child Guidance Clinic," *British Journal of Medical Psychology*, Vol. 41, Part 4 (December 1968), pp. 389–398.

46. Jaffe, Eliezer. "Effects of Institutionalization on Adolescent Dependent Children," *Child Welfare*, Vol. 48, No. 2 (February 1969), pp. 64–71.

47. Jaffee, Benson, and Fanshel, David. *A Follow-up Study in Adoption: Portrait of One Hundred Families.* New York: Columbia University Press, in press.

48. Jeffreys, Margot. *An Anatomy of Social Welfare Services.* London, England: Michael Joseph, 1965.

49. Jenkins, Shirley. "Duration of Foster Care—Some Relevant Antecedent Variables," *Child Welfare*, Vol. 46, No. 8 (October 1967), pp. 450–456.

50. ———. "Separation Experience of Parents Whose Children Are in Foster Care," *Child Welfare*, Vol. 48, No. 6 (June 1969), pp. 334–341.

51. ———, and Sauber, Mignon. *Paths to Child Placement—Family Situations Prior to Foster Care.* New York: Community Council of Greater New York, 1966.

52. Johnston, Ruth. "Some Casework Aspects of Using Foster Grandparents for Emotionally Disturbed Children," *Children*, Vol. 14, No. 2 (March–April 1967), pp. 46–52.

53. Jonassohn, Kurt. "On the Use and Construction of Adoption Rates," *Journal of Marriage and the Family*, Vol. 27, No. 4 (November 1965), pp. 514–521.

54. Jones, Betty L. "Non-Professional Workers in Professional Foster Family Agencies," *Child Welfare*, Vol. 45, No. 6 (June 1966), pp. 313–325.

55. Kadushin, Alfred. "Adoptive Parenthood: A Hazardous Adventure?" *Social Work*, Vol. 11, No. 3 (July 1966), pp. 30–39.

56. ———. "A Follow-up Study of Children Adopted When Older: Criteria of Success," *American Journal of Orthopsychiatry*, Vol. 37, No. 3 (April 1967), pp. 530–539.

57. ———. "Letter to the Editor," *Social Work*, Vol. 12, No. 1 (January 1967), pp. 127–128.

58. ———. "Reversibility of Trauma: A

Follow-up Study of Children Adopted When Older," *Social Work*, Vol. 12, No. 4 (October 1967), pp. 22–33.

59. Kenny, Thomas, Baldwin, Ruth, and Mackie, James. "Incidence of Minimal Brain Injury in Adopted Children," *Child Welfare*, Vol. 46, No. 1 (January 1967), pp. 24–29.

60. Kirk, David, Jonassohn, Kurt, and Fish, Ann. "Are Adopted Children Especially Vulnerable to Stress?" *Archives of General Psychiatry*, Vol. 14, No. 3 (March 1966), pp. 291–298.

61. Klein, Armin, Kofsky, Ellin, and Klein, William. "Behavior and Its Changes in the Residential Treatment of Children: A Preliminary Report," *Psychotherapy— Theory, Research and Practice*, Vol. 3, No. 2 (February 1966), pp. 14–20.

62. Kohlberg, Lawrence, LaCrosse, Jean, and Ricks, David. "The Predictability of Adult Mental Health from Childhood Behavior," in Benjamin Wolman, ed., *Hand Book of Child Psychopathology*. New York: McGraw-Hill Book Co., in press.

63. Kornitzer, Margaret. *Adoption and Family Life*. New York: Humanities Press, 1968. Pp. 13–14.

64. Lawder, Elizabeth, et al. *Post-Placement Functioning in Adoptive Families—A Follow-up Study of Adoptions at the Children's Aid Society of Pennsylvania*. Bryn Mawr, Pa.: Graduate Department of Social Work and Social Research, Bryn Mawr College, 1966.

65. Losbough, Bilie. "Relationship of E.E.G. Neurological and Psychological Findings in Adopted Children (75 Cases)," *American Journal of E.E.G. Technology*, Vol. 5, No. 1 (January 1965), pp. 1–4.

66. Low, Seth. "Foster Care of Children— Major National Trends and Prospects," *Welfare in Review*, Vol. 4, No. 8 (October 1966), pp. 12–21.

67. Luborsky, Lester. "Clinicians' Judgments of Mental Health: A Proposed Scale," *Archives of General Psychiatry*, Vol. 7, No. 6 (December 1962), pp. 407–417.

68. Maas, Henry S. "Children in Long-term Foster Care," *Child Welfare*, Vol. 48, No. 6 (June 1969), pp. 321–333.

69. ———, and Engler, Richard. *Children in Need of Parents*. New York: Columbia University Press, 1959.

70. McWhinnie, Alexina. *Adopted Children —How They Grow Up*. London, England: Routledge & Kegan Paul, 1967.

71. ———. *Adoption Assessments*. London, England: Standing Conference of Societies Registered for Adoption, 1966.

72. Maddi, Dorothy. "Recent Literature and the Children's Bureau Research Program." Chicago: School of Social Service Administration, University of Chicago, undated. Mimeographed.

73. Madison, Bernice, and Schapiro, Michael. "Long-Term Foster Family Care: What Is Its Potential for Minority Group Children?" *Public Welfare*, Vol. 27, No. 4 (April 1969), pp. 167–194.

74. Massarik, Fred, and Franklin, David. *Adoption of Children with Medical Conditions*, Research Department Report No. 1. Los Angeles: Children's Home Society of California, 1967.

75. Menlove, Frances. "Aggressive Symptoms in Emotionally Disturbed Adopted Children," *Child Development*, Vol. 36, No. 2 (June 1965), pp. 519–532.

76. *The Need for Foster Care—An Incidence Study of Requests for Foster Care and Agency Response in Seven Metropolitan Areas*. New York: Child Welfare League of America, 1969.

77. "Negro Attitudes toward Adoption in Hartford." New Haven: Connecticut Child Welfare Association, September 1965. Mimeographed.

78. North, G. E., and Kieffer, R. S. "Thematic Production of Children in Foster Homes," *Psychological Reports*, Vol. 19, No. 1 (January 1966), pp. 43–45.

79. Offord, D. R., Aponte, J. F., and Cross, L. A. "Presenting Symptomatology of Adopted Children," *Archives of General Psychiatry*, Vol. 20, No. 1 (January 1969), pp. 110–116.

80. Pappenfort, Donnell M., Dinwoodie, Adelaide, and Kilpatrick, Dee. "Children in Institutions, 1966: A Research Note," *Social Service Review*, Vol. 42, No. 2 (June 1968), pp. 252–260.

81. Parker, Roy A. *Decision in Child Care*. London, England: George Allen & Unwin, 1966.

82. Passingham, R. E. "A Study of Delinquents with Children's Home Background," *British Journal of Criminology*, Vol. 8, No. 1 (January 1968), pp. 32–45.

83. Pavenstedt, Eleanor (ed.). *The Drifter —Children of Disorganized Lower Class Families*. Boston: Little, Brown & Co., 1967.

84. Perlman, Robert, and Jones, David. *Neighborhood Service Centers*. Washington, D.C.: U.S. Department of Health, Education & Welfare, 1967.

85. Polsky, Howard, and Claster, Daniel. *The Dynamics of Residential Treatment.* Chapel Hill: University of North Carolina Press, 1968.

86. Pratt, Catherine. "Assembled Families," *Child Welfare*, Vol. 46, No. 2 (February 1967), pp. 94–98.

87. ———. *The Development of Group Foster Homes for Children in Long Term Care.* Washington, D.C.: Family & Child Services, U.S. Department of Health, Education & Welfare, June 1968.

88. Pringle, M. L. Kellmer. *Adoption—Facts and Fallacies.* London, England: Longmans, Green & Co., 1967.

89. Purvine, Margaret, and Ryan, William. "Into and Out of a Child Welfare Network," *Child Welfare*, Vol. 48, No. 3 (March 1969), pp. 126–135.

90. Raynor, Lois. "Agency Adoption of Non-White Children in the United Kingdom," *Race*, Vol. 10, No. 2 (October 1968), pp. 153–162.

91. Reece, Shirley, and Levin, Barbara. "Psychiatric Disturbances in Adopted Children: A Descriptive Study," *Social Work*, Vol. 13, No. 1 (January 1968), pp. 101–111.

92. Ripple, Lilian, *A Follow-up Study of Adopted Children.* Chicago: School of Social Administration, University of Chicago, April 1968.

93. ———. "A Follow-up Study of Adopted Children," *Social Service Review*, Vol. 42, No. 4 (December 1968), pp. 479–499.

94. Rock, John, Tietze, Christopher, and McLaughlin, Helen. "Effect of Adoption on Fertility," *Fertility and Sterility*, Vol. 16, No. 3 (June 1965), pp. 305–312.

95. Ruderman, Florence. *Child Care and Working Mothers.* New York: Child Welfare League of America, 1968.

96. Saltz, Rosalyn. *Evaluation of a Foster-Grandparent Program.* Detroit: Merill-Palmer Institute, May 1967.

97. Schaffer, H. R., and Schaffer, Evelyn B. *Child Care and the Family*, Occasional Papers on Social Administration No. 25. London, England: G. Bell & Sons, 1968.

98. Schwartz, Edward M. *A Comparative Study of Some Personality Characteristics of Adopted and Non-Adopted Boys.* Unpublished Ph.D. dissertation, University of Michigan, 1966.

99. Simon, Nathan, and Senturia, Audrey. "Adoption and Psychiatric Illness," *American Journal of Psychiatry*, Vol. 122, No. 8 (February 1966), pp. 858–868.

100. Skeels, Harold. "Adult Status of Children with Contrasting Early Life Ex-periences: A Follow-up Study," *Monographs of the Society for Research in Child Development*, Vol. 31, No. 3, Serial No. 105, 1966.

101. Solomon, Michael A. "Foster Parents' Perceptions of Foster Child's Roles," *Child Welfare*, Vol. 48, No. 4 (April 1969), pp. 202–211.

102. Standing Committee of Agencies Registered for Adoption. "Adoptees' Right to Know," *Child Adoption*, No. 53 (1968), pp. 30–31.

103. Star, Shirley, and Kuby, Alma. *Number and Kinds of Children's Residential Institutions in the United States.* Washington, D.C.: Children's Bureau, U.S. Department of Health, Education & Welfare, 1967.

104. Stringer, Elizabeth A. "Homemaker Service to Single-Parent Family," *Social Casework*, Vol. 48, No. 2 (February 1967), pp. 75–79.

105. Suzuki, Ryo, and Horn, Marilyn. "Follow-up Study on Negro-White Adoptions." Los Angeles: Los Angeles County Bureau of Adoptions, undated. Mimeographed.

106. Taylor, Joseph, Singner, Jerome, Kipnis, Dorothy, and Antrobus, John. "Attitudes on Foster Family Care in Contrasting Neighborhoods," *Child Welfare*, Vol. 48, No. 5 (May 1969), pp. 252–258.

107. Thomas, Alexander, Chess, Stella, and Birch, Herbert. *Temperament and Behavior Disorders in Children.* New York: New York University Press, 1968.

108. Thomas, Carolyn B. "The Resolution of Object Loss Following Foster Home Placement," *Smith College Studies in Social Work*, Vol. 36, No. 3 (June 1967), entire issue.

109. Turitz, Zitha. "A New Look at Adoption—The Current Developments in the Philosophy and Practice of Adoption," *Source Book of Teaching Materials on the Welfare of Children.* New York: Council on Social Work Education, 1969.

110. Tyler, Edward, Bonapart, Joseph, and Grant, Jeanne. "Occurrence of Pregnancy Following Adoption," *Fertility and Sterility*, Vol. 11, No. 6 (December 1960), pp. 581–589.

111. U.S. Department of Health, Education & Welfare. *Adoption in 1967*, Children's Bureau Statistical Series No. 92. Washington, D.C.: U.S. Government Printing Office, 1968.

112. ———. *Child Welfare Statistics—1967*, Children's Bureau Statistical Series No. 92. Washington, D.C.: U.S. Government Printing Office, 1968.

113. Wakeford, John. "Fostering: A Socio-

logical Perspective," *British Journal of Sociology*, Vol. 14, No. 4 (December 1963), pp. 335–346.

114. Watson, Kenneth. "The Manpower Team in a Child Welfare Setting," *Child Welfare*, Vol. 47, No. 8 (October 1968), pp. 446–454.

115. Welter, Marianne. *Adopted Older Foreign and American Children*. New York: International Social Service, 1965.

116. Wittenborn, J. Richard. *The Placement of Adoptive Children*. Springfield, Ill.: Charles C Thomas, 1957.

117. Wolins, Martin. "Child Care in Cross-Cultural Perspective—Final Report." Berkeley, Calif.: University of California, March 1969. Mimeographed.

118. ———. "Group Care: Friend or Foe," *Social Work*, Vol. 14, No. 1 (January 1969), pp. 35–53.

119. Williams, Gertrude. *Caring for People —Staffing Residential Homes*. London, England: George Allen & Unwin, 1967.

120. Witmer, Helen L., and Gershenson, Charles P. (eds.). *On Rearing Infants and Young Children in Institutions*, Children's Bureau Research Report No. 1. Washington, D.C.: U.S. Department of Health, Education & Welfare, 1967.

121. Zahn, Theodore P. "Word Association in Adoptive and Biological Parents of Schizophrenics," *Archives of General Psychiatry*, Vol. 19, No. 4 (October 1968), pp. 501–503.

COMMUNITY ORGANIZATION PRACTICE

By JACK ROTHMAN

In this chapter an attempt will be made to review recent significant professional and social science writings pertaining to community organization practice. Covered under the rubric of community organization will be social planning, local self-help activities sometimes referred to as community development, and social action programs based on more militant grass-roots indigenous movements. In this sense the scope of the treatment by Morris in the first volume of this series (63), which focused on social planning alone, is being broadened.

Since early 1964, the end of the period covered in the earlier review, there has been a burgeoning of work in community organi-zation. The social work literature in general has shifted from overriding concentration on clinical treatment methods to a concern with concepts such as social change, political action, social action, social policy, client advocacy, and the like. In the social sciences more attention has also been paid to problems of the poor and racial minorities and to programs and strategies aimed at changing their situation. Organizational theory has examined structures and programs in social welfare and social change. As part of this literature, an increasing number of research studies deal with issues pertinent to community organization practice.

The body of this chapter will be comprised of a review of a range of these empirical investigations. It will draw on material from thirty relevant journals covering the period 1964–68. These journals represent the disciplines of sociology, politi-

The research project on which this report is based is supported by NIMH Grant MH 16125-02. The author expresses thanks to an able group of research assistants who contributed immeasurably to this effort.

cal science, social psychology, and applied anthropology, as well as the professions of city planning, public administration, public health, and adult education, in addition to social work. It will not be possible to make a full summary here; the space allotted would preclude such treatment. Rather, the writer will select and present what he judges to be some of the more important or interesting findings. Breadth of coverage will be sought rather than intensity in a single practice area or discipline. The objective is to illustrate the utility of a broad literature cutting across several disciplines and professions as the source of a pool of research findings that may illuminate and guide community organization practice with respect to a variety of issues.

The difficulties of reviewing, if not synthesizing, so large a body of research, carried on with a variety of theoretical perspectives and purposes, should be apparent. Equally apparent is the need in practice for guidance that is based on systematic empirical inquiry. Thus in this chapter implications for action were drawn from each of the studies selected for review, although the studies were rarely replicated. Since the approach is obviously premature, the derived principles and guides to action should be seen as tentative—in actuality a set of hypotheses set forth for further testing by community organization practitioners and researchers. The state of relevant research is such that few problems have been studied systematically in more than one investigation, while at the same time the state of practice is such that guidance needs to be drawn from all available sources.

Planning Processes and Issues

Various theoretical and conceptual writings have been produced over the years regarding the process of planning. Research findings on the same subject have generally lagged behind the more expository literature. Here evidence will be presented from several research studies that illuminate a number of facets of planning.

Priority-Planning

Priority-planning has been a subject of discussion for a number of years in the social welfare council field. One study (11) traced the implementation of a priority plan in the Community Services Council of Indianapolis through close participant observation and interviews with staff members. Among other things it was found that the council made selective and partial rather than extensive use of priority recommendations, putting a recommendation into effect was often not contingent on its cost, and much dependence was placed on value-based judgmental processes rather than more systematic rational ones.

By and large allocators use those aspects of a priority plan to which they were predisposed originally. There is a greater tendency to use such a plan to hold back budget increases for low-status agencies than to reduce allocations of high-prestige agencies. "Often allocators use priorities as a facade for preserving the status quo" (11, p. 280). Practitioners should not expect a priority plan to generate new sources of finances through increasing the funding level, to transfer funds from strong and well-entrenched agencies to others, or to serve as an educational device for laymen in target agencies. Such a plan, however, does serve as a normative instrument for the planning staff and can speed up community action by legitimating the increase of services to which allocators are already predisposed. It was found that practitioners are more apt to utilize a priority plan when it contains minimal vagueness and imprecision, such as cloudy service definitions, confusing pagination, and unclear recommendations.

Organizational Form

Another study (78) examined certain structural arrangements that facilitated or hindered the planning process. This study was concerned with the question of what organizational form of city planning units is most effective, those under the jurisdiction of independent planning boards or those responsible to the chief executive. To answer this question, the authors surveyed 309 planning directors. The 201 usable responses came from 77 agencies responsible to the chief executive, 76 directors of independent planning commissions, and 48 directors of agencies that combined both structures.

The findings show that the major problem for independent planning directors is the lack of a person committed to "selling" the agency's plans or with a political obligation to promote recommendations. Directors of agencies with connections to the chief executive were more favorable to this arrangement, except in those instances when the executive was weak. The major finding of the study is that the promotion of planning is seen by professional planners as essentially a political process and that it is facilitated when there are close structural ties between the planning agencies and the chief executive.

The chief implication here is that when planning processes necessitate governmental-political action (legitimation and budget provision by the local governmental structure), then a direct structural linkage to the chief executive is desirable in achieving implementation of plans. Retention of a separate citizens' board at the same time may provide a safeguard against undue political influence in planning. Agencies might devise various formal and informal functional linkages to the office of the chief executive as a way of enlisting his support, recognizing that this may place some restraints on their autonomy.

Housing and Urban Renewal

Several studies have been made of the planning process in housing and urban renewal. Occasionally a practitioner serves local communities through a vantage point at the national level. One study (33) concerned itself with identifying variables that would predict a rural township's participation in federal renewal planning. The sample of townships that comprised the units of study consisted of a systematic random sample of all upstate New York townships with population densities of less than 875 persons per square mile. It was found that a township with an urban center located within it is more likely to have renewal plans than a township without such a center. Among the latter type of town, there is a greater probability of renewal plans if the town has a larger population, has a higher income, is closer to a metropolitan center, or has a planning or zoning board.

The implication for intervention is that in national or regional organizational planning for local services, the practitioner might assume that those townships that have an urban center already have renewal plans or would be easily subject to his efforts to establish these. He can also assume that for townships without renewal plans he will have an easier time influencing those that have a larger population, are closer to the metropolitan area, or have a higher income level. He should concentrate on these if he wants quick results or perhaps a contagion effect; he might concentrate on the others if he wishes to serve areas of greater resistance or incapacity to act. Encouraging the community to establish a planning or zoning board (social planning committee, manpower services study group) would appear to be a useful intermediate step in moving toward concrete plans.

Neighborhood Identity

A question is often raised concerning the functional and ethical issues involved in rebuilding inner-city slum neighborhoods and relocating residents in new areas. One study (93) investigated the extent to which black slum-dwellers have an attachment to their neighborhood as compared with an ethnic nationality group. Chosen for examination were (1) a census tract in Detroit that was occupied by almost all-black low-income residents living in largely substandard housing and (2) Italian residents of the West End area of Boston. The authors concluded that there is minimal attachment to home and neighborhood in inner-city black areas. In their view it would be possible to renew such areas without disrupting stable and viable social relationships; the major issue for the planner would be provision of adequate substitute housing. The reader should keep in mind that there may be variations in the study variables among neighborhoods—i.e., some black communities may have strong attachments and some ethnic communities weak ones. Degree of attachment rather than ethnicity would appear to be the critical factor.

In another study (79) it was found that what residents of a low-income project desire most is safety from a hostile and uncertain social environment. The home is viewed as a place of retreat from a threatening environment. The author suggests to planners that in designing housing for low-income populations esthetic considerations must be balanced by attention to security and order. There is also the implication that middle-class planners are removed from the life-space concerns of low-income people and ought to devise means of discerning these concerns if their planning is to be meaningful.

Service Expenditures

Planners are frequently concerned with the relationship of budgetary expenditures to the quality of services delivered to various population groups. One researcher (89) attempted to determine whether higher expenditures by state and local governments are associated with the quality of services found in these jurisdictions. Amount of expenditures was measured by such criteria as combined state and local general expenditures per capita, and quality of services, by criteria such as the number of teachers per hundred pupils. In general the author

found no direct relationship between expenditures and services and that the extent of state and local government spending does not have a pervasive effect on the character of public services.

This suggests that a planner or agency head desiring higher quality services should not always promote a generally higher level of spending in order to improve the overall quality of services. Rather, he should concentrate on improving the quality of services in specific areas of interest. Exceptions to this rule, as discovered in the study, include rehabilitation services, interstate highway completion, and payments of Old Age Assistance, Aid to Families with Dependent Children, and Aid to the Blind. Practitioners interested in these specific welfare areas might well promote generally higher expenditures with the anticipation of fallout in terms of quality of service in their areas of concern.

Another investigation of service expenditures (66) was based on a sample of all cities in Ohio with populations greater than 50,000. Twelve categories of expenditures were chosen from the *Compendium of Government Finance in 1961*. The items were ranked by amount of money spent on each in terms of both per capita expenditure and the percentage of the total budget. The budgetary items were then related to thirty-eight socioeconomic variables pertaining to the cities included in the study.

In general the following was found: (1) Higher socioeconomic status communities have lower per capita expenditures for police, fire protection, general control, water, and housing and urban renewal and have a higher percentage of expenditures for police, general control, highways, sewers and sanitation, and interest. (2) Older communities have higher per capita expenditures for health and hospitals, employee retirement, and parks and recreation and have a higher percentage of expenditures for employee retirement and health and hospitals. (3) More mobile communities have higher per capita expenditures for interest and urban renewal and have a higher percentage of expenditures for urban renewal.

From data such as these the planner is able to predict the level of support for given services or programs in the type of community in which he is located. Thus, if he is based in a mobile community, urban renewal is likely to absorb a relatively high proportion of the city budget. An awareness of this permits the planner to concentrate on program directions that maximize his chances of success.

Unintended Consequences

While the planning process attempts to evoke a highly rationalistic mode of operation, it can produce both unintended and undesired consequences, for example, as shown in a description of a community action program undertaken to improve the pattern of race relations in a largely segregated community in a depressed rural area of a northern state (39). The program was conducted through a university agency in a small community of 3,400 having a 40 percent black population. The agency philosophy was highly democratic, emphasizing wide community participation and the voluntary mobilization of community resources and skills. The project was conducted over a five-year period and included a research component consisting of unstructured interviews with residents, review of program documents, and participant observation. The study concluded that the pattern of race relations in this highly segregated community did not change at all as a result of this undertaking; rather, the feeling by the black residents that they were being exploited increased. Local merchants who were highly influential neither sought nor accepted egalitarian social arrangements. Their orientation toward the program was one of improving economic conditions within the framework of the status quo.

It is clear that a broad community involvement program can have unintended negative effects on race relations. In the present case this occurred because the racial goals were not clear, black leadership was weak, and the economic interests of the dominant business community were able to prevail. Since white business interests are ascendant in many small towns, "democratic" community development programs such as this are likely to be risky if the goal is improved race relations or the adjustment of racial inequalities. The planner should at least investigate to see whether dominant business interests will oppose or support black interests before undertaking a project with this type of program design.

Planning in Developing Countries

Planners in developing countries are often faced with policy choices regarding whether to emphasize community development goals (education, democratic values, and procedures) or economic goals, which are sometimes seen as conflicting objectives. The argument can be couched in terms of the long-standing professional debate concerning process versus task goals. A comparative study (70) of twenty-three countries was made using an index of democratic political development and a variety of measures of socioeconomic status. The authors conclude that certain levels of

basic socio-economic development appear to be necessary to elevate countries to a level at which they can begin to support complex, nation-wide patterns of political interaction, one of which may be democracy. Once above this threshold, however, the degree to which a country will "maximize" certain forms of democratic practice is no longer a function of continued socio-economic development. [70, p. 1007]

This finding is highly significant for planning in developing countries. It implies that a certain floor of economic well-being is necessary in order to encourage and sustain democratic political activity. In fact, such democratic functioning may be a direct correlate of a reasonably high level of economic development. The implication is that efforts to foster democratic practices may be futile in the face of an inadequate economic situation. In such a situation the planner might well direct his primary attention to economic considerations, viewing these as an intervening mechanism for achieving goals related to democratic practices.

Community Participation

The matter of community participation has been of long-standing interest in community organization practice, both in terms of an end to be pursued in its own right and also as an instrumental means toward other ends. Participation has been of special concern in community development efforts that emphasize self-help activities and in social action projects that attempt to stimulate mass involvement of indigenous groups as a way of impacting governmental and other bureaucratic structures. Participation has been associated to a large extent with two theoretical constructs in the social science literature—relative deprivation and status inconsistency, both of which will be covered here in depth.

Relative Deprivation

A number of researchers and theorists have held that the subjective feelings of deprivation and disadvantage have a greater effect on mobilizing people to better their conditions than do the objective circumstances of life. Matza writes:

. . . subjective feelings of deprivation depend on how one's own experiences compare to those close at hand, to what one has become accustomed in the past, or to what one anticipates. Thus, profound degradation in an absolute sense may be tolerated or even pass unnoticed if others close at hand fare no better or if one never had reason to expect any better. [57, p. 622]

Several studies have produced evidence tending to validate this proposition.

The data for one investigation (65) were taken from thirteen studies done in eight midwestern states (the core of the National Farmers' Organization membership) between 1962 and 1966, which permitted comparison of NFO members with similar farmers who were not members. The sample consisted of 8,700 subjects, about 1,200 of whom were NFO members. Conventional survey methods were used in the original studies (interviews, mailed questionnaires, and some group interviews). Compared with other farmers, NFO members were found to be generally in more advantaged economic circumstances, but they expressed greater dissatisfaction and were willing to use more drastic means to change institutions perceived as having detrimental effects. NFO members tended to have higher economic aspirations than nonmembers and to exhibit greater belief in the structural sources of their difficulties in achieving economic aspirations. The authors state that the principle of relative deprivation is at work in fostering organizational participation.

This suggests that the practitioner might look for initial participants in a social action-oriented social movement not from among the most deprived—those "at the bottom"—but rather from those who have risen to a somewhat higher economic level. Such individuals would most likely respond more easily to appeals to participate. Second, with other individuals, notions of deprivation and relative deprivation might be emphasized as a useful organizing tool. It is also important to point out to such persons structural rather than personal blockages to better life circumstances.

Another finding was that those who have experienced some prior success from participation in movements are most likely to participate, underscoring the possible desirability of seeking to achieve a number of short-term, even if relatively unimportant, successes. Finally, the study indicates that those involved in social movements tend to see change as a result of organized power. This suggests the use of strategies through which organizational power can be visibly exercised and demonstrated.

Another study (83) was based on interviews with 1,029 farm workers who were defined as living in poverty and a comparison group of middle- and upper-class farmowners. All subjects were from wheat-, fruit-, and vegetable-growing areas of the state of Washington. It was found that the workers, many of whom were migrants, were limited in upward mobility as a class because of lack of education and job skills and low income levels. Workers perceived that they were deprived to a greater extent than the growers (22 percent of the workers agreed that life was "unhappy and would not get better" as compared with only 6 percent of the growers). While the workers felt deprived, the small degree of deprivation they sensed may be associated with community isolation and the low social visibility that was true of the group, which had little contact with middle- and upper-class persons. The analysis of perceived deprivation revealed a false consciousness of one's objective position.

This has a number of implications in terms of organizing client groups from the poverty population. In the first place, it may initially be difficult to organize such groups because of their lack of awareness of their deprivation. Again, demonstrating actual deprivation may be a useful organizing tool (perhaps concentrating on a specific area of deprivation at any given time). Because of clients' greater awareness of poor life chances than of actual deprivation, this might be a concept around which to organize. Likewise, focusing on the needs of their children may be a powerful motivating force. Breaking up the pattern of isolation and bringing the group or its leaders in contact with middle-class persons and situations might intensify their feeling of deprivation. (In terms of services, the study underlines the need for educational and skill training programs for this population.)

Still another investigation (75) was based on a 1962 survey of members of the Social Credit Party in Quebec, with further documentation from other movements such as the Socialist and CCF parties in western Canada and the Poujadist movement in France. This investigator concludes that the poor are never the first to join new political movements, right or left. Movements and parties fail to enlist the support of the poor while such organizations are still in the formative stage and politically weak. The exception appears to be in conditions of acute economic crisis. A feeling of hopelessness seemed to account for low support and participation by the most poor in this study. Worry increased support of movements by other groups but reduced support by the poor.

A somewhat different approach to the problem is reflected in a survey of white and black colleges situated in neighboring cities in a southern state in which attitudes were explored regarding communism (43). The author found strong indications that deprivation, lower-class socioeconomic background, and black identity were not correlated with radical ideological acceptance. In actuality, lower-class persons and blacks were relatively intolerant of radical positions.

These studies taken together and when viewed with a substantial number of other studies yielding similar findings give impressive support to the concept of relative deprivation. More specifically, they point out that the most economically disadvantaged typically have had a low predisposition to support or participate in social movements. They suggest the principle of seeking organizational support and participation just above the lowest class level rather than at the bottom of the pyramid if the aim is efficiency, that is, maximal response in lower-class organizing for given amounts of recruitment effort.

Status Inconsistency

The concept of status inconsistency (and its counterpart, status crystallization) has also been associated in various ways with participation (45). The degree to which the various statuses that define a person's position in society are consistent or inconsistent for him is viewed as having a profound effect on his mental outlook and his predisposition to take action of various sorts.

One study (92) investigated participants in left- and right-wing student organizations in a large public university. Members of a leftist peace group and of Young Americans for Freedom were asked questions about their family background, class, political participation, and attitudes toward the war in Vietnam. Both groups appeared to manifest status inconsistencies, but of different types. The leftist group were of high socioeconomic status but identified themselves with the lower-status Democrats. The rightists were predominantly low-status individuals who identified themselves with the high-status Republican Party. (It might be noted here that status inconsistency cannot be viewed as giving an overall explanation because it does not account for another probably larger uncrystallized group that does not espouse radicalism.)

Another study (82) of political attitudes and behaviors of residents in the Eugene-Springfield area of Massachusetts found significant differences in extremist attitudes among low- and high-consistency groups. The authors suggest that a combination of high income and low education may predispose toward right-wing tendencies; a combination of low income and high education predisposes toward left-wing tendencies. Unrewarded persons with status inconsistency evidence the most discontent and are most prone to participation in social movements (30). (Unrewarded groups include those who are high in ethnicity but low in income or occupation and those who are high in education but low in income or occupation.)

Participation of the Poor

The period the United States has just passed through may be characterized as the era of "maximum feasible participation of the poor"—in rhetoric, if not in practice. Historically, social workers have been dedicated to the participation of low-income people in organizational activities related to improving their social position. Increasingly, recent research studies have spotlighted issues specifically related to participation of the poor, a suggestive sampling of which will be cited here.

Researchers interviewed 43 of the 48 candidates for seats on Cleveland's Council for Economic Opportunity (9). All came from areas designated as deprived and were economically below the defined poverty level. Those running for office belonged to voluntary associations and exhibited leadership, had many friends, voted regularly, were enthusiastic about the poverty program, wanted to help others, and saw themselves as equal. However, they did not possess the following characteristics: family stability, group consciousness as poor, strong feelings for the poor as oppressed, a view of the middle class as oppressors, or understanding of liberal politics and service programs. The characteristic of voting regularly seemed especially important in predicting candidacy.

This study may help the planner or organizer in predicting the characteristics of individuals who will seek offices as spokesmen of the poor. Individuals with the characteristics cited might be expected to turn up naturally, or if the planner wishes to stimulate candidacy, people with those characteristics might most easily be activated. Consistent past voting behavior is an especially good predictor. On the other hand, one would not expect people to participate simply because they lacked the characteristics cited in the second group, that is, evidenced family instability or lacked an understanding of liberal politics. The implication of the second group of characteristics is that spokesmen of the poor may be expected to need political education to increase their sophistication and social consciousness. In addition, there is an implication that the social activist will need aggressively to seek out individuals who have a more radical orientation but would not ordinarily or naturally desire to participate in establishmentarian politics. These guidelines are tentative, based on the assumption that the situation in Cleveland is similar to other metropolitan areas. Cross-community studies of programs of the Office of Economic Opportunity should be available in print shortly.

What is the relationship of participation in political organizations to the growth of political education and sophistication? A highly interesting and informative study examining this question was made of 300 members of the Italian Socialist Party (4). The author found that for the more highly educated members, greater political participation was associated with a "dramatic increase" in ideological sensitivity; for less educated members, in large measure lower-class individuals, there was no association between participation and this type of sensitivity. Low-income undereducated individuals appeared to continue to be at a disadvantage in interpreting events, developing and articulating alternatives, and addressing issues in ideological terms. According to this study, low-income people with low educational levels cannot be expected to develop political ideological sophistication through participation in political movements alone, although they can thereby acquire increased knowledge of political activities and processes. People with higher levels of education do not gain in this regard, having come to the situation with a basic pool of such information. This suggests that the practitioner who wishes to raise ideological sophistication on the part of a client group or constituency of low educational status must specifically educate them in ideological terms, either through formal classes or informal discussions. Ideological perspective is an input he himself might be expected to make or he might (1) link his client group with more-educated outside individuals or (2) bring such individuals into the situation as resources or participants.

Another revealing study (42) has to do with socialization into the political system toward the role of legislator. Family fac-

tors, personal predispositions, actual political participation, and the effect of certain events or individuals all acted as socializing agents that motivated individuals to seek political leadership. Early family influences accounted for political participation in the majority of instances (55 percent of the cases) of middle-class business and professional people. For those in low-income circumstances, 91 percent attributed their political activity to external factors in their adult lives.

This suggests to the organizer in low-income communities that there is a reservoir of viable adult leadership available in the population that he may be able to mobilize. The organizer, according to this study, should be alert to individuals with as yet undeveloped leadership potential, as well as to external events and conditions that might serve to trigger the movement of such individuals toward important political leadership roles.

Groups Other Than the Poor

The modes of participation of a range of groups other than the poor have been reported in the literature. Examples of a few of these will be described.

It was found that broad participation of the business community in voluntary associations is more likely in small towns than in large cities (74). The suggestion is that businessmen in small towns may be strongly motivated to participate in programs that emphasize their greater control of the economic environment, because they generally feel under greater economic threat than do businessmen in larger cities.

A study of desegregation of public transportation in the South singled out individuals who are more likely to participate in civil rights activities in that region (21). Persons who violated precedents by breaking patterns of segregation tended to a greater degree to be young people (especially among the blacks), males if white and females if black. It seems easier and less stressful in the South (at least in the past) for white males and black females to engage in activities that break caste-like norms.

There has been a growing interest in client groups to join organizations acting welfare organizations as well as of other institutions. The question of motivating client groups to join organizations acting in their behalf is of vital importance in making such organizations viable. A suggestive study was conducted in Israel, making note of the types of appeals different client groups normally used in dealing with officials of bureaucratic organizations (41). Typically, clients from traditional ethnic backgrounds tended to use altruistic appeals that were more passive, covered a narrower range of reasons, and were nonnormative, while those from more modern backgrounds tended to use normative appeals based on the target organization's goals and ideology. With the passage of time and with experience with organizations, traditional clients shifted to a greater degree to the use of normative appeals.

This study highlights the fact that different client groups tend to utilize different styles in their organizational participation. In working with such groups the practitioner must take these predilections into account. He may initially induce people to participate through an approach conducive to their shifting to more functional or aggressive strategies as they become ready for these. The suggestion made in the report is that when clients gain more experience with agencies, they tend to move toward more assertive modes of action. The practitioner might be attuned to this and do what he can to reinforce such natural tendencies when it is functional to do so.

Structural Variables

In addition to viewing patterns of participation of different population segments, a number of studies have examined participation from a structural point of view.

What structural variables are associated with what types of participation and what types of outcomes may be associated with different types or amounts of participation? Three studies bearing on these factors will be touched on briefly.

In a comparative analysis of participation levels and social welfare expenditures in forty different nations, a researcher discovered a strong positive correlation between political participation in voting and social security spending (20). Thus it is implied that the intervening variable of increased political participation may be a useful point of leverage for moving a nation toward more substantial welfare programs. (This no doubt oversimplifies by singling out two variables within a complex set of interrelated factors, but it provides at least one way of gaining leverage on the situation.)

In regard to another structural factor, it has been shown that states with stronger interest groups are more likely to be one-party areas, have legislative parties with weak cohesion, and be less industrial and urban (95). The suggestion is that practitioners located in such states might utilize heavy reliance on interest group activity to influence legislation.

Another investigator (28) found a positive relationship between interest group activity and the numbers of elected versus appointed commissioners and judges in a state. Practitioners in such states should be prepared to engage in more vigorous interest group strategies in the course of their work.

Social Action Strategies

Social action strategies utilizing confrontation, advocacy, and conflict have appeared in the social work and social science literature since the mid-1960s to a degree uncharacteristic of the previous few decades. In this section several studies that deal with aspects of these interventive techniques in community practice will be discussed.

In the previous section dealing with participation, a number of studies cited pertain equally to social action. The discussion of relative deprivation suggested types of individuals who might be receptive to social action approaches and ways of appealing to low-income people to join in such activities. Another population group from which to recruit potential activists was described in the treatment of status inconsistency. Here focus will be on a set of strategic guidelines to social action as suggested in some selected research reports.

Conflict

An exceedingly interesting and creative discussion of conflict is set down by a political scientist through examination of the communication pattern among top-level policy-makers of five European countries immediately before the outbreak of World War I (38). Content analysis was used to investigate the complete verbatim text of published documents dated between June 27 and August 4, 1914, that were signed by specified high policy-makers of Austria-Hungary, France, Great Britain, Germany, and Russia. While the context is national rather than local, the stages and dynamics of the conflict between contending parties (as stress increases) that are revealed appear to be highly pertinent for community organization practice. An intricate series of hypotheses are proposed by the author and tested carefully using quantitative methods. It will not be possible to go into the details in the space available here. For present purposes it might be just as well in this instance to skip a step and go on to derivations for practice from this research.

For the social action organization that is seeking to escalate the level of conflict, action implications are as follows: shorten the time period available to the other side for response, emphasize immediate goals, limit the range of alternatives available to the other side and its allies, overload the other side with communications and stretch its capacity to process these, aim the flood of communications at high-level personnel on the other side, disrupt the intraorganizational communication process of the other side. These tactics are derived from a description of the difficulties actually experienced by the parties involved as the level of stress increased. A practitioner who wishes to reduce tension would be advised to use these principles in reverse. Some lessons are also included for organizations against which conflict efforts are directed. Hypothetically they would operate in such a way as to counteract these initiatives through such devices as keeping their range of alternatives wide and fluid and perhaps becoming prepared to cope with a potential inundation of communications through employment of standby personnel to absorb some of the overflow.

An older study also examined the process of conflict. Here reference is to the well-known monograph by Coleman, which is based on a large number of case studies of community conflict (14). Coleman found that community conflicts typically pass through identical stages in a time-phased sequence. These stages can be described as follows: (1) single issue, (2) equilibrium of community relations is disrupted, (3) previously suppressed issues against opponent are allowed to appear, (4) more of opponent's beliefs enter into disagreement, (5) opponent appears totally bad, (6) charges are made against opponent as a person, (7) dispute becomes independent of the initial disagreement.

While this is a descriptive statement of the "natural" course of conflict, it also represents a prescriptive statement of likely steps to be followed by pressure groups. Ideas such as starting with concrete initial issues and personalizing these issues dramatically in terms of a specific individual are indeed tactics that seem to be followed by militant social action groups. Coleman's study suggests a conscious and disciplined utilization of these tactics rather than their recurrent rediscovery by each new group.

The impact on bureaucracies of pressure tactics by client groups may be viewed in another way. That is to say, the pattern of reaction by officials to pressure from clients may be charted and implications thereby derived. In a study of this type, sixty-seven officials of six social service organizations in Israel were interviewed regarding their customary responses to client pressure (6). It was found that practitioners respond to clients with individual forms of defense that are related to societal norms, with structural defenses that include joint defense group consolidation among professionals, or with the use of a "pressure specialist," that is, a practitioner who acts as a buffer between the clients and the other workers. Use of structural defenses was found to be associated with the degree of professionalization of the organization (the proportion of professionals to nonprofessionals employed).

In their responses professionals could be classified as pro-organization, pro-client, independent, or erratic (depending on the direction of greatest pressure). Independent behavior was most frequent in units with buffer defense, erratic behavior predominated in units with no structural defense, and pro-organization behavior was associated with joint (peer group) defense. When a social action group feels that opening options for independent performance by workers would aid their goals, they might encourage the buffer defense. When it seems desirable to disrupt the organization by fostering erratic behavior, individual forms of defense might be encouraged and structural defenses hindered. When general organizational policies are under attack, it would be well to limit peer group defenses, since this tends to foster conformity to organizational goals. From the standpoint of the profession, buffer defense in situations of client pressure seems to facilitate the exercise of independent or autonomous professional judgment that may support either organizational or client claims based on the merits of the issue.

This article indicates that organizational changes can come about as a result of direct pressure by clients on personnel in the field. As a consequence of multiple stresses that operate on such officials, they are vulnerable as well as in a position to bring about changes in organizational operations, despite constraining regulations of central headquarters. It is accordingly not necessary for client groups always to exert pressure at the inaccessible top in order to effect changes in human service organizations; intervention aimed at more available direct-service line personnel may also be effective.

Conflicting Demands of Constituencies

Carrying out a social action strategy may involve a wide range of complexities and even internal contradictions. In two articles (49, 50) based in part on the 1963–64 Harlem rent strikes in New York City, four distinct constituencies of a protest organization are delineated—internal organizational members, the communications media and general public, third parties who are potential allies or supporters, and target gatekeeper organizations. These four entities are viewed as different resources that are required to maintain general strategies, but each of which in its own right in order to be properly engaged requires different substrategies and perhaps different leadership styles. The author suggests that the conflicting demands of these constituencies create incompatible cross-pressures on the protest organizer that are perhaps impossible to resolve.

A combination tactic was used by Jesse Gray, the strike leader, in projecting the image to the public (through dramatic appeals via the mass media) of vulnerable tenants in danger, while the tenants actually remained fairly secure and within the legal process because Gray used a provision in the law that protected tenants against eviction if rent money was paid to the court. In doing this Gray reduced some of the dangers of organizational participation by the membership, while using dramatic militant appeals at the same time. Through this tactic Gray successfully met the needs of the mass media, aroused the target agency, and appealed to his members, satisfying competing constituent groups.

In leadership style, however, he had difficulty. Gray spent a good deal of time organizing groups and speaking throughout the city, thus neglecting administrative detail, failing to collect dues systematically, and alienating lawyers, who were often not paid. College students who staffed the rent strike offices helped this situation, but this sort of help, Lipsky points out, is transient and often not applicable with the modern emphasis on Black Power. A further difficulty in satisfying the conflicting demands of constituent groups arose with regard to the mass media. To satisfy the media's demands for "news," Gray often exaggerated the size and success of the protest; the mass media printed his claims, but later when they demanded documentation of these claims from him, he could not supply this. In the short run, through meeting the demands of his organizational members he had satisfied them, but in doing so he was labeled irresponsible by more established groups.

The target agency (in this the case New York City government) responded with symbolic rewards rather than significant changes in the protestors' situation. Programs were adopted in response to crisis that gave the impression of meeting the protestors' demands, but that lacked substance.

Rather than conclude from a case study of the rent strike situation that protest tactics are inherently bound to fail, one might instead draw the lesson that most protest movements do not take into account the constellation of substrategies and leadership styles that must be commanded by an organization in order to be effective. Each of the four key constituencies (discussed next) should be examined separately and distinct approaches toward them designed.

Key Constituent Groups

Illustratively, the practitioner might conceptualize leadership modes and tactics with regard to each constituent group as follows:

1. *Organizational members.* If these are deprived members of society who lack such customary gratifications from joining a group as improved status and money, the leader may have to adopt a militant style, promising rewards that will satisfy the members' needs for revenge and emotional release, for example. In the absence of immediate tangible rewards for participation, he will have to supply these intangible incentives.

2. *Mass media.* The worker should plan some organizational events and public tactics with an eye to what is news to the mass media; therefore, some of his tactics should be dramatic with perhaps a hint of conflict—e.g., demonstrations, sit-ins, sensational statements. In addition the worker must cultivate relationships with reporters assigned to his organization or to the area of civil rights or social problems and attempt to meet the reporters' special needs for news. He may try tactics such as letting the reporters know of events ahead of time (i.e., giving them a "scoop") or he may deliberately distort or enlarge the scope of his organization's activity in order to attract the media's interest.

3. *Third parties.* Appeals to third parties, which are likely to be established social welfare organizations or the more conservative civil rights organizations, must consider the long-term relationships and interdependencies these organizations are likely to have with target agencies, their modes of operating, which are likely to be less sensational than those of the protest agency, and their penchant for careful organization and administrative details. Appeal to these groups, then, may require that the protest organization adopt a more moderate leadership style (perhaps a different leader can be trained for these skills), the presentation of less dramatic

appeals to these groups, and the careful attention to administrative matters that these groups respect. With attention to these strategies, the leader of the protest organization who establishes relationships with third parties could then attempt to gain access to decision-making groups of the third parties or could attempt to use their influence with target agencies to gain access for the protest organization to decision-making bodies within the target agency.

4. *Target agency.* A combination of the cited strategies and leadership styles is likely to be necessary in moving the target agency—for example, dramatic protests involving the use of the mass media (in order to embarrass the target agency and provide negative publicity to which the agency is sensitive) combined with a less militant, organizationally conscious style in order to gain the long-term rewards of actual admission to decision-making bodies and the added support of third parties.

These strategies, the author suggests, should be considered short term, since protest as a tactic is a limited strategy because of its inherent difficulties in organizational maintenance and in meeting the conflicting needs of constituent groups.

Still another careful case study of the rent strikes produced a different observation (67). The author makes the point that the rent strikes failed because the social action organization became heavily involved toward the end in a complicated technical legal process. Most of its energies became enmeshed in court procedures, burning out its resources and dampening the spirits of members who were not given a continuing channel for active participation. The implication is that grass-roots activist groups should not engage with bureaucracies on their own terms, in their own arena of competence and strength. It is not possible for the grass-roots organization to bring to bear the organizational sophistication and technical resources that are involved in what has been termed "going the bureaucratic route." The suggestion is made that the styles and capacities

of formal organizations and of grass-roots groups are different and that the latter lose their driving force when they permit themselves to become enveloped in the style of the former.

Contextual Factors

Contextual factors such as community leadership patterns or immediate predisposing events may affect the capacity of an organization to mount social action projects or the outcome of such effort. For example, a study of a desegregation controversy in New Rochelle, New York, found that more lower-class parents became involved in transferring their children to integrated schools than did middle-class parents (53). This was in contrast to other studies which indicated that middle-class parents were more apt to aid desegregation programs. The authors state that the difference is explained by the prolonged and intense controversy in New Rochelle, which served to educate and mobilize the lower-class group. This period of conflict "awakened discontent of the lower stratum and set it in motion" (53, p. 88). The implication is that an atmosphere of controversy is a predisposing condition that lays the groundwork for lower-class participation in social action. Many social action projects requiring mass mobilization of people need the participation of this population.

Another predisposing condition appears to be instability in the leadership structure of the overall community. Gamson (29) studied eighteen New England communities that had made decisions about fluoridation of the community's water supply during the same period of a year and a half. Through interviews with 426 local informants and a review of pertinent documents, he was able to classify the communities into two groups, depending on whether or not they had engaged in intense or "rancorous" conflict. One of the major variables distinguishing the two sets of communities from one another was that in the rancorous situation there had been a shift in political leadership in the period preceding the fluoridation discussion. Accordingly, perhaps a good time to initiate a social action program is after a shift in community political leadership. Social action-oriented practitioners might select such communities for the initiation of programs or capitalize on such circumstances and times for beginning or intensifying programs within communities in which they are situated.

The pattern of community leadership across an action system may also affect social action outcomes. A thought-provoking study (57) is based on a comparative investigation of civil rights leadership in fourteen cities. Walker, in a previous study (90a), had suggested that competition among civil rights leaders tends to aid the black community's battle against segregation. McWorter and Crain (57) found in this study that organized competition among civil rights leaders led to intense activity but inadequate outcomes. Individual competition resulted in more sustained civil rights activities, but cities with no leadership competition seemed most capable of maintaining a disciplined drive for specific goals. The application principle exhibited here is that when a practitioner has specific social action objectives in mind he should work to minimize competition among relevant action groups and their leaders. Such competition presumably may be reduced through various mechanisms that enhance communication, bargaining, or coordination. When the objective is to increase the general level of activity rather than attain discrete action outcomes, then the practitioner might maintain or elevate the level of competition among groups.

Conditions Conducive to Local Movements

Often locality-based social action organizations devote their attention to neighborhood concerns under local sponsorship without considering possible limitations of such autonomous action. Light is shed on this issue by a study of fifty-two neighborhood associations in ten urban areas (3). There were four major findings: (1) All the associations had limited organizational resources (including operating funds), telephone service, and their own letterhead. (2) Three-fourths of the action issues of all associations are concerned with environmental or service improvements specific to a single neighborhood. (3) Associations with a high score on social action are found only in specific cities. (4) In the cities with high action score associations, nearly all neighborhood associations are predominantly black, factors within the Community Action Agency (CAA) have led to an agency-wide action-focused approach to neighborhood organization, and the activities of the neighborhood associations are linked to a larger pattern of black mobilization in the surrounding communities.

Certain conditions emerge as conducive to developing and sustaining grass-roots social action movements. Among these the following may be included: [1]

1. An agency-wide (citywide), specialized focus on neighborhood organization is more likely to result in forceful protest action by associations than a pattern that decentralizes such activities to individual neighborhood service centers.

2. The presence of a staff person with a specific commitment to organization for social change in a key administrative position within the agency may be an essential ingredient in developing such a pattern of organizational activities.

3. The employment of such an individual and the protection of his employment in the face of community criticism require that black community leadership be substantially represented in the original formation of the CAA and be represented in sufficient strength on the policy board to protect this organizational approach from community pressure.

---

[1] Comments are taken from personal communications from the researcher, David M. Austin.

4. In those cities in which there are neighborhood associations that use forceful protest methods there is an interassociation council among the CAA neighborhood associations that is created by the leadership of those associations and is not a part of the formal structure of the CAA.

5. The emergence of neighborhood associations that use forceful protest methods and the creation of an interassociation council involving predominantly black neighborhood associations is linked to a pattern of emerging mobilization within the black community in general. The lack of action mobilization within the black community outside the CAA is associated with a limited pattern of association action. A pattern of black mobilization that has moved to full-scale engagement in political competition, as in Cleveland, is also associated with a limited pattern of neighborhood association activity.

Certain national conditions also have been found to stimulate or sustain local social action programs, such as a rapid increase in social and political participation in a nation where socioeconomic conditions are deteriorating (69) or the existence of a national movement with characteristics including crystallized political and ideological objectives, intensive interaction among members across many spheres of life, and closeness to disadvantaged communities (73). The absence of the latter factors may account for the weakness of radical movements in the United States such as Students for a Democratic Society.

Two other subjects will be discussed briefly, one having to do with the effect on the individual of participation in social action activities and the other with community groups that may be predicted to be supporters of social protest movements.

Effects on the Individual

Various writers have commented on the possible beneficial effects on disadvantaged individuals of participation in activist pro-grams. It has been hypothesized that such involvement serves to eliminate feelings of powerlessness, improve morale, and foment a personal sense of mastery (77). While widely discussed and accepted (according to this reviewer's reading), this position until recently has not been subject to empirical verification.

A revealing search into this issue was conducted in a slum area of a northern city (46). AFDC mothers who belonged to a welfare rights organization were compared with another group of such mothers who did not belong but who resided in the same twelve-square-block neighborhood. Controls were maintained for age, education, work history, length of time in the organization, number of children, and number of organizational affiliations. Results showed a negative relationship between affiliation in the organization and feelings of powerlessness among this group of the poor. The author concludes that "affiliation in a welfare client organization appears to be a powerful weapon with which to combat powerlessness among the welfare poor" (46, p. 32). While this study does not prove conclusively the existence of a cause-and-effect relationship (despite the author's enthusiasm in this respect), it may be said that there is an association between participation and reduced feelings of powerlessness. Even if what is reflected here is that people who join such organizations have a greater feeling of mastery to begin with, it seems likely that others who are recruited into such groups will be affected by the attitudes and behavior of their peers.

As for potential supporters of social protest, a survey of residents in a midwestern college community indicated that one should look to those at the highest and the lowest educational levels (71). Individuals in the middle educational echelon (between eighth grade and graduation from college) are the poorest bets. Also, those who are politically alienated do not necessarily support social change movements; indeed, they may rather be found in the backlash activities. Other social categories likely to support protest activities include younger rather than older persons, men rather than women, Democrats rather than Republicans.

Decision-Making

Matters pertaining to community policies or program directions ordinarily require the use of a decision-making process. A number of research studies have explored this area, examining the role in decision-making of the chief elected or executive official as well as that of interest groups and the public-at-large. Structural and other variables have been associated with outcomes.

Role of the Mayor and City Manager

Rosenthal and Crain (81) examined the process by which decisions concerning fluoridation of drinking water were made. Questionnaires were sent to key informants in all cities with populations of 10,000–500,000 in which the city owned its water supply or controlled its treatment. The publisher of the largest newspaper was asked about the local political system and the level of controversy, the local health officer was asked about the details of the campaign, and the city clerk was asked about the results of the election if a referendum had been held. Data were also collected on population composition and the political structure.

It was found that the position taken by the mayor or city manager virtually determined the decision made by the local government, whether this was by action of a city council or by referendum. Mayors were more in favor of the adoption of fluoridation when the issue was less controversial, but at each level the mayor's decision seem to affect the outcome. Regarding city managers, the most important factor was their degree of professionalism —nonprofessional managers were more likely to support the issue when it was not

controversial, whereas professional managers were willing to take a stand in favor of it even in the face of opposition. The authors felt that the position taken by the mayor or city manager provided a cue for the rest of the community and that it was difficult to adopt fluoridation when the mayor or city manager was opposed or neutral.

The implication is that with an issue such as fluoridation that affects all or a major portion of the population, the practitioner desiring the adoption of a particular policy should place great stress on winning the support of the mayor or city manager. Almost all resources should be directed toward that goal, perhaps to the neglect of other activities. If the issue is controversial, it will be more difficult to win the support of the mayor and especially that of nonprofessional city managers. In the latter instance, special effort might have to be made to win the nonprofessionals' support or, in anticipation of defeat, to build some other approach. One way of gaining the nonprofessionals' support might be to neutralize, play down, or win over opponents so that the level of controversy is or appears to be mild. If it appears impossible to win over or neutralize the chief municipal officer with respect to a project such as this, it might be strategically wise to postpone or abandon the project and focus organizational resources on an undertaking more likely to succeed.

In another article (16) the same authors indicate that the fluoridation issue has the following properties: almost unanimous support among the elite and the medical profession, without, however, strong commitment from the former; opposition from an organized minority including health faddists and the radical right; and an uninformed general public that is neutral but cautious of possible side-effects of medical innovation. Fluoridation has a better chance of adoption, they indicate, when the local political structure has a centralized decision-making authority like a manager or a partisan mayor and when the level of citizen participation in decision-making is kept low. The implication is that with a "progressive" technical issue requiring official action but with little political capital for the politician, it would be well to keep the level of public awareness and attention low and aim for a centrally made decision without evoking broad public participation.

In a study of school desegregation by one of the same authors (17) a somewhat different pattern of decision-making was found. In this instance it was the school board, rather than its executive officer, that was most crucial in reaching decisions. This is probably because civil rights is not an area in which the superintendent's expertise is recognized or effective. School boards were found to be rather autonomous with respect to the superintendent and other community actors, and the board's first response was an accurate indicator of the outcome of the issue. Higher status boards and boards with fewer politically connected members were more apt to take a position favorable to desegregation. The implication for the practitioner is that for a higher probability of success in the issue of desegregation one should work through the board rather than cultivating or pressuring the superintendent. The practitioner ought to make the activities surrounding the first stage of the undertaking as impressive and favorable as possible, since the board appears to hold to its initial response in this area. According to this research, working to elect relatively high-status, nonpolitical board members would appear to be another useful avenue of effort.

Relevance of the Governor

A study of legislative action at the state level discovered the critical relevance of the governor, equivalent to the role of the mayor at the city level in fluoridation issues (52). In this instance all legislation introduced into the Tennessee General Assembly from 1957 to 1963 and supported or opposed by at least one interest group was investigated. Interest groups that were active in forging ties and alliances with other interest groups were found to be more successful than groups that failed to obtain such support. The governor's influence on those bills on which he took a stand was virtually complete, and a high correlation was found between gubernatorial support and interest group success. It seems clear that in a state with a strong governor a key element in successful decision-making on legislative issues is the governor's support, with a second important factor being an interest group's bargaining skill that permits it to form coalitions with other interest groups.

Another study of the legislative process (88) examined decisions of legislators in nineteen different states. The author was interested in determining those factors that affected a state agency's success in receiving favorable decisions from state legislatures with regard to financial appropriations. Data used included requests of 529 agencies in the nineteen states, the governor's recommendation, and the legislature's appropriation during portions of the 1965–68 time period. It was found that when the governor cut back severely on agency requests, he constitutionally had substantial veto powers. Agency requests for expansion are accepted by governors when there are a low state debt, high personal income, intense party competition, and high voter turnout. The legislature is likely to accept agency requests when there are low governmental spending and low state debt and to cut requests when there are high governmental spending and a small number of elected officials.

An agency seeking favorable action on an expanded budget should, according to this study, strive to win the support of the governor. High party competition and voter turnout are conducive to the governor's acceptance of agency requests. An unfavorable governor can be neutralized by limiting his veto power, limiting his tenure, and increasing the number of elected officials. These kinds of structural changes are, of course, substantial and difficult to achieve. In addition to this, an agency should be aware that there are certain economic circumstances in a state's history when favorable decisions on increased expenditures are likely to occur. These economic conditions include a relatively low level of state spending and debt and relatively high personal incomes. A practitioner working on the national level might select for concentration states that most closely approximate these conditions if he wishes to increase his chances of success in pursuing certain programmatic directions in the states.

City Council Decisions

Another useful study was concerned with factors associated with city council policy decisions in seventy-seven cities in the San Francisco Bay Area (37). Data were obtained concerning city size, density, growth, and resources. Interviews were held with city councilmen in 1966 and 1967 to determine policy orientations of different councils. Stages and levels of development for the different cities were charted. A number of different findings were obtained, among them that the larger a city's size and density, the more developed its policies are likely to be, and that a city's resource base was not correlated with its developmental stage.

Among the more important findings from a practice standpoint were the following: It was not true, as was anticipated by the authors, that the more diverse the problems perceived by a council, the more developed its city policy is likely to be. On the contrary, policy is more likely to develop from a few widely shared needs than from a large number of contending needs. Also, the more visible a problem is to councilmen, the more likely the problem will be incorporated into a later policy development.

The implication for the planner and program advocate is that if he wishes to promote a specific policy decision in a city council he should try to particularize it, make it visible, and gain wide support for it, while at the same time playing down contending program claims or making it appear as though there is considerable difference of opinion with regard to those. A narrow focus, agreement on the subject, and visibility seem to be useful guidelines to favorable decision-making in municipal governing bodies.

Influencing the Congress

Legislators are important in many welfare policy decisions; influencing their behavior is an important means of affecting outcomes. One study (12) analyzed roll call voting on domestic policy issues in the U.S. House of Representatives in the four Congresses during the Eisenhower Administration. The author concludes that two major clusters exist in voting behavior: (1) economic policy having to do with fiscal matters and issues of governmental control over private elements of the economic system and (2) welfare policy having to do with such matters as minimum wages, hospital construction, and unemployment compensation. It was found that the urban-industrial character of a congressman's constituency was a better predictor than party affiliation of his vote on social welfare, whereas party affiliation was a better predictor than constituency type with regard to voting on economic policy.

Interventive strategies are suggested as follows: If an organization or practitioner wishes to influence a congressman on economic policies such as governmental regulation or private business operations, he would in general best approach the issue through his party identification or through the party itself (keeping in mind that Republicans generally have opposed government intervention with respect to economic control). In an area in which the party in general is opposed to the policy being pursued by the practitioner, he might work through an individual party member with status or financial resources who deviates from the majority position. If social welfare is the issue on which the practitioner wishes to influence the congressman, he might operate through the constituency or interest and pressure groups within it such as unions and voluntary associations (keeping in mind that representatives from constituencies high in urbanization and industrialization generally support social welfare policy programs).

Political Issues

Occasionally decisions have to be made concerning potential candidates for political office. One study (32) offers excellent guidance regarding this. The author was interested in investigating the question of whether a candidate who had undergone a tough fight in a primary election is at a disadvantage when he faces an opponent who did not experience serious conflict in the primary. To test this proposition, Hacker examined all primary and general elections for governors and senators in the period 1956–64. Of the 220 relevant elections, 99 included a situation in which one of the candidates experienced a divisive primary whereas the other did not. When the two sets of elections were compared, Hacker concluded that the variables of incumbency and political tradition of the political jurisdiction were the significant ones and that "a divisive primary, in and of itself, bears little relation to a candidate's prospects at the general election," (p. 110). In addition, a large turnout for the primary was associated with later success in the general election.

Implications for intervention have to do with planners who wish to promote or support (openly or behind the scenes) candidates who are favorable to specific social policies. If the practitioner wishes a given party to succeed in the general election, but at the same time wishes to challenge

the present leadership through a primary fight, he may do so with least risk of later defeat if the party already holds office, if the electoral area already has a tradition of party support, or if a large turnout is achieved for the primary. In an opposition party in an unfriendly district, a primary fight is highly injurious in the general election, but this may be countered through stimulating a large turnout for the primary within that party. Of course, on another level primary contests may provide an educational medium for issues, irrespective of eventual election results.

What about the role of social workers in community decision-making regarding political issues? Interviews were conducted with executive directors of social work agencies in Durham, North Carolina, and their counterparts in Lansing, Michigan (36). The interviews centered on views and experiences of social work executives in terms of involvement in political issues and affairs. A number of hypothetical situations were presented for reaction, including a cut in the state budget in an area of the agency's concern, a legislative bill affecting the agency's operations, an individual seeking election who would help or damage the agency's program. The respondents indicated a clear avoidance of identification with political parties, a reluctance to campaign openly, and heavy reliance on professional associations and agency boards. There was a feeling that avoidance of partisan identification is necessary. Executives felt their roles in political decision-making to be limited to the performance of an expert analysis and taking part in organized advocacy of specific positions only through the established channels of the social agency and professional associations.

The implications are variable. On the one hand, this suggests the need to educate agency executives concerning the validity of more open political engagement and the provision of skills in this area. On the other hand, one might experience resistance and awkwardness in promoting such an

approach. A more immediate and pragmatic implication is that in attempting to
engage social agency executives in politically oriented action, one should encourage
those activities that can be accomplished
readily through agency boards and professional associations. These capitalize on
the existing readiness of executives to view
these as legitimate avenues of work. Such
action can serve to strengthen and reinforce more open and direct political action
geared toward the achievement of social
policies and programs. In addition, the
expertise and competence of the executive
might easily be drawn on in developing
anonymous position papers and technical
background materials in support of legislative bills and partisan campaign plat-
forms.

A similar perspective on social work
involvement in community issues is offered
in a study by Epstein (23). He found
that social workers do not perceive themselves as direct participants in social action
issues, but see this as the prerogative of
low-income individuals. They state that
they are more likely to take sides on issues
outside the social work realm, such as in
housing. As in the Heffernan study, they
conceptualize their role in the decision-
making process as offering expert testimony
or helping to coordinate activities. Rank-
and-file workers are more apt to favor
social action involvment, but do not perceive the extent of support for this within
the profession. Making the reality of such
support more manifest would be a way
of giving impetus to this activity among
social workers.

Setting Financial Goals

Closer to home, that is, to the welfare sector, two well-known social psychologists
have examined the dynamics of the process
by which financial goals are set in United
Fund campaigns (14). Some of the findings and implications are as follows:

1. Towns that have a consistent record

of failure have lower goals per capita than
successful towns; the former show a pattern of setting the same unattained goal
year after year. Such towns probably require some sort of additional financing to
meet social welfare needs, such as from
foundations or the state or federal government.

2. Raising the United Fund goal year
after year is an effective stimulus in "successful" towns, but goal-raising has no
effect in towns with a history of failure.

3. Actual welfare needs of towns have
little relationship to either goal-setting
(amount of goal) or to the town's record
of success or failure. However, another
factor is at work here—that is, towns with
high needs are probably less wealthy and
cannot set high goals although need is a
stimulus to higher goal-setting. These factors thus cancel each other out, leaving no
relationship.

Interorganizational Linkages and Relationships

In a community context formal organizations and primary-like groups are perhaps
the two major social units of relevance for
practice (51). Indeed, community organization practice may be defined in terms of
intervention into the linkage patterns among
organizational units in the community (25).
In this section several research studies that
treat the subject of interorganizational linkage will be examined.

Linking Diverse Organizations

The linking of diverse organizations into
operational coalitions often becomes an important but difficult practice objective. One
study (76) attempts to describe a successful
example of such an undertaking. This is
an analysis of the means by which Mobilization For Youth, a demonstration-research
project on delinquency control in New York
City's Lower East Side, was put into opera-

tion. It describes mechanisms by which a heterogeneous group of organizations, representing differing goals, geographic levels, and political interests, was forged into an organizational structure. The principles to be derived from the study for the practitioner interested in forming a coalition of highly diverse elements are as follows:

1. Keep ideas on a general level. "The specification of general ideas was evaded and therefore a source of potential stress on the collaboration was bypassed" (p. 205).

2. Stress innovation and experimentation. ". . . the themes of experimentation and innovation served to relax the logic of any set of ideas" (p. 205).

3. Build a large and/or multifaceted structure. ". . . the large, multifaceted character of the Mobilization program permitted participants to focus on aspects of the projects which were germane to their own interests, without requiring them to examine the total set of actions contemplated by the project" (pp. 205–206).

4. As an overall rule, keep the level of specification low. "Lack of specification, in short, facilitated discourse and muted differences" (p. 206).

One caution is in order here. On the basis of later experience, it is clear that the MFY structure was vulnerable when subjected to severe outside pressure. Hence those tactics that may permit formation of coalitions in the planning process may not make for a stable or strong structure in the program implementation stage. The procedures suggested may apply best to developing a coalition for a program that is fairly conventional or that is not likely to experience considerable external stress at a later time.

Occasionally a small organization attempts to introduce innovation into another organization over which it has limited authority or power. A case study (22) is presented of the program of the Vera Institute of Justice, an organization that attempts to change policies and procedures of the New York City Police Department. Vera is a small autonomous organization with no direct power over the police department, but with a record of success in influencing an organization that is highly independent and bureaucratized. The case study describes efforts to effect bail reform (to obtain release without bail for persons arrested for minor offenses) and police practices regarding issuance of summonses. The results of these efforts suggest tactics by which one formal organization with limited power can influence a large hierarchical organization that traditionally emphasizes its autonomy. The principles are as follows:

1. The Vera Institute used expertise and legitimacy, acquiring a highly qualified technical staff. It emphasized consensus based on expert power rather than coercion.

2. A long-term continuing relationship was maintained with persons in the target agency. With the lack of coercive power, referent power (trust, friendship) was exercised.

3. Projects were planned jointly with the target agency so that programs, by their own admission, were of benefit to that agency. A measure of cooptation was used in this instance.

4. Projects chosen were important but of low threat to the target organization's norms or values—for example, bail reform rather than a citizen review board.

5. There was considerable flexibility with regard to the type of staff employed for different projects. In addition, ample staff were made available by Vera to initiate projects so that new ventures could be undertaken by the police without an additional burden on their own staff resources.

6. The demonstration project approach put little pressure on the organization to commit itself to new practices on a systemwide basis until they had been validated adequately on a small-scale basis.

7. Finally, in an organization with a strong authority system, the change agency found it advantageous to work from the top down, acquiring approval and legitimation for each venture at the top of the hierarchy.

Considerable resources are necessary to

carry out an interorganizational influence pattern such as this. A change organization wishing to use such a strategy would have to limit itself to singling out one or two organizations as targets.

A welfare council's program may be viewed organizationally as a central unit in a federated structure attempting to influence its constituent units, but possessing little in the way of formal authority or power to enforce its wishes. Reference was made previously to use of a priority plan in a welfare council (11). Another report of this study treats the question of modes of influence used by the council to promote utilization of the plan by constituent member agencies (10). The author made an effort to record all known instances in which the council staff deliberately used the formal plan recommendations to influence decisions regarding seventeen fields of welfare service. Whenever possible, short follow-up interviews were conducted with the person who reported the utilization. Uses of the plan were analyzed with respect to such things as frequency and purpose.

It was found that staff used the priority recommendations most often to emphasize policy matters rather than informational ones. About half the utilizations were made for the purpose of direct intervention within the decision-making processes of various target agencies. In general staff used consensual tactics and long-term relationships with agencies, and intervened directly in change activities largely when they were participants in decision-making as members of boards or study groups in the target agencies.

There are a number of implications for organizations that play a coordinating role with target agencies in a federated structure that gives the change-coordinating agency little formal power. Assuming the patterns utilized in the council studied had some functional rationale, under such circumstances workers may find it useful to emphasize consensual tactics, establish long-term continuing relationships with target agencies as a means of maximizing referent

power, and obtain common membership in the target agency units (board, staff study group) as a way of directly influencing decision-making in that agency.

Effects on Quality of Service

The pattern of interorganizational linkage among social welfare agencies may materially affect the quality of services rendered to clients. Some indication of this is reflected in a survey of the rural black population in twelve small communities in North Carolina (59). Interviews were conducted in homes by black county agricultural and home economics agents and state extension specialists. Information was obtained on general background, extent of anomie, employment and educational history, and contact with three public agencies—the Agricultural Extension Service, area vocational schools, and the Employment Security Commission. A negative association was found between anomie scores and the extent of contact with agricultural extension or vocational schools. The converse was found with regard to anomie and contact with the Employment Security Commission. The investigators indicate that anomic individuals are often unemployed and economic need requires them to make use of employment services, even considering their general lack of knowledge of community resources and personal disorganization in capacity to use these.

The implication for practice is that employment services might use their auspices to channel individuals into other programs and services that may be necessary for the individual's overall social functioning. In part this may be accomplished through communication of information (via bulletin boards or flyers), having representatives of other services available to provide information, locating other services within or in immediate proximity to the employment service, or providing employment services jointly with other services that are found to be important for optimal rehabilitation.

The potency of the employment services to foster an ingathering of individuals deeply in need of a variety of social services should be capitalized on. Public welfare agencies may have some of these same characteristics.

Patterns of Relationship

Several studies have demonstrated the lack of coordination among social welfare agencies with consequent ill effects on programs and clients in areas such as mental health (18) and juvenile delinquency (62). A recent study (35) examined patterns of relationship between social control agencies of the authoritarian-punitive type (police, courts) and the humanitarian-welfare type (social work, schools). Personnel in each agency sampled responded to a self-administered questionnaire in which they were asked to indicate what action they took when in the course of their work they came upon a situation that concerned another agency. Did they (1) avoid or ignore the situation, (2) turn to someone else for help, or (3) take care of things themselves?

It was found that in general agency personnel avoid personnel of their own agency less and hold them in higher esteem than personnel of other agencies. Low intra-agency avoidance was found to be related more to high esteem than to normative prescriptions within the agency. The pattern of interaction in the social control agency system was highly voluntaristic. As a matter of fact, formal interdependence did not tend to decrease avoidance among agencies. Social workers from private and public agencies held prosecuting attorneys, court officials, and police in low esteem. Both court officials and police avoid public social workers more than any other group; they do not avoid private agency personnel as much as public social workers. The police department did not turn out to be one of the most avoiding agencies; actually, police were one of the least avoiding groups.

It is interesting that social workers held punitive agencies in low esteem but did not avoid them. Conversely, the punitive agencies were not as likely to rate social workers low in esteem, but avoided them more.

From the conclusions of this study it would appear that to improve interorganizational relations in a voluntaristic network such as this it would be more useful to increase esteem among units than to attempt more formal structural arrangements of association. Social workers would be advised to make heavy use of private agency personnel in contacts with police and the courts, since less resistance is likely to be encountered with such individuals. It is also suggested that the police department may be a more flexible and adaptable agency for social workers to relate to than professionals believe to be the case. Social workers' attitudes may play a larger role in hindering relationships than attitudes of police.

Structure and Delivery of Social Services

The end product of social planning in social work is often the delivery of goods and services to people in need. The purpose of planning is sometimes conceptualized as the rational and efficient organization and coordination of welfare programs. There has been much recent research treating this subject from a variety of perspectives.

Is Client Need the Basis of Service?

The basis of service has long been held to be client need, yet a disturbing number of studies have discovered that services are rendered on a basis other than this—and indeed sometimes counter to client need. Two of these investigations will be described illustratively. One (87) analyzed the characteristics of the blind population of the United States and of the agencies that serve this population, using demographic data and agency service documents. These data show a clear bias in favor of children and employable adults and against the elderly blind, who comprise the bulk of the blind population. About 90 percent of agencies place exclusive or primary emphasis on serving less than one-third of the blind population. Exceptions to this are agencies with new or independent sources of funding and those with more highly trained professionals.

There are a number of practice implications. In the first place, it is obvious that agencies need to be careful concerning whether they are serving the clients most in need of assistance. Recognizing that there is a tendency for social agencies to be moved by consideration other than client need, agencies should build in formal procedures to monitor their client-serving tendencies. There is an indication that organizations that wish to introduce innovations in agencies or select those that are most likely serving client need should look to agencies with independent funding and a greater number of highly trained professionals. Likewise, organizations seeking to ensure their capacity to serve populations in need should strive to incorporate these two features into their structure.

In the other study (72), interviews were conducted and observations made of the physical plants of all private agencies in Chicago providing group services to children and youths. Administrators as a group were found to hold stereotyped views of the difficulties and expenditures involved in serving the physically handicapped. From interviews with executives serving such clients it was determined that problems such as those foreseen were not based on reality. Experience in working with the handicapped only slightly influences the administrator's attitude. Services exist mainly in larger agencies, which have a greater range of programs, larger staffs, and a greater number of professionally trained workers.

It is shown again that social welfare agencies find reasons to serve persons other than those in greatest need of service. Administrators anticipate greater difficulties in pro-

viding specialized services than is the case, and cling to this belief even after experience with more needy client groups. Perhaps working through community pressure or higher decision-making units such as the agency's board of directors is the best means of influencing administrators. In seeking agencies that would be most receptive to innovating with specialized programs, an organization should look to those that are larger, have more-varied programs, have more staff members, and have a larger number of staff members with professional training. There might be a possibility of spread from these agencies to the others, especially if some of these agencies are standard-setters in the community.

Racial discrimination has been uncovered in the pattern of service delivery in the mental health field. In analyzing a series of studies in this field, one investigator (55) concludes that blacks as a group receive less treatment in mental hospitals and are less likely to receive psychotherapy; are more likely to receive somatic treatment, shock treatment, and custodial care; are likely to be labeled in racial stereotypes by therapists ("primitive controls," "desire to act out," "self-hate"); and are subject to slower and lower release rates.

Certain groups in the population are found to be more assertive in reaching out to agencies for mental health services. These include females, nonreligious individuals, people from urban settings, those from upper socioeconomic groups, and those of Jewish background (47). Another study of this nature (5) that examined a female population concluded that those failing to seek psychotherapeutically oriented services came from less sophisticated subcultures in which there was little use of psychiatric vocabulary; the resulting tendency was to express symptoms in physical rather than emotional terms. These women tended to be born in rural states, were more often housewives, were less likely to have gone to college or have worked, and were more likely to have husbands with nonprofessional and lower status occupations.

Thus clients present themselves at different rates in different ways for service, and one problem is related to how agencies evaluate and process applications for service. Economic as well as racial discrimination has been found to operate in such evaluation. Some 500 applicants for admission to a hospital for the retarded were studied, based on hospital records (64). It was found that admission was not based on extent of retardation. The most severely retarded were not given priority, rather, family income was the most closely related variable, higher income being associated with faster admission.

The point made previously about facility with psychiatric vocabulary is revealed in another study (80). Among patients applying for readmission to a mental hospital, those with ideologies favorable to psychiatry (expert and humane tendencies) as measured by the Nunnally-Osgood scale were more likely to be readmitted. The organization had a tendency to select patients whose ideology was more in tune with its own. Perhaps professionals assume that they can serve such patients most effectively—that is, effect more desired changes in the shortest period of time. (This assumption might also help account for biases in favor of children and employable adults rather than the aged in the previously cited services for the blind.) Such an assumption makes service goal as well as client need a criterion for acceptance for service. In effect, it leaves many persons in need unserved when services are not planned and coordinated for a total target population in need.

All these studies should give social workers and others in the human service and mental health professions pause concerning their use of rational, objective, client-centered procedures in the distribution of services. The use of systematic evaluative techniques is certainly called for. There may be many agencies that are sensitive and effective in these respects, but they apparently do not turn up when studies are made of the issues involved. (Or could it

be that social scientists and social work researchers are less than objective in the agencies they select for study?)

Treatment Effectiveness

Also disconcerting are the results of studies of treatment effectiveness among clients who are ultimately recipients of services. Two recent studies are of special interest. The better known is the Meyer-Borgatta-Jones examination of *Girls at Vocational High* (61). Following the use of rather rigorous and systematic measuring tools, the authors find it necessary to declare:

. . . no strong indications of effect are found and the conclusion must be stated in the negative when it is asked whether social work intervention with potential problem high school girls was effective in this instance. [61, p. 383]

While this study and its conclusions have been subject to intense criticism from the profession (56), its impact has been to cast a measure of scientific doubt on social work treatment methods.

Perhaps more damaging is the scrupulous study (91) of treatment in a public welfare agency in Elmira, New York. A control group that received standard welfare services was compared with an experimental group that had trained caseworkers with small caseloads, orientation toward family treatment, and linkages to a range of community resources.

The Geismar rating scale was used to evaluate movement during the experimental period, and this was cross-checked with the Hunt-Kogan scale. Use of nine dimensions of family functioning (such as family relationships, individual behavior, and economic practices) revealed no differences between the control and experimental groups. At least in this instance, intensive treatment by professional caseworkers was not an effective approach to improving the functioning of dependent hard-core families. Similar results were found in the Alameda County Welfare Department in California (81a).

When the client group is delinquent boys rather than dependent families, the conclusion is identical. After five years of reaching-out child guidance therapy, an experimental treatment group and a matched control group of boys were found to include the same number of serious delinquents (11). The researchers state:

This study offers no encouragement for the hope that child guidance therapy offers a means of materially reducing the incidence of serious delinquency in a population of boys selected by the Glueck Social Prediction Table as probable delinquents. [15, p. 170]

The authors indicate that there was also a lack of improvement of merely troublesome, as opposed to legally delinquent, behavior.

This set of findings is discouraging to social workers, especially when placed in the context that there are few if any positive empirical findings available to counterbalance the negative ones. One exception the author was able to locate in the literature evaluated the Neighborhood Improvement Project (NIP) in New Haven, Connecticut. A combined treatment design of family-centered casework, group work, and educational and recreational services appeared to improve the overall family for a treatment group of multiproblem families as compared with a control group of untreated families (29a). The implications for treatment personnel to reassess assumptions and methods are obvious. What might the implications be for the social planner? It is clear that he cannot have a high degree of confidence in establishing treatment programs to deal with social ills such as delinquency and dependency. At the same time other "sure-cure" nostrums are elusive. Perhaps what is suggested is that in the absence of adequate knowledge or technology a balanced variety of approaches might be applied to these kinds of problems, utilizing both "clinical" treatment methods operating at the level of individ-

uals and small groups and "social" treatment methods geared to community and societal intervention. Conventional as well as experimental programs should be considered and innovations encouraged. Within the clinical realm one would rely on numerous programmatic approaches to therapy in the absence of a given approach that enjoys strong validation.

Organizational Variables

Since 1964 attention has increasingly been paid to organizational variables affecting the provision of services. Only a few of these will be alluded to here.

Of interest is a study of sixteen public and private social welfare agencies in a large midwestern metropolis (2). Social welfare agencies were found to be characterized by a low or flat hierarchy of authority but at the same time by a low degree of staff participation in decision-making. In this study the question of workers' morale was probed, using the concept of alienation. Alienation was examined from two perspectives: alienation from the substantive job and alienation from expressive relations with others in the work situation. The degree of hierarchy was found to be correlated with both alienation from work and from expressive relations. Degree of participation in decisions and degree of codification or standardization of the task performance were found to be related to alienation from work, but not to alienation from expressive relations. Degree of rule observation was highly related to both kinds of alienation.

The implications are quite direct: To minimize work alienation, increase participation. To minimize expressive alienation, reduce hierarchy of authority. One may have active participation in decision-making but at the same time continue alienation from expressive relations. If tasks require a high degree of routine, standardized operations, alienation can be minimized by maximizing expressive relations. Since the degree of hierarchy is positively related in a general way to alienation, reducing the degree of hierarchy is a way of keeping morale high.

This discussion makes the assumption that high staff morale is "important," that it is related in some way to effectiveness in service outcome with clients. When one is assured of this relationship, the prescriptions stated might be implemented. However, one cannot accept the assumption at face value. A search into this question was carried out by the University of Chicago School of Social Service Administration at the Midway District Office of the Cook County Department of Public Aid (86). Variables that were manipulated included staff morale, staff activity, client change, and organization of work units. It was found that staff morale was not necessarily related to client outcome. Team organization of staff appeared to be a significant factor related to client outcome, revealing greater potency than reduced caseloads.

In another study of agency staff (8), it was found that social workers tend to lean toward a heavy bureaucratic orientation:

. . . the agency exerts a great deal of influence, as does the profession. Relatively speaking, both the clients and the community have less influence than profession or agency in the orientations of these workers. [8, p. 402]

In addition, social workers were found to be more bureaucratic than professional in outlook, in contrast to other professionals working in formal organizations. The researcher, Billingsley, feels that this posture may be harmful to effective service delivery, assuming that a more balanced orientation toward both professional and agency would be better. This is borne out in the research; workers with a mixed orientation were rated by their supervisors as most effective. The implication of this study is that attachment to and identity with agencies should be weakened in favor of greater identification with the profession.

From the discussion in the article, this may be accomplished through separating professional training from the agency and providing more possibilities for non-agency practice such as private consultation and attachment to autonomous indigenous groups.

Several studies have examined pathways into service, including informal and unofficial means by which referrals are made and simple services rendered (19, 44). The strong implication exists that social workers should capitalize to a much greater degree on informal networks in the delivery of services. Employment of indigenous paraprofessionals is one way this is being attempted. It has been found, however, that use of indigenous paraprofessionals is not the panacea it has sometimes been heralded as being. For example, paraprofessionals are closer in outlook to professionals than to the indigenous population they are meant to reflect (31). Also, doubt is cast on the effectiveness of such workers when they do achieve a high level of identification with clients.

One study cautions planners that "money isn't everything" in rendering service. It was found that the level of expenditure in the public field was not correlated with the quality of services offered (89). Nor is service per se the most helpful approach to clients. Sometimes it would be well to defer service if the context of its provision might produce ill effects. This is illustrated in a survey of 314 workers (a 10 percent random sample) who were displaced when the Packard plant in Detroit closed down its operations (1). Subjects were interviewed with respect to subsequent job history, political and social attitudes, and informal social participation. It was found that the most deleterious effects were on the "two-time losers"—those workers who obtained another job at a higher rate of pay and then lost it. These individuals scored highest in anomie, political alienation, and reduced involvement in social life. Those who remained unemployed continually had better adjustment scores than those who had to relate to status changes more than once.

The study suggests that protracted unemployment is better for the individual psychologically than fluctuating job and wage patterns. Hence manpower agencies should be cautious about placing clients in jobs that have a high risk of termination. They would be wiser, assuming absence of a personal economic emergency, to hold off placing clients into jobs until relative longevity on the job is assured. Also, in training programs projects should be undertaken with respect primarily to jobs that have a more stable character, and in job development activities emphasis should be on jobs that have relative stability. On a broader social policy basis manpower agencies might shift to applying to the pattern of employment fluctuation in the community some of the resources they devote to client placement.

Roles of the Practitioner

The practitioner himself is, of course, at the vortex of action in the performance of professional community organization functions. For this reason the professional literature abounds with writings having to do with the role or roles of the professional. Here again the writings have tended to be highly conjectural, with a paucity of hard evidence to buttress positions taken. Luckily, one is able to extract from a variety of sources research findings that provide a few empirical guidelines toward clarifying the question of practitioner roles.

Planning Styles

For example, Morris and Randall (64) report on a comparative study of planning for the elderly in seven different communities. Three distinct planning styles were discovered: (1) *The enabler*—much effort devoted to establishing and staffing com-

mittees. (2) *The demonstrator*—emphasis on implementing a single programmatic approach. (3) *Stimulator-innovator*— a "free-wheeling" style involving many interorganizational linkages; emphasis on prodding numerous already-established organizations and programs to do more than they were already doing for the aged.

The enabler style produced few programmatic results. The demonstrator style produced definite short-range successes, but few innovations. The stimulator style generated multiple short-range results, including innovations, in a variety of established agencies.

Practice implications for planning services and programs are quite obvious. If the practitioner is seeking delimited, predetermined programs, the demonstrator style would appear to be the method of choice. If the objective is innovation in programs and the stimulation of an existing agency's operation along the lines of a variety of short-term projects, then the stimulator-innovator style would seem to be indicated. Maximizing interorganizational linkage as in this latter style tends to maximize exchange and adoption of innovations. A study of national planning in a South American nation (26) arrived at a definition of an innovative planning role that is remarkably close to the Morris and Randall formulation.

Types of Administrators

In still another study (27), the styles of various governmental officials were investigated. Ninety-six top-level administrators and planners in eleven agencies at the federal and local levels in the United States and Canada were interviewed. Inquiries were made concerning the clienteles served by the agencies and their role in influencing the agency. In general it was found that administrators do not see public or community groups as a source of policy determination, preferring this to take place through the staff, internal boards, and other governmental bodies. Most administrators feel that they are influenced most by specific interest groups, not by the general public. Administrators were found to fall into three distinct types, each of which turned to different publics as sources of influence. The types and their influential publics were as follows:

Politico—an individual whose primary responsibilities are those of policy-making, defending the agency before the outside world, and responding to external pressure on the agency. Politicos are responsive to influence from a wide range of sources.

Administrator—an individual whose tasks involve general supervision of subunits and execution of agency programs, such as the deputy department head of a Canadian provincial department. Such individuals are responsive to influence from intraorganizational sources.

Professional—an individual whose responsibilities primarily involve the use of professional, technical, or scientific skills, such as the chief executive of a social welfare or highway department planning unit. Professionals are responsive to influence from professional associations.

This suggests not only a number of different role types but, equally important, a series of external interventive strategies for influencing practitioners, especially those attached to governmental agencies. In the first place, broad general public approaches are not likely to be effective. Second, one should analyze the style of the official and place him in the appropriate category: politico, administrator, professional. Several dicta follow: Attempt to reach the politico through a variety of sources (especially political ones). Attempt to influence the administrator through internal agency sources. Attempt to influence the professional through his professional associations and identity. Ultimate influence no doubt comes from the source that has direct authority over the official, such as the legislature or policy-making board.

Role Definition and Practice Outcome

As has been seen, practitioners' roles may be defined in various ways. Evidence suggests that clarity and agreement with regard to role definition may have an important bearing on practice outcomes. In an exploration of this issue, thirty county extension directors and their seventy-five county extension agents were interviewed with regard to a number of dimensions of the agents' role, for example, direction and coordination, extension relations, educational leadership, and personnel management (7). The degree of consensus between directors and agents regarding role expectations was assessed. In addition, state personnel rated the various directors in terms of efficiency in program development and implementation. It was found that county directors who were rated more effective had higher consensus on mutual role expectations with their county agents than was true for other county directors.

In practice terms, an effort should be made to spell out tasks and duties of supervisors and direct service practitioners and to foster mutual agreement concerning these. In this study it was found that explicit training of directors for new roles had a positive relationship to consensus on role expectations. The suggestion is that to increase organizational and practitioner effectiveness, time should be taken from operations to clarify roles and tasks, to increase training around these, and to provide a means by which consensus on role expectations can be reached through such means as orientation sessions, staff seminars, or sensitivity training groups.

The literature suggests that perhaps certain practitioners in their role performance underestimate the degree of influence or assertiveness that would be acceptable to key community influentials in the enactment of their roles (40). Two types of elites, business leaders and governmental leaders, were interviewed in Atlanta, Georgia, and Raleigh, North Carolina, with respect to their attitudes toward city planners. In general, favorable attitudes were expressed toward planning activities and planning roles. In Atlanta the opinion that planners should have greater influence was expressed by 73 percent of the governmental officials and 81 percent of the economic leaders; in Raleigh the percentages for these groups were 51 and 63 percent respectively. Governmental leaders were more likely to contact the professional planner for advice on planning matters than the board chairman; business leaders might not contact either one. In addition, there was evidence that involvement by elites in planning boards and programs tends to increase the favorableness of their attitude. The overall conclusion of this study is that certain types of planning activities (such as city planning) are viewed as legitimate by various community elites, and the practitioner has greater leeway in exercising his role in this connection than he perhaps takes advantage of.

Additional evidence is available indicating that practitioners occasionally have faulty perceptions of the expectations of other relative actors and accordingly underestimate their mandate and limit the impact of their role performance. A study (54) was made that compared the attitudes of the administrative leaders of the Oregon Education Association with the attitudes of the association's members and also examined administrators' perceptions of members' attitudes. It was found that there was a greater propensity to liberalism and to activism on the part of administrators than members. However, administrators tended to overestimate the degree of distance between themselves and the membership. That is to say, members were more liberal and action oriented than administrators viewed them as being: ". . . the teachers are more willing to join teachers' unions, political party organizations, or racial organizations (e.g., NAACP) than leaders believe them to be" (54, pp. 663-664). Sensing a difference in degree of liberal

orientation, the administrative leaders became overly cautious in assessing the options open to them. Better assessment tools would be useful for enabling the practitioner to discern attitudes and expectations of others and the boundaries imposed on his role performance.

A related finding came out of a study of planning in a semirural county that had a board made up of local citizens who were not sophisticated in their knowledge of planning (13). In this instance there was a rejection of the expert role of the planner and a reaffirmation of traditional rural institutions. The high disparity between the technical training and the experience of the planner and lack of information on the part of the board members were manifest and tended to block the extent to which the expert could be used by local people. Planners in rural settings might anticipate such reactions and minimize social distance between themselves and lay participants by playing down their use of "expert power" and utilizing to a greater extent other bases of power and influence. Alternatively, they might devote considerable energy to the training of board members in technical matters and extending the longevity on the board of those individuals who become better informed.

Practitioner As Linking Agent

The role of certain types of practitioners as "linking agents" has been discussed in the literature, especially when engaged in the role of a detached worker or detached expert in the execution of his responsibilities (51). It has been suggested that the detached worker has a position midway between the value system of the bureaucracy and the client population in whose immediate environment he tends to spend much of his professional time. An empirical test was made of this proposition through a survey of opinions held by different actors concerning what the ideal role of the public health nurse should be (34). Within non-metropolitan Missouri counties personal interviews were conducted with all public health nurses, random samples of the population in four selected counties, and central administrative personnel. The norms of the public health nurses were found to be intermediate to the positions of those at the central and local levels. The authors suggest that such an intermediate posture is the most comfortable one for incumbents of linking positions, and one might add hypothetically that this is probably the most functional role for such individuals to assume. It would seem advisable for bureaucratic organizations to train practitioners who are assuming linking roles to take a mediating position between the formal organization and local primary-like groups. The organization must also gear itself to expect and tolerate attitudes and behavior on the part of linking agents that veer away from its modal pattern in the direction of client groups.

Process Versus Task Role Performance

There has been considerable discussion in the literature regarding the merits and advantages of process (socio-emotional) versus task role performance in working with task-oriented groups such as committees and study groups. This area has been left clouded in murky rhetoric, but evidence has been produced that may help begin to clarify this issue (68). Groups of American and Indian students were brought together to discuss aspects of family life (child-rearing practices and the role of grandparents in the family) in which there are sharp differences of orientation in the two countries. The discussants were urged to reach some level of agreement within the time period allotted to them. Discussion leaders using different styles of intervention were assigned to the groups, which were structured on either a formal or infor-

mal basis. In the informal discussion setting task-oriented leaders were rated as more effective in achieving consensus; in the formal setting socio-emotional leaders were so rated. When the objective of the practitioner is to achieve consensus or a "meeting of the minds," the implication is that he should assume a role that counterbalances the atmosphere of the group setting. That is to say, in an informal setting he should take a more formal task-oriented role, while in a formal setting he should take a more informal socio-emotional-oriented role.

Relationships

Another aspect of practitioner role might be introduced here. In some types of practice, especially grass-roots work, a trusting relationship between the practitioner and community actors is important. In a gaming experiment (90) it was found that the establishment of relationships of trust was strongly associated with exposure of some aspect of the self. Individuals were able to establish trust by exposing themselves to one another and meeting each exposure with acceptance. It was necessary that both participants give something to the relationship before trust could be established. Yet most people were either unable to see that they could signal a desire to trust others by exposing themselves or were unwilling to take this risk. It would follow that when, to be effective in his work, a practitioner needs a trust relationship, he may take steps to initiate such a relationship by risking an exposure that can be accepted or rejected. He should also be alert to be accepting of signals of exposure by others so that trust may be established or sustained.

On the basis of an action-research project, Eugster (24) concludes that transfer of responsibility and skill from the practitioner to indigenous primary groups is crucial in locality development. In her

study the use of crisis situations was a significant factor in permitting this transfer
to be effected. The implication is that the
practitioner should be alert to such crisis
events or perhaps even help create them.

Multiple Role Orientation

Often the worker's role is referred to in
the literature in terms that suggest a given
mode of practice that uniformly covers all
circumstances and conditions. It would be
well to conceive of a multiplicity of roles
that may be used selectively by the same or
different practitioners with respect to different circumstances or at different phases
of a change process. This idea is brought
out cryptically in a study of decision-making in a metropolitan area (60). The authors studied twenty-two metropolitan planning decisions made in the Syracuse area
over a thirty-year period. One conclusion
of the work is that planning is "processual"
and requires a set of complementary roles—
initiators (idea men), influentials (to support a proposal), brokers (who gain support or effect compromises among various
formal organizations) and transmitters
(government officials and others who make
final decisions). This scheme suggests a
series of practitioner roles or resources
that a planning organization needs to command in order to be effective.

The Prospects for Community Organization Research

In this chapter a portion of recent professional and social science research providing some empirical bases for community
organization practice has been reviewed.
This review of the literature has been organized under seven rubrics, starting with
"Planning Processes and Issues" and ending with "Roles of the Practitioner." To
this extent studies in a wide range of disciplines and fields have been connected, for

practical purposes, with components of community organization practice.

Paucity of Community Organization Research

Through the years there has been a striking
paucity of research in community organization, a factor that has inhibited the development of this area of professional practice in
social work. In part this limited research
base can be attributed to the generally
marginal position enjoyed by community
organization in the profession, as reflected
by the relatively small percentage of practitioners occupying such positions, the low
number of students and faculty in the
specialty in schools of social work, a meager
curriculum—usually confined to a one-year
course of study—and a fairly unsophisti-
cated literature.

In addition, community organization
practitioners have tended to be strongly
action-oriented individuals, men of affairs,
often overburdened with a multitude of
pressures from diverse sources. Both because of practitioners' temperaments and
because of limited time some professional
niceties such as the production of research
and scholarly writings have tended to take
a back seat. A kind of anti-intellectualism
has also partially characterized the field in
the past. Community organization practitioners often allude to their work in such
terms as "operating by the seat of the
pants," both as a description of their practice and as a definition of the only possible
or useful way of engaging in this work. In
their classic book *The Dynamics of Planned
Change*, Lippitt and his associates (48)
speak of the difficulty they encountered in
locating suitable analytical case materials
pertaining to community intervention. They
state that the "split between those who act
and those who conceptualize was particularly and rather painfully conspicuous
among change agents working at the level
of community systems" (48, p. 17). In a
private communication to this writer by an

important social work policy planner, the following comment was made:

The longer I live, the more I think that people who are interested in social action and social change are either born that way or learn by practice, but they are not made that way alone by book learning. Perhaps I'm wrong. But I do believe that conceptualization of community organization tends to inhibit the community organizer. The latter is a doer, if he is to be effective.

The established "old-timers" in the field are joined in this position by the neophyte "New-Leftists" who arrive at the same place independently, based on a deep skepticism about social scientists and a conviction that the preferred route to knowledge or truth generally is through immersion in personal experience.

Even among community organizers and planners with research capabilities and responsibilities, agency pressures have forced preoccupation with "practical" studies that have had administrative planning purposes in a single community or agency but that have been unsuitable for generating generalizations concerning wider problems and processes. The reward system in the profession and norms among professional peers have not operated to stimulate or reinforce predilections toward research among community organization practitioners. Nor has there been a sense of identification with an allied profession that places a high value on research and theory in the same way, for example, that caseworkers have often related themselves to psychology or psychiatry.

An Optimistic Outlook

Despite this seemingly unhappy analysis, one may look ahead to the immediate future with considerable optimism. As stated by Morris in the analogous chapter in the previous edition of this volume, "Research in social planning is on the threshold of a new era" (63, p. 208). It appears that we are already in the early stages of an outpouring by social scientists of research studies pertaining to problems of community organization practice. Sociologists, social psychologists, and political scientists have all become preoccupied with a variety of subjects that formerly failed to engage their attention. Stimulated by the poverty program, the civil rights movement, and the phenomenon of student activism, a great number of studies have been undertaken on subjects such as participation of the poor, evaluations of social welfare and social action programs, student activism and black militancy, school desegregation, and the like. There is less tendency by social scientists to look askance at investigations into these pragmatic, policy-oriented matters. This trend has been given momentum by the push of younger members of the professions for relevance in scholarship and by the availability of grants for such research by the federal government and private foundations. Indeed, for the first time in memory money has been available for large-scale research into issues traditionally associated with concerns of community organization practice. The results of these studies have begun to be published and an increased output should be seen in the next year or two. The body of this chapter has attempted to demonstrate how the writings of social scientists conducting such studies may be harnessed to illuminate community organization practice.

Within the profession itself there has been a dramatic shift to an interest in planning, policy, prevention, and social action. Many more practitioners are working or writing in these areas. Courses of study in community organization have grown in an unprecedented way, bringing many new students and faculty members into this area and creating pressures for additional and more rigorous theoretical and empirical content. Doctoral programs in social work have been expanding and improving, many of them giving emphasis to planning and policy matters. Dissertation research can be expected as one product of these programs, another product being trained researchers who likely will carry with them a continuing interest in pursuing community organization research studies.

It is difficult at this time to predict the directions of community organization research in the near future. The social situation in the nation is exceedingly fluid, making uncertain the specific form that predominant problems may take and the amount and type of support that may be available for research. But what probably is predictable is that in volume and quality there will be a greater reservoir of research available to be drawn on to inform practice than heretofore has been the case.

REFERENCES

1. Aiken, Michael, and Ferman, Louis A. "Job Mobility and the Social Integration of Displaced Workers," *Social Problems*, Vol. 14, No. 1 (Summer 1966), pp. 48–56.
2. ———, and Hage, Jerald. "Organizational Alienation: A Comparative Analysis," *American Sociological Review*, Vol. 31, No. 4 (August 1966), pp. 497–507.
3. Austin, David M. "Organizing for Neighborhood Improvement or Social Change?" Unpublished doctoral dissertation, Florence Heller Graduate School for Advanced Studies in Social Welfare, Brandeis University, 1969.
4. Barnes, Samuel H. "Participation, Education, and Political Competence: Evidence from a Sample of Italian Socialists," *American Political Science Review*, Vol. 60, No. 2 (June 1966), pp. 348–353.
5. Bart, Pauline B. "Social Structure and Vocabularies of Discomfort: What Happened to Female Hysteria," *Journal of Health and Social Behavior*, Vol. 9, No. 3 (September 1968), pp. 188–193.
6. Bar-Yosef, R., and Schild, E. O. "Pressures and Defenses in Bureaucratic Roles," *American Journal of Sociology*, Vol. 71, No. 6 (May 1966), pp. 665–673.
7. Bible, Bond L., and McNabb, Coy G. "Role Consensus and Administrative Effectiveness," *Rural Sociology*, Vol. 31, No. 1 (March 1966), pp. 5–14.
8. Billingsley, Andrew. "Bureaucratic and Professional Orientation Patterns in Social Casework," *Social Service Review*, Vol. 38, No. 4 (December 1964), pp. 400–407.
9. Bowen, Don R., and Masotti, Louis H. "Spokesmen for the Poor: An Analysis of Cleveland's Poverty Board Candidates," *Urban Affairs Quarterly*, Vol. 4, No. 1 (September 1968), pp. 89–110.
10. Chetkow, B. Harold. "The Planning of Social Services Changes," *Public Administration Review*, Vol. 28, No. 3 (May–June 1968), pp. 256–263.
11. ———. "Some Factors Influencing the Utilization and Impact of Priority Recommendations in Community Planning," *Social Service Review*, Vol. 41, No. 3 (September 1967), pp. 271–282.
12. Clausen, Aage R. "Measurement Identity in the Longitudinal Analysis of Legislative Voting," *American Political Science Review*, Vol. 61, No. 4 (December 1967), pp. 1020–1035.
13. Clavel, Pierre. "Planners and Citizen Boards: Some Applications of Social Theory to the Problem of Plan Implementation," *Journal of the American Institute of Planners*, Vol. 34, No. 3 (May 1968), pp. 130–139.
14. Coleman, James. *Community Conflict.* Glencoe, Ill.: Free Press, 1957.
15. Craig, Maude M., and Furst, Philip W. "What Happens After Treatment? A Study of Potentially Delinquent Boys," *Social Service Review*, Vol. 39, No. 2 (June 1965), pp. 165–171.
16. Crain, Robert L., and Rosenthal, Donald B. "Structure and Value in Local Political Systems: The Case of Fluoridation Decisions," *Journal of Politics*, Vol. 28, No. 1 (February 1966), pp. 169–195.
17. ———, and Street, David. "School Desegregation and School Decision-Making," *Urban Affairs Quarterly*, Vol. 2, No. 1 (September 1966), pp. 64–82.
18. Cumming, Elaine. "Phase Movement in the Support and Control of Psychiatric Patients," *Journal of Health and Human Behavior*, Vol. 3, No. 4 (Winter 1962), pp. 235–241.
19. ———, Cumming, Ian, and Edell, Laura. "Policeman as Philosopher, Guide and Friend," *Social Problems*, Vol. 12, No. 3 (Winter 1965), pp. 276–286.
20. Cutright, Phillips. "Income Redistribution: A Cross-National Analysis," *Social Forces*, Vol. 46, No. 2 (December 1967), pp. 180–190.
21. Davis, Morris, Seibert, Robert, and Breed, Warren. "Interracial Seating Patterns on New Orleans Public Transit," *Social Problems*, Vol. 13, No. 3 (Winter 1966), pp. 298–306.

22. Doig, Jameson W. "Police Problems, Proposals and Strategies for Change," *Public Administration Review*, Vol. 28, No. 5 (September–October 1968), pp. 393–406.

23. Epstein, Irwin. "Social Workers and Social Action: Attitudes Toward Social Action Strategies," *Social Work*, Vol. 13, No. 2 (April 1968), pp. 101–108.

24. Eugster, Carla. "Field Education in West Heights," *Human Organization*, Vol. 23, No. 3 (Fall 1964), pp. 235–244.

25. Fellin, Philip, Rothman, Jack, and Meyer, Henry J. "Implications of the Socio-Behavioral Approach for Community Organization Practice," in Edwin J. Thomas, ed., *The Socio-Behavioral Approach and Applications to Social Work*. New York: Council on Social Work Education, 1967. Pp. 73–83.

26. Friedman, John. "Planning or Innovation: The Urban Case," *Journal of the American Institute of Planners*, Vol. 32, No. 4 (July 1966), pp. 194–204.

27. Friedman, Robert S., Klein, Bernard W., and Romani, John H. "Administrative Agencies and the Publics they Serve," *Public Administration Review*, Vol. 26, No. 3 (September 1966), pp. 192–204.

28. Froman, Lewis A., Jr. "Some Effects of Interest Group Strength in State Politics," *American Political Science Review*, Vol. 60, No. 4 (December 1966), pp. 952–962.

29. Gamson, William A. "Rancorous Conflict in Community Politics," *American Sociological Review*, Vol. 31, No. 1 (February 1966), pp. 71–81.

29a. Geismar, Ludwig L. "The Results of Social Work Intervention: A Positive Case," *American Journal of Orthopsychiatry*, Vol. 38, No. 3 (April 1968), pp. 444–457.

30. Geschwender, James A. "Status Inconsistency, Social Isolation, and Individual Unrest," *Social Forces*, Vol. 46, No. 4 (June 1968), pp. 477–484.

31. Grosser, Charles F. "Local Residents as Mediators Between Middle-Class Professional Workers and Lower-Class Clients," *Social Service Review*, Vol. 40, No. 1 (March 1966), pp. 56–63.

32. Hacker, Andrew. "Does a 'Divisive' Primary Harm a Candidate's Election Chances?" *American Political Science Review*, Vol. 59, No. 1 (March 1965), pp. 105–110.

33. Harp, John, and Gargan, Richard J. "Renewal Plans: A General Systems Analysis of Rural Townships," *Rural Sociology*, Vol. 33, No. 4 (December 1968), pp. 460–473.

34. Hassinger, Edward W., and Grubb, Charles E. "The Linking Role of the Local Public Health Nurse in Missouri," *Rural Sociology*, Vol. 30, No. 3 (September 1965), pp. 299–310.

35. Haurek, Edward W., and Clark, John P. "Variants of Integration of Social Control Agencies," *Social Problems*, Vol. 15, No. 1 (Summer 1967), pp. 46–60.

36. Heffernan, Joseph, Jr. "Political Activity and Social Work Executives," *Social Work*, Vol. 9, No. 2 (April 1964), pp. 18–23.

37. Heinz, Eulau, and Eyestone, Robert. "Policy Maps of City Councils and Policy Outcomes: A Developmental Analysis," *American Political Science Review*, Vol. 62, No. 1 (March 1968), pp. 124–143.

38. Holsti, Ole R. "The 1914 Case," *American Political Science Review*, Vol. 59, No. 2 (June 1965), pp. 365–378.

39. Janes, Robert W., and Byuarm, Samuel W. "The Effect of Voluntary Community Improvement Program on Local Race Relations," *Phylon*, Vol. 26, No. 1 (September 1965), pp. 25–33.

40. Jennings, M. Kent. "Planning and Community Elites in Two Cities," *Journal of the American Institute of Planners*, Vol. 31, No. 1 (February 1965), pp. 62–68.

41. Katz, Elihu, and Danet, Brenda. "Petition and Persuasive Appeals: A Study of Official Client Relationships," *American Sociological Review*, Vol. 37, No. 6 (December 1966), pp. 811–821.

42. Kornburg, Allan, and Thomas, Norman. "The Political Socialization of National Legislative Elites in the United States and Canada," *Journal of Politics*, Vol. 29, No. 4 (November 1965), pp. 761–775.

43. Kosa, John, and Nunn, Clyde Z. "Race Deprivation and Attitude Toward Communism," *Phylon*, Vol. 25, No. 4 (Winter 1964), pp. 337–346.

44. Kurtz, Norman R. "Gatekeepers: Agents in Acculturation," *Rural Sociology*, Vol. 33, No. 1 (March 1968), pp. 64–70.

45. Lenski, Gerhard. "Social Participation and Status Crystallization," *American Sociological Review*, Vol. 21, No. 4 (August 1956), pp. 453–464.

46. Levens, Helene. "Organizational Affiliation and Powerlessness: A Case Study of the Welfare Poor," *Social Problems*, Vol. 16, No. 1 (Summer 1968), pp. 18–32.

47. Linn, Lawrence S. "Social Characteristics

and Social Interaction in the Utilization of a Psychiatric Outpatient Clinic," *Journal of Health and Social Behavior*, Vol. 8, No. 1 (March 1967), pp. 3–14.

48. Lippitt, Ronald. *The Dynamics of Planned Change*. New York: Harcourt, Brace & Co., 1958.

49. Lipsky, Michael. "Protest as a Political Resource," *American Political Science Review*, Vol. 62, No. 4 (December 1968), pp. 1144–1158.

50. ———. "Rent Strikes: Poor Man's Weapon," *Trans-action*, Vol. 6, No. 4 (February 1969), pp. 10–15.

51. Litwak, Eugene, and Meyer, Henry J. "The School and the Family: Linking Organizations and External Primary Groups," in Paul F. Lazarsfeld et al., eds., *The Uses of Sociology*. New York: Basic Books, 1967. Pp. 522–543.

52. Longley, Lawrence. "Interest Group Interaction in a Legislative System," *Journal of Politics*, Vol. 29, No. 3 (August 1967), pp. 637–658.

53. Lutchterhand, Elmer, and Weller, Leonard. "Social Class and the Desegregation Movement: A Study of Parents' Decisions in a Negro Ghetto," *Social Problems*, Vol. 13, No. 1 (Summer 1965), pp. 83–88.

54. Luttbeg, Norman R., and Zeigler, Harmon. "Attitude Consensus and Conflict in an Interest Group: An Assessment of Cohesion," *American Political Science Review*, Vol. 60, No. 3 (September 1966), pp. 655–666.

55. Maas, Jeanette P. "Incidence and Treatment Variations Between Negroes and Caucasians in Mental Illness," *Community Mental Health Journal*, Vol. 3, No. 1 (Spring 1967), pp. 61–65.

56. MacDonald, Mary E. "Reunion at Vocational High: An Analysis of Girls at Vocational High: An Experiment in Social Work Intervention," *Social Service Review*, Vol. 40, No. 2 (June 1966), pp. 175–189.

57. McWorter, Gerald A., and Crain, Robert L. "Subcommunity Gladiatorial Competition: Civil Rights Leadership as a Competitive Process," *Social Forces*, Vol. 46, No. 1 (September 1967), pp. 8–21.

58. Matza, David. "Poverty and Disrepute," in Robert K. Merton and Robert A. Nisbet, eds., *Contemporary Social Problems*. New York: Harcourt, Brace & Co., 1966. Pp. 619–669.

59. Marsh, C. Paul, Delan, Robert J., and Riddick, William L. "Anomia and Communication Behavior: The Relationship Between Anomia and Utilization of Three Public Utilities," *Rural Sociology*, Vol. 32, No. 4 (December 1967).

60. Martin, Roscoe C., et al. *Decisions in Syracuse*. Bloomington, Ind.: Indiana University Press, 1961.

61. Meyer, Henry J., Borgatta, Edgar F., and Jones, Wyatt C. "An Experiment in Prevention Through Social Work Intervention," in Edwin J. Thomas, ed., *Behavioral Science for Social Workers*. New York: Free Press, 1967. Pp. 363–383.

62. Miller, Walter B. "Inter-Institutional Conflict as a Major Impediment to Delinquency Prevention," *Human Organization*, Vol. 17, No. 3 (Fall 1958), pp. 20–30.

63. Morris, Robert. "Social Planning," in Henry S. Maas, ed., *Five Fields of Social Service: Reviews of Research*. New York: National Association of Social Workers, 1966. Pp. 185–208.

64. ———, and Randall, Ollie A. "Planning and Organization of Community Services for the Elderly," *Social Work*, Vol. 10, No. 1 (January 1965), pp. 96–103.

65. Morrison, Denton E., and Steeves, Allan D. "Deprivation, Discontent and Social Movement Participation: Evidence on a Contemporary Farmers' Movement, The NFO," *Rural Sociology*, Vol. 32, No. 4 (December 1967), pp. 414–434.

66. Mosotti, Louis H., and Bowen, Don R. "Community and Budgets: The Sociology of Municipal Expenditures," *Urban Affairs Quarterly*, Vol. 1, No. 2 (December 1965), pp. 39–58.

67. Naison, Mark. "The Rent Strike in New York," *Radical America* (November–December 1967), pp. 7–49.

68. Nayar, E. S. K., Touzard, Hubert, and Summers, David A. "Training, Tasks and Mediator Orientation in Heterocultural Negotiations," *Human Relations*, Vol. 21, No. 3 (August 1968), pp. 283–295.

69. Needler, Martin C. "Political Development and Socioeconomic Development: The Case of Latin America," *American Political Science Review*, Vol. 62, No. 3 (September 1968), pp. 889–898.

70. Neubauer, Deane E. "Some Conditions of Democracy," *American Political Science Review*, Vol. 61, No. 4 (December 1967), pp. 1002–1010.

71. Olsen, Marvin E. "Perceived Legitimacy of Social Protest Actions," *Social Problems*, Vol. 15, No. 3 (Winter 1968), pp. 297–310.

72. Pappenfort, Donnell M., and Kilpatrick,

Dee Morgan. "Opportunities for Physically Handicapped Children: A Study of Attitudes and Practice in Settlements and Community Centers," *Social Service Review*, Vol. 41, No. 2 (June 1967), pp. 179–188.

73. Petras, James, and Zeitlin, Maurice. "Miners and Agrarian Radicalism," *American Sociological Review*, Vol. 32, No. 4 (August 1961), pp. 578–586.

74. Photiadis, John D. "Social Integration of Businessmen in Varied Size Communities," *Social Forces*, Vol. 46, No. 2 (December 1967), pp. 229–236.

75. Pinard, Maurice. "Poverty and Political Movements," *Social Problems*, Vol. 15, No. 2 (Fall 1967), pp. 250–263.

76. Piven, Frances Fox. "Dilemmas in Social Planning: A Case Inquiry," *Social Service Review*, Vol. 42, No. 2 (June 1968), pp. 197–206.

77. ———. "Resident Participation in Community-Action Programs: An Overview," in George A. Brager and Francis P. Purcell, eds., *Community Action Against Poverty*. New Haven: College & University Press, 1967. Pp. 151–160.

78. Rabinovitz, Francine F., and Pattinger, S. Stanley. "Organization for Local Planning: The Attitudes of Directors," *Journal of the American Institute of Planners*, Vol. 33, No. 1 (January 1967), pp. 27–32.

79. Rainwater, Lee. "Fear and the House-as-Haven in the Lower Class," *Journal of the American Institute of Planners*, Vol. 32, No. 1 (January 1966), pp. 23–31.

80. Raphael, Edna E., Howard, Kenneth I., and Vernon, David T. A. "Social Process and Readmission to the Mental Hospital," *Social Problems*, Vol. 13, No. 4 (Spring 1966), pp. 436–441.

81. Rosenthal, Donald B., and Crain, Robert L. "Executive Leadership and Community Innovation: Fluoridation," *Urban Affairs Quarterly*, Vol. 1, No. 3 (March 1966), pp. 39–57.

81a. Rudoff, Alvin, and Piliavin, Irving. "Aid to Needy Children: A Study of Types and Responses to Casework Services," *Community Mental Health Journal*, Vol. 5, No. 1 (February 1969), pp. 20–29.

82. Rush, Gary R. "Status Consistency and Right-Wing Extremism," *American Sociological Review*, Vol. 32, No. 1 (February 1967), pp. 86–92.

83. Rushing, William A. "Aspects of Deprivation in a Rural Poverty Class," *Rural Sociology*, Vol. 33, No. 3 (September 1968), pp. 269–287.

84. Sabagh, George, Eyman, Richard K., and Cogburn, Donald. "The Speed of Hospitalization: A Study of a Pre-Admission Waiting List Cohort in a Hospital for the Retarded," *Social Problems*, Vol. 14, No. 2 (Fall 1966), pp. 119–128.

85. Sample, William C. "The Findings on Client Change," *Social Service Review*, Vol. 41, No. 2 (June 1967), pp. 137–151.

86. Schwartz, Edward E. "The Field Experiment: Background, Plan and Selected Findings," *Social Service Review*, Vol. 41, No. 2 (June 1967), pp. 115–136.

87. Scott, Robert A. "The Selection of Clients by Social Welfare Agencies: The Case of the Blind," *Social Problems*, Vol. 14, No. 3 (Winter 1967), pp. 248–257.

88. Sharkansky, Ira. "Agency Requests, Gubernatorial Support and Budget Success in State Legislatures," *American Political Science Review*, Vol. 62, No. 4 (December 1968), pp. 1220–1231.

89. ———. "Government Expenditures and Public Services in the American States," *American Political Science Review*, Vol. 61, No. 4 (December 1967), pp. 1066–1077.

90. Swinth, Robert L. "The Establishment of the Trust Relationship," *Journal of Conflict Resolution*, Vol. 11, No. 3 (September 1967), pp. 335–344.

90a. Walker, Jack. "The Functions of Disunity: Negro Leadership in a Southern City," *Journal of Negro Education*, Vol. 32 (1963), pp. 217–236.

91. Wallace, David. "The Chemung County Evaluation of Casework Service to Dependent Multiproblem Families," *Social Service Review*, Vol. 41, No. 4 (December 1967), pp. 379–389.

92. Westby, David L., and Beaungart, Richard G. "Class and Politics in the Family Backgrounds of Student Political Activists," *American Sociological Review*, Vol. 31, No. 5 (October 1966), pp. 690–692.

93. Wolf, Eleanor P., and Lebeaux, Charles N. "On the Destruction of Poor Neighborhoods by Urban Renewal," *Social Problems*, Vol. 15, No. 1 (Summer 1967), pp. 3–8.

94. Zander, Alvin, and Newcomb, Theodore, Jr. "Group Levels of Aspiration in United Fund Campaigns," *Journal of Personality and Social Psychology*, Vol. 6, No. 2 (June 1967), pp. 157–162.

95. Zeigler, Harmon. "Interest Groups in the States," in Herbert Jacob and Kenneth Vines, eds., *Politics in the American States*. Boston: Little, Brown, 1965. Pp. 101–147.

FAMILY SERVICES
AND CASEWORK

By SCOTT BRIAR

The closing passages of the review of research in the family service field that appeared in the first volume of this series(7) were written in the summer of 1964 under the shadow of redwoods high in the Sierra Nevada Mountains. It is now the summer of 1969, and the first lines of this attempt to bring the earlier review up to date are also being written in the awesome stillness of a redwood forest. In those five years, a short time by almost any standard, the priorities in social work, social welfare, and the social order have changed far beyond what anyone could have imagined. Sitting here, in fact, it seems to the writer that the only things that have not changed deeply are these timeless redwoods. All else seems profoundly different.

In those five years we have been witness to the assassination of three men who represented the best hopes of millions, the eruption of rage and violence of such intensity that it threatens to destroy our cities, the end of the university's dispassionate insulation from the more virulent aspects of political and social turmoil, and

the brave beginning and whimpering decline of an ambitious War on Poverty.

It is important to keep these changes in mind, since they have affected social work and social welfare and therefore the family service field. Not only have these changes influenced social work and social welfare directly, they have also altered our sense of what matters. Some issues that earlier seemed central now appear less important, perhaps even trivial, while other issues, such as racism, which were hardly visible in the literature five years ago, have moved to the center of the stage.

In a time of rapid change it is also important to take note of continuities. Perhaps only in that way can the precise significance of these changes be appreciated. Thus this review will follow the path defined by the previous one. That is, the field of view will be limited to the private family service agency and the research since 1965 that bears on it and its work. Research conducted outside social work and social welfare will not be reviewed but will be brought in by allusion. The vast literature

108

pertaining to the family as an etiological factor in the genesis of all manner of psychological and social ills will not be reviewed. For the most part, material reviewed will be restricted to published works. And this review seeks to be representative rather than exhaustive, especially in areas where a large number of studies have been reported.

One departure from the framework of the previous review should be noted: A somewhat less restricted definition of "research" will be followed in this review, not because the reviewer has relaxed his methodological biases, but out of concern that the stringent standards followed in the previous review may have eliminated exploratory efforts that exposed important avenues for research. This chapter, then, will review social work research related to (1) the private family service agency, (2) methods of intervention in the family service field, (3) family disorganization, and (4) social policy pertaining to the family.

The Family Service Agency

It is probably accurate, although perhaps painful, to suggest that the private family agency is relatively less important in the network of social welfare services than it was five years ago. This is so not because of any specific changes in family agencies themselves, but for other reasons.

First, the increase in social welfare programs and agencies, spawned directly or indirectly by the War on Poverty, simply means that there are more agencies offering similar or functionally equivalent services. In short, the family agency has more competitors than it had before.

Second, social casework, the stock-in-trade of the family agency, no longer is so dominant in social work as it once was, although this is a difference more in emphasis than numbers, since the bulk of social workers and social work students still are caseworkers. In any event, what some regard as an effort to discredit casework in

recent years has hardly enhanced the status of those agencies that offer mainly casework services.

Third, when the poor were given an opportunity, as they have been in recent years, to decide what services they wanted, the services offered by family agencies were not often high on the list. However, family agencies did respond positively to the War on Poverty in a variety of ways, from the extension of their traditional services in low-income neighborhoods to the creation of highly innovative programs.

The searching, penetrating analysis of the mission of the private family agency and its place in the social service system called for in the previous review has not appeared, although the need for it is, if anything, greater than ever. The long-standing promise that the private family agency, by virtue of its autonomy and flexibility, could best serve as a center of experimentation and innovation for services that then would be transferred to the public sector when their utility was demonstrated appears increasingly to have been a myth. In a recent analysis of this subject, Schorr (68) showed in area after area that the major social service innovations have tended to come from the public rather than the private sector.

Why this should be so is at this juncture largely speculative, but at least one student of the private agency field has expressed a similar view. Levin (42), writing on the mission of the voluntary agency, labeled as myths many of the special characteristics attributed to voluntary agencies, including the notion that they are active and adept at experimentation and demonstration. Where to go from there is not clear. Levin seeks mainly to legitimate a concept of voluntary agencies or autonomous direct-service agencies serving the purposes of small special interest groups, with no necessary commitment to serve a wider community, to fill in the gaps left by other programs, or to engage in experimentation and demonstration. It is not the place of this review to analyze that view of the private agency, except to note that if Levin's conception prevails, one consequence will be less research and fewer contributions to knowledge from private family agencies.

As was found at the time of the previous review, research on the family agency continues to be concentrated in two areas, organizational efficiency and patterns of service. A conspicuous and important difference, however, is that descriptive surveys have increasingly been replaced by innovative demonstrations, especially in the area of organizational efficiency.

Organizational Efficiency

Cost analysis studies, which were prevalent in the period covered by the previous review, have declined markedly, although scattered studies of this type have been reported in individual agencies, such as the one conducted at the Baltimore Jewish Family and Children's Service (28). The decline in such studies is not surprising in view of the repetitious similarity of findings obtained from different agencies—for example, "that caseworkers devoted only about one-third of their time to interviews with clients" (7, p. 11). What is more important is that the manifested concern with cost analysis studies has been carried another step forward in a few efforts to experiment with more efficient and less costly patterns of agency organization.

The most dramatic example of these innovative demonstrations was reported by Comess and O'Reilly (14). They described a small family agency in West Covina, California, that had to close after only four and a half years of operation because of a lack of funds, in spite of heavy community demand for the counseling services offered by the agency. A decision was made to reopen the agency with a radically different pattern of organization. A tiny staff was employed, consisting of a director and one secretary. Counseling services were provided by experienced social workers in the community who, acting essentially as private practitioners, worked and were paid on an hourly basis. A broad fee scale was established, including provision for waiver of fees. The outcome in efficiency was dramatic. The cost of an interview was reduced to $10.00, compared to a cost of $21.00 when the agency was organized along more traditional lines. Waiting lists were eliminated, since in the face of increased demands for service the agency simply made fuller use of the time of the contract workers or called on additional workers. The cost to the community was reduced, partly because of the reduction in interview costs, but also by an increase in income from fees (65 percent of the agency's income came from fees). Comess and O'Reilly also report that these benefits enhanced the agency's image in the community and generated a strong *esprit de corps* in the agency. This reviewer is familiar with similar experiments in northern California with comparable effects and benefits.

It might be said that the Comess-O'Reilly model limits the function of the family agency to that of a facility for the private practice of casework, which some years ago Cohen said the private family agency had become (13). However, to the extent that family agencies do offer such services, this model has much to commend it from the standpoint of efficiency and perhaps even quality of service given.[1] And even in those family agencies that perceive their mission in much broader terms, this model of organization for the counseling component of their programs deserves serious consideration and experimentation.

Two other focuses of active research related to organizational efficiency in the period covered by the previous review—recording and supervision—have diminished or moved in directions less directly related to the question of efficiency. For ex-

---

[1] As Comess and O'Reilly reported, the contract workers tend to be experienced workers capable of independent practice. One benefit not mentioned is that such workers are often willing to work evenings and weekends, thus making service more accessible to many clients.

ample, probably the most important study of the past five years concerning recording is the effort in Seattle to develop a system for case recording by code (70). In this project the gains in efficiency, if any, were incidental. The main object was to record case material in a form that would be more accessible to research, in order to "bring under scrutiny the precise nature of social work intervention"(70). Two- to four-digit codes were developed to index five sets of information: (1) person contacted, (2) mode of contact, setting, who initiated contact, and interpersonal base of contact, (3) duration of contact, (4) diagnostic category, and (5) major interventive techniques. Seaberg reported that recording with this system took one-fourth the time previously devoted to process recording and yielded an immense saving in data collection and processing (the recording system was developed as an aid in evaluating the demonstration project in which the system was used).

The potential benefits of such a system could be substantial, and it is a hopeful sign that somewhat similar efforts have been made elsewhere (23). For if a satisfactory system of this type could be developed and used uniformly by all service agencies in a community, the gain in knowledge about service patterns and their effectiveness could be enormous, provided the system included an assessment of case outcome, even measured crudely.

A major obstacle is the compromises that must be made in developing such a code. The problem is not so much that of reducing complex phenomena to a set of categories and numbers, but rather the conceptual and theoretical compromise that must be made in choosing which categories to use. For example, what theoretical orientation should shape the choice of diagnostic and interventive categories? On the one hand there is the problem of theoretical bias, and on the other hand, the fact that the shifts in theoretical perspective that occur frequently in social work would soon render the system passé. For these reasons, such systems should seek to use descriptive

categories, the simpler the better—an ideal not realized in the Seattle project, as inspection of the code categories reveals.

No significant studies of supervision have appeared since the last review. Apparently the plea in the previous review for studies of this thorny and consequential aspect of social agency organization had little or no effect on research activity. One must assume that the important contribution of supervisory practices to staff turnover and service cost remains as it was described five years ago.

Some experiments have been reported showing that reducing the length of casework interviews, especially at intake, lowers costs, increases the agency's service capacity, and reduces waiting lists without lowering the quality of service (36, 73). While experiments of this sort may seem mundane, they are quite valuable in that they discover significant benefits to be gained from simple changes in easily modifiable practices.

Service Patterns

Major studies of patterns of service in family agencies have been limited largely to demographic descriptions of the client population served and, in part at least, represent efforts to respond to the alleged disengagement of family agencies from the poor. The largest of these studies was conducted at Community Service Society of New York and reported by Coursey, Leyendecker, and Siegle (17). The sample consisted of all cases assigned for continuing service as of March 31, 1964 ($n = 1,102$ cases). The study sought to determine the socioeconomic status of the clients served and reported that 50 percent of the clients had insufficient incomes. On the basis of these findings Coursey et al. concluded that the agency "has not turned away from the poor" (p. 338).

However, one problem with this study was that an eight-point rating scale developed for this project was used as the measure of socioeconomic status. Basically the scale reflected the ratio of family living costs to net weekly income as determined by raters from information contained in case records. In principle at least this approach to determining socioeconomic status is more rational for the purposes of such studies than measures limited to deviations from arbitrary income levels (e.g., the poverty line). As is well known, an annual income of $5,000 for a family of four does not have any uniform meaning—with such an income some families live comfortably while others are poor, depending on other circumstances. The approach utilizing the ratio of living cost to net income is more relativistic of course, but that would not be a problem if population base rates were available, which they are not. Consequently, in the absence of such base rates there is no way to tell whether the conclusion drawn by Coursey et al. should be accepted, since it is not known what proportion of the New York City population has "insufficient income" as measured in this study.

A finding that casts further doubt on the authors' conclusion is the underrepresentation of certain ethnic groups: 55 percent of the sampled clients were white, 38 percent were black, and only 6 percent were Puerto Rican. Thus, with reference to the question of whether the family agency reaches disadvantaged groups, even if family agencies serve a higher proportion of low-income clients than some critics have claimed —and it appears from this study, in spite of the questions raised, that the Community Service Society does serve a high proportion of low-income persons—then, at least in this one agency, other disadvantaged groups are greatly underrepresented in the client group.

Of course the study reported by Coursey et al. holds for only one agency, albeit a large one. As one would expect, the patterns differ for agencies in other communities. Janowicz (34) reported a similar study conducted in a New Haven family service agency. The findings are not strictly comparable to the CSS study because different measures of socioeconomic status were utilized, but using the Hollingshead two-factor index of social class, Janowicz found that well over half the caseload were in Classes IV and V, the lowest classes. Comparison of data collected in different years (1954–55 and 1961) indicated the class distribution of cases remained relatively stable, with a slight increase in cases from Class III and a slight decrease in Classes I and II. During the same period the proportion of black clients (20 percent of intake, 25 percent of continuing caseload) also remained constant even though the black population in the community tripled during that period.

In discussing the New Haven findings Janowicz raised the central question: Whom should the family agency serve? Should the demographic characteristics of the client group correspond to the distribution of these characteristics in the community? This is a fundamental question, but at the moment probably an unanswerable one, since a rational answer would require a clearer sense of the mission of family agencies than now prevails. The answer toward which Janowicz leans—namely, that the private family agency should serve mainly middle-class clients, leaving the upper-class clients to private practitioners and the low-income clients to public agencies— requires a better rationale than the one Janowicz provides (middle-class clients use the services of the agency more effectively and efficiently than do lower-class clients) if it is to escape the charge of class bias. As it stands, Janowicz's position simply confirms the charges made by some of the principal critics of the family service agency (12), namely, that potential clients are expected to fit the service preferences and patterns of the agency, not vice versa.

New Directions

However, during the period reviewed here many family agencies ventured away from conventional patterns and styles of service, with the result that the field is much more heterogeneous than it was five years ago. Spurred partly by the War on Poverty, a number of family agencies across the country have moved to extend their services into urban ghettos and poverty target areas (1, 32, 70, 76). In some instances this move has meant little more than the establishment of outposts in poor neighborhoods, but in others more radical changes in service styles were established.[2] It is too early to say what the effects of these developments have been and will be, but one of the few studies of that question that have appeared indicates that the impact can be deep and, for staff, disquieting (76). In fact, in the agency studied, traditional services and the new programs oriented to a poor area continued as parallel developments, with little integration and some antagonisms between them.

The development of brief service methods, a trend that had just started at the time of the last review, in 1964, has gained momentum, assisted by several demonstration projects, of which the most important is the one conducted at the Community Service Society and reported by Reid and Shyne (62). That study (discussed in greater detail later in this review) found that brief service is generally superior to extended service. Hopefully these conclusions will influence family agency practice in the next several years, with important benefits for clients and for the service capacity of agencies that adopt the brief service pattern.

Finally, Family Service Association of America has initiated several projects designed to bring research and practice closer together (75), to improve neighborhood conditions(63), to describe marital counseling practices (16), and to develop inno-

vative methods of service to aged clients (20). Such efforts, although difficult to execute and coordinate, should be encouraged since the payoff is likely to be more substantial and solid than studies conducted in one agency alone, except for those few large agencies with resources to support a sophisticated research program.

Needed Research

There are signs that private family service agencies have entered a period of transition. Where present trends will lead is difficult to discern, for only the most sketchy information is available about the impact of current trends on agencies and even about details on the trends themselves. What is clear is that the field is stirring itself; there are movements toward client populations previously neglected, toward a broader concern with the neighborhood and the community, and toward more effective and efficient methods of service.

In a time of change, when directions are not clear and predictions are hazardous, what might research contribute of use to family agencies? Probably the most important and most needed studies are those that expose and illuminate the possibilities opened by the new directions that are being explored. However trite this may be, a period of change *is* a period of opportunity, in this case an opportunity to discover and develop new and vital roles for private family agencies in a period characterized by an understandable and legitimate preference for public programs and a relative decline in resources for private agencies. To fail to consider these opportunities is to overlook the potential inherent in the considerable resources already invested and available for use in family agencies. Such research is a task for policy analysis, a technique still more an art than a science (83), but which nevertheless can provide valuable and useful insights. A study or studies of this sort probably could best be launched by FSAA, since the perspective

---

[2] Oakland, California, provides an example of the former pattern. Caseworkers from the local family agency were attached to neighborhood service centers scattered through the target areas. Across the bay in San Francisco, the family service agency developed a program that departed radically from conventional patterns of service.

should be broad and national. The practical value of such studies would inhere in the guidelines they could provide for shaping current trends in rational and purposeful rather than haphazard directions.

Social Work Intervention

Both in volume and certainly in significance, studies of social work intervention have dominated research in the family service field over the past five years. Research attention has focused on continuance, short-term casework, and techniques of intervention, but probably the most significant investigations in this area were the several major studies of effectiveness.

Effectiveness

Three major studies of the effectiveness of social work intervention in the family field have appeared since publication of the first volume in this series. The first of these, *Girls at Vocational High* (53), has attracted considerable attention both within and, to a lesser extent, outside the profession. Although the study was not conducted in a family service agency, its central concern is with the effectiveness of social casework, the primary service offered by most family agencies. Opinions about this study have ranged from the view that it is a fair, conscientious, and careful effort to demonstrate the effectiveness of casework (67) to the belief that the study is so faulty in its failure to approximate the appropriate conditions for effective casework practice that the study findings can be disregarded (29). Such widely divergent interpretations are understandable inasmuch as it has been claimed that the study provides a reasonably rigorous test of the effectiveness of casework and since, if the latter claim is correct, the findings permit only one general conclusion: persons receiving casework services show no significant gains over comparable persons who do not receive such

services. With that much at stake, it was to be expected that the study would be carefully scrutinized for possible weaknesses.

Probably the most thorough critique was Macdonald's essay review (50); since that review is readily available, Macdonald's analysis will not be repeated in full here. Among the numerous weaknesses that Macdonald saw in the study, two were central for her and also for Herstein (29), another critic: (1) Appropriate motivation for casework was lacking since the girls who became clients did not ask for help but were invited to accept it. (2) Since casework is not a unitary method, but is actually many things, it cannot be tested without further specification and differentiation—one can only test *a* casework method, not *the* casework method, since the latter does not exist.

The second criticism is more telling than the first. The motivation issue ignores the reality that caseworkers have worked for many years with clients who did not ask for help (e.g., in corrections, psychiatric hospitals, and protective service programs) and have claimed to be effective under these conditions. Moreover, in recent years some caseworkers have advocated preventive programs in which potential clients would be invited to use casework services, much as were the girls at Vocational High. It may be that caseworkers are more effective with clients who ask for help, but that remains to be demonstrated. On the other hand, the criticism that casework practice is not unitary but varies greatly with the worker and other factors seems well taken. The hitch is that a differentiated, measurable typology of casework practice has not been formulated; consequently, the authors of *Girls at Vocational High* cannot be faulted for failing to make such differentiations, however important such classifications may prove to be when they have been developed.

But these and other criticisms do not detract from the findings of the study, which can be rephrased as follows: Whatever the caseworkers in the study did with the girls who were invited to use their services, the caseworkers' interventions did not have a measurably significant effect on a variety of outcome measures.[3] That finding can be countered only by other studies showing significant positive effects.

The perfect study has not been done, but the two other major studies of casework effectiveness that have appeared since *Girls at Vocational High* do not suffer from some of the weaknesses found in the latter. The Chemung County study, although conducted in a public welfare agency, was an effort to test the effectiveness of casework methods developed in private family agencies for helping multiproblem families (9). These methods had been described in detail in the literature (56, 79, 80), and an effort was made in this project to be sure that they were followed as formulated in previous projects.

Professionally trained, experienced caseworkers were used, their caseloads were small and protected, and cases were randomly assigned to the project. Two control groups were used, both randomly selected from the same population as the experimental group. One control group served in the usual manner, while the second was a "hidden control" that became known to agency staff only at the conclusion of the project. Two outcome measures were used, the Geismar family functioning scale and the CSS movement scale. Two independent sets of ratings on the Geismar scale were obtained, one by raters selected and supervised by Geismar, the other by raters at CSS. An important feature of the design was that two experts rated the quality of casework service provided to the demonstration cases. These experts found the quality of casework slightly below average for trained caseworkers but still above average for regular public assistance workers.

---

[3] The use of multiple outcome measures is one of the virtues of the research design in *Girls at Vocational High*. This practice increases the probability of finding some effects, if there are any. While this stacks the deck in favor of the interventions introduced, it is justified by the general weaknesses of available outcome measures.

In other words, the quality of service was less than would have been desirable for an evaluative study but hardly low enough to discount the study, especially in view of evidence showing that the demonstration cases received much more intensive service than controls.

The study findings reveal no significant differences in outcome between the demonstration and control groups. While a slight positive trend favoring the demonstration group was found, closer analysis revealed that this trend was attributable largely to a marked change in one of the demonstration cases. Thus the net result of this project is to add one more to the growing list of studies that failed to show positive results from casework services.

The Chemung County study was published in 1968, some sixteen years after the original multiproblem family demonstration project began in St. Paul (9). In those sixteen years scores of similar projects were launched across the country, costing millions of dollars. The Chemung County study could have been conducted and reported at least ten years ago. If it had been, the results might have altered the rapid spread of multiproblem family projects so that the money and effort expended on such projects could have been used more productively, for example, to discover and test other methods of serving these families. The fact that the study was not done earlier and that even now its results may not be heeded speaks to the schism between research and practice in social work. And the fact that the study could and should have been done earlier speaks to the social cost of that schism to the profession, the public, and, most of all, to the clients who continued to receive ineffective services when other, possibly more effective, services might have been developed and tested. Such is the price of the persistent failure in social work to regard all new methods as untested experiments that must be subjected to rigorous evaluation from the beginning.

The published report of the Chemung County study is a curious, perhaps even unique, research report. The methodology and findings of the study are reported in the *last* of seven chapters. Except for a brief overview of the study in the first chapter, the rest of the book consists of interpretations of the meaning to be attached to the study findings. Several of the later chapters are essentially attempts to explain away the findings and thereby preserve the efficacy of the practice methods used. Much less attention is given to the possibility that the findings are valid and to the consequences that would follow from that possibility.

The third major study during this period was *Brief and Extended Casework* by Reid and Shyne (62). In this research, Reid and Shyne sought to determine the relative effectiveness of brief as compared to extended casework. A brief service program was established, and clients were randomly assigned to that program or to the regular casework program of the agency, on which no time limits were imposed. A variety of outcome measures were used. The findings clearly revealed that, for the types of clients included in this study, brief service was generally more effective than extended casework. Moreover, not only did a higher proportion of brief service cases show positive improvement, but fewer showed deterioration as compared to cases that received extended casework.

The Reid-Shyne study goes beyond previous studies of casework effectiveness in one important respect. "Is casework effective?" —the question addressed in *Girls at Vocational High* and in the Chemung County study—is an important and legitimate question. However, it is not an especially useful question for practitioners, since it admits of only two definitive answers: yes or no. Either answer is important for evaluative purposes, but neither is very informative to the practitioner. If the answer is yes, presumably the practitioner gains the comfort that comes from the knowledge that his activities are helpful. But if the answer is no, the practitioner is left with a serious dilemma. He has been told that his methods are not effective, but not what he may do to improve them. For that reason, perhaps it is not surprising that practitioners have ignored these studies or have denied their validity—the alternative, for them, would be to close up shop!

The Reid-Shyne study goes a step beyond the question of effectiveness to ask which of two methods is more effective. Consequently their results point a direction for casework practitioners to follow in order to maximize their effectiveness. More generally, effectiveness studies could be made more attractive to practitioners if researchers put their questions in a form that would yield more useful information to the practitioner. Of course, it remains to be seen whether the Reid-Shyne study will have a greater impact on practice than previous effectiveness studies, even though it did yield information that practitioners can apply and that, if applied, would make a substantial difference both in effectiveness and, what is more, in savings of time and effort. Also, it should be emphasized that the general level of effectiveness achieved by caseworkers in the Reid-Shyne study still is far short of what would be required for caseworkers to feel sanguine about their methods.

Apart from a few scattered small-scale studies (for example, see 54 and 71), these three studies constitute the major research on casework effectiveness in the past five years. This does not diminish their importance, for they are major studies indeed.

The future direction of social work research in this area is not entirely clear. It is to be hoped that future studies will follow the lead of the Reid-Shyne study and put questions in a form that will increase their information value for practitioners. One area of active research that will bear fruit in the next few years is the work on the application of behavior modification principles to social work being conducted by Thomas and his co-workers at the University of Michigan (78) and, to a lesser extent, at Berkeley (41). This research, some of which is discussed later, tends to produce concrete, pragmatic, and immediately applicable tools for the practitioner. Although there is considerable resistance to the behavior modification approach among social workers, its demonstrated effectiveness will make it increasingly difficult for practitioners to ignore these principles and techniques.

Continuance

One of the active and productive areas of investigation during the period covered by the previous review was research on the factors associated with client continuance and discontinuance in casework. This subject has continued to receive some attention, but in a rather limited way, and certainly not to the extent that the promise of the earlier research deserved.

Fowler (24) reported data on continuance collected from five family agencies in two metropolitan areas in New York State. The findings are consistent with previous studies in that the proportion of continuers (i.e., those clients who continued beyond the third interview) was low (from 30 to 40 percent). In contrast to many previous studies, Fowler's data made it possible to identify what he calls "planned continuers," that is, clients who were expected by staff to continue. Nevertheless, separate analysis of this group did not increase the continuance rate appreciably, for only 42 percent of the planned continuers continued beyond the third interview.

Fowler did find the following specific factors to be positively associated with higher rates of continuance: (1) discussion of fees with the client in the initial interview, (2) making a specific second appointment, and (3) an intake pattern in which the worker who conducts the intake interview also continues with the case. On the other hand the educational level, size, and experience of the staff were found to be unrelated to continuance.

In another study Clement (11) also found some concrete factors associated with continuance in family agency cases involving parent-child relationship problems. Specifically, such cases were more likely to continue if (1) the client received strong support from the referring agency before and after the initial interview, (2) the child was seen by the caseworker sometime before the fourth interview, (3) the caseworker expressed strong empathy for both mother and child in at least one of the interviews with the mother, and (4) the caseworker maintained a central focus on parent-child problems in all interviews with the mother.

The Fowler and Clement studies carry forward the promise of earlier research in the sense that both identify factors associated with continuance that have to do with specific actions that can be taken by caseworkers (e.g., the intake worker also carries the case if continued service is needed) to increase continuance rates—provided, of course, that the associations found in these studies turn out to be predictive.

Other studies of continuance have added depth to the understanding of continuance-discontinuance derived from previous research (18, 38). David (18), for example, found that continuance is positively associated with social class, which is consistent with previous studies. However, David also found no association between social class and degree of consensus between caseworker and client regarding the nature of the client's problem. The latter finding is difficult to understand, since a number of studies have shown that worker-client consensus and continuance are strongly associated.

Probably the most ambitious study of continuance during the past five years—using a weighted sample of 2,289 cases from 280 agencies—was conducted by Rosenblatt and Mayer (65). Surprisingly, the most powerful factor associated with continuance in this study was city size: the larger the city in which the agency was located, the higher the rate of discontinuance. This factor seemed to overwhelm all other factors considered in this research, including client social class. Unfortunately, some of the factors found in other studies (e.g., consensus between client and worker) were not examined because data on them were not available (Rosenblatt and Mayer used data originally collected for other purposes). In any event, the Rosenblatt-Mayer study indicates that client continuance-discontinuance is a more complex phenomenon than it first appeared to be.

These few, relatively scattered, studies of continuance do not add up to a concentrated research program. That is unfortunate because of the significance of the problem and because of the payoff in directly applicable findings that some studies of the subject have yielded.

On the other hand, there are some indications that a closely related subject, brief service, may be beginning to receive the systematic research attention it deserves. The ambitious and important study by Reid and Shyne (62) was reviewed earlier in this chapter, and other, less significant studies such as the one by Warren (82) have been reported. Given the increasing interest in brief service among practitioners, more research in this area can be expected, and as the findings of Reid and Shyne indicate, the benefits of such research can be substantial.

Methods of Intervention

Ultimately, to be maximally useful, practice research must reach the question of the precise effects of specific interventive acts. The question: Is brief service more effective than extended service? is useful to practitioners, but far more useful would be questions that identify in detail the conditions in the intervention situation that are associated with specific desired changes in the client. Only through answering questions of that sort can social work develop empirically grounded change methods. At the time of the previous review, few systematic studies of this kind had been conducted—the literature consisted mostly of case reports and theoretical discussions.

That picture has changed for the better in the past five years, for a fair number of studies of interventive methods have appeared. None of these studies is major, either in ambitiousness or discovery, but together they add up to the emergence of research in a crucial and long-neglected area. For that reason the modesty and weaknesses of many of these studies are less important than the fact that they were done.

For some years Hollis has been at work on a typology of casework treatment, and some of the research using this typology has appeared in recent years. Hollis (33) reported some basic work on the coding and application of the typology. Reid (61) tested and confirmed hypotheses concerning the differential use of the techniques in the typology as a function of the experience of the caseworker and the degree of disturbance in the client. Variations in use of the procedures in the Hollis typology as a function of the client's value orientation were reported by Turner (81). And Ehrenkranz (21, 22) found that caseworkers tended to use different procedures in joint as compared to individual interviews.

As these studies indicate, the typology can be applied reliably, and use of the procedures in the typology by practitioners does vary in relation to important variables in the practice situation. And since logically the first step toward the development of a relevant diagnostic typology should be the construction of an intervention typology, Hollis's work is important as a first move in that direction.[4] Unfortu-

---

[4] The function of a diagnostic typology, for the practitioner, is to make it possible to select the most effective interventive method from the array available to him. Consequently the steps to construction of a diagnostic typology should be as follows: (1) identification and description of the array of interventive methods available to the practitioner, (2) empirical determination of the effect of each method on clients representing the array of problems confronting the practitioner, (3) constructing a parsimonious diagnostic typology differentiating the clients (or problems) who were helped most by each method.

nately, the potential contribution of this work is diminished by certain limitations in the typology itself and by the sorts of questions addressed in the research conducted on it thus far. The typology is defined in psychological terms and therefore does not adequately subsume more socially directed procedures. And it is predicated on an insight theory of individual change, the validity of which is questionable. The research conducted thus far on the typology has focused on correlates of variations in the use of these procedures by practitioners. But the question: When do caseworkers use these procedures? is considerably less important and useful than the question: When *should* they use them? And only research focused on the differential effects of these procedures on a wide range of clients can be expected to answer the latter question.

A second direction taken in the newly emerging research on interventive methods consists of studies of family-centered approaches. Again, these studies are few in number and modest in their conclusions, but they indicate that a widespread development in casework is beginning to receive systematic study. Schreiber (69) attempted to evaluate the effectiveness in a family agency of the family therapy approach developed by Jackson and Satir (66).

Fifty-nine families treated with this approach were rated for their degree of movement on five dimensions: (1) communication, (2) role functions, (3) individual responsibility, (4) integration of differences, and (5) unity and cohesion. Since there was no control group, it is impossible to assess the meaning of the outcomes reported, except for the relative differences in movement among the five dimensions rated. The greatest movement was found on the dimensions of communication (61 percent of the families), role functions (49 percent), and individual responsibility (51 percent); least movement occurred on the integration and unity dimensions. These findings are consistent with the heavy emphasis on communication and role

clarification in the Jackson-Satir approach. At the same time, the claim by Jackson and Satir that improved communication leads to improvement in other areas of family functioning is not supported by these findings or by Schreiber's report that only 40 percent of the families showed improvement in "total family behavior."

Despite the weaknesses of this study, it is one of the few reported attempts to study the effectiveness of the Jackson-Satir approach (or any school of family therapy for that matter). It is a commentary on the triumph of faith over science that in all the years that Jackson and Satir have successfully extended the influence of their approach on the clinical field they have never reported an evaluation of the effectiveness of their methods, nor have they ever been called to account for this deficiency. Once again practitioners have charted a course without checking to see whether it leads anywhere.

Langsley et al. (40) used a control group and somewhat harder outcome measures to assess the effectiveness of family-centered crisis-oriented treatment. Although the study was conducted in a psychiatric setting, it is mentioned here because of the interest in the crisis-oriented approach in the family service field. Baseline data were collected from 150 families that had a member admitted to a psychiatric hospital.[5] Seventy-five families were assigned to the experimental project and 75 "control" families received traditional service. Ratings on a social adjustment inventory and a personal functioning scale were made at the time of admission and again three and six months later. In addition data were collected on readmission rates and length of hospitalization following treatment.

Controls were found to have a slightly but probably not significantly higher number of readmissions and substantially longer

---

[5] A larger sample (300) is planned; this article is an interim report based on results for the first 150 families.

periods of hospitalization when readmitted than did experimentals. Whether the latter difference was due to the treatment methods used or simply to the fact that these families were the objects of an experimental program is impossible to say, but the failure to find any substantial differences between experimentals and controls on the measures of social adjustment and personal functioning makes it doubtful that the therapeutic method accounted for the differences in rate and duration of readmissions.

Krill (39) studied the use of family interviewing at intake as a diagnostic tool. Review of twenty cases led him to conclude that use of this technique led to a more family-oriented view of the presenting problems for both staff and the family members themselves. These results are only suggestive since no comparison cases were used.

Brandreth and Pike (6), Bounous (5), Cooke (15), and Young (84) reported assessments of marital counseling. Since none of these studies utilized control groups, the outcome findings are again difficult to interpret (moreover the Cooke study involved only three cases). Of these studies, the most precise was that by Brandreth and Pike, who reported that some improvement was found in 62 percent of the cases—some studies of psychotherapy have reported improvement rates that high for untreated groups. Bounous took the still unusual step of interviewing clients as well as workers in marital counseling cases. He found that caseworkers tended to overestimate client perceptions of problem severity and underestimated client hopefulness, sense of personal responsibility, and support of significant others.

Mayer and Timms (52) attempted to elicit more general information about the client's perspective in social casework through interviews with working-class clients of the Family Welfare Association in London. Comparison of worker and client perceptions led the researchers to conclude that they "were dealing with two different cultural systems when it came to coping with problems—the worker system and the client system" (p. 16). They note that both systems make sense if one accepts their initial, but quite different, premises. The social workers followed a "causal approach" to problem-solving: that discovery of the cause makes constructive action possible. The working-class clients, on the other hand, were not interested in causes because they felt nothing could be done about them; instead they had a preference for suppressive techniques for solving problems. As a result of these divergent viewpoints, clients often misunderstood or were confused about the meaning of the worker's comments or actions (e.g., silence was interpreted as disinterest, nods and smiles as agreement) and dissatisfied with their counseling experience. Just as the workers assumed that clients shared their assumptions about problem-solving, clients assumed that workers shared *their* assumptions. Mayer and Timms suggest that it might help if workers would attempt to explain to clients what they are doing and why, a practice not followed by the workers in this study.

Use of Groups

Group methods have been used in family agencies for some time, but only recently have they received any substantial research attention. Dillon (19), Mabley (49), Pattison (57), and Ganter and Polansky (27) reported studies of the use of groups in the intake-diagnosis stage of treatment. All these reports speak favorably about this use of group methods, although specific evidence attesting to its superiority over alternative methods or its differentiated utility is lacking. The one exception is Mabley, who found that group intake procedures increased the rate of continuance slightly over the rate achieved with the intake procedures used elsewhere in the agency.

Other Services

In recent years many family agencies have expanded their activities to incorporate a variety of new programs and projects, although as yet few of these projects have been described in print. One of the most ambitious of these was Project ENABLE (Education and Neighborhood Action for Better Living Environment), which was funded by the Office of Economic Opportunity and sponsored by the Family Service Association of America, the National Urban League, and the Child Study Association of America (63). Project ENABLE sought to form discussion groups in low-income neighborhoods throughout the country. The intent was that these groups would discuss local neighborhood conditions and what might be done to improve them; it was expected that the discussions might become a stimulus to action. Over 300 such groups were formed in some sixty cities under the auspices of 100 family agencies and National Urban League affiliates. Since research was integral to the project, a staggering amount of data was accumulated (e.g., 11,587 personal interviews were conducted), enough to justify the claim in the project report that ENABLE research offers the "richest material now available on working with lower class parents" (p. 8).

This mass of data was subjected to careful, competent analysis. Unfortunately, the results seem disproportionately small compared to the effort that went into the project and the research. Most of the analysis centered on two areas: (1) correlates of rates of attendance at meetings and (2) attitudinal change among project participants. Attendance was remarkably high, considering what others have said about the difficulty of interesting low-income persons in groups of this sort. Con-

siderable research analysis was devoted to an effort to discover factors associated with attendance. The main findings were that rates of attendance were higher in the South than the North and varied inversely with the size of the agency. The meaning of these two findings is unclear, and the report offers little to illuminate them.

The findings are similar to those of a study of continuance reviewed earlier in this chapter (63). In that study Rosenblatt (who was research director of ENABLE) reported that the larger the city, the higher the rate of client discontinuance. One possible explanation is the somewhat higher degree of personalization of service that may occur to a greater extent in smaller communities and rural areas. And there is some material in the ENABLE report to suggest that staff in rural areas come to know their clients in a more personal way. But this is only speculation—a clearer explanation of these findings must await further research.

Sizable changes in participants' attitudes were found, even though the groups met only eight to ten times (the percentage of groups showing attitudinal change in desired directions ranged from 47 to 76 percent on the six items used). Attitudinal change tended to be highest in groups with high stability and attendance and to vary directly with the educational level of participants. Still, the most striking finding is that so many low-income persons participated so regularly. For reasons that are not clear, OEO support was withdrawn after only one year of field operation—a mystery in view of the obvious success of the program and the careful research done. Another mystery is why more family agencies did not develop such programs on their own before or since.

Much of the content of the discussions in these groups amounted essentially to family life education, an activity in regard to which family agencies seem to have been both singularly well suited and peculiarly uninterested. For those agencies that are engaged in programs of family life education, Rosenblatt's report contains useful information about factors affecting rates of attendance and participation.

Some family agencies, in developing programs directed to low-income groups, have —among other things—developed projects in connection with public housing units. A study of the effectiveness of one such program was reported by Lewis (47) and Siff (72). (Although not actually conducted in a family agency, this project is similar to others that were.) It was an effort to improve the housekeeping practice of "families in public low cost housing who were in danger of lease cancellation because of chronic poor housekeeping"(72, p. 25). A sample of such families were randomly assigned to control and experimental groups; families in the experimental group became the object of a program of services intended to improve their housekeeping practices. Outcome results showed no significant differences between experimental and control families, although the trend favored the experimental group. Comparison with a sample of "excellent housekeeping" families suggested some differences between the two groups that might be useful in developing other service programs directed to related problems with a similar population.

Future Trends

As indicated earlier, the research on methods and techniques tends to be scattered and tentative, but it is a beginning. As could be predicted, the tighter the design and the more specific the measures used, the more useful the findings of such studies. On the horizon, but not yet in print at the time of this review, are efforts to apply behavior modification principles in the family agency field (see, for example, 78). The dramatic successes and special amenability to rigorous research of this interventive approach suggest that it will improve both practice and research in the family service field (2, 25).

Family Organization and Disorganization

The research possibilities inherent in the social worker's unique access to certain groups of families remains, unfortunately, an unrealized potentiality. Studies of the family and of family disorganization in particular seem to have declined in social work over the past five years.

The Multiproblem Family

Research related to the multiproblem family concept, the most active area of study at the time of the previous review, has dwindled virtually to the point of extinction. And the Chemung County study (9), reviewed earlier in this chapter, which found the interventive methods developed out of research on the multiproblem family to be ineffective, probably presages the end of this research theme. For the research that was done was concerned less with describing and analyzing such families than with classifying them and assessing their responsiveness to interventions presumably tailored to their special needs. Moreover, the value biases implicit in the concept of the multiproblem family have become more apparent and increasingly unacceptable to many persons, much as many reacted to what they regarded as an invidious bias in Moynihan's analysis of the black family (55, 60). The concept of the multiproblem family carried, for many, the implication that the causes of the problems resided in these families themselves, rather than in the social conditions that may have produced their problems. Consequently the concept gave rise to therapeutic programs rather than efforts to change social conditions.

The Black Family

Moynihan was accused of a similar bias; that is, it was said that he located the sources of problems in black families within the black family itself. This criticism seems valid for the multiproblem family concept, but not for the Moynihan report. What Moynihan claimed was quite the opposite. He attempted to show that certain problems of family disorganization that appear in black families are the result of social conditions especially affecting these families, and, further, that the "normal" course of social processes will not ameliorate these problems. Consequently, for Moynihan, extraordinary *social* measures—such as the provision of income and jobs—are required to deal with these problems. It should be said that while this criticism is not appropriate to Moynihan's analysis, his report can be criticized validly on other grounds.

Partly stimulated by the Moynihan report, the black family became an important focus of attention for social scientists, and a few social work researchers contributed to the research that developed in association with the interest in black families. Billingsley's work on the subject (4), while containing little original or new data, pulled together material from a variety of sources to trace the historical origins of black family patterns and, among other things, to show that it is inaccurate to speak of *the* black family, since a variety of family types and patterns exist in the black community. A similar conclusion is reached by Herzog in her review of research bearing on the question of the alleged breakdown of the black family (30).

However, neither of these studies nor others done by social workers approaches the penetration and insight of studies done outside the field, such as the work of Liebow (48) or Rainwater (59). The point is not that social work research on black families should equal or exceed in quality the work done by others, but rather to reemphasize that social work's special access to black (and other) families has not produced a rich literature that would add to the general body of knowledge on the subject. The failure of social work research to make a major contribution to knowledge in an area of central concern to the profession undoubtedly has many causes. In part it probably has to do with the low value attached to research by social workers, as shown in Rosenblatt's survey (64). Added to this attitude is the rather narrow, noninstitutional view of the family that Gabler and Otto found in their review of the social work literature (26).

Cohesion in Marriage

In contrast to the public welfare field, where a number of major studies of families were conducted by, for example, Podell (58), Stone and Schlamp (77), and Levinson (46), only a small and rather scattered array of studies of the family has emanated from the family service field during the past five years. Levinger continued his research on cohesion in marriage with studies showing that disclosure of feelings and degree of agreement between husband and wife were positively associated with marital satisfaction (43, 44, 45). Katz also found a strong relationship between agreement and marital satisfaction (35). Herzog prepared an excellent and useful review of research on fatherless families (31); more reviews of this sort would help to bring to the attention of the field relevant research conducted outside the field and published in journals not ordinarily read by social workers. And Siporin conducted an informative study of families that underwent bankruptcy proceedings (74). Siporin's study was descriptive, but such studies are fundamental and useful in developing detailed knowledge about the interaction between families and social organizations and institutions.

One has the strong impression that social workers in the family service field work without close familiarity with the extensive research on the family being conducted outside the field, principally in sociology. To be sure, it may be that much of this research is not directly relevant to family service practices, but greater familiarity with it might affect social workers' perspective on the family and, through that shift, lead to new programs directed to aspects of family life and family problems currently slighted or ignored.

Social Policy and the Family

In the previous review in the first volume of this series, family policy appeared to be one of the most exciting and promising areas of research activity in the family service field. Although only a few studies had been done at that time, they offered a fresh perspective that opened intriguing and fruitful avenues for further investigation. Because of that high promise, the lack of activity in this area during the five-year period under review is disappointing.

However, the reasons for the decline of research on family policy are not difficult to discover. Policy analysis is a newly emerging research area, and as yet few social work researchers are engaged in it. During the past five years, social work policy analysts have been preoccupied with the problems that have dominated this period, namely, poverty, income maintenance, racism, public welfare, and political and social conflict. And these preoccupations have resulted in several important policy studies (3, 37, 51).

The Moynihan report generated a flurry of debate over the proposal for a national policy to strengthen the black family (55, 60), and some social work researchers contributed to this discussion (4, 30). For a time it appeared that family policy might become a central issue for national attention. But the negative reaction to Moynihan's conclusions, described in the previous section of this chapter, also discredited, unfortunately, the parallel notion that a national effort to strengthen the family as an instiution is necessary in order to cope effectively with a variety of social problems.

Such an argument was advanced in the one major family policy study conducted during the past five years. Schorr, in *Poor Kids* (68), marshalled evidence to show the central role of the family in poverty and the effects of poverty on the family. Against that background Schorr analyzed the major income maintenance proposals in terms of their capacity to strengthen the family in certain crucial areas. Schorr's analysis led him to favor a family allowance as an essential component of any program intended to eliminate poverty. Similar arguments were subsequently advanced at a conference on family allowances (10) and by Briar (8). Although these arguments receded into the background because of the attention received by the negative income tax concept, the emphasis on the family in President Nixon's 1969 welfare proposals may precipitate renewed attention to the effects of various income maintenance schemes on families.

The lack of policy-oriented research on the family—apart from the studies conducted in public welfare—is singularly unfortunate, since it could easily be argued that policy research should have highest priority in the family service field. Most social workers would share with many others the belief that the family plays a vital role in many matters of central concern to social welfare. It is demonstrable that social welfare programs and policies affect, in one way or another, the lives of families. Yet little is known about what these effects are and even less about what it might be necessary to provide if the family is to be strengthened, and no one has clearly assumed this mission of inquiry.

Here, then, is a function that the family service field could assume, a function that could have national as well as local impact and one that could infuse the field with the sense of mission it seems to be seeking. Such a step would entail some reallocation of resources in the family agency field, but the payoff could be substantial. Project ENABLE represented a tentative move in this direction (63), demonstrating that (1) cooperative ventures involving a number of family service agencies can be conducted successfully, with considerable national and local benefits, and (2) family agencies can successfully conduct programs directed to a broader concern with family life in the community than traditional service patterns have had. This project demonstrated potentialities in the family service field that could be exploited to make the field a more influential force in shaping social policies affecting the family.

Conclusions

A recurrent theme throughout this review has been the observation that the volume of research in the family service field is substantially less than it was at the time of the previous review five years ago. There are several reasons for this state of affairs. First, the previous review covered a much longer time period and therefore drew on research spanning several decades. Second, with the appearance in recent years of new types of social welfare programs and agencies, the private family agency has become relatively less important; whereas once it was a principal source of ideas and practice methods for social work generally, it is now but one of many. Third, the number of researchers in social work and social welfare remains quite small, so that the amount of work that can be done in any one field is limited. An added factor is that the scope of social work and social welfare has been expanded considerably. Finally, the attention of researchers tends to be attracted to national concerns, and in recent years these have not focused centrally on the family.

But the lessened volume of research does not diminish the importance of the work that was done. Several trends emerge that have considerable significance for the family service field and for social work generally.

First, the effectiveness of one of the mainstays of the family service field and of social work—social casework—was the object of several major studies. In spite of various efforts to discredit them, the generally discouraging results of these studies cannot be ignored for long without damaging the credibility of the profession. At the same time, those who would use these findings to diminish or perhaps even eliminate the casework function fail to recognize the widespread need for the kind of individual service casework attempts to provide. The problem posed for casework by these studies is how to increase its effectiveness. One of the evaluative studies, by Reid and Shyne (62), indicates that greater use of short-term methods will increase effectiveness and efficiency. Another promising avenue for increasing the effectiveness of casework is to be found in the behavior modification approach, yet to be applied in the family service field to any extent. The effectiveness of this approach can no longer be doubted, and its generalizability to the kinds of behavioral problems encountered in the family service field seems well established (78).

Second, the national preoccupation with the problems of low-income groups stimulated family agencies to develop new programs directed to these groups. Research describing and evaluating these developments has just begun to appear and indicates, as in Project ENABLE (63), that private family agencies can effectively launch basically different approaches to problems they have traditionally attempted to solve in other ways.

Third, the failure to generate descriptive, analytical studies of families, their problems, and the forces affecting them remains a serious handicap for the family service field. Only on the basis of such studies could the field speak authoritatively about the family, its problems, and its needs. If it could speak authoritatively on these matters, the family service field could fill an important gap in social policy development. The family therapy movement, which might have moved in that direction, has not done so and is not likely to because of its narrow focus on certain processes internal to the family. Any movement in the direction proposed here would require that family agencies divert more of their resources to research, policy analysis, and social action.

Fourth, one is still given the strong impression, also evident at the time of the last review, that family service agencies go about their business unaware of the mainstream of research on the family in sociology, social psychology, and economics. This isolation would have to be ended if family agencies sought to assume a broader role vis-à-vis the family and its problems.

Finally, the research reported during the past five years seems to be characterized by more rigor and sophistication than the studies covered in the previous review. For example, control groups, use of an array of measuring tools, and hypothesis-testing are more prevalent now than they were five years ago. This can only be a good sign, since it means—among other things—that the findings reported can be accepted with greater confidence.

If research progress in the family service field has been uneven during the past five years, progress is nevertheless unmistakable. And if important questions have gone unattended, others have been examined in a more searching way than ever before. Given the magnitude of the problems embraced by social welfare and the extremely limited research talent and resources available, perhaps one could not ask for more in a few short years.

REFERENCES

1. Ambrosino, Salvatore. "A Family Agency Reaches Out to a Slum Ghetto," *Social Work*, Vol. 11, No. 4 (October 1966), pp. 17–23.
2. Bandura, Albert. *Principles of Behavior Modification*. New York: Holt, Rinehart & Winston, 1969.
3. Bell, Winifred. *Aid to Dependent Children*. New York: Columbia University Press, 1965.
4. Billingsley, Andrew. *Black Families in White America*. Englewood Cliffs, N.J.: Prentice-Hall, 1968.
5. Bounous, Ronald C. "A Study of Client and Worker Perceptions in the Initial Phase of Casework Marital Counseling." Unpublished doctoral dissertation, University of Minnesota School of Social Work, 1965.
6. Brandreth, Alice, and Pike, Ruth. "Assessment of Marriage Counseling in a Small Family Agency," *Social Work*, Vol. 12, No. 4 (October 1967), pp. 34–39.
7. Briar, Scott. "Family Services," in Henry S. Maas, ed., *Five Fields of Social Service: Reviews of Research*. New York: National Association of Social Workers, 1966. Pp. 9–50.
8. ———. "Why Children's Allowances?" *Social Work*, Vol. 14, No. 1 (January 1969), pp. 5–12.
9. Brown, Gordon E. *The Multi-Problem Dilemma*. Metuchen, N.J.: Scarecrow Press, 1968.
10. Burns, Eveline (ed.). *Children's Allowances and the Economic Welfare of Children*. New York: Citizens' Committee for Children, 1968.
11. Clement, Robert G. "Factors Associated with Continuance and Discontinuance in Cases Involving Problems in the Parent-Child Relationship." Unpublished doctoral dissertation, University of Chicago School of Social Service Administration, 1964.
12. Cloward, Richard A., and Epstein, Irwin. "Private Social Welfare's Disengagement from the Poor: The Case of Family Adjustment Agencies," in Mayer N. Zald, ed., *Social Welfare Institutions*. New York: John Wiley & Sons, 1965.
13. Cohen, Nathan E. *Social Work in the American Tradition*. New York: Dryden Press, 1958.
14. Comess, Leonard J., and O'Reilly, Patrick. "Private Practice Approach in a Family Service Agency," *Social Work*, Vol. 11, No. 2 (April 1966), pp. 78–83.
15. Cooke, Philip W. "A Study of Husband-Wife Behavior and Behavioral Change When Joint Interviewing is Employed as the Method of Therapy in Marriage Counseling." Unpublished doctoral dissertation, University of Pennsylvania School of Social Work, 1964.
16. Couch, Elsbeth H. *Joint and Family Interviews in the Treatment of Marital Problems*. New York: Family Service Association of America, 1969.

17. Coursey, Patricia, Leyendecker, Gertrude, and Siegle, Elsie. "A Socioeconomic Survey of Family Agency Clients," *Social Casework*, Vol. 46, No. 6 (June 1965), pp. 331–338.

18. David, Gerson. "The Relationship between Social Class and Length of Treatment of Families Served by a Family Service Agency." Unpublished doctoral dissertation. University of Pittsburgh Graduate School of Social Work, 1966.

19. Dillon, Vera. "Group Intake in a Casework Agency," *Social Casework*, Vol. 46, No. 1 (January 1965), pp. 26–30.

20. "Editorial Notes: More Services for the Aging," *Social Casework*, Vol. 50, No. 5 (May 1969), p. 295.

21. Ehrenkranz, Shirley. "A Study of Joint Interviewing in the Treatment of Marital Problems: Part I," *Social Casework*, Vol. 48, No. 8 (October 1967), pp. 498–502.

22. ———. "A Study of Joint Interviewing in the Treatment of Marital Problems: Part II," *Social Casework*, Vol. 48, No. 9 (November 1967), pp. 570–574.

23. *Family Unit Register*. St. Paul: Greater St. Paul United Fund and Council, undated.

24. Fowler, Irving A. "Family Agency Characteristics and Client Continuance," *Social Casework*, Vol. 48, No. 5 (May 1967), pp. 271–277.

25. Franks, Cyril M. (ed.). *Behavior Therapy: Appraisal and Status*. New York: McGraw-Hill Book Co., 1969.

26. Gabler, John, and Otto, Herbert A. "Conceptualization of Family Strengths in Family Life and Other Professional and Family Living," *Journal of Marriage and the Family*, Vol. 26, No. 2 (May 1964), pp. 221–222.

27. Ganter, Grace, and Polansky, Norman A. "Predicting A Child's Accessibility to Individual Treatment from Diagnostic Groups," *Social Work*, Vol. 9, No. 3 (July 1964), pp. 56–63.

28. Goldman, Milton. "An Agency Conducts a Time and Cost Study," *Social Casework*, Vol. 45, No. 7 (July 1964), pp. 393–397.

29. Herstein, Norman. "The Latest Dimension of Social Work Research," *Social Casework*, Vol. 50, No. 5 (May 1969), pp. 269–275.

30. Herzog, Elizabeth. "Is There A 'Breakdown' of the Negro Family?" *Social Work*, Vol. 11, No. 1 (January 1966), pp. 3–10.

31. ———, and Sudia, Cecelia E. "Fatherless Homes—A Review of Research," *Children*, Vol. 15, No. 5 (September-October 1968), pp. 177–182.

32. Hoffman, Mary Ellen. "An Agency Begins Service Under the Economic Opportunity Act," *Social Casework*, Vol. 46, No. 8 (October 1965), pp. 472–476.

33. Hollis, Florence. "The Coding and Application of a Typology of Casework Treatment," *Social Casework*, Vol. 48, No. 8 (October 1967), pp. 489–497.

34. Janowicz, Ruth. "Whom Should the Family Agency Serve?" *Social Casework*, Vol. 48, No. 2 (February 1967), pp. 85–94.

35. Katz, Myer. "Agreement on Connotative Meaning in Marriage," *Family Process*, Vol. 4, No. 1 (March 1965), pp. 64–74.

36. Kiler, Norine. "Half Hour Intake Interviews." Unpublished report, Family Service Agency of San Bernadino, Calif., 1966.

37. Kramer, Ralph. *Participation of the Poor*. Englewood Cliffs, N.J.: Prentice-Hall, 1969.

38. Krause, Merton. "Comparative Effects on Continuance of Four Experimental Intake Procedures," *Social Casework*, Vol. 47, No. 8 (October 1966), pp. 515–519.

39. Krill, Donald F. "Family Interviewing As an Intake Diagnostic Method," *Social Work*, Vol. 13, No. 2 (April 1968), pp. 56–63.

40. Langsley, Donald G., Pittman, Frank S., III, Machotka, Pavel, and Flomenhaft, Kalman. "Family Crisis Therapy—Results and Implications," *Family Process*, Vol. 7, No. 2 (September 1968), pp. 145–158.

41. Lawerence, Harry. "The Effectiveness of Group-Directed versus Worker-Directed Style of Leadership in Social Group Work." Unpublished doctoral dissertation, University of California School of Social Welfare, Berkeley, 1967.

42. Levin, Herman. "The Essential Voluntary Agency," *Social Work*, Vol. 11, No. 1 (January 1966), pp. 98–106.

43. Levinger, George. "Marital Cohesiveness and Dissolution: An Integrative Review," *Journal of Marriage and the Family*, Vol. 27, No. 1 (February 1965), pp. 19–28.

44. ———, and Breedlove, James. "Interpersonal Attraction and Agreement: A Study of Marriage Partners," *Journal of*

Personality and Social Psychology, Vol. 3, No. 4 (April 1966), pp. 367–372.

45. ———, and Senn, David J. "Disclosure of Feelings in Marriage," *Merrill-Palmer Quarterly*, Vol. 13, No. 3 (July 1967), pp. 237–249.

46. Levinson, Perry. "Attitudes Toward Dependency: A Study of 119 AFDC Mothers," *Welfare in Review*, Vol. 2, No. 9 (September 1964), pp. 17–18.

47. Lewis, Harold. "Etiology of Poor Housekeeping Among Low Income Public Housing Families," *Journal of Marriage and the Family*, Vol. 26, No. 2 (May 1964), pp. 224–225.

48. Liebow, Elliott. *Tally's Corner*. Boston: Little, Brown & Co., 1966.

49. Mabley, Albertina. "Group Application Interviews in a Family Agency," *Social Casework*, Vol. 47, No. 3 (March 1966), pp. 158–164.

50. MacDonald, Mary E. "Reunion at Vocational High: An Analysis of *Girls at Vocational High: An Experiment in Social Work Intervention*," *Social Service Review*, Vol. 40, No. 2 (June 1966), pp. 175–189.

51. Marris, Peter, and Rein, Martin. *Dilemmas of Social Reform*. New York: Atherton Press, 1967.

52. Mayer, John E., and Timms, Noel. "Working Class People's Reactions to Casework Treatment: A Preliminary Report." Talk given to Research Council, New York Chapter, National Association of Social Workers, May 1968.

53. Meyer, Henry J., Borgatta, Edgar F., and Jones, Wyatt C. *Girls at Vocational High: An Experiment in Social Work Intervention*. New York: Russell Sage Foundation, 1965.

54. Most, Elizabeth. "Measuring Change in Marital Satisfaction," *Social Work*, Vol. 9, No. 3 (July 1964), pp. 64–70.

55. Moynihan, Daniel P. *The Negro Family: The Case for National Action*. Washington, D.C.: Department of Labor, Office of Planning & Research, March 1965.

56. Overton, Alice, and Tinker, Katherine H. *Casework Notebook*. St. Paul: Greater St. Paul United Fund and Council, 1959.

57. Pattison, E. Mansell, Courias, Peter G., and Mullin, Dee. "Diagnostic Therapeutic Intake Groups for Wives of Alcoholics," *Quarterly Journal of Studies on Alcohol*, Vol. 26, No. 4 (December 1965), pp. 605–616.

58. Podell, Lawrence. "Families on Welfare in New York City." Seven-part report. New York: Center for Social Research,

Graduate Center, City University of New York, 1967 and 1968. (Mimeographed.)

59. Rainwater, Lee. "Crucible of Identity," *Daedalus*, Vol. 95, No. 1 (Winter 1966), pp. 172–216.

60. ———, and Yancey, William L. *The Moynihan Report and the Politics of Controversy*. Cambridge, Mass.: MIT Press, 1967.

61. Reid, William J. "Client and Practitioner Variables Affecting Treatment," *Social Casework*, Vol. 45, No. 10 (December 1964), pp. 586–592.

62. ———, and Shyne, Ann W. *Brief and Extended Casework*. New York: Columbia University Press, 1969.

63. Rosenblatt, Aaron. "Attendance and Attitude Change: A Study of 301 Project ENABLE Groups." New York: Family Service Association of America, April 1968. (Mimeographed.)

64. ———. "The Practitioner's Use and Evaluation of Research," *Social Work*, Vol. 13, No. 1 (January 1968), pp. 53–59.

65. ———, and Mayer, John E. "Client Disengagement and Alternative Treatment Resources," *Social Casework*, Vol. 47, No. 1 (January 1966), pp. 3–12.

66. Satir, Virginia. *Conjoint Family Therapy*. Palo Alto, Calif.: Science and Behavior Books, 1964.

67. Schorr, Alvin. "Mirror, Mirror on the Wall . . .," *Social Work*, Vol. 10, No. 3 (July 1965), pp. 112–113.

68. ———. *Poor Kids*. New York: Basic Books, 1966.

69. Schreiber, Leona E. "Evaluation of Family Group Treatment in a Family Agency," *Family Process*, Vol. 5, No. 1 (March 1966), pp. 21–29.

70. Seaberg, James R. "Case Recording By Code," *Social Work*, Vol. 10, No. 4 (October 1965), pp. 92–98.

71. Siegel, Natalie. "A Follow-up Study of Family Clients: An Example of Practitioner-Director Research," *Social Casework*, Vol. 46, No. 6 (June 1965), pp. 345–350.

72. Siff, Hilda. "Services to Families Being Evicted From Public Low-Rent Housing," *Welfare in Review*, Vol. 2, No. 10 (October 1964), pp. 25–26.

73. Simmons, Robert E. "The Brief Interview as a Means of Increasing Service," *Social Casework*, Vol. 48, No. 7 (July 1967), pp. 429–432.

74. Siporin, Max. "Bankrupt Debtors and Their Families," *Social Work*, Vol. 12, No. 3 (July 1967), pp. 51–62.

75. Smith, Neilson F. "A National Experi-

ment in Staff Development," *Social Casework*, Vol. 48, No. 9 (November 1967), pp. 556–562.

76. Stein, Irma. "The Impact of the Western Addition Project on the Counseling Department of the Family Service Agency of San Francisco." Unpublished report, Family Service Agency of San Francisco, 1968.

77. Stone, Robert C., and Schlamp, Frederic T. "Characteristics Associated with Receipt or Nonreceipt of Financial Aid from Welfare Agencies," *Welfare in Review*, Vol. 3, No. 7 (July 1965), pp. 1–11.

78. Thomas, Edwin J. (ed.). *The Socio-Behavioral Approach and Applications to Social Work*. New York: Council on Social Work Education, 1967.

79. Tinker, Katherine H. "Casework with Hard-to-Reach Families," *American Journal of Orthopsychiatry*, Vol. 29, No. 1 (January 1959), pp. 165–171.

80. ———. *Patterns of Family-Centered Treatment: A Descriptive Study of 30 FCP Closed Cases*. St. Paul: Greater St. Paul United Fund and Council, 1959.

81. Turner, Francis J. "A Comparison of Procedures in the Treatment of Clients with Two Different Value Orientations," *Social Casework*, Vol. 45, No. 5 (May 1964), pp. 273–277.

82. Warren, Effie. "Study of Short Term Cases." Cleveland: Family Service Association of Cleveland, October 1963. (Mimeographed.)

83. Wildavsky, Aaron. "Rescuing Policy Analysis from PPBS," in *The Analysis and Evaluation of Public Expenditures: The PPB System*, Vol. 3. Washington, D.C.: Joint Economic Committee, Congress of the United States, 1969. Pp. 835–864.

84. Young, Mary Louise. "Marital Counseling with Affection Deprived Spouses," *Social Casework*, Vol. 47, No. 9 (November 1966), pp. 571–574.

NEIGHBORHOOD CENTERS AND GROUP WORK

By WILLIAM SCHWARTZ

In the writer's previous review of research in the neighborhood center field, written for the first volume of this series (199), some problems in defining the field were identified and note was made that

group work is practiced not in a unified field of service but in a loose assortment of agencies with diverse traditions and purposes . . . an array of different objectives and client groups, as well as a wide gamut of commitments ranging over the fields of education, recreation, social service, psychotherapy, and social reform. [199, p. 144]

The writer noted further that the global character of agency objectives, the agencies' view of themselves as both social movement and social service, their emphasis on ends without a corresponding curiosity about means, all served to inhibit both the pursuit of research and the use of research from other fields. The effort to assess the relevance of scientific work from other disciplines was in itself a formidable task:

When agency purposes are so all embracing and ill defined, when the client group is almost unlimited, and when the "client" concept itself includes not only the people but the vehicles in which they move together (the family, the group, the neighborhood), the relevant scientific data are encyclopedic. [199, p. 145].

At the same time it was pointed out that these agencies—the *building-centered* "Y"s, settlements, Jewish centers, and boys' clubs and the *program-centered* Scouts, Campfire Girls, B'nai B'rith Youth Organization, and others—are built into the American urban scene and emerged historically from the same impulses that created the social welfare field and the social work profession (196).

As such, they have a potential as yet only barely realized for affecting deeply the scope and quality of the social welfare performance where it is most needed. Much will depend on the extent to which these agencies can follow both the field and the profession into a closer working relationship with science and research. [199, pp. 144–145]

At this time, some six years later, both the pattern and the promise remain essentially the same, although there are some signs of movement in certain quarters. The field of service is still vaguely defined and the agencies have characteristically taken on even more functions without first clarifying those they already had. The volume of research is still thin, the production sporadic, and the study themes unconnected and atheoretical. On the other hand there is evidence of a growing "official curiosity" about questions emerging from agency practice; some sectors report what seem to be serious attempts to institutionalize research rather than leaving it to occasional bursts of individual effort. In addition several of the young practitioners now moving into doctoral work have taken with them their interest in direct practice and have begun to produce published accounts of their dissertation research in this area. Finally, some long-standing work in which the neighborhood centers have been much involved—notably the street club projects of the past two decades—have recently matured and produced some significant scientific findings. These trends should become clear as the specific studies are reviewed in the pages that follow.

The decision to extend this review's scope from neighborhood centers (the sole subject of the earlier chapter) to group work—from the traditional agencies to other settings for social work practice with groups—stems partly from the fact that six years is a short follow-up period and this provided an opportunity to use a broader compass that would help to enlarge and enrich the material under review. Actually, the writer had laid the basis for this approach in the earlier chapter, in which much of the classical small group research that has affected group work thought and practice both in the neighborhood centers and elsewhere was included. In this spirit, the writer has again tried to catch up some

of the more relevant studies made by other fields and disciplines interested in the dynamics of small group behavior.

An Overview

Our search for studies—helped by students and other friends—took us through the 1964–69 issues of 125 periodicals in the fields of social work, education, recreation, psychology, psychiatry, rehabilitation, public welfare, and crime and delinquency, among others. In addition, we examined national agency house organs, recent research anthologies, and mimeographed accounts of work as yet unpublished. The yield, as indicated, was not large and yet there was no intent to report it all. Rather, we have tried to develop a sense of what has been happening since the earlier review and to highlight the major trends and research directions of the past few years. In making the choice of work to report we may have missed some studies that should in fairness have been included, and to these researchers we apologize. Certainly, in the use of mimeographed accounts of work in progress we will inevitably reflect a bias in favor of work being done close to home and miss a great deal of what is going on elsewhere. Selected student research has been used without any systematic review of this work throughout the country being attempted. Throughout, the choice of studies has been guided as before by Zimbalist's definition of social work research as any effort to collect and analyze data in a planned attempt to answer questions and test hypotheses arising out of the planning and practice of relevant agencies (255, p. 12).

While research reviews are still scarce, reviews of the literature have been appearing in greater number. The "state-of-our-knowledge" articles have been especially helpful in assessing the quality of scholarship in the field and calling attention to the areas that need more light. Silverman (208), for example, examined all the group work articles published between 1956 and 1964 in *Social Work, Social Service Review,* and *Social Welfare Forum;* his attempt was "to identify some of the strengths and weaknesses in the literature and consequently suggest fruitful areas of inquiry for the future" (208, p. 56). To do this he sorted his material into two major categories—the kinds of knowledge with which the authors were concerned and the professional sources from which they drew their references. He found a high proportion of the content to be descriptive of specific programs and service settings, rather than technical and practice oriented. And he found too that his authors drew little from the scientific journals in sociology, social psychology, and other social science disciplines.

In a similar analysis of the broader field of social work knowledge, Taber and Shapiro (223) used a one-issue-a-year sample from *Social Work, Social Casework,* and *Social Service Review* and examined 124 articles covering about fifty years of the periodical literature. Their conclusions for the field as a whole were both similar to and somewhat more encouraging than those reached by Silverman for the group work sector. Their findings are as follows:

The increasing interest of the field in reliable knowledge is indicated by the findings. While reports of practice experience accounted for over half the empirical material, the reports became more generalized and less personal in recent years. Evidence of borrowing knowledge from other fields was found in the use of recognized authorities, concepts, and theories for exposition or interpretation . . . . On the other hand, the findings could not be interpreted as showing progression toward "relatively well-confirmed theory." The theory and concepts found were used for exposition and there were no attempts to revise concepts or to develop and add to theory in a systematic way. Research reports were few and were not related to each other or to a common frame of reference. [223, p. 106]

Arkava's (5) examination of the relationship between social work knowledge and practice traced the history of the effort to

organize social work knowledge. He described "the three faces of social work" as its "art form face," "empirical technology face," and "scientific face," pointing out that the field must move toward closer connections among practice, values, and knowledge, rather than trying simply to extrapolate knowledge directly from its practice experience.

Other works provided useful references and research collections. Rostov's review of the literature on group work in the psychiatric hospital (185) classified articles by their emphasis on background information, goals, functions, relationship to other services, relationship to social service, and implications for practice. She noted, as Silverman did later, that she found little cross-referencing among authorities:

Although much has been written on the subject of group work in the psychiatric hospital, there is a notable scarcity of references by one writer to others. Each writer describing a program tends to write as if his is the first and only one of its kind that has been tried. [185, p. 29]

And she pointed out, also as would Silverman, that the work was essentially descriptive rather than theoretical, and that little attention was paid to the technical problems of practice.

Walton's (244) review of research on the community power structure was an interesting attempt to find generalizations about the methodological and substantive correlates of different power arrangements. There were other useful reviews that will be mentioned as their area of investigation comes under consideration in the pages that follow.

Several research collections have gathered studies together around themes of importance to social workers in general and group workers in particular. The memorial volume published by the National Association of Jewish Center Workers after the untimely death of Irving Canter (25, 26) was both a fine tribute to the moving spirit in the development of research on the Jewish community centers and an important addition to the literature on that subject. Thomas's *Behavioral Science for Social Workers* (226) and Zald's reader in social welfare institutions (254) were also valuable resources. The January 1965 issue of *Journal of Social Issues* combined a number of articles in pursuit of

three interrelated purposes: to encourage comparative studies of the new emerging poverty intervention bureaucracies; to contribute to the elaboration of the strategic variables in the system of poverty; and to make our organizational efforts in the "war on poverty" increasingly congruent with our enlarging understanding of such organizations and their focus of effort, improving the lot of the poor. [113, pp. 1, 2]

The United States government continues to publish bibliographies and reviews on current social themes important to social workers in the neighborhood setting. Several recent publications were especially thorough and informative. From the U.S. Public Health Service came four annotated bibliographies on training methodology (234, 235, 236, 237), two on in-service training for key professionals in community mental health (230, 231), a publications catalog on community health services (232), and a comprehensive bibliography on human deprivation (233), embedded in an exhaustive summary of the issues, review of research, and account of the literature from biological, psychological, and sociological perspectives. From the U.S. Children's Bureau, the annual *Research Relating to Children* is an inventory of work in progress (229). The Department of Agriculture has provided a well-selected bibliography on the literature on the poor (142). And, in another sphere of interest, the Department of the Interior issues an annual "reference catalog" of research in progress in the field of outdoor recreation (159).

Other reports of research in progress were obtained from agency associations such as the Community Council of Greater New York (41), the National Federation of Settlements and Neighborhood Centers (178), the Center for Community Research of the Associated YM-YWHAs of Greater New York (34), the National Council of the YMCAs (9), Boy Scouts of America (14), and others. Attention should also be called to a new quarterly journal first issued in the winter of 1969: the *Journal of Leisure Research*, published by the National Recreation and Park Association, 1700 Pennsylvania Avenue, N.W., Washington, D.C.

Finally, researchers will be grateful for Casper's ingenious new *KWIC (Key-Word-In-Context) Index* (32, 33) of journal articles relevant to group work practice. Two volumes have now appeared, encompassing the years 1965 through 1968, and those who take the trouble to master the device itself will find it a valuable tool for digging out specific issues and themes from the group work literature.

Studies will be presented here in much the same order as in the last review and under the same rubrics whenever possible, so that the reader may follow more easily the unfolding of the various research themes over the years and make comparisons between old and new trends. The major headings will be as before: (1) the client and his problems, (2) the agency as an institution of service, (3) neighborhood and community problems affecting service, (4) the worker and social work practice with groups, and (5) evaluations and outcomes.

The Client

Like most institutions in these times, the neighborhood centers have been drawn into deeper involvement with the social problems that surround them. In the process the centers have continued to grow more and more related to the social welfare enterprise, and as they do the client concept takes increasing primacy over that of the member (199, p. 146). This may explain why the flood of "market research"—stressing dropout rates, membership analyses, activity "buying habits," and other "consumer" approaches—has diminished to a trickle. Correspondingly there is a larger output of research on special problems and populations that need attention. No doubt the spur of antipoverty financing over the past decade has jogged this development, and it remains to be seen whether the more recent drying up of many of these federal sources will result in a retreat to the more traditional preoccupations.

Participation

The question of "Who participates?" seems to have been relegated to a subordinate role; it appears as part of other studies, but it drew relatively little attention compared to the intense interest shown earlier. Something has been lost in this, since study of participation has often reflected the connections between agency service and the social scene.

The Yankelovich survey commissioned by the National Executive Board of the Boy Scouts of America asked, "Is Scouting in Tune with the Times?" and found that "while Scouting is highly regarded as part of the American scene, it has some serious problems in attracting and holding today's youth" (109, p. 2). The problems cited are interesting, for they apply to the wide range of youth-serving agencies. In discussing their discovery that the program "fit" becomes less close as the boys grow older, the researchers note: "As boys mature Scouting does not point the way toward contemporary American adulthood; it points the other way toward childhood" (109, p. 2). Nearly a quarter of all boys between the ages of 8 and 18 are now members of the Boy Scouts of America, but an additional 25 percent have expressed a liking for the program while either dropping out or failing to join at all. The inhibiting factors are given by respondents as overorganization, irrelevant programming, inaccessibility in poor and nonwhite neighborhoods, leadership insensitivity, and interest

in coeducational activities. The responses reflected the difficulties of most of the group- and youth-serving agencies and in particular their failure to offer services perceived as exciting by older adolescents and young adults.

Simon's analysis of the girl-boy imbalance in the B'nai B'rith Youth Organization (209) begins with a concern about the constant membership figure of Aleph Zadek Aleph boys as against the rising entry rate of B'nai B'rith girls; he proceeds to examine the BBYO and adult B'nai B'rith statistics and concludes:

The higher the concentration of Jews in a given area, the lower the percentage of affiliated Jewish males in the area as compared to Jewish females and this is true of adults as well as adolescents but more true of adolescents. [209, p. 6]

Simon notes also that "males tend to be users of facilities while females become users of services" (209, p. 8) and speculates further about inhibiting factors that may keep adolescents from using service and may be especially deterrent to males: overorganization, the stress on "Jewish" programming, the agency's apparent disinterest in open approaches to the problems of dating and sex, and the boys' interest in smaller groups, among others. As with the Scouts and the "Y"s, there is the recurring idea that the age of single-sex agencies may be over:

Perhaps we ought to conclude that the time has come for the B'nai B'rith Youth Organization to merge its programs on the adolescent as we did on the Young Adult level and not to be concerned with separate or different programs for boys and girls. [209, p. 15]

Essentially these are recruitment studies out of which the field often derives valuable insights about client needs and patterns of agency use. In another tradition are the sociological researches that come from outside the field of practice and serve the agencies by illuminating social participation phenomena at work in the general community. In this category are Pope's study of the relationship between social participation and economic deprivation (168) and Kraus's research on black participation in public recreation and the administrative practices that affect such participation (119). Pope studied high-seniority white workers in a single factory, obtaining work histories that provided data about the number and duration of unemployment and layoff periods and relating these to participation in voluntary associations and attendance at union meetings and church services. Middle-aged (45–54) and blue-collar workers were overrepresented in the high-deprivation group, and Pope found that participation in formal associations was indeed negatively related to cumulative economic deprivation. Interestingly, the better educated, younger, and higher income workers showed the strongest inverse relationship between economic deprivation and participation in voluntary associations.

Kraus, working under the sponsorship of New York's Center for Urban Education, gathered data from supervisors and directors of recreation in the park and recreation departments of the five boroughs of New York City, as well as from park and recreation administrators in twenty-four suburban communities in New York, New Jersey, and Connecticut. Using structured interviews, analysis of printed brochures and reports, ethnic maps, meetings with specialists, and direct observation of programs and facilities, Kraus developed information on black participation patterns, administrative problems and practices, the relationship between public recreation programs and other community activities in the areas of antipoverty, civil rights, and school desegregation, and the extent of employment of blacks as leaders, supervisors, and administrators in public recreation. The region under study includes some 13.5 million people, of whom 2.5 million are between the ages of 5 and 19. Kraus chose for his study suburban communities with a population of more than 10,000, with public recreation departments operating under full-time year-round leadership, and with nonwhite populations of at least 7 percent.

In his background chapter Kraus traced the growth of public recreation in the United States, citing the expansion of public funds devoted to such programs (from $262 million in 1948 to $894 million in 1960) and the proliferation of public agencies concerned with providing recreational facilities and services (over 3,000 throughout the country by 1966). He also reviewed the history of discrimination in both private and public recreation, giving instances of segregated patterns of service in "Y"s, settlements, Scouts, and neighborhood centers: "Thus we find, in the North as well as in the South, a conscious pattern of separation between the races, both in public and private recreation programs" (119, p. 13). He then proceeded to describe the progress of civil rights in the field of recreation and the efforts to desegregate facilities in northern cities, pointing out that "the relationship between racial disturbance and inadequate recreation facilities is only one aspect of the broad problem of recreational opportunity for Negroes" (119, p. 19).

Kraus's findings covered a wide range of concerns. On *patterns of participation* in activities he found "a striking contrast between the reported recreational involvements of Negro and white participants" (119, p. 31), with blacks tending to dominate in track and field, swimming, basketball, and boxing and to participate less in tennis, golf, archery, and bocce, "which are of an individual or dual nature and which have certain social-class connotations" (119, p. 31). Blacks were lightly represented in programs designed for physically handicapped, blind, and retarded children, with involvement well below their estimated proportion of the population. In the case of outdoor activity, blacks made widespread use of inexpensive and unstructured programs and participated little in the more costly pursuits. Kraus concluded:

Both in terms of the kinds of choices they make and the overall percentages of their participation, it therefore may be said of Negroes as a group that their pattern of recreational involvement differs widely from the white-community population. [119, p. 32]

On *participation by age groups* he found "a striking shift of interest and involvement according to age levels" (119, p. 32), with extremely high participation by those under 12, especially in the neighborhood playgrounds, high teen-age activity in most programs (except for the suburbs), and declining participation by black adults and older people. On *integration within programs,* although

recreation is regarded within the professional literature, and in programs of professional training, as a means of achieving racial or ethnic integration in community life [the] findings of this study indicate . . . that these claims are generally not realized. [119, p. 32]

Team segregation follows neighborhood patterns, especially among teen-agers and adults, and "the entire field of athletic competition, as reported by many directors, is characterized by increasing racial antagonism and examples of conflict . . ."(119, p. 33).

Regarding *administrative problems related to race,* Kraus's respondents perceived the situation in different ways: the directors in suburban communities tended to blame black youths for their "aggressive behavior" and "racial antagonism"; city administrators, on the other hand, tended to ascribe their problems to the fact that white residents often withdrew from programs in which blacks became involved. In both settings the administrators, invariably white, found themselves working with heavily segregated programs, predominantly black, especially in the evening centers.

On *equality of opportunity* all the directors emphasized de jure accessibility of all facilities and resources, while offering many instances of de facto exclusion, tension, and white resistance. Facilities in and near black neighborhoods were asserted to be equal in quality, but closer examination

disclosed that these were usually of the most basic type, while the more attractive and diversified facilities were located at a distance from the older town center where the black population resided. Recreation directors reported that black residents tended to be less persistent in making demands for improved resources, but offered instances in which antipoverty groups had in fact mobilized such pressure in black neighborhoods.

Serious criticism of these antipoverty agencies emerged in Kraus's examination of the *relationship with other community agencies;* directors often scored them as "troublemakers" and charged that they represented unnecessary competition for both staff members and the children to be served. Contacts between the public recreation agencies and neighborhood groups representing blacks were found to be "superficial" except for the widespread hiring of Neighborhood Youth Corps trainees financed by the Office of Economic Opportunity. Kraus also found, interestingly for these times, that recreation directors often felt it "improper" to make special efforts to attract specific ethnic and racial groups in the community. "Most indicated that they publicized their programs with all groups, and anyone who attended was welcome"(119, p. 35).

On the *employment of Negroes* Kraus reported, not unexpectedly, that blacks are substantially represented, that they are employed at the lower levels of pay and responsibility, and that most directors said they would like to change this but that "it was difficult to locate qualified personnel with the proper academic background" (119, p. 35).

And finally, on *recreation and school desegregation,* recreation directors reported:

The present practice is to bus Negro children back to their home neighborhoods almost immediately at the close of the school day . . . rather than permit them to remain for extracurricular or other organized recreation activities. This procedure suggests that desegregation efforts have been seen narrowly in terms of academic involvement, rather than in terms of achieving the broader benefits of social integration as well. [119, p. 35]

Kraus concludes with a quotation from a director:

It seems to me that 80 per cent of our program problems are related to this matter of race relations—one way or another. Yet, most of us treat it about on the level of deciding what refrigerating unit to buy for an artificial ice rink. [119, p. 36]

Needs and Interests

When the neighborhood centers undertake to study membership needs and interests, they generally reserve their greatest curiosity for the adolescent population. Teenagers are not only their most complex and ambivalent consumers, they have also historically carried the major burden of the agencies' educative and character-building aspirations. Thus studies of adolescents' program preferences, attitudes toward the agency, and other perceptions abound. There is, however, some recent evidence that the work is moving to a higher level of sophistication, focusing less on "market research" and more on a scientific interest in the discovery of psychological and social need.

Levin's (127) scholarly review of research on adolescents and its implications for practice is one such sign; coming from a top administrator of the Chicago Jewish Community Centers, one of the largest neighborhood center complexes in the country, it speaks well for the emergence of an official curiosity about scientific and technical questions related to service. Levin examines the research on adolescent psychology, the subcultural and contracultural perspectives, generational differences in the Jewish family, value similarities and contrasts within the family, the development of sexual activity, problems of Jewish identity within the larger culture, and other factors. In his discussion of findings the emphasis on service is clear—in his call for

the recording of practice; for the need to respond to adolescents' "urge to find their own identity, their own goals, their own means" (127, p. 30); and for more research and pooling of information among the centers.

The Jewish centers have in fact produced a number of studies of adolescents over the past five years; Carp (31) compiled a list of such research carried on between 1962 and 1966. An evaluation by Deutschberger (44) of four such studies conducted in Savannah, Georgia (39), Youngstown, Ohio (114), Wilkes-Barre, Pennsylvania (84), and Montreal, Canada (65), raised some basic questions about the applicability of findings and the relationship between local studies and the development of a usable picture of "the present realities of American Jewish teenage life" (44, p. 23). These and similar studies initiated in Pittsburgh (250), New Orleans (220), and New York (30) vary in the range of their interest, from a broad concern with psychosocial problems in the current American scene to a narrower focus on the patterns of Jewish identification and belongingness. In a later section of this chapter a closer look will be taken at some of these studies in the context of group identification.

In the broader field of adolescent study, Bachman and his associates at the Survey Research Center of the Institute for Social Research in Ann Arbor, Michigan, have issued the first volume of their report on a longitudinal study of high school boys, launched under the sponsorship of the United States Office of Education in June 1965 (8). In this first volume they provide an overview of the purpose and design of the research, its relationship to other nationwide youth studies, the conceptual framework, measurement procedures, analytical strategies, and the "major substantive interests to be explored in the study, including the study of schools as organizations" (8, p. iv).

Schwartz and Merten (195), in an "anthropological approach to the youth culture," held that contrary to the model of the youth culture as a contra-culture . . . its reality as a subculture does not rest on its power to repudiate or undermine basic adult values. We shall argue that peer-group interaction is guided by expectations which do not govern the behavior of other members of the community. [195, p. 453]

They made their initial contacts through a youth survey agency and established subsequent relationships by tracing friendship networks. Data were obtained from field observation of peer groups in their natural environments and from intensive interviews with selected informants. The researchers found that "adolescent conceptions of the validity of adult goals and values are . . . largely independent of the standards they use to estimate the relative excellence of their peers" (195, p. 459). The adolescents' judgments of personal worth were closely linked to standards of masculinity and femininity. The adolescents described two different life-styles, labeling them "hoody" and "socie" (the researchers perceived a third, residual "conventional" style), and within the two major styles they drew vertical status positions related to how well the individual lives up to the group's standards. The authors concluded:

We do not hold that the youth subculture is a closed normative system. The normative integrity, coherence and identity of a subculture is not always based upon estrangement from the larger culture nor does it always reside in social organizations which resist integration into larger society. . . . We suggest that the core of the youth culture resides in its distinctive evaluative standards. They endow the adolescent status terminology with qualities and attributes which do not dominate adult status judgments. . . . Finally, our approach emphasizes the element of free cultural play in the genesis of the youth culture. . . . [There are ways in which] the meanings inherent in the adolescent normative order transcend the requirements of simple adjustment to the exigencies of life. [195, p. 468]

Finally, those interested in the literature on the urban adolescent will find a valuable resource in Gottlieb and Reeves's annotated bibliography and discussion of the literature (75). Their work is divided

into sections that include the adolescent as consumer, his social institutions, his peers, his preparation for adulthood, "the world in which he lives," and the subject of deviant behavior. They have also included a section on the adolescent subculture, an area of study to which the neighborhood centers may yet make an important contribution from their practice. Taken as a whole, in fact, the research on adolescent needs and behaviors—including the street club studies to be discussed later—is reaching a point at which it will no longer be possible to plead lack of evidence as a reason for operating purely from practice wisdom.

Interest in the preadolescent child produced the next largest volume of research, and several of the national program agencies have been active in this area. Withey and Smith (249) reported a study supported by the National Council of the Boy Scouts of America as part of an extensive study of children carried out by the Survey Research Center of the Institute for Social Research at the University of Michigan. This long-term series of youth studies has included a national survey of 14–16-year-old boys, two national studies of girls, and a national study of boys aged 11–13 (199, pp. 146–149).

In this study Withey and Smith sought

to describe as fully as possible the needs, problems, interests, activities and preferences of boys at the age level that Cub Scouting hopes to serve. The picture should be as broadly descriptive as possible, and it should be useful to any group that is interested in this age level. [249, p. 2]

The families chosen were from a national cross-section of those with a boy aged 8–10 in grades two through six of public, private, or parochial schools; it was estimated that this grade and school dimension included 98 percent of boys in this age range. The respondents were selected through a process of multistage probability sampling that developed a total national sample of about 1,000 families—500 in which only the mother was interviewed and 500 in which boys and fathers were also engaged. Focus of the study was on the mother as the major source of information about the children.

Responses to the elaborate questionnaire constituted a detailed account of family characteristics, leisure-time activities, attitudes toward competitive activity, participation in sports and athletics, characteristics favored by parents, their estimates of how they influence their children, their estimates of the age at which children's values are formed, the boys' organizational involvements, and similar data. An attempt was also made to develop categories encompassing the dimensions of rural-urban, urban-suburban, race, religion, and social class.

The chapter accounts follow the thread of the interview, and there is a mass of information too detailed to be summarized here; the report itself makes no effort to develop overall patterns or conclusions. However, the findings themselves are thought provoking, reaching as they do for a wide range of opinions and attitudes and searching for class and racial differences on issues such as parental aspirations, mother-father comparisons, organizational behavior of both parents and boys, and many other significant areas. While many of these questions emerge from the organizational, recruitment-oriented interest of a membership agency, there is evidence here of how such a vested interest can mobilize the resources and technical expertise necessary to generate data of general practice interest.

The Boys' Clubs of America reported on a study (157) of 7–10-year-old members, describing the third and final phase of their National Needs and Interests Study begun in 1958. Here data were derived from the observation of members engaged in activities at four selected Boys' Clubs, chosen to represent a large metropolitan area, a large industrial city, a small industrial city, and a suburban area. One hundred and sixty boys, 40 from each club, were thus observed by student workers especially trained to record activity and interaction among boys and their leaders. The analysis yielded data in five categories —descriptive information, boys' activities in the clubs, boys' likes and dislikes, evaluation of boys' attributes, and boy-leader relationships.

Again the findings are too far ranging to be summarized here, but although the agency pointed out that the sample was not to be considered representative, some of the findings have relevance for those interested in the work of neighborhood centers. It was found, for example, that a large percentage of the boys (86 percent) came from intact families, and that almost half joined before they were 7 years old. With regard to activities, it was shown that the point of entry—first and second choices of activity—was the low-organized games focusing on physical forms of play. The largest number of boys played in groups throughout their four choices of activity, and group play was more likely to be engaged in by the older boys. The highest percentage of boys were judged to be "cooperative," and "very little spontaneity or frustration was observed. Only 3% were said to exhibit any signs of leadership" (157, p. 33). In assessing the quality of "leaders' contact with boy," the highest percentage of contacts (17 percent) was "to reprimand," the next highest (16 percent) was "to instruct," and the next (10 percent) was "regarding behavior to other boys." At the bottom of the scale was "friendly gesture" (4 percent).

A valuable contribution to the study of latency-age boys was made by Hess (90), who, under the auspice of the Boy Scouts of America, contributed a comprehensive review of research and theory on this age group. His review

recognizes the lack of interest of personality theorists in the 7–10 period, but emphasizes the importance of these years as a time for developing social behavior and orientation toward school and work. It is also a time when a wide range of basic attitudes are laid down. [90, p. 3]

The survey is divided into chapters covering an overview, psychosocial issues in
development, "models and masculinity,"
values and attitudes, interests and leisure,
gangs, groups and social interaction, an
annotated bibliography, and a general bibliography of 142 items. This is yet another instance of what emerges as the
membership agencies turn to scientific
methodology in an effort to instruct themselves about the lives and needs of their
members.

With regard to the older groups, almost
no systematic study of needs and interests
could be found since the several researches
on young adults reported in the earlier
review (199, p. 149). This applied not
only to the neighborhood centers and program agencies, but to the published group
work literature, which is still mostly descriptive in its accounts of the work in this
area.

Special Problems and Populations

The search of the literature turned up considerable evidence that the neighborhood
centers are increasingly taking on special
populations for service. Much of the work
has not yet produced research; the accounts
are enthusiastic but unsystematic and the
"findings" are generally unsupported by
data. Nevertheless some results have begun to accrue: the older work—especially
the study of street club youths—is beginning to yield a body of tested knowledge,
and there are enough reports of study in
the newer areas so that findings can be
submitted in a few categories beyond those
used in the last review.

Identification and belongingness.
The social work research on group identification and ethnic self-awareness has remained largely a monopoly of the Jewish
agencies. Despite the burgeoning of group
consciousness among blacks, Puerto Ricans,
and other minority groups throughout the
country, neighborhood center research has

not yet focused on them. The situation
remains much as it was when the writer
noted in the earlier review that

interest in the problems of minority group
members vis-à-vis the larger culture is, of
course, not restricted to the Jewish agencies;
settlement and other neighborhood workers
are continually concerned with these problems. . . . However, no evidence of any
systematic study of these issues in these settings could be found. [199, p. 151]

Jewish center research on these questions
varies from community to community, but
there is a fairly common thread running
through the investigations. A central
theme has been the development of indexes
designed to measure the degree of Jewish
group identification. Population samples are
then compared (members and nonmembers,
participants and nonparticipants, males and
females, parents and children, members and
professionals), and implications are drawn
for agency program and practice. Lazerwitz (123), describing a study conducted
at the Jewish Community Centers of Metropolitan Chicago, identified ten indexes of
Jewish identification: (1) religious behavior, (2) pietism—involving "those religious
items which are at a more intensive level
than the standard ones," (3) Jewish education, (4) attitudes toward and involvement
with the state of Israel, (5) Jewish organizational activity, (6) degree of acceptance
of traditional religious beliefs, (7) concentration of friendship and courtship behavior among Jews, (8) intention to provide one's children with a Jewish education,
(9) the "Jewishness" of one's childhood
home, and (10) the overall index—"a composite of the nine specific indices" (123,
p. 19). Respondents were grouped into four
categories—dues-payers (*members, N =*
102), nonmembers who attended in the past
year (*attending nonmembers, N = 134*),
previous members who did not attend in
the past year (*past members, N = 68*), and
those who had never joined and did not
attend during the past year (*nonattending–
never members, N = 210*).

Combining the Index of Activity with
the Index of Jewish Identification, it was

found that members had the largest high-level percentages in nine of the ten measures. Similarly the attending nonmembers provided the largest medium-level percentages in nine of the ten measures. Lowest in identification were those in the past members category, and, interestingly, it was found that the nonattending–never members, while distinctly below the top-identification group, were nevertheless second in the ranking. It was concluded from these figures that "it is most likely that Chicago JCCs attract more identified Jews and then proceed to strengthen their already strong identifications" and further "the often repeated statement that JCC members are like other Jews or are less active in the religious realm is false" (123, p. 38). Amid a considerable amount of other data, the study also produced some interesting comparisons of center members and their workers, on which the author comments as follows:

On one hand, JCC members are somewhat more religiously oriented and far more traditional in Jewish outlook than past and present Center professionals. On the other hand, the group workers are the more inclined to express their Jewishness through Zionism and their children's Jewish education. Do we find here some insight into possible sources of misunderstanding between Center group workers, members, and the remainder of the Jewish community? Does the membership of JCCs view with alarm their iconoclastic group workers while these professionals regard the members as unthinking, backward-looking Jews? [123, p. 24]

The studies of Jewish adolescents previously mentioned were fairly uniform in their general line of inquiry, their access to large samples of their universe, and the consistent picture they produced of Jewish middle-class adolescents and their connections with the issues of Jewish belongingness and group survival. Hefter (84) described a Jewish center study in Wilkes-Barre, Pennsylvania, in which the adolescents expressed security with non-Jews, a high degree of outgroup dating, and a "liberal approach" to Jewish belief and custom, while at the same time showing belief in God, curiosity about Judaism, a rejection of intermarriage, and a friendship pattern in which their closest relationships were limited to Jews. The conclusion was as follows:

There were no trends to a wholesale abandonment of their Jewishness . . . [but] a dilution of the specific elements of traditional Judaism . . . which could in time weaken their sense of Jewish identification. [84, p. 68]

In Pittsburgh Yaillen (250) used procedures similar to those of the Wilkes-Barre survey and found that the responses given by the Pittsburgh adolescents were "strikingly similar" to those revealed by the Wilkes-Barre effort. There was an important difference bearing on parental attitudes, and Yaillen felt that this might reflect community size: "The worry parents have in smaller communities about Jewish values produces behavior towards these values which the parents in a larger community take for granted or disregard" (250, p. 7). In addition Yaillen's inquiry into the youngsters' use of the agency yielded

a virtual tie between a desire for recreation and individual development, when first and second choices are added up. In fact . . . it is rather obvious that these teens are asking for help in growing up as individuals. [250, p. 7]

A study in New Orleans (220) found that the adolescents' own definition of "good Jew" emphasized most strongly their self-identification as Jewish, belief in God, knowledge of the fundamentals of Judaism, and membership in a temple or synagogue, in that order. About half the respondents thought it necessary to marry within the group, although interfaith dating was high, "with the proportion rising to 93% by the 12th grade." The agency was used largely for athletics, "general recreation," and as a gathering-place for ingroup courting and friendship.

In Savannah, Georgia, a study of adolescents, parents, and advisers of local youth groups found strong evidence of a "Jewish teen culture" in which the youngsters identified Jewishness in terms of specific tasks and problems rather than abstract or traditional constructs (39). It was found that the adolescents were generally mistaken when they tried to identify parental attitudes on secular matters, but most often correct when they guessed at parental opinions on issues of Jewishness. The researchers also arrived at some interesting similarities and differences when they compared advisers' and parents' perceptions of various questions affecting the work with adolescent youths.

In Youngstown, Ohio, Kaplan and Walden (114) found that their adolescent respondents viewed the center both as an object of rebellion in their search for independence and as a setting offering a "dependency relationship analogous to the adolescent's position in the family" (114, p. 19). This study probed a number of apparent contradictions and ambivalences with implications for center practice: the youngsters offered "to make friends" as a major reason for joining club groups, but reported that few "meaningful" friendships were formed; parents idealized developmental and growth needs of their children, but were "non-supportive at points of direct confrontation"; parents gave lip-service to individuality, but were fearful of nonconformity. It was concluded that "many of the findings cast doubts as to the Center's effectiveness in working with its adolescent population. The Center is only one institution within the context of the wider community" (114, p. 20). The authors also expressed the familiar concern about the tension between the recreational and the educational-developmental concepts of agency function:

For the adolescent, the Center is not consciously seen as a place where growth needs and objectives are being met. This is the professional perspective. The adolescent simply seeks a setting in which he can meet friends, have fun and socialize with members of the opposite sex. Considering physiological changes, world uncertainty and pressures at home and school, is it any wonder that teenagers conceive of the Center merely as a place where they relax and perhaps unwind? Desirable or not, these factors seem to color the adolescent's image of the Center. [114, p. 21]

Garfinkle's Montreal study (65) was a sophisticated investigation with a wide range of inquiry and a useful review of the literature. He surveyed 500 adolescents aged 14–17 in residence at eleven summer camps during the 1964 season— a group that comprised 6 percent of the Jewish adolescent community of Montreal. Garfinkle asked questions about their "social values and spheres of social activity," "the relevant sociological or psychological dimensions related to Y membership or participation," and "aspects of Y experience [that] tended to attract or repel membership and participation" (65, p. 1). He found that in his sample peer group acceptance was the dominant social value; "the peer group is clearly telling its members to cultivate social rather than intellectual or athletic skills"; non-"Y" clubs were the dominant social spheres; and, while those from the higher socioeconomic group were more likely to be "Y" members, lower middle-class youngsters were more likely to be participants. Garfinkle explained this by showing data to indicate that "the lower middle class seems more achievement oriented, while the upper middle class [is] more status oriented" (65, p. 107). The study indicated that the "Y" was attracting adolescents who were below average in Jewish identification and that those scored as average were dropping out at a faster rate than they came in. Those who scored above average seemed to have been attracted to other groups and settings. The data amassed in the Montreal study carried many implications for program modification, and the discussion of it by Boeko (16) is a detailed example of the efforts of practitioners to draw practice and program from research findings.

Finally, Carp (30) reported a pilot study in which he used the Taylor Anxiety Scale (derived from the Minnesota Multiphasic Personality Inventory), Hollingshead's Index of Social Class Position, and other measures with a 300-member sample of adolescents in the program of the East Flatbush–Rugby YM-YWHA in New York City. His inquiry was concerned with adolescent anxiety, Jewish identification, and social attitudes and values and he attempted to correlate these variables with those of age, sex, and social class. Some interesting connections were found: girls were more anxious than boys; anxiety increased in the higher social classes; there were no male-female differences on attitudes toward maintaining a "Jewish home" —a responsibility traditionally entrusted to the woman in the family; a "low" sense of values existed on issues such as cheating versus honesty, ends versus means, material things versus happiness, and similar alternatives; and, on the perceptions of the agency and its service, there was little inclination to favor more Jewish programming, regardless of age and class differences.

The studies reported have produced considerable data, much of it thought provoking to those at work in the field. At this stage of development the research is inconclusive and fragmented, but it carries a good deal of interest for its rudimentary attempts at design, its efforts to order the questions, and the nature of its curiosity.

The hard-to-reach. This term itself has already grown strange, expressing as it does the early frustrations of the neighborhood centers in their efforts to serve youngsters who would not respond to the orderly and traditional rules of the agency game. The image of unreachability has by now given way to the realities of considerable practice and research showing that these youths were in fact accessible to any serious effort to reach them. In the past few years some of the most ambitious street club projects and research investigations have been brought to a conclusion and the findings issued. Books are beginning to emerge summarizing and synthesizing the processes and results of street club practice during the past generation.

Short and Strodtbeck's *Group Process and Gang Delinquency* (206), published in 1965, presented the results of a rigorous and comprehensive street club investigation conducted over a five-year period in a collaboration between the Detached Worker Program of the YMCA of Metropolitan Chicago and the Department of Sociology of the University of Chicago. The book discusses the theoretical traditions of street club work and the study of delinquent gangs; the research design and the authors' "departure from conventional notions of research strategy"; the researchers' attempt to bring data to bear on the various theories of gang behavior such as those generated by Cohen (38), Miller (151), and Cloward and Ohlin (37); data designed to "decipher the puzzle of self-conception" in the group context and how the boys' self-concepts affected their group behavior; the early discovery that "delinquent episodes are related to status-maintaining mechanisms within the group"; the group-process emphasis in their findings —the effects of group norms on group responses to status threats, the relationship between social disabilities and delinquent behavior, and other factors; and a summary of the group-process perspective in the context of more recent theoretical formulations (206, pp. vii, viii).

The method and substance of this research are too varied to summarize here, but the "group-process perspective" with which the authors emerge is rich in implications for group work program and practice. The authors' own summary of their position on this theme is as follows:

We have turned to the face-to-face context of behavior for further guidance and precision. We accept in principle the idea that structural differentiation in the culture of the larger society gives rise to subcultures of social classes characterized by conditions of life which are productive of differential rates of criminal behavior. The focus of this book is on hypotheses relating to mechanisms by which norms and values associated with structural variation become translated into behavior. Between *position in the social order*, including detailed knowledge of the subculture which this implies, and *behavior* there intervene processes of interaction between individuals in groups. For delinquency theory, we feel it is particularly important to link peer-group process and community relations. It is these group-community interactions which impart to delinquent behavior so much of its apparently *ad hoc* character. [206, pp. 269, 270]

The Chicago Youth Development Project, conducted by the Chicago Boys' Clubs with an evaluation team from the Institute for Social Research of the University of Michigan, issued a report in 1964 describing the action program and the research design (147). Reporting as it does work at the halfway mark, much of its interest lies in its account of the relationship between the program and the research, in the "action-research" collaboration that has characterized work with street clubs since its inception.

Too often the role of the researcher in an action-research project, such as the CYDP, is akin to the role of the archeologist digging through successive levels of an ancient civilization in the hope that he may salvage enough artifacts to reveal the nature of a bygone era. Frequently the meaning of the artifacts, and the relations between them remain problematic because the connecting links required for an accurate interpretation are missing. . . . It is the aim of the CYDP research program to not only evaluate the action program in terms of the changes reflected in the target population, but also to interpret the degree of change effected in relation to the operating causes and effects of the action program. . . . The inquiry of the research program is addressed not only to *what* happened, but also to *how* it happened. [147, p. 50]

This plan is notably achieved in Caplan's (28) ingenious "near-success" concept, to be described later in this chapter in the section on evaluation and outcomes. In its description of research procedures the 1964 report is valuable in presenting its perspectives on the use of record materials, the treatment of arrest data, the interview program, use of the Advisory Committee, the activities analysis, the "crucial determinants" study, and other factors.

Another long-range investigation of work

with acting-out youths—although not with street clubs—is in the process of completion at the Seattle Atlantic Street Center, Seattle, Washington. Ikeda (107), the principal investigator, has issued a summary of the final report, and the progress reports of 1967 (46) and 1968 (47) carry collections of documents covering different aspects of the research and action programs. Emphasis is on the effort "to assess the effectiveness of assertive social work among acting-out junior high school boys by comparing performance on school and community indices of experimental group to control group" (107, p. 1). The researchers found that although no differences were produced between the experimental and control groups in the frequency of school disciplinary contacts,

there is a trend favoring a reduction in the severity of the type of school disciplinary contacts for experimentals, and . . . by the end of the project there was a significant difference in the average severity of disciplinary contacts for the experimental group as a whole in the school environment. [107, p. 3]

The agency was also able to rule out the possibility that the differences were due to "favorable labeling on the part of teachers" (107, p. 3). Berleman and Steinburn's evaluation of the project results (11) will be discussed in a later section of this chapter.

To return to the street club scene, Jansyn (111) reported a study in which he tried to

illuminate some of the ways in which variations in group activity are related to internal processes of the group and variations in group structure over time. Knowledge of such processes aids in the understanding of the episodic character of gang delinquency. [111, p. 600]

His findings, very much in the group process tradition, pointed to the fact that delinquency in the corner group was often generated as a result of declining solidarity: "The solidarity of the group is important to the boys and its decline beyond a certain level is threatening to them" (111, p. 613). He found too that the boys found it easier to act as a group in a delinquent manner than in a conventional one, and he concluded that the behavior of street corner boys might be understood as activities pursued in reaction to their concern about their own instability as a peer group.

There are, of course, many studies of this nature now going on throughout the country, deriving their interests from many theories and traditions, adding to them, and producing valuable insights for the use of practitioners. It is anticipated that these will be making their contributions to the literature for a long time to come. And as they continue, the tasks of summarizing, synthesizing, and theorizing will become increasingly crucial. Bernstein (12) and Spergel (216) have made contributions to this end.

Bernstein studied a wide range of approaches to work with street groups in different communities, touching the conditions of work, expectations, limitations, theoretical perspectives, relationship to other community services, characteristics of workers, research problems, and other issues. He visited nine cities—Chicago, Cleveland, Los Angeles, San Francisco, Detroit, New York, Philadelphia, Washington, and Boston—interviewing street workers, supervisors, executives, court and police personnel, psychiatrists, school officials, researchers, and groups of youths and their parents. His findings were voluminous, ranging over all of the major issues and providing a kind of encyclopedic view of the historical, theoretical, administrative, programmatic, and practice-oriented perspectives at work over the past two decades. The chapter on research reviews the major findings and calls attention to the fact that little systematic study has been devoted to the problem of method and the skills of street club practice. Bernstein concludes with a discussion of the major sociological problems affecting the ways in which "delinquency is woven into the texture of our society" (12, p. 149).

Spergel's *Street Gang Work: Theory and Practice* is a scholarly and thoroughgoing analysis of practice—"an effort to examine what the street worker does, and what he should do, in his practice with delinquent and potentially delinquent street groups" (216, p. vii). Written from the perspective of an erstwhile street worker and supervisor, the book is divided into two major sections—the development of theory and an analysis of street work practice. The approach is textlike in the best sense of the term, providing a compendium of the major sociological dimensions in gang work and proceeding in Part II to offer a manual of practice on specific tasks like "initiating the relationship," "dealing with the sense of deprivation," decision-making in the group, programming, "terminating the relationship," and others. The book also moves into tasks related to work with individuals, working with other systems (family, neighborhood groups, police, courts, schools, and others), and supervising the street work program. The general approach to street work practice is illustrated in Spergel's concluding remarks:

Street work may be viewed as a fundamentalist orientation of social organizations to helping people. The basic idea of street work is reaching out to people in need, by the simplest and most direct means possible, to provide service of almost unlimited scope and high personal identity. . . . In the final analysis, the program mobilizes the community's faith in the goodness of and capacity for positive change in its most aggressive, deviant youths. [216, p. 224]

As might be expected, the newest hard-to-reach youths to arouse the interest and concern of the neighborhood centers are members of the "hippie" community. It might also be anticipated that the greatest impetus for studying the problems of this group may emerge from the agencies most closely engaged with middle-class segments of the population.

Solomon (213), working for the Center for Community Research of the Associated YM-YWHAs of Greater New York, conducted a pilot study of hippies in the East Village section of New York City. Motivated partly by the apparent attractiveness of drugs to certain sectors of Jewish mid-

dle-class youths and Jewish center constituencies, the researchers moved to test
the feasibility of collecting personal data
from hippie youths through the use of
structured interviews, to develop information on individuals and social structures in
the hippie community, and to construct a
working definition of the term hippie itself.
Five indigenous hippie interviewers were
recruited, trained, and deployed to interview 51 of their fellows in the East Village
area. Later their data were augmented by
returns from a questionnaire on drug abuse
published by a hippie newspaper and submitted to the research center for its analysis.

Solomon's findings covered a wide range
of questions. Demographically, his respondents were between 18 and 25, with
the females averaging almost three years
younger than the males; the majority had
attended college for a while; most reported
fathers as being professionals, executives,
or administrators, with annual incomes over
$10,000; and over one-third were Jewish,
most of whom were males. Drug use was
high, with exposure to heroin being low,
most admitted to selling as well as using,
and the order of drug use seemed to run
from marijuana to hashish to LSD to
methedrine.

The national sample taken from the newspaper study indicated "a tendency for both
groups of data to exhibit more similarities
than differences in demographic characteristics and patterns of drug use among respondents" (213, p. 46).

In terms of the meaning attached to being a
"hippie," responses generally can be sub-
sumed under 2 categories of reaction to
alienation from the norms and values of the
dominant society. These categories are: (1)
perceptions of powerlessness and (2) feelings
of self-estrangement. [213, p. 12]

There will be more along these lines as
agencies continue to make advances toward
these youngsters who, very much like the
street club youths, need help badly but can
only be served on their own turf and in
their own style.

The handicapped. The integration of
handicapped children into the regular programs of the neighborhood centers has been
a focus of agency interest for some years
now; the pace of this activity seems to be
accelerating and some formal research efforts are beginning to yield results. Further, whereas in the past attention seemed
to be given mainly to the physically handicapped, there seems now to be a newer interest in the integration of the mentally
retarded. Overall the center of attention
is the younger child, with little given to
the adolescent or the adult.

The apparent increase in such activity is
not yet cause for considerable optimism,
according to a study Pappenfort and Kilpatrick (160) made of group work programs for physically handicapped children
in Chicago. They interviewed administrators
and examined facilities in 95 agencies, of
which 19 had programs for the physically
handicapped and 42 others had some handicapped children in their regular programs;
less than 1 percent of the total agency population was handicapped. Some marked
differences were found between agencies
with programs and those without, administrators of the latter tending to stereotype
the difficulties of programming for the
handicapped and to foresee problems unre-
ported by agencies that had such programs.
They found too that the larger the agency
the more likely it was that it provided services for children with a range of different
handicaps.

The New York Service for the Orthopedically Handicapped reported a study of
230 children who participated in a two-year
demonstration of the effects on physically
handicapped children of organized group
activities in community centers and settlements (221). The researchers hypothesized that the children's home and school
functioning, as well as their self-images,
could be improved by participation in after-
school activity with nonhandicapped peers.
They further believed that such integration
could be achieved without special staff,
training, or equipment. Results showed

some of the sought-for benefits to the children, but there were many indications that such programs could not be carried on without special staff and facilities. The report lays several action-research problems at the door of the centers, pointing up difficulties agencies experience in disciplining themselves for rigorous program evaluation. Articles by Deschin (42) and Robbins and Schattner (180) have explained some of the processes and problems of this research in greater detail.

The most intensive study of the integration of physically handicapped children into ongoing groups in a neighborhood center was undertaken by the Associated YM-YWHAs of Greater New York at the Mosholu-Montefiore Community Center in New York City, supported by a three-year grant (1962–65) from the U.S. Children's Bureau. Forty-seven physically handicapped children aged 7–14 were placed in existing groups within the center's junior program; the service was augmented with casework and medical consultation to the children, parents, and staff. Directing the research, Holmes (96, 100) used trained observers who accompanied the integrated groups, interaction recording, before-and-after questionnaires designed to elicit parental attitudes, and a number of other measures. He was able to document a "positive and significant impact" on the children, providing data on improvements in adaptive behavior, coping attitudes, social skills, and self-esteem. He further found that the parents developed more realistic and less fantasied appraisals of their children's potentials.

Holmes's interest in group process and in leadership behavior yielded additional findings about the worker skills and group structures through which integration of the handicapped was best achieved. In fact, his developing curiosity about the more general problems of group process resulted in the finding of some important connections between the study of special groups and the study of all groups. His distinction between collections and groups should serve

as a useful guide to researchers who need to understand that the mere structural fact of physical integration, without skilled attempts to help the group members come together, may not constitute integration at all or achieve any of the effects hypothesized about it.

The project has been prolific in turning out papers and materials explicating various research problems and procedures and reporting other aspects of the study. Holmes reported on the structured observational schema used in the measurement and evaluation of social interactions in the children's groups (102). Holmes and Smolka (104) described a comparison of attitudes toward child-rearing among mothers of handicapped and nonhandicapped children, finding no support for hypotheses of difference either in the before or after measures, but some evidence of differences in certain subtest scores. In all, the work of Holmes and his associates at the Center for Community Research of the Associated YM-YWHAs of Greater New York is an example of the developing involvement of a segment of the neighborhood center field in the tasks of scientific research.

Added to the work with the physically handicapped, some findings have begun to appear regarding work with mentally retarded children and their parents. Ramsey (171) reviewed a number of studies in which group methods were used to help the parents of these children and found that only three of the fifteen studies utilized objective criteria for measurement. In analyzing the variables of greatest interest to the researchers, Ramsey named the following: modes of recruitment and group formation, size of groups, length of sessions, time span of the group experience, types of group leadership, and the range of group purposes from the structured and formal information-giving to the unstructured counseling and therapy orientation. All studies reported at least partial success, and progress was found in the areas of feeling-ventilation, sharing of practical advice, mutual reassurance, and reality-testing. Ramsey concluded that the studies were generally so poorly designed as to prohibit replication and comparison, and he suggested more taxonomic descriptions of population variables that might affect outcomes; more precise descriptions of group structure, functions, and goals; more information about methods of working; and more objective measures of change.

Schreiber (191), of the Association for the Help of Retarded Children in New York City, reported a program in which 300 retarded children, adolescents, and adults were offered admittance to leisure-time programs in neighborhood agencies. As against the integration orientation, these groups were organized homogeneously, establishing a study population of 25 to 30 groups of mentally retarded clients. Schreiber and Feeley (192), under the same aegis, established and observed a group of siblings of retarded children, working entirely with adolescent siblings between the ages of 13 and 17. The Boy Scouts of America surveyed the number and program disposition of handicapped boys and found 111,100 boys in fifteen categories of handicap, with higher representation of blind, deaf, and mentally retarded children than are found in the general population (222). Fox (56), for the Associated YM-YWHAs of Greater New York in collaboration with the Child Study Association of America, has described a program currently under way to establish and study educational group experiences for parents of retarded children. He reports also that New York State is designing an Institute for Basic Research in Mental Retardation.

The National Institute of Child Health and Human Development (156, pp. 95–96) has been studying the effects of parental counseling on the mentally retarded child. They have reported several emergent trends: parents are more accurate in estimating the child's present abilities than his future adaptability, certain styles of counseling do better in affecting these estimates of future adaptation, parents whose estimates of present ability are poor manage their child

less successfully, parents often view the child's difficulties as being separate treatable problems such as poor speech or poor coordination, and counselors often reinforce this view by discussing the child as if his retardation were in fact the sum of separate handicaps (156, p. 95).

The Jewish Community Centers Association of St. Louis conducted an integration study of retarded children similar in scope and discipline to that of the New York Associated YM-YWHAs on the physically handicapped. Flax and Pumphrey (54) and, in a more detailed report, Pumphrey, Goodman, and Flax (170) described a research project financed by the National Institute of Mental Health for a five-year period beginning in 1965. The study was designed "to determine the feasibility of including educable mental retardates (EMRs) in regular Center programs" (54, p. 2), testing the extent to which EMRs could participate with and be tolerated by normal children in the ongoing group activities. Seventy diagnosed EMRs (defined by state law as having IQs between 48 and 78) new to the agency were registered for activities in the period 1965 through 1968. The children were referred by parents, JCC staff, schools, social agencies, and other retardates. The sample consisted of 46 males and 24 females aged 6 through 17, with socioeconomic backgrounds ranging from welfare to upper-class families; 50 of the children were living with both parents; 59 were white and 11 black; 55 were non-Jewish; and the majority had additional handicaps such as poor vision, poor speech, bad coordination, and proneness to seizures. Children and parents were interviewed and placed in activities ranging over day camp, social clubs, resident camp, special interest groups, and athletic groups; 52 of the children chose additional activities at a later point.

A control for each EMR was selected randomly from the group of which he was a member. Measures used were a group participation form, social adjustment rankings, observation schedules, and case histories. The findings were generally favorable to integration, with some interesting complexities. For example, a factor analysis of workers' responses to the group participation scale yielded three independent dimensions of individual performance that explained 87 percent of the common variance among the items—aggressive acting-out, evidence of belongingness and comfort, and behavior directed toward the leader. The EMRs were found not to differ significantly from their controls on the first and third dimensions—aggressiveness and behavior directed toward the leader—but were rated lower, at the .001 level of significance, on the belongingness and comfort factor. The general conclusion was as follows:

The behavior of two-thirds of the retarded children studied intensively was well within the range of that of the normal children. On the average, their behavior was no more aggressive or focused on adults than that of the other children. Since EMRs were no more inclinded to be involved in episodes which caused concern than were other members, but less involved in positive incidents, it seems clear that an optimal expectation for most EMRs would be that they can achieve a level of functioning somewhere among the lower half of a group's total membership. [170, pp. 159, 160]

The researchers also reported a highly favorable reaction from the normal children, their parents, and the staff to the participation of the EMRs.

The aging. The studies at hand are geared mainly to the task of testing the limits of involvement of older people in community activity, as both consumers and providers of service. At Brandeis University's Florence Heller Graduate School for Advanced Studies in Social Welfare, Lambert, Guberman, and Morris (120) set out to test some common assumptions about the role of older citizens in community service. Financed by the Chronic Disease Program of the U.S. Public Health Service, the study sought to determine the extent to which older people were willing and able to participate, and the kind of opportunity

structure that existed if they did. The researchers interviewed 297 people in a suburban community of metropolitan Boston, a random sample of all noninstitutionalized residents 65 years of age and over. To assess the opportunity potential, they interviewed the executives of nineteen health and welfare agencies in the community and developed other techniques for involving agencies and old people's organizations in collaborative work on the project itself.

The researchers found that the manpower potential of the aging, considered by itself, was "large enough to make tremendous inroads upon current manpower shortages" (120, p. 44) if transportation, some expenses, and some payment were provided. The old people's task preferences called for interpersonal communication rather than mechanical or physical work, they wanted emotional support and the feeling that the work was needed, not make-work, and they asked for tasks that were specific and feasible. The factors differentiating those who would participate and those who would not were previous volunteer experience, educational level, and self-perception of health; no differences were found with respect to age, sex, and employment status. On the question of availability of opportunity and the extent to which such opportunities were consonant with old people's needs and interests, the researchers found the prospects "rather dismal." They found old people to be underrepresented in full-time paid, part-time paid, and volunteer categories; they were mostly in clerical and maintenance categories. In the case of volunteers, "neither the volunteer nor his function was vital to the goals of his agency" (120, p. 50). No agency had trouble finding aged volunteers, but most found reasons for not being able to use them. "The older volunteer is viewed as an intrusion into the well-organized functioning of an agency. He has three strikes against him; he is a lay person, he is old, and he is a volunteer" (120, p. 50).

Tuckman (228) studied factors related to frequency of attendance at the Adult

Health and Recreation Center operated by the Division of Mental Health of the Philadelphia Department of Public Health. He found only two statistically significant factors—health and distance of residence—and failed to find any significance in the factors of age, sex, race, marital status, or education.

Rosenblatt (183), in interviews with 250 older people on New York's Lower East Side, found that "potential volunteers are somewhat younger, healthier, and more neighborly than persons without interest in volunteer activities. They also enjoy life more and make more plans for the future" (183, p. 90). His conclusions also stress the importance of agency commitment to training and job satisfaction for the older volunteer.

In Long Beach, California, Miran and Lemmerman (152), for the Jewish Community Center and Jewish Family Service, surveyed an older adult population for information on home and neighborhood, work and income, leisure-time pursuits, medical care and health, social and emotional adjustment, and need for additional services. They found some excess of leisure time and need for help with transportation, but essentially

a portrait of an older adult community with comparatively good state of health—physically, socially, emotionally and economically —one that reverberates with intellectual curiosity and a desire for new experiences. [152, p. 34]

The preschool child. When the government accepted—and financed—the proposition that children living in poverty often suffer deprivation in their early childhood learning and need compensatory education before they enter the public schools, the neighborhood centers became a prime setting for the new programs that were implemented. Project Head Start was established by the Office of Economic Opportunity in the summer of 1965 and centers throughout the country have been closely involved with it since that time. Nevertheless, only a small portion of the Head Start research

has as yet emanated from that quarter. In New York there was activity by the Center for Community Research of the Associated YM-YWHAs, which examined two such programs conducted for eight weeks in the first summer of Head Start operation.

Holmes's report of this activity pointed out the following:

These summer programs, and indeed all of the summer Headstart programs, were designed to offset or overcome some of the deficits among children from disadvantaged homes who were scheduled for public school kindergarten or first grade classes starting in the fall of 1965. More specifically, the aim of these programs was to offer the participants a pre-school experience which would help them to learn about the demands of school and teacher, to develop their social skills through participation in an organized group experience with their peers, and to increase the level of their cognitive skills through participation in a wide variety of interesting and stimulating play activities. [97, p. 1]

Holmes thus set out to measure changes in cognitive functioning, patterns of play, and fantasies about peers and adults. Foiled in his effort to do a before-and-after study by the not untypical lateness of the grant award, he studied the ending phase using all of the Head Start children and a matched group of controls. He also followed up at a later point to test for any latent effects that might appear after initial exposure to school.

Thirty-six Head Start children were matched with sixty nonparticipants along the dimensions of age, sex, ethnic background, previous schooling, number of siblings at home, presence or absence of father or mother, and occupation of the major wage earner. Holmes used cognitive measures, projective devices, and a structured observational scheme to observe the children at play. He found significant gains among the Head Start children on cognitive measures and social behavior:

There was an increase in behavior which was directed toward a fostering of solidarity with others, with a marked decrease in random, non-purposive, and merely passive "responding" behavior. In other words, at the end of program the goal of the interaction was more likely to be social and affiliative, and less likely to be random or recipient. [97, p. 5]

On the projective device significant differences were found between the participants and the controls on four dimensions —quality of interaction between the characters in the stories, degree of investment of the main characters in the activities, the affect with which the activity was invested, and the degree to which it was constructive or destructive. The Head Start children described the principal characters as being more involved than did the controls, but they also showed more instances of negative interaction, more negative affect, and more destructive fantasies. Holmes's comment on this is as follows:

Clinically, this finding is striking. It suggests that the initial experience of being in an organized group study has a civilizing effect on behavior, i.e., a decrease in the instances of aggressive behavior is accompanied by an increase in the instances of aggressive fantasies. Thus, hostile impulses are, through this type of experience, less likely to be acted upon and more likely to be represented in fantasy. In other terms, they are more likely to be under the control of the ego. [97, p. 6]

In the follow-up study two months after the children's entrance into school, Holmes found that the differences were eradicated and Head Start children had lost their lead. Surprisingly, however, they had not lost their educational gains; the nonparticipants had simply caught up. Holmes's comment was as follows:

These findings are not surprising. The first two months of this type of experience are so different from the child's experience in the home, that they have a dramatic effect on fantasy, and on behavior. Both the school and the Head Start program, as it was conducted, are primarily organized nursery school play experiences and, as such, have a great deal in common. It is possible that the first two months of school are so dramatic for children who previously have had no such experience that this was, in fact, the worst time for a recomparison. . . . possibly, if tested at the end of the year, the Head Start

children would show more consistent growth than the controls, as a function of the previous summer's experience. [97, p. 7]

In the following year the Associated "Y"s carried forward three new six-month Head Start programs, and Holmes and Holmes (103) studied different classes of participants. Their study groups were defined as follows: (1) the *self-referred*, whose families had sought out the program on their own initiative, (2) the *sought-after*, who responded to active reaching-out by the study staff, (3) the *nonparticipants*, who were contacted by staff but did not enroll in the program, and (4) the *controls*, who were nonparticipating middle-class children with no nursery school experience. The researchers found that the self-referred children were more similar to the middle-class children than to either of the other two categories; that the sought-after and nonparticipant children, although somewhat older, did most poorly; and that the middle-class children, even when younger, did better on the cognitive tests than any of the others. Differences found among the parents reflected closely those found among the children. The researchers' experience also impressed them with the importance of personal contact as a device for recruiting potential users of these kinds of programs. They concluded by calling for comparative studies of "class-integrated" versus "100% disadvantaged" programs and for further research into the reliability of teachers' ratings of children.

The growing concern about the educational preparation of the preschool child has also focused attention on the role of the mother in providing learning experiences in the home. Karnes and his associates studied "the effects of short-term parent training as reflected in the intellectual and linguistic development of the children" and found significant differences between the children and their controls on the Stanford-Binet Individual Intelligence Scale (115, p. 174). They concluded:

Mothers of low educational and low income level can learn to prepare inexpensive educational materials and to acquire skills for using such materials to foster the intellectual and linguistic development of their children at home. [115, p. 182]

The mothers were paid to attend the sessions, were actively involved in the classroom work, and worked closely with visiting teachers.

Finally, Brittain (18) reviewed several studies of preschool enrichment programs and their effects on the children. He found that although most of the studies reported positive gains, there has been a general inconsistency about whether these gains were maintained over time. Many have concluded that the failure to sustain progress is in large measure a function of the isolation of the family from the enrichment experience of the child.

The school deviant. In the last few years public schools in many communities have turned to the small group as an extracurricular activity for helping children who are having trouble in the classroom. Leadership for these groups has been drawn from many sources: where there are caseworkers in the system they have been asked to broaden their service, group workers have been attracted into a number of school social work departments, neighborhood clinics have been enlisted to provide consultation and leadership, and neighborhood centers and public schools have increasingly been developing working relationships designed to provide the necessary small group skills and leadership. Again, the programmatic development precedes the research and study by many years and the literature is still largely descriptive.

One of the first systematic efforts to study the work in this area came from a research team at the University of Michigan School of Social Work (187, 240). Financed by the national Office of Juvenile Delinquency and Youth Development, the President's Committee on Juvenile Delinquency and Youth Crime, and the National Institute of Mental Health, the researchers studied five public school systems in which

group work practitioners were integrated into school social work services to assist malperforming pupils. They began with the proposition that "malperformance patterns should be viewed as *resultants of the interaction of both pupil characteristics and school conditions*" (240, p. 4) and proceeded to study the role of the social workers in the system, the concept of malperformance itself, and the school conditions reflected in the grading patterns, system of sanctions, and dropout phenomena. Among the findings reported were differential and discriminatory grading patterns in the non-college-preparatory curriculum, "a variety of negative sanction to curb malperformance" (187, p. 23), and a disproportionate number of dropouts among boys, blacks, those from working-class families, those with lower IQs, poor readers, low achievers, and those in the non-college-preparatory curriculum. They concluded:

The findings from this study and demonstration effort provide substantial support for the proposition that pupil malperformance is most usefully viewed as a consequence of adverse school-pupil interactions. Both within-school and between-school variations were noted in teachers' perspectives, in group services, in curriculum placement patterns and outcomes, in grading practices, and in pupil careers. . . . The school itself may maintain or even generate the very malperformance it seeks to eliminate by offering limited opportunity for educational attainment . . . by judging pupils adversely because of attributes which are independent of their actions . . . through unwise use of control practices, and by making it exceedingly difficult for the pupil to "find his way back" once he has been defined as a malperformer. [187, p. 26]

Schafer (188) elaborated the theoretical position of this study, offering an "interactional view" that stressed the social definition of malperformance and the self-fulfilling prophecies that develop from the labeling of deviant acts and the enforcement of norms. Finally, the research team produced a "Pupil Behavior Inventory" designed to draw systematic information about teachers' judgments of malperformers' classroom behavior (241). The

PBI was first considered as a response to an earlier need of Detroit's Neighborhood Service Organization to classify pupils referred by the schools for problems defined as misbehavior and underachievement.

The most thorough research effort in this category was undoubtedly the well-known *Girls at Vocational High* (149), a study of the effectiveness of social work services in treating "potential problem cases" referred by a school to a social agency. The inclusion of group counseling in the treatment design was of considerable interest to those working with groups in school systems. Since this was an evaluative study, it will be discussed later in the section on evaluations and outcomes.

The family. The literature and research on the family group is growing rapidly, as is the interest of social workers in the family as a unit of service. Lennard and Bernstein offer an entry into this research from the perspective of the "clinical sociologist" (125, pp. 83–141). Leader (124) reviewed some of the major issues confronting the family therapist. And, closest to the immediate concerns of the neighborhood centers, Kraft and Chilman (118) reviewed a number of programs and studies of parental education in low-income families. Hardy's monograph on *The YMCA and the Changing American Family* (82) is an account of one agency's experience in working with families over the past century.

The most recent connections between the neighborhood agencies and family work have been strengthened by Project ENABLE, of which a review was presented in the December 1967 issue of *Social Casework* (144). An acronym for Education and Neighborhood Action for Better Living Environment, the effort began in September 1965 and was "the first nationwide demonstration designed and implemented by voluntary social agencies to be funded by the Office of Economic Opportunity."

ENABLE was planned as an effort to forge a new tool for reaching and serving families living in poverty by drawing from the combined expertise and resources of three national organizations: the Child Study Association of America, the Family Service Association of America, and the National Urban League. Expertise in parent education through small group discussion, casework knowledge of individual behavior and family relationships, and skill in community organization were joined in a team approach to help parents discover the strengths within themselves and the resources in their communities to change the situations in which they live and rear their children. [144, p. 609]

Rosenblatt and Wiggins (184) interviewed 4,219 participants in the program, 1,644 nonattenders, and 939 persons who had refused participation. They sought to find the extent to which they were reaching low-income parents in greater proportion than had previous programs, whether they were drawing only the more stable segment of the lower-class families, and whether they could find differences between regular attenders and dropouts. They found that ENABLE had indeed reached a client group that was more deprived than those served previously by FSAA and CSA; there was no evidence that the ENABLE program was reaching only the most advantaged sections of the disadvantaged: "Indeed, there is reason to believe that many of the more enterprising neighborhood residents refused to join ENABLE groups" (184, p. 646). And they found that the project was "slightly less successful in retaining as regular members Negroes and Mexican-Americans and persons with less than twelve years of schooling than whites and those with more education" (184, p. 646). Rosenblatt (182) also reported an evaluative study of attitudinal changes among project participants; this will be reviewed later in this chapter.

Out of a demonstration project on Social Group Work with Parents financed by the U.S. Children's Bureau, Glasser and Navarre (72) developed a description of the one-parent family and the structural variables intervening between their poverty and their single-parenthood. They noted that little study has been made of this subject:

This seems to be a significant omission in view of the major change of the structure of family life in the United States during this century, and the large number of one-parent families classified as poor. [72, p. 98]

These structures are designated as those of task, communication, power, and affection. In drawing implications for policy and practice, the researchers discussed the need for institutionalizing emotional supports, social outlets, task-oriented groups, provision of male figures, and the subsidization of child care and housekeeping services. They also stressed public services aimed at "diverting family dissolution."

The Group As Client

Although there is still little small group research coming out of group work and the neighborhood centers, the academic study of small groups continues to flourish and the body of knowledge to grow. A by-product of this activity is the increased sophistication of the research compilations and reviews themselves as they become more related to specific research problems and dimensions. McGrath and Altman (140), financed by the Behavioral Sciences Division of the Air Force Office of Scientific Research, published a classification system for organizing and synthesizing information on small group research. Their account contained a case history of their nine-year program of study, some perspectives on the small group field, a discussion of specific research relationships tested in a sample of 250 studies reviewed, annotation of those studies, and a comprehensive bibliography of small group studies up to 1962.

Gerard and Miller (68) reviewed the literature of small group research produced between 1963 and 1966 ("the problem of organizing the research on group dynamics remains insoluble"), beginning with a general overview in which they pointed out that none of the new ideas that have appeared in the past three years has catalyzed or focused the activities of researchers to the extent that contributions of Sherif, Lewin, Asch, Heider,

and Festinger have mobilized effort in the past. [68, p. 288]

The major interest of small group researchers was indicated as still being in the areas of cooperation-competition and interpersonal attraction, and they went on to review studies concentrating on internal group processes (attraction, problem-solving, conformity and social influence, reinforcement effects, and cooperation-competition) and structural characteristics (communication channels, power structure, leadership and membership characteristics).

Among the other important reviews and bibliographies that appeared were Raven's collection of 3,500 items of small group research (173), Deutsch and Krauss's review of theoretical approaches to problems in social psychology (43), Hoffman's summary of the literature on group problem-solving (94), Allen's description of work on the relationship between situational factors and conformity (4), Glanser and Glaser's review of work on communication networks (71) and the regular evaluations and summaries of studies in game theory appearing in the *Journal of Conflict Resolution*. Other reviews will be mentioned later in the context of specific research categories to be discussed.[1]

In recent years two major areas of study have become especially attractive to group work practitioners: (1) the so-called encounter, sensitivity, and T-group phenomena have increasingly found their way into agency practice and (2) systems theory has undergone elaboration as it has been applied to social work practice. In the sensitivity field, Gifford's "Sensitivity Training and Social Work" (69) was a valuable evaluation of applications of, strengths of, and

---

[1] Some new journals should also be noted: The old *Journal of Abnormal and Social Psychology* was cleft to produce the *Journal of Abnormal Psychology* and the *Journal of Personality and Social Psychology*; the latter is now a primary source for small group research. The *Journal of Applied Behavioral Sciences* is an outlet for work on T-group and sensitivity training, *Trans-action* is of a more popular cast, and the *Journal of Experimental Social Psychology* will also be relevant to group workers.

problems involved in using the work in that field. Schein and Bennis (189) and Bradford, Gibb, and Benne (17) have produced comprehensive expositions of the method and the research on which it is based. Bach (7) wrote an account of the marathon group and its assumptions. In the systems field Buckley (24) edited a source book on the subject and Lathrope (121) tried to bring

the application of systems logic to some of the problems encountered in day-by-day social work practice. . . . In a search for bridging ideas, it [the paper] attempts some guidelines, raises some cautions, lists some advantages, suggests some habits of mind, and investigates some concepts stemming from systems theory. [121, p. 1]

Moving to the research on some specific problems of group process and structure, the following are a few of the studies recently completed and of specific interest to group workers and their agencies:

The individual in the group. Heslin and Dunphy (89) examined 450 small group studies for dimensions relevant to member satisfaction. They found three major variables—status consensus, perception of progress toward group goals, and perceived freedom to participate. Status consensus involved agreement of members about the statuses of the leader and of each other and was facilitated by having a leader who was high on both group task and group maintenance functions. Perceptions of progress facilitated goal attainment, followed by more member satisfaction. And the members felt more satisfaction when there were more—and more fluid—communication channels within the group. Parker (161), working in a locked ward of a Veterans Administration hospital, found that patients with different psychiatric problems used and benefited from groups in certain specific ways varying in quality of contacts, social integration, and social feeling.

Ganter and Polansky (63) tried to predict a child's suitability for individual treatment from his participation in a diagnostic

group. Defining accessibility as capacity for insight, motivation for change, trust in the worker, and freedom to communicate feelings, they found significant differences on some factors and no differences on others. Important were the ability to talk of painful feelings, identification of the clinic's purpose, sustained activity spans, responsiveness to worker controls, and dependence on the group worker. Not significant were amount of verbalization, direction of responses to other children, flexibility of responses, and attractiveness of the child to the worker. They concluded that the potential of the diagnostic group for predicting accessibility to individual treatment was well demonstrated.

Medow and Zander (148) found in a laboratory experiment that "central" members —those whose actions were needed by fellow members in order to move themselves— did exceed peripheral members in task involvement, self-perception as having more responsibility for outcomes, and desire for the successful performance of the group.

Goodchilds and Smith studied "the wit and his group" and found that "the prediction that a wit will have a relatively positive self-image is supported in the first investigation" (73, p. 28). They found that wits were nonconforming and relatively independent of social norms.

Kazzaz (116) studied the role of the "champion of the cause," describing him, in the Bennis and Shepard framework, as counterdependent during the dependency phase and overpersonal during the intimacy phase of group development.

Levinger (130), in the context of the study of complementarity among married couples, found that structural descriptions of the partners' personalities were less significant than describing these people in interaction with each other. Tharp (224), discussing Levinger's comments on this score, reinforced the need for a situational perspective on complementarity, and Gerard and Miller stated:

The issues involved here reach far beyond the study of the marriage relationship. The fact that such ferment is occurring in the study of dyadic relations may presage a new stimulus-centered look at the broad field of dynamics. [68, p. 297]

Group composition. Problems of group composition were dealt with by Levine (128) and Shalinsky (203) in doctoral dissertations. Levine sought to determine factors related to "interpersonal balance" —when members could be highly attracted to each other and still be free to disagree with each other—and found that age similarity was the only factor related to a desirable state of high-attraction/low-agreement imbalance, except when those under study were married.

Shalinsky (203, 204), in an experimental field study conducted at a children's summer camp, used Schutz's (193) theory of Fundamentl Interpersonal Relations Orientations (FIRO) to seek out factors in the relationship between group composition and "selected aspects of group functioning which have relevance for social group work" (204, p. 42). By grouping campers according to Schutz's three basic needs—inclusion, control, and affection—he created groups deemed compatible and incompatible and then used measures to study four aspects of group functioning—interpersonal attraction, attraction to the group, cooperative behavior, and group productivity. He found support for several of his hypotheses: that (1) more of the compatibles liked each other than did the incompatibles, (2) members of the compatible groups tended to see each other as more attractive, (3) groups of compatibles showed more cooperative behavior, and (4) the compatibles were more productive in competitive tasks. Certain subgroup assumptions were not borne out, raising the question of whether subgrouping is actually a phenomenon related to decline in cohesiveness. Shalinsky concluded that his hypotheses were substantially supported and that FIRO theory is valuable as an approach to group composition in group work practice. The work also included a review and discussion of grouping criteria, as these are elaborated in the literature.

Franseth and Koury's (57) survey of grouping research and its relationship to pupil learning is a summary of nationwide studies on grouping practices in the elementary schools. It deals with ability groupings, normal versus increased range of individual differences, some assumptions underlying grouping by ability, sociometric formations, and some philosophical questions raised by the grouping of children for learning purposes.

Patterns of group interaction. Feldman's doctoral research (50, 52), also located in the summer camp setting, sought to relate certain forms of group integration to variables of power, leadership, and conforming behavior. Defining group integration as the social interaction pattern among members, he examined *normative* integration, in which there is a high consensus about group-relevant behavioral norms; *interpersonal* integration, in which the interaction is based on the members' liking for each other; and *functional* integration, based on specialized activities that meet group requirements. His finding of a high correlation between functional and interpersonal integration was an interesting comment on the popular mode of polarizing the expressive and task-oriented functions.

For the groups studied, it was found that functional integration and interpersonal integration are highly correlated in a positive direction. That is, groups characterized by effective goal attainment, pattern maintenance, and external relations, and in which responsibility for performance of those functions is distributed among many members, tend to be characterized by high degrees of reciprocal liking. Conversely, groups that are relatively ineffective in the performance of such functions, or in which responsibility for their performance has been monopolized by one or a few members, tend to manifest low levels of interpersonal liking. [50, p. 45]

Bjerstedt (15) studied another aspect of group interaction—the "rotation phenomenon"—in which children tend to rotate the responsibility for tasks, showing what Bjerstedt calls a proper respect for social justice and representing an aspect of the children's "interaction competence." He found that the rotation phenomenon was positively related to other forms of interactional competence and could be used as an indicator of such general competence in group interaction.

Group size. On this factor O'Dell (158) found that in formed leaderless groups the pace and pleasure of group interaction increased as the groupings grew from two to five: "The inhibition that characterizes the dyad is shared also by the triad and, to a decreasing degree, by groups of larger size." Indik (108) investigated the relationship between organizational size and member participation and found that "the results confirm the earlier findings that organizational size is significantly negatively related to member participation in our three sets of organizations" (108, p. 345).

Stages of group development. Tuckman (227) reviewed fifty articles on the developmental sequence in small groups, divided them by setting, and suggested a synthesis descriptive of social and interpersonal group activities.

Group cohesiveness. Lott and Lott (135) surveyed the literature of the past fifteen years, examining work on the determinants and consequences of interpersonal attraction. Goodman (74), at the Jewish Community Center in St. Louis, studied the attractiveness of adult groups to their members and found that in groups led by trained social workers, members tended to respond less favorably to the agency and more to the staff, while the reverse was true of groups that were staffed only to render occasional program and administrative assistance.

Group decision-making. Hall and Williams (79) compared procedures used in established and ad hoc groups and found that the latter tended to resolve differences through compromise while the established groups were more creative and "view conflict as symptomatic of unresolved issues." Handlon and Parloff (80) investigated the specific mechanisms that enhance the production of "good" ideas, finding that a low-critical atmosphere does not necessarily produce the ideas but does increase the probability that they will be reported out when they occur.

Group influences. The earlier work by Festinger, Pepitone, and Newcomb (53) on deindividuation in the group had found that people tended to be much less conservative in revealing themselves in a group than when they were alone, and this had considerable interest for group workers. In this tradition, Wallach, Kogan, and Bem (243) studied the "risky-shift" phenomenon, finding that the group process tends to push decisions in a risky, rather than a conservative, direction; group decision-making reduces the responsibility felt by members, who feel a shared responsibility with others. Thus the group tends to risk more, with more chance of failure, than does an individual acting on his own decision. Taking the problem a step further, Alker and Kogan (3) found, in three studies conducted with women in college sororities, that discussion alone is not a sufficient condition for the risky-shift phenomenon. When groups converged strongly on standardized ethical norms, the shifts tended to become conservative, whereas those groups that achieved consensus on particularistic unethical alternatives showed shifts toward greater risk-taking.

Finally, group workers will be interested in two studies of nonverbal communication. Exline, Gray, and Schuette (49) found situational variations in people's willingness to engage in mutual glances, and Miller, Banks, and Ogawa (150) sought to identify the relationships between feelings and facial expressions.

The Agency

Following the pattern of the chapter in the first volume of this series (199), agency studies will be presented in three categories: attempts to define agency *function*, studies of internal *structure*, and research on the *program* through which agencies carry out their work. Although the output remained meager, there were a few studies that may lead the way toward more disciplined work in this area.

Function

Research on agency function has often been designed to probe the perceptions, or "image," of the agency held by its users and nonusers in the surrounding community. In this tradition, Alcabes (2) devoted his doctoral research to a study of

differential perceptions and patterns of use of a complex of Neighborhood Centers by the households of one community—the Lower East Side of New York City. The findings bear upon issues arising from a recurrent dialogue between Neighborhood Centers and their critics as to the centers' effectiveness with the slum community they serve. [2, p. 17]

Alcabes sought to discover (1) the social characteristics of community residents who used and did not use the neighborhood centers, (2) the social characteristics of those who discussed important problems with staff as compared with those who did not, and (3) residents' perceptions of the centers as friendly or alien, positive and negative, and the effect of these perceptions on residents' tendency to discuss important problems with staff.

The study was based on data obtained in a larger survey conducted by Mobilization For Youth in 1961 to develop demographic and attitudinal data on the population of the Lower East Side. The area contains eleven large centers and a number of smaller ones adjunctive to churches and synagogues. Alcabes treated this complex of

agencies as one center, "as if they constituted one organization with many branches" (2, p. 45). He conducted interviews in 988 of the 1,252 households selected for the MFY survey, a 79 percent completion rate. Measures were developed for determining residents' awareness and use of the center and their problem-sharing processes.

Alcabes found that 80 percent of the households were aware that a center existed nearby, about half of these had made use of the center, and lower-class families were least likely to be aware that the center existed. He also found that the centers were currently in use by about half of those who had ever used them, lower-class blacks were overrepresented among those who continued to use center resources, and users who had no clear conception of agency staff were more likely to drop out. About a third of the current users shared personal, family, or community problems with staff, and the sharers were overrepresented among households in higher socioeconomic classes, those with no grade school children, and persons who had lived in the community for many years. The households most accessible to the centers were those containing adolescent children. Alcabes concluded that the centers showed a "relatively high recruitment efficiency":

The critics' charge that the Center selectively recruits middle class households or lower class households with middle class mobility orientation is not substantiated by study findings. The study provides evidence that several factors other than class and mobility orientation are important in determining which households are selected by the recruitment process. However, for some phases of the recruitment process, class does produce an effect in the direction charged by Center critics (the higher the class the higher the recruitment). . . .
When the use phases of the recruitment process are considered, charges that the Center over-recruits middle class Whites or lower class households with middle class mobility orientation become untenable. The effect of class or mobility upon Center use is neither strong nor consistently in the expected direction. Two major factors appear most closely related to Center use: length of residence and composition of household.

Location and type of housing, and ethnicity also bear some relation to Center use. [2, pp. 158–159]

Alcabes' findings ran counter to the recent tendency, reported in the earlier review (199, pp. 146–148), to describe the disengagement of the neighborhood centers from the most needy segments of the population. As such it should feed the controversy and hopefully stimulate further careful research of this nature.

Levin (126) analyzed a number of "image" studies conducted by Jewish centers in New York City, Newark, Chicago, and Los Angeles. He concluded that there was a "fairly universal consensus" about the differences in perception of agency function between the professionals and members of the community.

The data suggest to us that anyone who holds the concept that the membership and the community at large see us as primarily a social group work agency which furthers and fosters individual growth and development and enhances and supports Jewish identification and Jewish values is living, like Alice, in a kind of Wonderland. [126, p. 190]

Levin identifies the points of difference as follows: while the professionals stress Jewish identification and personality development, the community sees the agency as a place for recreation and physical activity; while the professionals hold the image of a family agency, the community perceives the center as primarily a service to children; and while the staff members envisage a broad range of educational, cultural, and social activities designed to develop leadership and participation, the adults invest a substantial portion of their involvement in the health club, cultural arts, interest groups, and social groupings. The professional emphasis on social group work is superseded by a trend toward special interest groups, and the stress on Jewish identification produces a situation wherein "our verbalization far exceeds our practice" (126, p. 207). In short, the professionals tend to speak of the center as a way of life rather than as a variety of specific services. Levy (133) has also explored

this range of functional images and its "disparities between idealizations and experience of center personnel."

The need of the neighborhood centers to find a vital function in today's intense struggle for racial democracy produced several studies of problems and strategies. Drake (45) surveyed agency programs and practices on race relations for the National Federation of Settlements and Neighborhood Centers (NFS). Moved by criticism of agency paternalism and rigidity, NFS authorized a study that would stimulate local self-assessment and tap five aspects of agency experience: (1) degree of commitment to integration, (2) integration at the board level, (3) integration at the staff level, (4) modes of social action, and (5) their reactions to the "militant mood" within the civil rights movement. Drake took data from 56 agencies in an interview sample and 86 centers in a general sample that responded to mail questionnaires. The report emerged in a series of case presentations and discussions of community conditions and settlement reactions in Atlanta, Chicago, Philadelphia, Rochester, and other cities. It concluded with a set of guidelines designed to provide agency direction and responsibility during periods of "rapid change in race relations."

For the YMCAs Harlow (83) reported a study of the merger process in which black branches were closed as part of a move toward integration with all-white branches. Here again the emphasis was on racial integration, and here too the study report took the form of case discussion. "It follows the sequence of events from an exploration of early catalytic incidents, the factors behind the incidents, and other contributing causes to the actual closing of the Branch" (83, p. 1).

In another YMCA study Foster and Batchelder (55) examined three different modes of "Y" response to the pressure for racial integration—those agencies that adopted open policies and worked to implement them, those that gradually desegregated without any official policy, and those that, in disagreement with the national council, maintained segregated programs and facilities. They found that the agency image held by "Y" leadership was frequently quite different from that perceived by others in the community, that white and black leadership communicated poorly, and that

many of the YMCA leaders interviewed in this study felt that the YMCA should not practice racial discrimination, but also made it clear that they felt no responsibility for actually achieving racial integration. [55, p. 30]

These were the people who "make no issue of race," but simply "accept people as they come."

The flow of agency self-studies and surveys designed to relate agency resources to community need seems to have narrowed to a trickle; some of these have already been reported in the various categories presented earlier. The Chicago Jewish Community Centers have been engaged in a comprehensive self-study the final report of which has not yet been received. Holmes (98) surveyed parental interest in nursery school services in three New York communities served by Jewish centers; he found the study rewarding, locating a substantial need that had hitherto been unrevealed and identifying some of the conditions under which it could be met.

Structure

Zald's analysis of "organizations as polities," directed specifically to community organization agencies, had many implications for the neighborhood centers (253). "These concepts and propositions are designed to explain some of the determinants of agency processes and, consequently, the styles and problems of professional practice" (253, p. 56). Four interrelated concepts formed the core of his analysis: that (1) organizations have constitutions, (2) these constitutions serve a constituency that is not the clientele but those groups that

control the agency and to whom the executive is most responsible, (3) the community organization agency wishes to affect target populations, other organizations, and centers of decision-making, and (4) the community agencies exist among other agencies and have "foreign relations" that can facilitate or impede their goals.

Zald offered a number of testable propositions, among them the following: (1) To the extent that an agency is heavily dependent on its constituency, it is likely to develop a constitution that gives little room for discretion. (2) The greater the knowledge differential between staff and constituency, the more likely that staff autonomy will be great and the constituency consulted only on "boundary" conditions. (3) Middle- and upper-class constituencies are more apt to work by persuasion and informal negotiation, while lower-class-based organizations will more likely resort to direct action, open propaganda, and agitation. (4) The more an agency has a constituency made up of agencies, the more difficult it is to develop commitment to an action program and the more likely that the agency will serve as a clearinghouse for information and coordination. The analysis is provocative and evokes many of the classic problems and frustrations of the neighborhood group-serving agencies. Zald's "sociological reader" on the social welfare institutions (254) will also be a valuable resource for those interested in the structure of neighborhood agencies and its implications for practice.

In somewhat the same vein Warren (246) identified two constituencies in the "community decision organizations": the input constituency consisted of those parties to which the organization owed responsibility in determining its policies and programs and the output constituency was composed of the appropriate targets of service. Warren found that these two populations were often at variance on specific decisions made by a community organization.

The notion of lay sponsors and boards of directors as constituencies to be served rather than as representative bodies responsible to their clients and members is an effort to align some of the old ideas about agency structure with some persistent realities. The concept may stimulate research designed to explain and document some long-standing inconsistencies between theory and practice in the neighborhood agencies.

On the study of boards of directors and their characteristics, Massarik and Okin (146), for the Jewish Centers Association of Los Angeles, developed a portrait of their board members by age, education, occupation, patterns of religious identification, organizational membership, modes of involvement and influence, satisfactions and dissatisfactions with the board member role, and other factors. They found that their board member was not likely to identify with a specific sect or party in the Jewish community, that his influence tended to be localized to the center itself rather than to Jewish community policy in the larger scene, and that he believed strongly that a small central clique made most of the important decisions. They also found that the "exceptionally satisfied" board member was regarded by others as central and that those perceived as near-central were *less* likely to view their role as exceptionally satisfying than those who were clearly on the fringe. The exceptionally satisfied board members were more likely to report that they had frequent contacts with center executive staff. Only about one in five of the board members believed that he had an almost complete understanding of center philosophy and purpose.

Levy, at the Yeshiva University School of Social Work, sought to uncover elements of knowledge and skill "requisite for effective professional practice with social agency boards" (132, p. 6). He did a content analysis of thirteen process records written by as many center executives to describe their work at a single board meeting. The analysis yielded an inventory of issues with which these agency boards are occupied and he was able to identify—and illustrate with record excerpts—a number of helping roles used by the executives in their direct practice with their boards. Levy emerged with a concept of enabling that he felt was close to the helping role as it is generally understood in other groups and other agencies.

Program

Program studies of depth and general applicability are still hard to come by, and there is little cross-fertilization among the agencies except by way of broadly descriptive accounts published in the various house organs. Mogulof (153) tried to take some more specific measures of a program ingredient much discussed in the Jewish centers:

The observer of the Jewish Center field "knows" that centers vary in their Jewish practices and that communities, agencies and their leadership also vary. Could this "knowledge" be made specific in the form of hard data? Could patterns of Jewish achievement and patterns of situational variance be linked to each other statistically so as to suggest that their concurrence was not happenstance? [153, p. 102]

He sent a mail questionnaire including 112 items of Jewish practice and questions dealing with selected variable characteristics to 102 Jewish centers. These were centers that were not linked to synagogues, had autonomous boards of directors, and were not located in Canada or in the metropolitan areas of Los Angeles, Chicago, or New York. The Guttman scale procedure was used to analyze the data, the centers were rated on a continuum from low to high level of Jewish practices, and an effort was made to associate these ratings with characteristics of the general community, the Jewish community, the welfare community, the agency, and the agency leadership.

Mogulof found that in communities marked by a profusion of other cultural patterns centers are more likely to distinguish their practices, achieving a higher level of Jewish content. In communities where Jews had a higher representation on the Community Chest than in the general population, the centers were less likely to distinguish their practices. Other high-level indicators were the center's ability to finance its own operations, a high-density Jewish population, and less extensive welfare community contacts by center leadership. Having hypothesized that "center linkage to the welfare community would be associated with relative failure in the achievement of Jewish goals, and linkage to the Jewish community would be associated with their most successful pursuit," Mogulof concluded that "the findings indicate that one must know a good deal more about the Jewish community before hypothesizing that strong linkage to it is associated with higher levels of distinguishing practices" (153, p. 112). He pointed out that the center field may have considerable difficulty accepting the possibility that two of its major goals may be irreconcilable— the strengthening of Jewish practices and the reinforcement of its connections to the social welfare community.

Brodsky (19) developed data on participation of the Jewish community centers in activities related to the urban crisis. He surveyed 73 centers in 61 cities in the United States and found that "a large majority of Jewish Community Center executives believe that involvement of their Centers in appropriate urban-crisis-related activities is a valid expression of Jewish commitment and values." Centers were involved in three ways: (1) direct services to minorities and disadvantaged groups, including Head Start programs, day care centers, tutorial programs, work training opportunities, camping, and intergroup programming, (2) center participation in Community Action Programs, and (3) public affairs programming involving educative and legislative activity.

For the YMCAs Hardy (81) provided a summary of a national study of work with families in which it was discovered that the goals of the program were unclear, there was little lay involvement, and "there is little coordinated effort in bringing the resources of the Association to bear on fam-

ily needs" (81, p. 2). He provided program-planning and systematic study guidelines for the development of "Y" work with families. Also for the YMCA, Lucci (136) studied the "Y"s' work with college students, examining the extent and distribution of campus work, the characteristics of leaders and members, the religious orientation of the "Y"s, the relationship between college attributes and "Y" effectiveness, and some implications for policies and practices.

The Boy Scouts of America studied nationwide reactions to their Cub Scout program through the perceptions of scoutmasters (201), Webelos den leaders (247), and the den mothers and Cub Scouts themselves (155). It was found that the tenure of Cub Scout leaders is short, that the emphasis of cubmasters and den mothers is focused heavily on ends and goals, that few of the leaders are trained in the courses supplied by the Scouts, and that while most packs operate uniformly in basic organization and activity, there is considerable variation in the wide range of recommended practices.

The ambiguities surrounding the functions and purposes of the neighborhood centers continue to obstruct efforts to study their structures and processes in depth. The formulation of clear research questions and central theoretical issues is still inhibited by unresolved arguments about whether these agencies are meant to serve as social agencies, social movements, class-homogeneous social clubs, or some definable combination of these.

The Community

The community role of the neighborhood centers has been changing rapidly in the past few years. With the growing national emphasis on local action groups, it may in fact be said that the neighborhood center is no longer at the center of its neighborhood. It has, rather, taken its place within a complex of local community services geared to group activity—ranging from the federally financed CAPs to the "neighborhood service centers" to the community mental health programs to other efforts designed to move hitherto detached and isolated services into the streets and alleys of poor urban neighborhoods (35). At the same time the centers themselves have thrown renewed energy into the work outside their own walls, seeking to become more engaged with militant indigenous groups and to take a part in the activism around them. Further, as other community services have involved themselves in working with groups—in public welfare, child guidance clinics, the schools, ghetto hospitals, and others—the old-time neighborhood center monopoly as the group-serving agency has been broken up.

Thus as we begin with the rubrics of the earlier review—*the community survey, selected social problems,* and *measuring need* —it will soon become apparent that these categories no longer yield the results of bygone years. We will then move on to present some of the more recent—and relevant —work dealing with group services in neighborhoods. The research is still thin, but there is much writing and theorizing, and some of this points with promise to lines of investigation for the future. Trying to stay clear of the territory that belongs to the chapter on community organization, we will describe a few studies on problems of *neighborhood organization* from the perspective of the neighborhood centers, and we will conclude with some work dealing with *related neighborhood services.*

The Community Survey

As noted in the earlier review, the large-scale social survey designed to investigate community needs and bring them to the attention of the people was a major social welfare instrument in the early part of the present century. Its use has dwindled in recent years, but agencies continue to survey their populations and communities in more limited ways and for more specific purposes. Holmes (95) discussed his use of such devices in the agencies comprising the Associated YM-YWHAs of Greater New York. Citing the demographic studies undertaken by his staff, he pointed out that these have a kind of "preresearch" character, leading toward more productive research designs.

There is no study aim save the collection of data descriptive of the broad memberships of the Associated Y's centers. The variables are not conceptualized except in so far as we have a general notion of what to look for in making any demographic study. There are no hypotheses formulated and there are no sampling requirements save the expectation that all members will be represented on the questionnaire. The variables, as such, are uncontrolled; we want to collect descriptive measures, not to control variables. Similarly, there is no research design as such since this is a preparatory survey. [95, pp. 100–101]

Solomon and Friedman (214) summarized the returns of these Associated "Y" studies over the period 1966–68, providing demographic profiles of each of eight centers reporting to them. They included population information on employment status, age, religious education, religious affiliation, attendance at religious services, participation in Jewish organizations, and patterns of center use. Holmes (99) reported a study of Jewish population mobility in a New York City neighborhood. Using telephone and in-person interviews with Jewish families living in the southeast Bronx, he probed attitudes toward the neighborhood, intentions to move out, and views about the construction of a new agency in the community. He found that those who intended to move were young, had children, and were of a high socioeconomic status.

Selected Social Problems

A reading of the literature suggests that this is a time in which more energy is being put into redefining the problems that the agencies should be studying than in the study of the problems themselves. In such periods historical research is a much-needed commodity, and the field has not been prolific in this area. Gans's reading of settlement history to find a new focus for its work (62) created considerable discussion when it appeared (13). Weissman and Heifetz (248) reviewed the history of the country's oldest settlement—University Settlement on New York's Lower East Side—to illustrate the eras of major concern from the early stress on social reform to the "youth-centered approach" to its current participation in the War on Poverty. They end by calling for an "adult-centered program" emphasizing organized community action and the study of social problems on which it is based: "Settlements cannot do everything, but they can do a great deal more for the urban Negro and Puerto Rican adult than simply take care of his children" (248, p. 49).

Hillman's "People, Places, and Participation" (91), part of a study of local community structure and civic participation financed by the National Commission on Urban Problems, was a sociological examination of the problems attached to citizen participation in the urban scene. The study was conducted by the staff of the National Federation of Settlements and Neighborhood Centers and produced a document that discussed the origins, characteristics, and living patterns of people in slum neighborhoods; the values, conditions, and limitations of civic participation; and the "good community," which encompasses five major factors: (1) the absence of nuisances and freedom from physical fear, (2) adequacy and availability of transportation, (3) sufficiency of public services, (4) provision for the enjoyment of leisure, and (5) wide distribution of political power among skilled and competent groups organized for cooperative action.

One of the more significant studies of a specific and growing social problem was Herman and Sadofsky's examination of nine youth-work programs conducted in major cities throughout the country (88).

After the termination of the work-training programs for youth undertaken during the Great Depression, more than twenty years elapsed before any comparable programs were created to serve the vocational needs of out-of-school, out-of-work, disadvantaged youth. It was only three years ago that the first of this new group of youth-work programs opened its doors. Similar programs were subsequently established in a large number of cities across the country. Many of these programs received their original impetus from the President's Committee on Juvenile Delinquency and Youth Crime as well as support from the Office of Manpower, Automation and Training (OMAT) for their vocational components. [88, p. v]

Using interviews and workshops the authors undertook a broad survey of the problems of operating youth-work programs, reviewing the tasks of planning, setting objectives, dealing with interagency battles for control, staff training, and others. The chapter on research documents some of the difficulties of conducting effective study programs, pointing out:

All but one of the executives interviewed in this study believed that research had failed to fulfill its functions in respect to the work program. In fact, at the time they were visited, three of the nine work programs studied had not acquired a research capability of any kind. One program had subcontracted its research to a nearby university, which . . . had provided useful observations that had been incorporated in the plans for the program's next year of operations. The five remaining work programs had their own research staffs, but these staffs had produced little of value, in the opinion of our respondents. [88, p. 165]

Measuring Need

In the tradition of the "Youth Project Yardstick" reported from the Welfare Council of Metropolitan Los Angeles by Carter and Frank in the early 1950s, as well as other index-building attempts described in the earlier review (199, pp. 166–168), Staley (217) developed a "recreation needs instrument" as part of a 1966 study of recreational needs and services in south-central Los Angeles. He developed a resources index compounded of the number of professional staff hours per year per 1,000 residents in a given neighborhood, acreage of neighborhood recreation centers per 1,000 residents, and the number of centers per 10,000 persons. His need index consisted of figures on a population of 5–19-year-olds, population density, median family income, and juvenile delinquency rate. With the use of a "C-Scale," he developed scores that related needs to resources and established need priorities for recreational services, neighborhood by neighborhood. His report also included a review of similar attempts to measure recreational and youth needs in American cities over the past twenty years.

In the issue of the journal following that in which Staley's article appeared, Hendon (85) raised some important questions about the value of such studies and the actual relationship between human need and recreational programming. He pointed out that the index was designed to determine neighborhood priority claims within a condition of scarcity. However, he asked, what is meant by *need,* and if recreational resources are increased, what has been said about the human problems they are supposed to meet? He stated:

We do not know precisely what the relationship is between a given recreational program and human development. We do not know because we have had no extensive explorations of the relationship between particular recreation programs and behavior. [85, p. 189]

Hendon called for an exploration of social and psychological attitudes toward programs such as the Little League, behavioral inputs, parental attitudes, the learning processes involved, the impact of the experience, and other factors. He also criticized the study for its restriction to youths, its use of population density as a criterion, and its assumption that recreation is in some way responsive to problems of delinquency. Stating that current recreational conceptions are class bound and emphasize middle-class forms and structures, Hendon

concluded that there is little basis on which to plan recreational facilities "until we approach a point where we can say that expanding recreation resources in a particular way will satisfy a particular set of behavioral criteria for the persons affected"(85, p. 191).

Staley's reply in the same issue (218) further sharpened the dichotomy between structural and process-oriented concerns. He denied having asserted that there is a a causal relationship between recreational programs and human behavior and stated that the instrument does not promise to eliminate social problems but simply to indicate that needs exist, that certain social characteristics and resources are related to those needs, and that tensions may be reduced through providing recreation in areas of maximum pressure. He pointed out that there are quantitative and qualitative measurements and his index is in the former category. Staley's emphasis on structural solutions—more facilities—and Hendon's insistence on analyzing the nature and quality of these structures bear upon an important issue, one that is rarely examined by any of the human relations professions.

Neighborhood Organization

Neighborhood center professionals have always been interested in the literature on community power structures, perhaps because their agencies have always found it so difficult to mobilize power as an effective instrument of practice. Walton (244) analyzed 33 studies dealing with 55 communities:

The purpose of this paper is to review a substantial portion of the existing literature on community power in order to identify what generalizations, if any, can be drawn concerning the methodological and substantive correlates of various types of community power structure. [244, p. 430]

He came to several conclusions about the nature of this work, including the proposition that "the type of power structure identified by studies that rely on a single method may well be an artifact of that method" (244, p. 438).

Neighborhood workers will also be interested in Litwak and Meyer's discussion of the relationship between bureaucratic organizations and community primary groups:

The general problem we wish to discuss is how bureaucratic organizations and external primary groups (such as the family and neighborhood) coordinate their behavior to maximize social control. It will be argued in this paper that mechanisms exist to coordinate the two forms of organizations, and that these mechanisms of coordination can be systematically interpreted by what we will call a "balance theory of coordination." It will also be argued that this "balance theory" provides a formulation to account for current empirical trends more adequately than traditional sociological theories. [134, p. 246]

Running counter to the prevailing theory that bureaucracies and primary groups, and especially the nuclear family, are inherently antithetical in goals and atmosphere, Litwak and Meyer suggest that "these forms of organization are complementary and that each provides necessary means for achieving a given goal" (134, p. 248). Their balance theory states that maximum social control occurs when coordinating mechanisms develop between organizations and primary groups that balance their relationships in such a way that they are neither too intimate nor isolated from each other. Their search of the literature identified eight mechanisms of coordination currently in operation. Among these are the "detached expert approach," typified by the street club worker who bridges the structures of agency and primary group, and the "settlement house approach," in which facilities, proximity, and professional workers establish a "change-inducing milieu." This effort to develop a theoretical orientation to the task of building bridges between people and their organizations is an important contribution to the advocacy-versus-mediation controversy, more often carried on in rhetorical than in scientific terms.

Hillman and Seever (92), of the Na-
tional Federation of Settlements Training Center, examined the character of neighborhood organization through interviews, questionnaires, and case material drawn from NFS affiliates in 93 cities. The report raised all of the basic questions, examined agency experiences in detail, and offered guidelines for agency practices in the areas of citizen participation and neighborhood organization.

Related Neighborhood Services

The trend toward the location and integration of services in the heart of a neighborhood is the most recent expression of the reaching-out impulse of the last generation. March(145) summarized the shortcomings of present social service distribution and developed four models designed to offer greater neighborhood participation, more highly articulated services, and an extension of service beyond the individual to the family and the neighborhood. The models include centers for advice and referral, diagnostic centers, centers for "one-stop, multipurpose neighborhood service," and coordinated networks of service systems.

Perlman and Jones(166) reviewed the experience of six neighborhood service centers for a definitive HEW publication. They developed a working definition of this kind of agency, including information and referral; advocacy to protect client interests in their use of other agencies; certain concrete services such as legal aid, day care, employment counseling, and others; and the organization of groups for collective action. They also discussed the role of research in these programs, cited the paucity of resources, and questioned, as had Herman and Sadofsky(88) in the youth-work field, the weakness of research in this area.

The community mental health center is another major neighborhood service phenomenon, and its literature has been growing rapidly in the past few years:

1. Vacher(239) reviewed over 45 journals published from 1957 to 1968 and ab-

stracted articles specific to ten major areas of mental health center operation.

2. Roen and his associates (181) developed and validated an instrument designed to measure "community adaptation" and to serve as a tool for the evaluation of community mental health programs. The community adaptation concept, constructed to operationalize the client's interaction with his environment, was geared to wide application.

3. Richart and Millner studied factors affecting admission to a community mental health center and found that the "regulatory influence" of secure social statuses such as parent, spouse, or employee made such people "less likely to become or remain psychiatric patients than those persons with less tangible positions in life"(179, p. 29).

4. Hinkle, Cole, and Oetting described their efforts at the Southeast Wyoming Mental Health Center to make "research and evaluation, which is quite often a 'spare-time' activity in most mental health centers, an integral part of the ongoing program at Cheyenne"(93, p. 130).

5. Peck and Kaplan(164), in a theoretical discussion of the dynamic exchange between individuals and their groups, pointed out that "the small group has the unique property of enabling us to retain sight of the individual in crisis while we try to gain access to those aspects of his social milieu which are concomitantly involved."

6. The *Community Mental Health Journal*, for seven issues between the spring of 1965 and the winter of 1966, carried a "Program Developments" section that focused on built-in research components. The section seems to have been discontinued after that time.

The interest of the traditional public agencies in the use of groups as a medium of service is illustrated most dramatically by the growing involvement of public welfare programs throughout the country. *Public Welfare* used its October 1968 issue to document this development, publishing summaries of programs across the nation and featuring an account by Schwartz(197)

of a four-year process designed to integrate group services in the Bureau of Child Welfare of the New York City Department of Welfare (now the Department of Social Services). Subsequently Feldman (51), also in *Public Welfare*, reported on an exploratory study of group service programs instituted by six public welfare agencies, analyzing factors related to the initiation and development of these programs.

The neighborhood center seems to have gained strength rather than lost it from the breakdown of the old group work agency monopoly. As an established member of a new and growing family of group-oriented services, the center should perhaps have had more to teach. But there are signs, of which the Alcabes study(2) is an example, that the advent of the newer services will involve the center in new investigations that will help to pull together its working experiences over the past seventy-five years and draw generalizations from these.

The Worker

A major development of the past few years was the wide interest in paraprofessionals and their contribution to service in the neighborhoods. The literature on the subject is still largely ideological and hortatory, but there is some recent movement toward systematic role appraisal and analysis. This development has had its counterpart in a growing concern about the differential use of professional manpower and there is some work to report in this area. Beyond that there is evidence that the study of practice itself is at last becoming an object of some scientific interest, mostly in the field of doctoral research.

Continuing to stay close to the format of the earlier review, we will report the studies in three categories: those related to paid, full-time *professionals;* work on *nonprofessionals,* substituting this rubric for "volunteers" and including material on paraprofessionals; and findings from studies of *method* and the nature of group practice. When the data are thin, some of the subrubrics used in the last review will be abandoned.

Professionals

The neighborhood centers have always been sensitive to the possibility that, while they "are apparently well suited to introduce young people into the social work arena [they] may not promise the kind of professional experience that would attract them into the field of service in which they began"(199, p. 172). Pins's finding that their recruitment role yields only a small return was disconcerting(167).

Following this line of inquiry, Greene, Kasdan, and Segal(76) probed the attitudes toward Jewish center careers of Jewish second-year group work students who had been placed in centers during their first year of training. Thirty-one students in six graduate schools of social work in the New York metropolitan area served as respondents, and the researchers found considerable disaffection: only half of the students felt that the center's goals and purposes were made explicit to staff, three-quarters felt the agencies were unclear in their purpose, more than half felt that social group work principles played little or no part in program-planning, there was a good deal of rejection of and ambivalence about Jewish programming, and they found the social work role in the center confusing and wanted more direct practice by professional staff. The authors concluded that "the Jewish Community Center has to become a more exciting and dynamic setting if it is to attract professional social workers" (76, p. 175).

Related to this area of investigation is the study of occupational mobility, and Scotch(200) built his doctoral research on some problems opened up by Herman(86) in the latter's 1959 study of the mobility of Jewish community center professionals. Scotch pointed out that when Herman did his study the turnover problem in the Jewish center field was an internal one; the

field, "in effect, was a closed system of employment" and when a worker left one job he moved to another in the same field. More recently workers are tending to leave the field:

The annual rate of moveout is on the increase, thus shrinking the total number of workers with MSW's. The circulation pattern of workers in the field of social work is virtually one way in terms of movement of workers away from the JCCF [Jewish community center field] with no reciprocal exchange. The future plans of those now working in the JCCF with reference to career commitment would indicate further dwindling of the MSW segment of the JCCF work force to an increasingly smaller percentage. [200, p. 2]

Scotch studied all the graduate social workers employed by the Jewish Community Centers of Chicago for three months or more during the period from 1947 through June of 1967. He was able to enlist all but one of a total population of 141, giving him a response rate of close to 100 percent. Scotch found that the one-way movement of trained social workers out of the Jewish center field "is not so much a product of disenchantment with the JCCF as such but rather, the recent emergence of a number of highly competitive alternative career opportunities" (200, p. 8). Other factors were the newer social work emphasis on institutional change, the emergence of community organization as a more attractive area of work, the shift in emphasis to treatment and problem-solving practice rather than "preventive goals," and the problems of financing professional education.

On the matter of professional manpower utilization, the YMCA's "Preparing for the Seventies" called for a study of their total manpower development program "in view of the crisis in employed leadership"(169, p. 6). Holmes(101), for the Staff Utilization Committee of the Manpower Commission of the National Jewish Welfare Board, interviewed 44 staff members at different levels in eight centers of various sizes in five different states. He found that professional personnel tended to feel that a disproportionate amount of time was required for administrative tasks and not enough for professional activity of appropriate scope and depth, "thus reducing the workers' over-all effectiveness as professionals"(101, p. 36). The committee also produced a number of other studies, all of which are pulled together and summarized by Warach(245).

Nonprofessionals

Books about and anthologies of material on the indigenous nonprofessional have been multiplying, and those by Pearl and Riessman(163), Reiff and Riessman(174), and Grosser, Henry, and Kelley(78) may serve as entries into this field of study. Seidler's paper on the supervision of nonprofessionals(202), prepared as part of an NFS study for the National Commission on Urban Problems, is a good brief introduction to the tasks of incorporating these workers into agency services.

Sobey devoted her doctoral research to a survey of 185 NIMH-financed projects using over 10,000 nonprofessionals; her inquiry was concerned "with the nature, the extent, and the consequences of use of nonprofessionally trained persons in a particular group of projects funded for the purpose of experimenting in new manpower uses"(211, p. 1). The settings ranged "from isolated state mental hospitals to central city community centers, schools and social agencies caring for the young and old, the mentally ill, and those highly vulnerable to emotional disturbance," and the study questions included extent of use, titles, ratio to professional staff, and characteristics of age, sex, race, and educational level, among others. Combining interviews and site visits, she produced a comprehensive array of findings, including the following: the largest single group of projects (39 percent) were in the psychiatric hospitals, paid and volunteer nonprofessionals were represented about equally, the majority of the projects produced a 6:1 ratio

favoring nonprofessionals, adults and young adults predominated with limited use made of adolescents and the aged, and the majority of workers were high school graduates, making those with less education an important untapped manpower resource.

Sobey concluded that the boundary lines between the mental health disciplines, as well as the traditional divisions between professional and nonprofessional functions, are blurring. Also less distinct are the lines between the various nonprofessional aide groups; they are all "performing caretaking, therapeutic and community-oriented functions with little evidence of concern that they are moving out of their traditional roles"(211, p. 286). Sobey(212) added another valuable resource with her annotated bibliography on volunteer services in mental health from 1955 to 1969; her introduction gave a historical perspective on voluntarism, some current trends in the field, and the scope of the bibliography. Her book on the "nonprofessional revolution" in mental health is in press at this writing(210).

Some research has begun on role analysis of the indigenous nonprofessional; research on this has, in fact, begun much more quickly than similar investigations in the heyday of the volunteer. Levinson and Schiller(131) conceptualized the agency structure as a three-level pyramid with forms of participation at each level; they identified the key issues as classification of nonprofessionals, simplification and standardization of social work tasks, and the attempt to connect the "discrepant roles" emerging from where the indigenous nonprofessional is heading and the point from which he left.

Gannon(61) examined the nonprofessional role as it was defined by a group of indigenous workers in the Domestic Peace Corps program of the Harlem community in New York City (HDPC). The HDPC was engaged in the recruitment and training of nonprofessionals to work in the social service agencies of central Harlem. From 150 corpsmen and about half of the agencies served, they drew a clear picture of worker aspirations and role implications: the most common reason given for joining was career advancement, the most common response to questions about life satisfaction was related to career and occupation, the most frequent criticisms of HDPC were the low pay and limitation of work hours, and there was dissatisfaction about the quality of the relationship with the professionals. The status of indigenous personnel was poorly defined and seemed to lead to undesirable consequences:

A source of strain for most workers was the ambivalence within the structure of HDPC regarding the volunteer or employee status of the Corpsmen. This was reflected in difficulties over wages, job benefits and transferring to another job after one's term of service with the Corps is finished. [61, p. 359]

Grosser(77), at MFY, administered a survey questionnaire on perceptions of the neighborhood to community residents, MFY professionals, and indigenous staff workers, with all staff members being asked to predict how the residents would answer the questions. He found that the professionals differed from the residents on many issues related to deprivation, the professionals were most optimistic about the efficacy of social action, the community residents were most optimistic about the chances for success of individual poor persons, indigenous staff perceptions were closer to those of the community residents than were those of the professionals, and the indigenous staff members predicted the responses of community residents more accurately than did the professionals.

Grosser also found, however, that although indigenous staff responses were more like those of the residents than were those of the professionals, on a high proportion of items the indigenous workers were also closer to the professionals than they were to the residents. This suggested that those selected to work in a professional agency were in many ways more like the middle-class professional than the lower-

class client. This finding, similar in some important ways to Gannon's data on the Harlem corpsmen, has implications for those who see the "para" as a step toward becoming "professional" rather than as a fixed and permanent role—a "career for the poor."

Specht, Hawkins, and McGee(215), in the Community Development Demonstration Project of Richmond, California, made an important contribution to role and skill analysis when they required all of their "subprofessionals" to keep casebooks of their daily work. The examination of these materials was informal but yielded beginning information on the subprofessionals' tasks, the institutional contacts they were making, and the kinds of skills they were called on to exercise. The researchers found that these workers were required to use skills in interviewing, diagnosis, referral, advocacy, and "brokerage," and often served as a bridge between clients and the institutions. The authors called for more precise means of measuring skills and competence, lest a large number of subprofessional workers be backed into low-paying and unrewarding jobs no matter how great their increasing abilities.

Moving from the indigenous nonprofessional to the more classic frame of reference of the volunteer, several studies explored the roles and characteristics of this category of personnel. Cantor(27), for the Research and Demonstration Center of the Columbia University School of Social Work, followed 111 VISTA Volunteers from the beginning of training through their first four months in jobs located in forty-three different urban projects across the nation. These volunteers, selected randomly by the Washington office from a pool of eligible applicants, were almost all 25 years old and under (90 percent), with two-thirds ranging in age from 20 to 23; girls slightly outnumbered boys; most were white, single, and came from affluent middle-class backgrounds; they were college educated and some had advanced professional training; most had parents who were managers, professionals, and semiprofessionals. On their VISTA jobs the volunteers worked mainly with blacks, children, and young people, and they served in several ways:

as *bridges* between the ghetto and the world outside; as *catalysts* activating neighbors in social action; as *service agents* giving concrete help to individuals and groups; as *innovators* and *gadflies* within the agency trying out new services, criticizing the status quo; and as *symbols* of mobility and concern offering a contact with the outside world. [27, p. 5]

Although somewhat over half indicated that their satisfactions outweighed their frustrations, "almost all had some frustration to tell":

The major frustrations the volunteers reported . . . related to the nature of their job, agency, relationships with clients and their own personal misgivings. As noted, many Volunteers came to their agencies with the preconception that a VISTA job involved going into the homes and organizing for social action. They were uneasy about their service jobs. Others were concerned with the fact that they did not see immediate results. Some felt that they were not fully utilized or that the agency was too structured and limiting. Volunteers were less bothered by their own agencies than by the fact that other agencies in the community blocked action or did not do their jobs. [27, pp. 44-45]

There were other findings, related to on-the-job training, use of available staff in different ways, supervision, and the impact of neighborhood conditions on the volunteers. "VISTA Volunteers are in no sense indigenous workers" and "culture shock is as real for most VISTA Volunteers as for Peace Corpsmen"(27, p. 47).

Schwartz(194), in a doctoral study, surveyed the volunteer program of the Associated YM-YWHAs of Greater New York, examining the nature of volunteer service, the satisfactions derived from the work, and volunteers' role perceptions together with those of the professional staff. She found:

The volunteer does not go to the Y primarily to carry out the aims of the agency. He or she goes to satisfy personal purposes related to personal development and educa-tion. He is happy to do this while helping the agency, but he is likely to judge the Center on the basis of how well the volunteer program serves him. [194, p. 83]

Schwartz also found that staff members higher up in the hierarchy tended to express more appreciation for the volunteer's contribution, but "these were not the staff members who most frequently worked with volunteers or had the most contact" with them (194, p. 85).

Johnson(112) studied the use of volunteers in community service in North Carolina, developing data on motivation, characteristics, specific contributions, the role of retired and lower income groups, relationships with professional staff persons, and staff willingness to use volunteers in the expansion of social services. Carp(29) investigated the differences among volunteers, older workers, and nonworkers in a population of applicants for public housing for the aged. She found that workers scored as being happier and more self-satisfied than either volunteers or nonworkers on all measures.

The results suggest that, if volunteer service is to become an effective substitute for work, attention must be paid not only to its time-filling, time-scheduling activity and sociability components, but also to the purchasing power and the social value inherent in payment. [29, p. 501]

Method

There are signs that the long-awaited interest in the study of practice has begun to appear, both in social work and in related professions. In the field of education Gage (59) edited a superb collection of research pieces on the practice of teaching from which all of the helping professions can learn a great deal. Gage's own chapter on paradigms of research on the teaching process(60) and Broudy's analysis of the historical development of pedagogical concepts (21) are of particular interest to social workers seeking ways of approaching the study of the helping process in groups. Of interest too will be Strupp and Bergin's bibliography of 2,741 items of research in individual psychotherapy, with a major emphasis on studies using a research design and reporting quantitative results(219). They pointed out that "the growth of the field is documented by the fact that the earlier compilation [published by Strupp in 1964] included about 1,000 references whereas the present one, four years later, lists almost three times that number"(219, p. v). The bibliography is indexed by content categories, using rubrics of client, method, and process, among others.

In social work a growing body of doctoral students has begun to produce some fairly substantial contributions to the study of practice with groups. Fresh from their own practice in the neighborhood centers and other settings, many have turned their curiosity loose on problems of method and the output is beginning to mount. Without trying to do a comprehensive review, the writer will describe briefly a few of these studies to give some sense of the kinds of problems they are undertaking.

Garvin(66, 67) investigated the effects of "contractual agreement" between workers and their group members on reciprocal obligations and the role of the worker. Defining contract as "a set of agreements between the worker and the group members regarding the problems to be dealt with in their interaction as well as the means to be utilized in this process"(67, p. 127), he hypothesized that high agreement between workers and members would be associated with a higher quality of performance by both. He found that although all of the variances could not be explained in contractual terms, "the over-all conclusion of this study is that the existence of the 'contract' . . . is an important correlate of worker activity and group movement"(67, p. 145). Brown(22), also working on the contract theme—which promises to become an increasingly popular research subject— found that early attention by the worker to the problem of mutual expectations seemed to produce significant reductions in the amount of time spent on testing, allowing

the groups to move to their work more rapidly.

Horowitz(106) and Morgan(154) worked to define the specific techniques of intervention used by social workers in group situations. Horowitz explored the reactions of group workers to hypothetical instances of deviant behavior and tried to trace the effects of selected variables on the workers' projected behavior; he found that his "Study Model" was a useful instrument for differentiating dimensions of worker behavior. Of considerable interest too was the fact that he could derive no meaningful differences between socialization and treatment groups; a high consensus was found on the modes of intervention for the two types. Morgan, analyzing critical incidents reported by professionally trained workers in a New York City neighborhood center, developed a classification system of interventive techniques used with groups and with individuals in groups.

Other method-oriented doctoral investigations were reported by Cleminger(36), who studied group workers' skill in assessing their members' perception of the worker's role (an aspect also related to the contractual theme); Peirce(165), who developed and tested some conceptual models of elements of group practice; Ishikawa (110), who investigated three variables of group workers' verbal acts through time— to whom they were addressed, the nature of the problem situation, and the group resources called on; and Lawrence(122), who, in the classic "leadership style" line of inquiry, tested the effects of group-directed versus worker-directed approaches toward changing the food-buying practices of welfare recipients.

Mention should also be made of a master's degree thesis produced by Agueros and eight associates at the Columbia University School of Social Work(1). Using an analytical instrument previously devised by Schwartz(198), these students isolated and classified over 500 specific helping acts reported by group workers, caseworkers, and community organization practitioners in three statuses—untrained, student, and professional—thus creating nine categories for study and comparison. They stated:

The attempt is also made to develop some understanding of the complex of factors in which these acts are embedded: to whom they are addressed, the stimuli that set them off, workers' modes of interpreting these stimuli, the hoped-for client responses, and the kinds of assumptions on which these acts are based. The total effort is designed to see as deeply as we can into the detailed events of the helping process, as these events are perceived by the social workers themselves. [1, p. 25]

Comparing the nine worker categories on each of the variables mentioned, the researchers produced a host of subtle and suggestive findings: caseworkers, with high internal consistency among the three degrees of training, were triggered by feeling stimuli significantly more than were group or community workers; group workers tended to be highly susceptible to nonverbal stimuli; the acts of community organization workers tended to be less feeling oriented and more related to advising their clients and providing information intended to be useful; untrained workers were highest on the dimension of directive acts; the three student categories were the most internally consistent in their responses; professionals tended to produce interpretations that related strongly to clients' perceptions of their own situations and to clients' avoidance patterns. In their conclusion the students raised questions about whether the various methods (group work, casework, and community organization) are in some way geared to producing different work-styles, the relationship between work-style and personal styles, and the possibility of effecting comparisons between the workers' and clients' conceptions of what constitutes a helping act. The study also offered a review of the practice research literature and an annotated bibliography of practice studies in social work and related disciplines.

Other studies of group practice were reported from a number of different agency settings. Klein and Snyder(117) studied the work-style phenomenon in the context of gang work, examining the practice of ten detached workers assigned by the Los Angeles Probation Department to the most active gang neighborhoods in the county. They found that interworker variability on practice and the use of time was high, and they concluded that "the agency must build into its structure and program a system for tolerating variability in worker styles." (P. 68.)

Gilbert(70) reported a study of the role of the neighborhood coordinator in the CAP sponsored by the Pittsburgh Mayor's Committee on Human Resources. He probed the question of whether these coordinators were advocates or, as Rein and Riessman(175) had put it, "the cement that binds distributors and consumers," or whether "they operate in a vague shadowland somewhere between these two" (70, p. 136). The study examined these stances carefully and operationally and concluded:

The coordinators have mastered the essential political and social tools for operating under conflicting pressures in the public spotlight . . . [they] walk the tightrope between advocate and middleman . . . [and] to maintain this balance, they become masters at negotiation, accommodation, and manipulation of citizens and agency staff. [70, p. 144]

From the mental hospital field Yalom and his associates contributed to the research on the contract theme by showing that "anxiety stemming from unclarity of the group task, process, and role expectations in the early meetings of the therapy group may, in fact, be a deterrent to effective therapy"(251, p. 426), and that pretherapy preparatory sessions were able to reduce much of this anxiety. Also from the psychiatric setting, Becker and his associates(10) studied the differences between led and unled therapy groups and found that in the smaller groupings

the presence of a high-status leader, such as a psychotherapist, leads to less spontaneity, more self-consciousness, and more inhibition. . . . When the size of the group was increased and the role of the participants changed by adding family members to the groups, the inhibiting effect of the therapist's presence was modified, making the activity level of the meetings similar, in some ways, to that of unled group meetings. [10, p. 50]

In a VA hospital in Houston, Rothaus, Johnson, and Lyle(186) assigned 49 psychiatric patients to group discussion roles either similar to their usual behavior (role repetition) or opposite to their usual behavior (role reversal). They found that passive patients found the role reversal process most difficult, but that role reversal resulted in the greatest feeling of satisfaction for all participants. Further, those assigned to active roles felt more responsible for the group than those assigned to silent ones.

From the camping field Ramsey(172) tested a program designed to produce social and interpersonal activity among mental patients selected from the Texas state mental hospital system. The program was designed to implement the concept that the social structure and processes of the patient community are the essential treatment agents, and Ramsey found a high degree of corroboration for this theory in his examination of worker-patient relations and in his follow-up studies. Levine(129), for the Mental Hygiene Clinic of Henry Street Settlement in New York City, studied the clinic's program of "treatment in the home" and found that efforts to bring mental health skills into the homes of multiproblem families did effect changes in the ways in which parents responded to their children, as well as leading to improved behavior in the children.

On the classic directive-nondirective dimension, Shaw and Blum(205) worked with ninety male undergraduates assigned to eighteen five-member groups. On the same three tasks, nine groups worked under directive leadership and nine under nondirective. The researchers reported:

This experiment shows clearly that directive leadership is more effective than nondirective when the task is highly structured, that is, when there is only one solution and one way of obtaining this solution. . . . However, on tasks that require varied information and approaches, nondirective leadership is clearly more effective. On such tasks the requirements for leadership are great. Contribu-

tions from all members must be encouraged and this requires motivating, advising, rewarding, giving support—in short, nondirective leadership. [205, p. 241]

Thomas(225) and Bruck(23) offered points of departure for the developing study of behavioral approaches to social work practice, both individually and in groups. Thomas related to social work practice the techniques of positive reinforcement, extinction, differential reinforcement, response-shaping, and punishment, and attacked the "mistaken conceptions" that associate such techniques with manipulation and mechanism: "Knowledge is itself ethically neutral and values become engaged only when knowledge is used"(225, p. 25).

Bruck's review of the theory and practice of behavior modification defined the basic tenets "accepted by most behaviorists," evaluated their claims of success, discussed their conception of the individual and the meaning of neurosis, and pointed up some areas of applicability to social work practice. The language of these theorists is strange to most social workers and the frame of reference difficult to handle, but the controversy has grown increasingly lively and may soon produce some valuable practice research in social work as it has in related fields.

The systematic study of practice recording is still in its infancy. Wakeman(242), working out of the Seattle Atlantic Street Center, used high-speed computers to analyze the quality of street worker activity.

While the keeping of narrative, process, and summary records has served a very useful purpose—and probably always will remain an intrinsic part of the social work education process—the recent and burgeoning development of high-speed computers has introduced a new means for recording social work activity. [242, p. 54]

Garfield and Irizarry(64) described their use of an instrument—the "Record of Service"—that was designed to draw from the worker an account encompassing both the specific focus of his service and the techniques used in carrying it out. From the University of Michigan School of Social

Work a Practice Skill Assessment Instrument was offered that gives "quantitative measures of selected aspects of student performance in field instruction"(238). And Shulman's *A Casebook of Social Work with Groups*(207) represented a rare effort to use record materials as a teaching-learning bridge between theory and practice in the helping process. His twenty-seven "interactional techniques" are drawn from theoretical models and illustrated by written accounts of practice.

Concluding with the area of training and supervision, the annotated bibliographies issued by the U.S. Public Health Service on training methodology(234, 235, 236, 237) and on in-service training for key professionals in community mental health (230, 231) have already been mentioned. The neighborhood centers will also be interested in the research reported by the Boys' Clubs of America on their "executive program"—a nationwide effort to establish in-service training for executive and supervisory personnel(176, 177). On a theoretical level, French and his associates(58) systematically applied Homans's formulation on the human group (105) to problems of staff training in group service agencies. Pointing out that

theory to guide social work practice will develop more rapidly and productively by building on theoretical efforts going forward in the underlying sciences of human behavior, rather than by formulating theory primarily on the basis of observation and analysis of practice [58, p. 379],

they held the Homans frame of reference up against a training program for camp counselors, clerical staff relationships in a group work agency, and the pattern of professional versus volunteer staffing in a community center.

Evaluations and Outcomes

In this final category the picture is that of a few rigorous efforts in a fairly unproductive field. Herman's (87) discussion of the problems of evaluating work training programs for unemployed youths cited the general frustrations of defining criteria of success, using researchers who are unfamiliar with the programs and hence unable to establish the proper categories for data collection, the scientific interest in "basic" research that often obscures the curiosity about specific program data and statistics, and the problems involved in generating reasonable conclusions from specific events.

Brooks(20) described the evaluation process in CAPs, identifying the tasks of determining the extent of goal achievement, fixing the relative importance of the program's key variables, and distinguishing these from variables external to the program and active on it. He also defined levels of evaluation and discussed the various constraints on evaluative research: the long-standing tensions between action and research; the arbitrary boundaries that separate the social sciences from one another; the ethical necessity for the feedback of findings into the program itself, thus changing the very phenomena under study as they are being studied; the brief life expectancies of most projects, creating a pressure for quick results; and the openness of the systems under study, where "the community is *not* a laboratory in which all the variables can be carefully controlled and manipulated at will"(20, p. 39).

It seems fairly clear at this point that the antipoverty programs have failed to live up to the research promises embedded in their grants. However, it may be that the adding-up is still going on and that more productive statements will be forthcoming as many of these projects draw to a close.

Movement Studies

From the Chicago Youth Development Project, Caplan(28) has offered what seems to be a landmark attempt to integrate the study of outcomes and processes so that one may understand the relationship between the two.

The present study is less concerned with outcome effects as such than it is with the process of behavioral change and with factors that regulate the course of such change through time among subjects involved in a treatment intervention project. Specifically, the major point of interest is the change in behavior of youth who are exposed to a program of counseling and pragmatic help designed to improve their personal and social adjustment; how they change over time; the relationship of behavior changes to program input; and how client and treatment agent behavior are affected by the very interaction system they create. [28, p. 64]

The subjects were 109 inner-city boys being counseled by three experienced street gang workers; each boy was at Stage 5 or above of an eight-stage program adjustment scale developed for an earlier investigation. Going up the scale, Stage 5 was "receptivity to personal counseling," Stage 6 was the ability to demonstrate "meaningful relationship" with the worker, Stage 7 involved "commitment and preparation for change," and Stage 8 called for "transfer and autonomy" (the success stage and the final, rather than instrumental, goal). The variations of treatment input were measured on a "Blood, Sweat, and Tears (BST) Scale," operationalized on six points extending from "minimal worker input" involving only routine recreational and social services to "the supreme effort," calling for a high degree of intimacy and an intensive work level.

The researchers found, as they had in a previous investigation, a striking "near-success pile-up" with 71 percent of the boys in Stages 6 and 7 one year after Stage 5 classification; only 7 percent were in Stage 8 at that time. The study then took some ingenious and creative directions as the researchers turned to explore the "near-success" phenomenon. Was Stage 8 disproportionately small because the study ended too soon for the "additive change model to produce its final summation effects"? The data showed that 89 percent of the subjects had moved to a numerically higher

stage through time; however, after Stage 7 the movement was *negative* and there was a backsliding effect followed by a "rebound phase" in which the boys' movement headed back toward Stage 7. Thus it was not a question of time: "in fact, Stage 8 classification after the initial progress through the adjustment stages, became increasingly *less* likely with each successive iteration of the backsliding orders"(28, p. 77).

After further analysis of the complex factors affecting the tendency *nearly* to succeed in taking on the "final change behaviors advocated by the treatment program," Caplan suggested that "instrumental changes proceed independently of or are basically incompatible with the final objectives they are designed to produce." The youngsters can be reached, but "because of the services and favors proffered, there may be considerably more advantage in being 'reached' repeatedly than in being changed"(28, p. 83). And again: "The subjects seemed to have a special affinity for accepting help and a special disaffinity for 'success' in terms of those behaviors which the program ideally wished to produce"(28, p. 85).

Although Caplan noted that "there may be good reason for the [client's] unwillingness to adapt to the external demands required for program success"(28, p. 85), it seemed clear that there was inadequate recognition of the fact that the failure of Stage 8 was a function of the success criteria themselves rather than of the treatment process. If one stopped short of the global and overreaching claims often established for client-worker success, the so-called near-success stage could be accepted as a far more realistic appraisal of what can be achieved by the professional helping process. It seemed clear that in this instance the boys' positive moves were related to stages that reflected the workers' desire to *help*; as soon as the workers began to try to *change* their clients into socially acceptable models (Stage 8), the boys rebelled and forced the workers to persist in their helping behavior. Caplan's interest in the processes of work is stimulating throughout: at one point he draws a fascinating picture of a kind of *folie à deux* between worker and client in which each is "creature and creator of a self-perpetuating drama built upon an interweaving of reciprocal interaction effects"(28, p. 86).

Although not strictly in this category, Maas's(137) inquiry into the connections between preadolescent peer relations and the adult capacity for intimacy would be relevant here. Using the files of a longitudinal study of 248 children born in Berkeley in 1928 and 1929 who were assessed periodically from infancy through adolescence and again at age 30, Maas selected 44 adults who were judged to be at either end of a continuum of capacity-incapacity for intimacy. Evidence of adult capacity for intimacy was the scored distributions on two items of the 100-item California Q-sort deck: Item 35 on warmth, capacity for close relationships, and compassion; and Item 48 on "keeps people at a distance" and "avoids close interpersonal relationships." Independent sorting by two judges, using a third in instances of low agreement, and a search for clearly contrasting cases yielded selection of 22 males (10 "warm" and 12 "aloof") and 22 females (14 warm and 8 aloof). Maas then analyzed the preadolescent peer relations of these men and women. The data were derived from interviews conducted with the subjects during their school years. Maas found the following:

There are enduring friendships during preadolescence in both male subsamples—the warm and the aloof. In other aspects of the composition of the peer networks, however, there are notable differences between the warm and the aloof males, and differences in the nature of their interaction with peers. [137, p. 165]

Warm males who had a "chum" had only one, while aloof males tended to have two in sequence, with much evidence of "spoiled friendships" in the aloof male subsample. Warm males tended to have relationships with age-peers and older boys, while aloof males tended to move toward those younger than themselves. Warm males named girls as playmates, while aloof males did not. And aloof males tended to be critical, pejorative, and controlling, explaining somewhat their preference for younger boys. Among the females Maas found fewer differentiating antecedents. The major differences between the warm and aloof females lay in their early attitudes toward boys and in the number of playmates they had at age 12, with a lessening number for the aloof females by that age.

Maas concluded that there were different preadolescent contexts for males and females in developing the capacity for adult intimacy. For the males it seemed to be associated with constancy of enduring friendships, early familiarity with girls, less superordination and rivalry, and being sought after by high-status peers. For the females it was associated with early outgoingness with boys and a large and constant number of playmates. The evidence seemed to support theory on preadolescents' capacity for close and enduring friendships; however, it did not support the proposition that having a preadolescent chum is an essential precondition for the development of the adult capacity for intimacy. Rather, it was the *spoiling* of such friendships that seemed to characterize the aloof adult males. Maas also found that in the larger peer networks reciprocity and collaboration were least characteristic of the aloof males. He concluded with a reminder that he was not trying to establish

causal connections between these antecedent and subsequent human conditions. Many factors, such as temperament, the age of sexual maturity, family relations, and subcultural socialization, not touched on in this paper, probably contribute to the nature of interpersonal relations with peers in both preadolescence and adulthood. [137, p. 172]

Craig and Furst(40) studied the outcomes of boys for whom predictions of future delinquency had been made using the Glueck Social Prediction Table. Those who were judged to have a 50 percent or greater chance of becoming delinquent had been referred for treatment at a child guidance clinic, and these 29 boys and their families had been in therapy over a four-year period. The researchers found few differences between the treatment and the control groups, except that the average age of declared delinquency was two years higher in the treatment group. They concluded:

This study offers no encouragement for the hope that child guidance therapy offers a means of materially reducing the incidence of serious delinquency in a population of boys selected by the Glueck Social Prediction Table. [40, p. 171]

Macdonald(139) reviewed the New York City Youth Board's test of the table itself, examining both its original and its revised forms in the light of its demonstrated usefulness over the years. She concluded that "high predictive power was not demonstrated by the first table and has not been shown for the new one"(139, p. 182). Further:

Whether any screening device to identify future delinquents could be used effectively and with proper safeguards remains to be seen. Certainly, effective help for all children when they need help is a more desirable objective. Certainly we now know more about identifying troubled children than about helping them. Clearly the Youth Board's publication of a "Manual" is premature, if not irresponsible, promotion of a screening device that has not yet been proved. [139, p. 182]

From Nashville, McLarnan and Fryer (141) reported on the second year of a research and demonstration project sponsored by the University of Tennessee School of Social Work and the Wesley House Centers and financed by the U.S. Public Health Service. The project was designed

to help young married couples who are residents in low-rent public housing complexes improve in their performance of family roles. . . . Social group work was selected as the primary method of social work to be used in the demonstration project. Social casework and informal education services were included as additional means of effecting change. [141, p. 1]

The interim report encompassed dimensions of group structure, norms, program, worker function, individualization, and some problems of establishing a clear contract for work.

Program Evaluation

It is beyond the scope of this chapter to render a detailed description of the controversial study by Meyer, Borgatta, and Jones of *Girls at Vocational High*(149). Reviews and discussions abound, ranging from that in the *Washington Post* of March 17, 1966, stating that social workers were "writhing" under the "challenge to their work," to the technical professional reviews of Macdonald(138), Schorr(190), and others. The authors introduced the study rationale and objectives as follows:

This book describes a study of the consequences of providing social work services to high school girls whose record of earlier performance and behavior at school revealed them to be potentially deviant. Over the course of four years girls with potential problems who entered a vocational high school in New York City were identified from information available to the school. From this pool of students a random sample of cases was referred to an agency where they were offered casework or group counseling services by professional social workers. A control group was also selected at random from the same pool of potential problem cases in order that a comparison could be made between girls who received service and similar girls who did not. Since all these girls were identified as potential problem cases, they may be considered latent or early detected deviants. Services to them consisted in efforts to interrupt deviant careers. [149, p. 15]

The group aspects of the treatment program were somewhat clouded in the authors' description and it is often difficult to understand exactly what happened; apparently the consultants were changed and the groups re-formed, following which there was "almost exclusive use of group approaches after the first phase of the project" (149, p. 149). There are no record excerpts given on which to base any judgments about the quality of individual or group techniques, but the evidence seems clear that both the initial referrals and the "contracts" were vague:

The specific nature and etiology of their problems were not known at the time of selection and referral. There was no indication of how the girls felt about their problems or whether they were willing or able to attempt to find new and more constructive ways of coping with them. [149, p. 119]

Later, as more concrete tasks were taken on in the groups, the girls' sense of satisfaction seemed to rise:

The workers continually received comments from the girls regarding their attitudes toward the groups. Aldena Wray, after being in a group for six months, credited her new-found confidence directly to the group experience. Other girls were amazed that they were able to talk about their problems in a group and frequently expressed it. After the group experience, several girls mentioned the meaning it had for them. One girl, Edith Casper, had nothing to say while a member of the group, but when she was seen individually much later by a caseworker she gave an unusually good report of many things that had happened in the group and reported on various areas in which she had been helped by the group discussion. . . .

Even some girls whom the workers thought they had failed to reach later returned to the agency asking for help with concrete problems, such as employment. [149, p. 146]

In the end, however, the general conclusions were fairly dismal. Although the researchers indicated that "the findings are not entirely negative," the overall judgment was that "with respect to all of the measures we have used to examine effects of the treatment program, only a minimal effect can be found"(149, p. 204). It is important to recognize that despite the weaknesses of the study and the harshness of the professional reaction, the research effort was a major and a rigorous one, and it created nationwide discussion of a critical subject—the scientific evaluation of social work practice.

Berleman and Steinburn(11) described the pretest phase of an evaluation of a delinquency prevention program begun in 1962 by the Seattle Atlantic Street Center (46, 47) and financed by NIMH for a five-year period. The authors maintained that although the pretest did not represent a real test of the service, it was an opportunity to establish a rigorous technique not generally used in such a program. In the context of another, unnamed, delinquency prevention project, Aronson and Sherwood (6) reviewed the efforts of the research branch to evaluate various aspects of the program. Again the action-research tensions come through explicitly and in detail.

Rosenblatt(182) conducted an extensive study of attendance and attitudes of participants in 301 Project ENABLE groups throughout the country. Processing enormous amounts of attendance and interview data, he found regional differences in attendance, favoring the North, and higher attendance figures emerging from smaller cities and smaller agencies. Measuring attitudinal changes on six items of opinion, he reported on the complex variations, both positive and negative, associated with factors of attendance, group stability, and background characteristics, as these applied to each of the six items. His conclusions were positive, encompassing the rethinking of parental attitudes, the lessening of family isolation, the rise in community action, and other effects.

In the related arena of the Head Start activity, Mann and Elliot(143) studied the 1967 summer Head Start program in seven rural Oklahoma communities and found significant differences between first- and last-week tests. They concluded that although their sample was small, there were indications that the experience had a substantial effect on the cognitive functioning of the children involved.

Endres(48), having offered study-discussion groups as a device for working with disadvantaged parents in Indiana, found that parental self-evaluation yielded evidence of increased confidence and satisfaction. Finally, those interested in both group psychotherapy and the techniques of evaluation will wish to examine Patterson's review of evaluative studies in this area over the past twenty years(162).

Agency Impact

The study of agency effectiveness has never been an area of considerable activity among the neighborhood centers, and now that the classic self-study device has fallen into relative disuse, the output is close to nil. However, Zalba and Stein's report of a study designed to develop a "systematic methodology" for assessing agency effectiveness is an event of some importance to the neighborhood agencies(252). Using two family agencies judged to have high standards of practice, the researchers identified agency input goals on the basis of a content analysis of agency documents and interviews with key staff persons. They then collected data at the "crucial decision points" affecting the screening of clients and judged a sample of 160 cases for treatment success and the development of indexes for the quality of agency output. Normal production data for a given quarter were used to develop indexes of quantity. The conclusions and recommendations are explicit in their instructions relative to use of the model in other settings.

Conclusion

It would be difficult to characterize the complex pattern of the work described in this chapter and to assess its positive and negative aspects in simple terms. Certainly the gaps are still large, the continuity weak, and the commitment spotty. But there can be no doubt that the picture is more developed than it was a half-dozen years ago, and there are several places in which the "official curiosity" called for in the earlier review is growing rapidly. In other settings as well research activity is growing beyond the hobby status to incorporation into the job analysis of the agency itself.

In his chapter in the first volume of this series the writer pointed out:

Ultimately, much will depend on the developing relationship between the neighborhood centers and the social work profession. When the agencies continue to clarify their conceptions of service, they will be increasingly less occupied with questions of faith and doctrine and more with the problems of science. [199, p. 184]

We believe that there was further movement in this direction in the last six years, and indeed such movement seems bound to continue as the agencies are drawn closer to the increasingly desperate problems of war, frustration, and poverty that surround them.

REFERENCES

1. Agueros, Julie, et al. "A Study of Social Work Practice: An Exploratory Investigation into the Nature of the Helping Process." Unpublished master's thesis, Columbia University School of Social Work, 1965.
2. Alcabes, Abraham. "A Study of a Community's Perception and Use of Neighborhood Centers." Unpublished doctoral dissertation, Columbia University School of Social Work, 1967.
3. Alker, Henry, and Kogan, Nathan. "Effects of Norm-Oriented Group Discussion on Individual Verbal Risk-Taking and Conservation," *Human Relations*, Vol. 21, No. 4 (November 1968), pp. 393–405.
4. Allen, V. L. "Situational Factors in Conformity," in Leonard Berkowitz, ed., *Advances in Experimental Social Psychology*. New York: Academic Press, 1965.
5. Arkava, Morton L. "Social Work Practice and Knowledge: An Examination of Their Relationship," *Journal of Education for Social Work*, Vol. 3, No. 2 (Fall 1967), pp. 5–13.
6. Aronson, Sidney, and Sherwood, Clarence. "Researcher Versus Practitioner: Problems in Social Action Research," *Social Work*, Vol. 12, No. 4 (October 1967), pp. 89–96.
7. Bach, George R. "The Marathon Group: Intensive Practice of Intimate Interaction," *Psychological Reports*, Vol. 18, No. 3 (1966), pp. 995–1002.

8. Bachman, Jerald G., et al. *Youth in Transition. Volume I: Blueprint for a Longitudinal Study of Adolescent Boys.* Ann Arbor: Survey Research Center, Institute for Social Research, University of Michigan, 1967.

9. Batchelder, Richard L., and Buckley, Earle R. (eds.). *YMCA Year Book and Official Roster 1969.* New York: Association Press, 1969.

10. Becker, Robert, et al. "Influence of the Leader on the Activity Level of Therapy Groups," *Journal of Social Psychology,* Vol. 74, No. 1 (February 1968), pp. 39–51.

11. Berleman, William C., and Steinburn, Thomas W. "The Execution and Evaluation of a Delinquency Prevention Program," *Social Problems,* Vol. 14, No. 4 (Spring 1967), pp. 413–423.

12. Bernstein, Saul. *Youth on the Streets: Work with Alienated Youth Groups.* New York: Association Press, 1964.

13. Berry, Margaret E. "Mr. Gans Is Challenged" (Points and Viewpoints), *Social Work,* Vol. 10, No. 1 (January 1965), pp. 104–107.

14. "Bibliography of Research Service Studies." Chicago: Boy Scouts of America, 1969. Mimeographed.

15. Bjerstedt, Ake. "Interaction Competence Among Children: The Rotation Phenomenon in Small Groups," *Journal of Psychology,* Vol. 61, First Half (September 1965), pp. 145–152.

16. Boeko, Jack. "Application of a Survey of the Montreal Jewish High School Population," in "Research Papers, National Association of Jewish Center Workers." Papers presented at the National Conference of Jewish Communal Services, Atlantic City, N.J., 1967. New York: National Association of Jewish Center Workers, 1967. Pp. 45–51. Mimeographed.

17. Bradford, L. P., Gibb, J. R., and Benne, Kenneth D. *T-Group Theory and Laboratory Method.* New York: John Wiley & Sons, 1964.

18. Brittain, Clay V. "Preschool Programs for Culturally Deprived Children," *Children,* Vol. 13, No. 4 (July–August 1966), pp. 130–134.

19. Brodsky, Irving. "The Role of the Jewish Community Center in the Urban Crisis," *Associated YM-YWHAs of Greater New York 11th Annual Report, 1968.* New York: Associated YM-YWHAS of Greater New York, 1968.

20. Brooks, Michael P. "The Community Action Program as a Setting for Applied Research," *Journal of Social Issues,* Vol. 21, No. 1 (January 1965), pp. 29–40.

21. Broudy, Harry S. "Historic Exemplars of Teaching Method," in N. L. Gage, ed., *Handbook of Research on Teaching.* Chicago: Rand McNally & Co., 1963. Pp. 1–43.

22. Brown, Leonard N. "Social Workers' Verbal Acts and the Development of Mutual Expectations with Beginning Client Groups." Unpublished doctoral dissertation, Columbia University School of Social Work, 1970.

23. Bruck, Max. "Behavior Modification Theory and Practice: A Critical Review," *Social Work,* Vol. 13, No. 2 (April 1968), pp. 43–55.

24. Buckley, Walter (ed.). *Modern Systems Research for the Behavioral Scientist.* Chicago: Aldine Publishing Co., 1968.

25. Canter, Irving. "Implications of Developments in the Behavioral Sciences for Practice in Jewish Group Service Agencies," *Journal of Jewish Communal Service,* Vol. 41, No. 2 (Winter 1964), pp. 155–167.

26. ———— (ed.). *Research Readings in Jewish Communal Service.* New York: National Association of Jewish Center Workers, 1967.

27. Cantor, Marjorie. "Tomorrow is Today: A Study of VISTA in Urban Poverty, Summary and Implications." New York: Columbia University School of Social Work, Research and Demonstration Center, 1967. Mimeographed.

28. Caplan, Nathan. "Treatment Intervention and Reciprocal Interaction Effects," *Journal of Social Issues,* Vol. 24, No. 1 (January 1968), pp. 63–88.

29. Carp, Frances. "Differences Among Older Workers, Volunteers and Persons Who Are Neither," *Journal of Gerontology,* Vol. 23, No. 4 (October 1968), pp. 497–501.

30. Carp, Joel. "Value Systems of the Jewish Adolescent: A Research Report," in "Conference Papers, Annual Conference of the National Association of Jewish Center Workers," Philadelphia, May-June 1965. New York: National Association of Jewish Center Workers, 1965. Pp. 82–91. Mimeographed.

31. ————. "A List of Selected Reports of Research Projects Conducted in Jewish Community Centers and YM-YWHAS" in "Research Papers, National Association of Jewish Center Workers." Papers presented at the National Conference of Jewish Communal Services, May 1966. New York: National Association of

Jewish Center Workers, 1966. Pp. 55–62. Mimeographed.

32. Casper, Max. *The Helping Person in the Group: A KWIC (Key Word in Context) Index of Relevant Journal Articles, 1965–1966.* Vol. 1. Syracuse, N.Y.: Syracuse University School of Social Work, 1967.

33. ———. *The Helping Person in the Group: A KWIC (Key Word in Context) Index of Relevant Journal Articles, 1967–1968.* Vol. 2. Syracuse, N.Y.: Syracuse University School of Social Work, 1969.

34. Center for Community Research. "Newsletter." New York: Associated YM-YWHAs of Greater New York, July 15, 1969. Mimeographed.

35. Chetkow, B. Harold. "Some Factors Influencing the Utilization and Impact of Priority Recommendations in Community Planning," *Social Service Review,* Vol. 41, No. 3 (September 1967), pp. 271–282.

36. Cleminger, Florence. "Congruence Between Members and Workers on Selected Behaviors of the Role of the Social Group Worker." Unpublished doctoral dissertation, University of Southern California School of Social Work, 1965.

37. Cloward, Richard A., and Ohlin, Lloyd E. *Delinquency and Opportunity: A Theory of Delinquent Groups.* Glencoe, Ill.: Free Press, 1960.

38. Cohen, Albert K. *Delinquent Boys: The Culture of the Gang.* Glencoe, Ill.: Free Press, 1955.

39. "Community Self-Study for Jewish Youth." Compilation of documents. Savannah, Ga.: Savannah Jewish Council and National Jewish Welfare Board, 1966. Mimeographed.

40. Craig, Maude and Furst, Philip. "What Happens after Treatment? A Study of Potentially Delinquent Boys," *Social Service Review,* Vol. 39, No. 2 (June 1965), pp. 165–171.

41. *Current Research in Voluntary Social and Health Agencies in New York City: 1969.* New York: Research Department, Community Council of Greater New York, 1969.

42. Deschin, Celia S. "Implications for Schools of a Demonstration Project to Integrate Orthopedically Handicapped Children in Community Centers with their Nonhandicapped Peers." Paper presented at the Research Council of the American School Health Association, Miami Beach, Florida, October 1967.

43. Deutsch, Martin, and Krauss, R. M.

Theories in Social Psychology. New York: Basic Books, 1965.

44. Deutschberger, Paul. "On the Results of Four Recent Studies of Jewish Teenagers," in "Research Papers, National Association of Jewish Center Workers." Papers presented at the National Conference of Jewish Communal Services, Atlantic City, N.J., May 1967. New York: National Association of Jewish Center Workers, 1967. Pp. 20–24. Mimeographed.

45. Drake, St. Claire. *Race Relations in a Time of Rapid Social Change.* New York: National Federation of Settlements & Neighborhood Centers, 1966.

46. "Effectiveness of Social Work with Acting-Out Youth: Fifth Year Progress Report." Seattle, Wash.: Seattle Atlantic Street Center, 1967. Mimeographed.

47. "Effectiveness of Social Work with Acting-Out Youth: Sixth Year Progress Report." Seattle, Wash.: Seattle Atlantic Street Center, 1968. Mimeographed.

48. Endres, Mary. "The Impact of Parent Education through Study-Discussion Groups in a Poverty Area," *Journal of Marriage and the Family,* Vol. 30, No. 1 (February 1968), pp. 119–122.

49. Exline, Ralph, Gray, David, and Schuette, Dorothy. "Visual Behavior in a Dyad as Affected by Interview Content and Sex of Respondent," *Journal of Personality and Social Psychology,* Vol. 1, No. 1 (January 1965), pp. 201–209.

50. Feldman, Ronald A. "Determinants and Objectives of Social Group Work Intervention," *Social Work Practice, 1967.* New York: Columbia University Press, 1967. Pp. 34–55.

51. ———. "Group Service Programs in Public Welfare: Patterns and Perspectives," *Public Welfare,* Vol. 27, No. 3 (July 1969), pp. 266–271.

52. ———. "Three Types of Group Integration: Their Relationships to Power, Leadership, and Conformity Behavior." Unpublished doctoral dissertation, University of Michigan, 1966.

53. Festinger, Leon, Pepitone, A., and Newcomb, Theodore. "Some Consequences of Deindividuation in a Group," *Journal of Abnormal and Social Psychology,* Vol. 47, No. 2 (April 1952), pp. 382–389.

54. Flax, Norman, and Pumphrey, Muriel. "Serving Educable Mentally Retarded Children and Youth in Regular Center Groups," *Jewish Community Center Program Aids,* Vol. 30, No. 3 (Summer 1969), pp. 2–5.

55. Foster, Barbara R., and Batchelder, Richard L. *Report of the 1965–1966 YMCA Interracial Study.* New York: Research and Development Services, National Board of YMCAs, 1966.

56. Fox, Murray. "Considerations in Developing a Demonstration Program in Parent Education in Child Rearing Practices for Mentally Retarded Children." New York: Associated YM-YWHAs of Greater New York, 1968. Mimeographed.

57. Franseth, Jane, and Koury, Rose. *Survey of Research on Grouping as Related to Pupil Learning.* Washington, D.C.: U.S. Department of Health, Education & Welfare, 1966.

58. French, David G., et al. "Homans' Theory of the Human Group: Applications to Problems of Administration, Policy, and Staff Training in Group Service Agencies," *Journal of Jewish Communal Service,* Vol. 40, No. 4 (Summer 1964), pp. 379–395.

59. Gage, N. L. (ed.). *Handbook of Research on Teaching.* Chicago: Rand McNally & Co., 1963.

60. ———. "Paradigms for Research on Teaching," in Gage, ed., *Handbook of Research on Teaching.* Chicago: Rand McNally & Co., 1963. Pp. 94–141.

61. Gannon, Thomas. "The Role of the Non-professional in the Harlem Domestic Peace Corps," *Sociology and Social Research,* Vol. 52, No. 4 (July 1968), pp. 348–362.

62. Gans, Herbert J. "Redefining the Settlement's Function for the War on Poverty," *Social Work,* Vol. 9, No. 4 (October 1964), pp. 3–12.

63. Ganter, Grace, and Polansky, Norman. "Predicting a Child's Accessibility to Individual Treatment from Diagnostic Groups," *Social Work,* Vol. 9, No. 3 (July 1964), pp. 56–63.

64. Garfield, Goodwin P., and Irizarry, Carol R. "The 'Record of Service': A Way of Describing Social Work Practice," in William Schwartz and Serapio R. Zalba, eds., *The Practice of Group Work.* New York: Columbia University Press, 1970.

65. Garfinkle, Max. "Survey of Montreal Jewish High School Population." May 1965. Mimeographed by the author.

66. Garvin, Charles. "Complementarity of Role Expectations in Groups: Relationship to Worker Performance and Member Problem Solving." Unpublished doctoral dissertation, University of Chicago School of Social Service Administration, 1968.

67. ———. "Complementarity of Role Expectations in Groups: The Member-Worker Contract," *Social Work Practice, 1969.* New York: Columbia University Press, 1969. Pp. 127–145.

68. Gerard, Harold B., and Miller, Norman. "Group Dynamics," in Paul R. Farnsworth, Olga McNemar, and Quinn McNemar, eds., *Annual Review of Psychology.* Vol. 18. Palo Alto: Annual Reviews, 1967. Pp. 287–332.

69. Gifford, C. G. "Sensitivity Training and Social Work," *Social Work,* Vol. 13, No. 2 (April 1968), pp. 78–86.

70. Gilbert, Neil. "Neighborhood Coordinator: Advocate or Middleman?" *Social Service Review,* Vol. 43, No. 2 (June 1969), pp. 136–144.

71. Glanser, Murray, and Glaser, Robert. "Techniques for the Study of Group Structure and Behavior: II. Empirical Studies of the Effects of Structure in Small Groups," *Psychological Bulletin,* Vol. 58, No. 1 (January 1961), pp. 1–27.

72. Glasser, Paul, and Navarre, Elizabeth. "Structural Problems of the One-Parent Family," *Journal of Social Issues,* Vol. 21, No. 1 (January 1965), pp. 98–109.

73. Goodchilds, Jacqueline D., and Smith, Ewart E. "The Wit and his Group," *Human Relations,* Vol. 17, No. 1 (February 1964), pp. 23–31.

74. Goodman, Mortimer. "Preliminary Study of Social Work Intervention with Adults in Social Groups in the Jewish Center," in "Research Papers, National Association of Jewish Center Workers." Papers presented at the National Conference of Jewish Communal Services, Atlantic City, N.J., May 1967. New York: National Association of Jewish Center Workers, 1967. Pp. 25–43. Mimeographed.

75. Gottlieb, David, and Reeves, Jon. *Adolescent Behavior in Urban Areas: A Bibliographic Review and Discussion of the Literature.* New York: Free Press of Glencoe, 1963.

76. Greene, Alan, Kasdan, Barry, and Segal, Brian. "Jewish Social Group Work Students View the Jewish Community Center Field as a Placement and Career," *Journal of Jewish Communal Services,* Vol. 44, No. 2 (Winter 1967), pp. 168–176.

77. Grosser, Charles. "Local Residents as Mediators Between Middle-Class Professional Workers and Lower-Class Clients," *Social Service Review,* Vol. 40, No. 1 (March 1966), pp. 56–63.

78. ———, Henry, William E., and Kelley, James G. (eds.). *Nonprofessionals in*

the Human Services. San Francisco: Jossey-Bass, 1969.

79. Hall, Jay, and Williams, Martha S. "A Comparison of Decision-Making Performances in Established and Ad Hoc Groups," *Journal of Personality and Social Psychology*, Vol. 3, No. 2 (February 1966), pp. 214–222.

80. Handlon, Joseph, and Parloff, Morris B. "The Influence of Criticalness on Creative Problem-Solving in Dyads," *Psychiatry*, Vol. 27, No. 1 (February 1964), pp. 17–27.

81. Hardy, James M. *Planning for Impact: A Guide to Planning Effective Family Programs.* New York: Association Press, 1968.

82. ——. *The YMCA and the Changing American Family.* New York: Department of Research and Planning, National Council of YMCAs, 1965.

83. Harlow, Harold C., Jr. *Racial Integration in the Young Men's Christian Associations.* New York: Research and Planning Department, National Council of YMCAs, 1962.

84. Hefter, Sy. "The Wilkes-Barre Survey Results," in "Research Papers, National Association of Jewish Center Workers." Papers presented at the National Conference of Jewish Communal Services, Atlantic City, N.J., May 1967. New York: National Association of Jewish Center Workers, 1967. Pp. 67–73. Mimeographed.

85. Hendon, William S. " 'Determining Neighborhood Recreation Priorities': A Comment," *Journal of Leisure Research*, Vol. 1, No. 2 (Spring 1969), pp. 189–191.

86. Herman, Melvin. *Occupational Mobility in Social Work: The Jewish Community Center Worker.* New York: National Jewish Welfare Board and the Research Institute for Group Work in Jewish Agencies of the National Association of Jewish Center Workers, 1959.

87. ——. "Problems of Evaluation," *American Child*, Vol. 47, No. 2 (March 1965), pp. 5–10.

88. ——, and Sadofsky, Stanley. *Youth-Work Programs: Problems of Planning and Operation.* New York: Center for the Study of Unemployed Youth, Graduate School of Social Work, New York University, 1966.

89. Heslin, Richard, and Dunphy, Dexter. "Three Dimensions of Member Satisfaction in Small Groups," *Human Relations*, Vol. 17, No. 2 (May 1964), pp. 99–112.

90. Hess, Robert D. "The Social and Psy-

chological Development of Six to Ten-Year Old Boys: A Review of Research and Theory." Chicago: Boy Scouts of America, 1963. Mimeographed.

91. Hillman, Arthur. "People, Places and Participation." New York: National Federation of Settlements and Neighborhood Centers, 1969. Mimeographed.

92. ——, and Seever, Frank. *Making Democracy Work: A Study of Neighborhood Organization.* New York: National Federation of Settlements and Neighborhood Centers, 1968.

93. Hinkle, John, Cole, Charles, and Oetting, E. R. "Research in a Community Health Center: A Framework for Action," *Community Mental Health Journal*, Vol. 4, No. 2 (April 1968), pp. 129–133.

94. Hoffman, L. R. "Group Problem Solving," in Louis Berkowitz, ed., *Advances in Experimental Social Psychology.* New York: Academic Press, 1965. Pp. 99–132.

95. Holmes, Douglas. "Bridging the Gap Between Research and Practice in Social Work," *Social Work Practice, 1967.* New York: Columbia University Press, 1967. Pp. 95–108.

96. ——. "Integrating the Handicapped Child: Report of a Research and Demonstration Program," *Journal of Jewish Communal Service*, Vol. 43, No. 2 (Winter 1966), pp. 182–188.

97. ——. "An Objective Evaluation of Certain Aspects of 'Operation Headstart.' " Paper presented at the Eastern Regional Conference, Child Welfare League of America, Atlantic City, N.J., March 1967. Mimeographed.

98. ——. "Potential Use of Associated Y's Nursery Schools." New York: Associated YM-YWHAs of Greater New York, 1969. Mimeographed.

99. ——. "Study of Jewish Population Mobility in the Bronx River Area." New York: Associated YM-YWHAs of Greater New York, 1967. Mimeographed.

100. ——. "A Study of the Problems of Integrating Physically Handicapped Children with Non-Handicapped Children in Recreational Groups." 2 vols. New York: Associated YM-YWHAs of Greater New York, 1966. Mimeographed.

101. ——. "A Study of Staff Utilization: Final Report." New York: National Jewish Welfare Board, 1967. Mimeographed.

102. ——. "The Use of a Structured Observational Schema in Evaluating the Impact of Integrated Social Experiences

upon Orthopedically Handicapped Children." Paper presented at a meeting of the American Psychological Association, Chicago, September 1965. Mimeographed.

103. ———, and Holmes, Monica Bychowski. "An Evaluation of Differences Among Different Classes of Head Start Participants." New York: Associated YM-YWHAS of Greater New York, 1966. Mimeographed.

104. ———, and Smolka, Patricia. "A Comparison Between the Attitudes Towards Child Rearing Among Mothers of Orthopedically Handicapped and Non-Handicapped, Pre-Adolescent Children." Paper presented at a meeting of the American Psychological Association, Chicago, September 1965. Mimeographed.

105. Homans, George C. *The Human Group.* New York: Harcourt, Brace & Co., 1950.

106. Horowitz, Gideon. "Worker Interventions in Response to Deviant Behavior in Groups." Unpublished doctoral dissertation, University of Chicago School of Social Service Administration, 1968.

107. Ikeda, Tsuguo. "Final Report Summary: Effectiveness of Social Work with Acting-Out Youth." Seattle, Wash.: Seattle Atlantic Street Center, 1968. Mimeographed.

108. Indik, Bernard. "Organization Size and Member Participation: Some Empirical Tests of Alternative Explanations," *Human Relations,* Vol. 18, No. 4 (November 1965), pp. 339–350.

109. "Is Scouting in Tune with the Times?" Reprint from *Scouting Magazine.* Chicago: Boy Scouts of America, undated.

110. Ishikawa, Wesley. "Verbal Acts of the Social Worker and their Variations Through Time in Release-planning Discussion Group Meetings." Unpublished doctoral dissertation, University of California School of Social Welfare, Los Angeles, 1968.

111. Jansyn, Leon R. "Solidarity and Delinquency in a Street Corner Group," *American Sociological Review,* Vol. 31, No. 5 (October 1966), pp. 600–614.

112. Johnson, Guion Griffis. *Volunteers in Community Service.* Chapel Hill: North Carolina Council of Women's Organizations, 1967.

113. Kaplan, Berton H. "Social Issues and Poverty Research: A Commentary," *Journal of Social Issues,* Vol. 21, No. 1 (January 1965), pp. 1–10.

114. Kaplan, Martin, and Walden, Theodore. "Adolescent Needs and Center Objectives." Paper presented at the Annual

Meeting of the National Conference of Jewish Communal Services, Philadelphia, June 1965. Mimeographed.

115. Karnes, Merle, et al. "An Approach for Working with Mothers of Disadvantaged Preschool Children," *Merrill-Palmer Quarterly,* Vol. 14, No. 2 (April 1968), pp. 174–184.

116. Kazzaz, David S. "The Champion of the Cause and the Challenge of Supervising his Anti-Leader Role," *American Journal of Psychiatry,* Vol. 125, No. 6 (December 1968), pp. 737–742.

117. Klein, Malcolm, and Snyder, Neal. "The Detached Worker: Uniformities and Variances in Work Style," *Social Work,* Vol. 10, No. 4 (October 1965), pp. 60–68.

118. Kraft, Ivor, and Chilman, Catherine S. *Helping Low-Income Families Through Parent Education: A Survey of Research.* Washington, D.C.: Children's Bureau, U.S. Department of Health, Education & Welfare, 1966.

119. Kraus, Richard. *Public Recreation and the Negro: A Study of Participation and Administrative Practices.* New York: Center for Urban Education, 1968.

120. Lambert, Camille, Jr., Guberman, Mildred, and Morris, Robert. "Reopening Doors to Community Participation for Older People: How Realistic?" *Social Service Review,* Vol. 38, No. 1 (March 1964), pp. 42–50.

121. Lathrope, Donald E. "Making Use of Systems Thought in Social Work Practice: Some Bridging Ideas." Paper presented at the Conference on Current Trends in Army Social Work, Denver, Colo., September 1969. Mimeographed.

122. Lawrence, Harry. "The Effectiveness of a Group-directed vs. a Worker-directed Style of Leadership in Social Group Work." Unpublished doctoral dissertation, University of California School of Social Welfare, Berkeley, 1967.

123. Lazerwitz, Bernard. "The Jewish Identification of Chicago Jewish Community Center Members and Non-Members," in "Research Papers, National Association of Jewish Center Workers." Papers presented at the National Conference of Jewish Communal Service, Detroit, Michigan, June 1968. New York: National Association of Jewish Center Workers, 1968. Pp. 16–39. Mimeographed.

124. Leader, Arthur L. "Current and Future Issues in Family Therapy," *Social Service Review,* Vol. 43, No. 1 (March 1969), pp. 1–11.

125. Lennard, Henry L., and Bernstein, Arnold. *Patterns in Human Interaction.* San Francisco: Jossey-Bass, 1969.

126. Levin, Morris. "An Analysis of Study Material on the Image of the Jewish Community Center Held by Membership and the Community," in Irving Canter, ed., *Research Readings in Jewish Communal Service.* New York: National Association of Jewish Center Workers, 1967. Pp. 190–207.

127. ———. "A Survey of Research and Program Developments Involving Jewish Adolescents and the Implications for JCC Service." Chicago: Jewish Community Centers of Chicago, 1969. Mimeographed.

128. Levine, Baruch. "Factors Related to Interpersonal Balance in Social Work Treatment Groups." Unpublished doctoral dissertation, University of Chicago School of Social Service Administration, 1968.

129. Levine, Rachel A. "Treatment in the Home," *Social Work,* Vol. 9, No. 1 (January 1964), pp. 19–28.

130. Levinger, George. "Note on Need Complementarity in Marriage," *Psychological Bulletin,* Vol. 61, No. 1 (January 1964), pp. 153–157.

131. Levinson, Perry, and Schiller, Jeffry. "Role Analysis of the Indigenous Nonprofessional," *Social Work,* Vol. 11, No. 3 (July 1966), pp. 95–101.

132. Levy, Charles S. *The Executive and the Jewish Community Center Board.* New York: National Jewish Welfare Board, 1964. Mimeographed.

133. ———. "Professional Practice in the Jewish Community Center: Disparities Between the Idealizations and Experience of Center Personnel," in "Research Papers, National Association of Jewish Center Workers." Papers presented at the National Conference of Jewish Communal Services, Atlantic City, N.J., May 1967. New York: National Association of Jewish Center Workers, 1967. Pp. 1–19. Mimeographed.

134. Litwak, Eugene, and Meyer, Henry J. "A Balance Theory of Coordination Between Bureaucratic Organizations and Community Primary Groups," in Edwin J. Thomas, ed., *Behavioral Science for Social Workers.* New York: Free Press, 1967. Pp. 246–264.

135. Lott, Albert J., and Lott, Bernice E. "Group Cohesiveness as Interpersonal Attraction: A Review of Relationships with Antecedent and Consequent Variables," *Psychological Bulletin,* Vol. 64, No. 3 (September 1965), pp. 259–309.

136. Lucci, York. *The Campus YMCA: Highlights from a National Study.* New York: National Board of YMCAs, 1960.

137. Maas, Henry S. "Preadolescent Peer Relations and Adult Intimacy," *Psychiatry: Journal for the Study of Interpersonal Processes,* Vol. 31, No. 2 (May 1968), pp. 161–172.

138. Macdonald, Mary E. "Reunion at Vocational High. An Analysis of *Girls at Vocational High: An Experiment in Social Intervention,*" *Social Service Review,* Vol. 40, No. 2 (June 1966), pp. 175–189.

139. ———. "Verdict Before Trial: A Review of the Test by the New York City Youth Board of the Glueck Social Prediction Table," *Social Service Review,* Vol. 39, No. 2 (June 1965), pp. 172–182.

140. McGrath, Joseph E., and Altman, Irwin. *Small Group Research: A Synthesis and Critique of the Field.* New York: Holt, Rinehart & Winston, 1966.

141. McLarnan, Georgiana, and Fryer, Gideon W. *Improving Decision-Making of Young Low-Income Couples.* Nashville: University of Tennessee School of Social Work and Wesley House Centers, 1967.

142. Maida, Peter R., and McCoy, John L. *The Poor: A Selected Bibliography.* Miscellaneous Publication No. 1145. Washington, D.C.: U.S. Department of Agriculture, Economic Research Service, May 1969.

143. Mann, Edward, and Elliot, Courtney. "Assessment of the Utility of Project Head Start for the Culturally Deprived: An Evaluation of Social and Psychological Functioning," *Training School Bulletin,* Vol. 64, No. 4 (February 1968), pp. 119–125.

144. Manser, Ellen P., Jones, Jeweldean, and Ortof, Selma B. "An Overview of Project ENABLE," *Social Casework,* Vol. 48, No. 10 (December 1967), pp. 609–617.

145. March, Michael. "The Neighborhood Center Concept," *Public Welfare,* Vol. 26, No. 2 (April 1968), pp. 97–111.

146. Massarik, Fred, and Okin, Leo. *Patterns of Board Leadership: A Study of the Jewish Community Center Board Members of Los Angeles, California.* New York: National Jewish Welfare Board, 1964.

147. Mattick, Hans W., and Caplan, Nathan S. *The Chicago Youth Development Project: A Descriptive Account of its Action Program and Research Designs.* Ann Arbor:

Institute for Social Research, University of Michigan, 1964.

148. Medow, Herman, and Zander, Alvin. "Aspirations for the Group Chosen by Central and Peripheral Members," *Journal of Personality and Social Psychology,* Vol. 1, No. 3 (1965), pp. 224–228.

149. Meyer, Henry J., Borgatta, Edgar F., and Jones, Wyatt C. *Girls at Vocational High: An Experiment in Social Work Intervention.* New York: Russell Sage Foundation, 1965.

150. Miller, Robert E., Banks, James H., Jr., and Ogawa, Nobuya, "Role of Facial Expression in 'Cooperative-Avoidance Conditioning' in Monkeys," *Journal of Abnormal and Social Psychology,* Vol. 67, No. 1 (July 1963), pp. 24–30.

151. Miller, Walter B. "Lower Class Culture as a Generating Milieu of Gang Delinquency," *Journal of Social Issues,* Vol. 14, No. 3 (1958), pp. 5–19.

152. Miran, Bernard B., and Lemmerman, Mervin N. "Older Adult Population Study and Demonstration Project," in "Research Papers, National Association of Jewish Center Workers." Papers presented at the National Conference of Jewish Communal Services, Washington, D.C., May, 1966. New York: National Association of Jewish Center Workers, 1966. Pp. 21–35. Mimeographed.

153. Mogulof, Melvin. "Toward the Measurement of Jewish Content in Jewish Community Center Practice," *Journal of Jewish Communal Services,* Vol. 41, No. 1 (Fall 1964), pp. 101–113.

154. Morgan, Ruth. "Intervention Techniques in Social Group Work." Unpublished doctoral dissertation, Columbia University School of Social Work, 1966.

155. National Council, Boy Scouts of America. *Cub Scouting: Practices and Attitudes in Packs and Dens.* Princeton, N.J.: Opinion Research Corporation, 1964.

156. National Institutes of Health. *Research Highlights, National Institutes of Health, 1966.* Public Health Service Publication No. 1613. Washington, D.C.: U.S. Department of Health, Education & Welfare, 1966.

157. *Needs and Interests Study of 7–8–9–10 Year-Old Boys' Club Members.* New York: Boys' Clubs of America, 1964.

158. O'Dell, Jerry W. "Group Size and Emotional Interactions," *Journal of Personality and Social Psychology,* Vol. 8, No. 1 (January 1968), pp. 75–78.

159. *Outdoor Recreation Research, A Reference Catalog, 1967.* Washington, D.C.: Bureau of Outdoor Recreation, U.S. Department of the Interior, 1968.

160. Pappenfort, Donnell, and Kilpatrick, Dee Morgan. "Opportunities for Physically Handicapped Children: A Study of Attitudes and Practice in Settlements and Community Centers," *Social Service Review,* Vol. 41, No. 2 (June 1967), pp. 179–188.

161. Parker, Rolland S. "Patient Variability as a Factor in Group Activities on a Maximum Security Ward," *Psychiatric Quarterly,* Vol. 39, No. 2 (April 1965), pp. 265–278.

162. Patterson, Mansell. "Evaluation Studies of Group Psychotherapy," *International Journal of Psychiatry,* Vol. 4, No. 4 (October 1967), pp. 333–343.

163. Pearl, Arthur, and Riessman, Frank. *New Careers for the Poor.* New York: Free Press, 1965.

164. Peck, Harris, and Kaplan, Seymour. "Crisis Theory and Therapeutic Change in Small Groups: Some Implications for Community Mental Health Programs," *International Journal of Group Psychotherapy,* Vol. 16, No. 2 (April 1966), pp. 135–149.

165. Pierce, Francis. "A Study of the Methodological Components of Social Work with Groups." Unpublished doctoral dissertation, University of Southern California School of Social Work, 1966.

166. Perlman, Robert, and Jones, David. *Neighborhood Service Centers.* Washington, D.C.: Office of Juvenile Delinquency & Youth Development, U.S. Department of Health, Education & Welfare, 1967.

167. Pins, Arnulf M. *Who Chooses Social Work, When and Why?* New York: Council on Social Work Education, 1963.

168. Pope, Hallowell. "Economic Deprivation and Social Participation in a Group of 'Middle Class' Factory Workers," *Social Problems,* Vol. 11, No. 3 (Winter 1964), pp. 290–300.

169. "Preparing for the Seventies." Chicago, Ill.: National Board of YMCAs, 1968. Mimeographed.

170. Pumphrey, Muriel W., Goodman, Mortimer, and Flax, Norman. "Integrating Individuals with Impaired Adaptive Behavior in a Group Work Agency," *Social Work Practice, 1969.* New York: Columbia University Press, 1969. Pp. 146–160.

171. Ramsey, Glenn V. "Review of Group Methods with Parents of the Mentally Retarded," *American Journal of Mental*

Deficiency, Vol. 71, No. 5 (March 1967), pp. 857–863.

172. ———. "Sociotherapeutic Camping for the Mentally Ill," *Social Work,* Vol. 9, No. 1 (January 1964), pp. 45–53.

173. Raven, B. H. *Bibliography of Small Group Research.* Technical Report No. 15, 3d ed. Los Angeles: University of California at Los Angeles, 1965.

174. Reiff, Robert, and Riessman, Frank. *The Indigenous Non-Professional.* New York: National Institute of Labor Education, 1964.

175. Rein, Martin, and Riessman, Frank. "A Strategy for Antipoverty Community Action Programs," *Social Work,* Vol. 11, No. 2 (April 1966), pp. 3–12.

176. *A Report on the Executive Program, Part I.* New York: Boys' Clubs of America, undated.

177. *A Report on the Executive Program, Part II.* New York: Boys' Clubs of America, undated.

178. "Research and Demonstration Projects Reported by Members of the National Federation of Settlements, 1962–1965." New York: National Federation of Settlements and Neighborhood Centers, April 1965. Mimeographed.

179. Richart, Robert, and Millner, Lawrence. "Factors Influencing Admission to a Community Mental Health Center," *Community Mental Health Journal,* Vol. 4, No. 1 (February 1968), pp. 27–35.

180. Robbins, Harold, and Schattner, Regina. "Obstacles in the Social Integration of Orthopedically Handicapped Children," *Journal of Jewish Communal Services,* Vol. 45, No. 2 (Winter 1968), pp. 190–199.

181. Roen, Sheldon, et al. "Community Adaptation as an Evaluation Concept in Community Mental Health," *Archives of General Psychiatry,* Vol. 15, No. 1 (July 1966), pp. 36–44.

182. Rosenblatt, Aaron. *Attendance and Attitude Change: A Study of 301 Project* ENABLE *Groups.* New York: Family Service Association of America, 1968.

183. ———. "Interest of Older Persons in Volunteer Activities," *Social Work,* Vol. 11, No. 3 (July 1966), pp. 87–94.

184. ———, and Wiggins, Lee M. "Characteristics of the Parents Served," *Social Casework,* Vol. 48, No. 10 (December 1967), pp. 639–647.

185. Rostov, Barbara W. "Group Work in the Psychiatric Hospital: A Critical Review of the Literature," *Social Work,* Vol. 10, No. 1 (January 1965), pp. 23–31.

186. Rothaus, Paul, Johnson, Dale I., and Lyle, F. A. "Group Participation for Psychiatric Patients," *Journal of Counseling Psychology,* Vol. 11, No. 3 (Fall 1964), pp. 230–240.

187. Sarri, Rosemary C. "Group Approaches to Enhancing Pupil Performance." Paper presented at Wisconsin School Social Workers Association, Madison, April 1968. Mimeographed.

188. Schafer, Walter E. "Deviance in the Public School: An Interactional View," in Edwin J. Thomas, ed., *Behavioral Science for Social Workers.* New York: Free Press, 1967. Pp. 51–58.

189. Schein, Edgar H., and Bennis, Warren G. *Personal and Organizational Change Through Group Methods.* New York: John Wiley & Sons, 1965.

190. Schorr, Alvin L. "Mirror, Mirror on the Wall . . ." (Book Review Essay), *Social Work,* Vol. 10, No. 3 (July 1965), pp. 112–113.

191. Schreiber, Meyer. "Community Recreation Resources for the Mentally Retarded," *Training School Bulletin,* Vol. 62, No. 1 (May 1965), pp. 33–51.

192. ———, and Feeley, Mary. "Siblings of the Retarded—A Guided Group Experience," *Children,* Vol 12, No. 6 (November-December 1965), pp. 221–225.

193. Schutz, William C. *FIRO, A Three Dimensional Theory of Personal Behavior.* New York: Holt, Rinehart & Winston, 1958.

194. Schwartz, Florence S. "Profit Without Pay: Volunteer Activity in Community Centers," in "Research Papers, National Association of Jewish Center Workers." Papers presented at the National Conference of Jewish Communal Services, Atlantic City, N.J., 1967. New York: National Association of Jewish Center Workers, 1967. Pp. 74–91.

195. Schwartz, Gary, and Merten, Don. "The Language of Adolescence: An Anthropological Approach to the Youth Culture," *American Journal of Sociology,* Vol. 72, No. 5 (March 1967), pp. 453–468.

196. Schwartz, William. "Group Work and the Social Scene," in Alfred J. Kahn, ed., *Issues in American Social Work.* New York: Columbia University Press, 1959. Pp. 110–137.

197. ———. "Group Work in Public Welfare," *Public Welfare,* Vol. 26, No. 4 (October 1968), pp. 322–370.

198. ———. "Identification of Worker Re-

sponses in Group Situations." Memorandum to Gertrude Wilson et al., Chicago, 1958. Mimeographed.

199. ———. "Neighborhood Centers," in Henry S. Maas, ed., *Five Fields of Social Service: Reviews of Research.* New York: National Association of Social Workers, 1966. Pp. 144–184.

200. Scotch, C. Bernard. "The Impact of Alternative Job Opportunities for MSW's Upon the Manpower Resources of the Jewish Community Center Field," pp. 64–97. Paper presented at the Annual Conference of the National Association of Jewish Center Workers, Detroit, Michigan, June 1968. Mimeographed.

201. "Scoutmasters' Reactions to Cub Scouting." New Brunswick, N.J.: Research Service, Boy Scouts of America, 1964. Mimeographed.

202. Seidler, Morris. "Employment and Supervision of Non-Professionals." Chicago: National Federation of Settlements and Neighborhood Centers, 1968. Mimeographed.

203. Shalinsky, William. "The Effect of Group Composition on Aspects of Group Functioning." Unpublished doctoral dissertation, Western Reserve University School of Applied Social Sciences, 1967.

204. ———. "Group Composition as an Element of Social Group Work Practice," *Social Service Review*, Vol. 43, No. 1 (March 1969), pp. 42–49.

205. Shaw, Marvin E., and Blum, Michael S. "Effects of Leadership Style Upon Group Performance as a Function of Task Structure," *Journal of Personality and Social Psychology*, Vol. 3, No. 2 (February 1966), pp. 238–241.

206. Short, James F., Jr., and Strodtbeck, Fred L. *Group Process and Gang Delinquency.* Chicago: University of Chicago Press, 1965.

207. Shulman, Lawrence. *A Casebook of Social Work with Groups: The Mediating Model.* New York: Council on Social Work Education, 1968.

208. Silverman, Marvin. "Knowledge in Social Group Work: A Review of the Literature," *Social Work*, Vol. 11, No. 3 (July 1966), pp. 56–62.

209. Simon, Edwin. "The AZA Program and Membership—the Problems We Face, the Membership Imbalance." Paper presented at the National Staff Conference of the B'nai B'rith Youth Organization, Washington, D.C., January 1968. Mimeographed.

210. Sobey, Francine S. *The Nonprofessional Revolution in Mental Health.* New York: Columbia University Press, 1970.

211. ———. "Non-Professionals in Mental Health Service: Objectives and Functions in Projects Funded by the National Institute of Mental Health." Unpublished doctoral dissertation, Columbia University School of Social Work, 1968.

212. ———. *Volunteer Services in Mental Health: An Annotated Bibliography, 1955 to 1969.* Publication No. 1002. Washington, D.C.: National Institute of Mental Health, National Clearinghouse for Mental Health Information, 1969.

213. Solomon, Theodore, "A Pilot Study Among East Village 'Hippies.' " Monograph 35. New York: Associated YH-YWHAs of Greater New York, 1968. Mimeographed.

214. ———, and Friedman, Arlene. "The Associated 'Ys' Demographic Study: Summary of Returns, March 1966–January 1968." New York: Associated YM-YWHAs of Greater New York, 1968. Mimeographed.

215. Specht, Harry, Hawkins, Arthur, and McGee, Floyd. "Case Conference on the Neighborhood Sub-Professional Worker: Excerpts from the Casebooks of Sub-Professional Workers," *Children*, Vol 15, No. 1 (January-February 1968), pp. 7–11.

216. Spergel, Irving. *Street Gang Work: Theory and Practice.* Reading, Mass.: Addison-Wesley Publishing Co., 1966.

217. Staley, Edwin J. "Determining Neighborhood Recreation Priorities: An Instrument," *Journal of Leisure Research*, Vol. 1, No. 1 (Winter 1969), pp. 69–74.

218. ———. " 'Determining Neighborhood Recreation Priorities': A Reply," *Journal of Leisure Research*, Vol. 1, No. 2 (Spring 1969), pp. 193–194.

219. Strupp, Hans H., and Bergin, Allen E. *Research in Individual Psychotherapy: A Bibliography.* Public Health Service Publication No. 1844. Washington, D.C.: U.S. Department of Health, Education & Welfare, 1969.

220. "A Study of Jewish Adolescents of New Orleans." New Orleans: Jewish Welfare Federation of New Orleans, August 1966. Mimeographed.

221. "Summary of a Demonstration Project to Integrate Orthopedically Handicapped Children in Community Centers with their Nonhandicapped Peers." New York: New York Service for the Orthopedically Handicapped, undated. Mimeographed.

222. "A Survey of Boys with Physical or Mental Handicaps Who Are Members of the Boy Scouts of America." New Brunswick, N.J.: Research Service, Boy Scouts of America, 1960. Mimeographed.

223. Taber, Merlin, and Shapiro, Iris. "Social Work and Its Knowledge Base: A Content Analysis of the Periodical Literature," *Social Work*, Vol. 10, No. 4 (October 1965), pp. 100–106.

224. Tharp, Roland G. "Reply to Levinger's Note," *Psychological Bulletin*, Vol. 61, No. 2 (February 1964), pp. 158–160.

225. Thomas, Edwin J. "Selected Sociobehavioral Techniques and Principles: An Approach to Interpersonal Helping," *Social Work*, Vol. 13, No. 1 (January 1968), pp. 12–26.

226. ——— (ed.). *Behavioral Science for Social Workers.* New York: Free Press, 1967.

227. Tuckman, Bruce W. "Developmental Sequence in Small Groups," *Psychological Bulletin*, Vol. 63, No. 6 (June 1965), pp. 384–399.

228. Tuckman, Jacob. "Factors Related to Attendance in a Center for Older People," *Journal of the American Geriatrics Society*, Vol. 15, No. 5 (May 1967), pp. 474–479.

229. U.S. Department of Health, Education, and Welfare, Children's Bureau. *Research Relating to Children.* Bulletin 24. Washington, D.C.: Clearinghouse for Research in Child Life, 1969.

230. U.S. Department of Health, Education, and Welfare, Public Health Service. *Annotated Bibliography on Inservice Training for Allied Professionals and Nonprofessionals in Community Mental Health.* Washington, D.C.: U.S. Government Printing Office, 1969.

231. ———. *Annotated Bibliography on Inservice Training for Key Professionals in Community Mental Health.* Washington, D.C.: U.S. Government Printing Office, 1969.

232. ———. *Community Health Service, Publications Catalog, 1969 Edition.* Public Health Service Publication 1907. Washington, D.C.: U.S. Government Printing Office, March 1969.

233. ———. *Perspectives on Human Deprivation: Biological, Psychological, and Sociological.* Washington, D. C.: National Institute of Child Health and Human Development, 1968.

234. ———. *Training Methodology, Part I: Background Theory and Research: An Annotated Bibliography.* Washington,

D.C.: U.S. Government Printing Office, 1969.

235. ———. *Training Methodology, Part II: Planning and Administration: An Annotated Bibliography.* Washington, D.C.: U.S. Government Printing Office, 1969.

236. ———. *Training Methodology, Part III: Instructional Methods and Techniques, An Annotated Bibliography.* Washington, D.C.: U.S. Government Printing Office, 1969.

237. ———. *Training Methodology, Part IV: Audiovisual Theory, Aids, and Equipment, An Annotated Bibliography.* Washington, D.C.: U.S. Government Printing Office, 1969.

238. University of Michigan School of Social Work. *Practice Skill Assessment Instrument.* Ann Arbor, Mich.: Campus Publishers, 1967.

239. Vacher, Carole Doughton. *The Comprehensive Community Mental Health Center: An Annotated Bibliography.* Public Health Service Publication 1980. Chevy Chase, Md.: National Institute of Mental Health, 1969.

240. Vinter, Robert D., and Sarri, Rosemary C. "Malperformance in the Public School: A Group Work Approach," *Social Work*, Vol. 10, No. 1 (January 1965), pp. 3–13.

241. ———, et al. *Pupil Behavior Inventory: A Manual for Administration and Scoring.* Ann Arbor: Campus Publishers, 1966.

242. Wakeman, Roy P. "Using Data Processing to Analyze Worker Activity," *Social Work Practice, 1965.* New York: Columbia University Press, 1965. Pp. 54–64.

243. Wallach, Michael A., Kogan, Nathan, and Bem, Daryl J. "Diffusion of Responsibility and Level of Risk-taking in Groups," *Journal of Abnormal and Social Psychology*, Vol. 68, No. 3 (March 1964), pp. 263–274.

244. Walton, John. "Substance and Artifact: The Current Status of Research on Community Power Structure," *American Journal of Sociology*, Vol. 71, No. 4 (January 1966), pp. 430–438.

245. Warach, Bernard. "Findings on Staff Utilization in Jewish Community Centers and Proposed Recommendations." New York: National Jewish Welfare Board, 1968. Mimeographed.

246. Warren, Roland. "The Interaction of Community Decision Organizations: Some Basic Concepts and Needed Research," *Social Service Review*, Vol. 41, No. 3 (September 1967), pp. 261–270.

247. "Webelos Den Leaders' Reactions to the

Webelos Program." New Brunswick, N.J.: Research Service, Boy Scouts of America, 1964. Mimeographed.

248. Weissman, Harold H., and Heifetz, Henry. "Changing Program Emphases of Settlement Houses," *Social Work*, Vol. 13, No. 4 (October 1968), pp. 40–49.

249. Withey, Stephen B., and Smith, Robert L. *A National Study of Boys Eight to Ten Years Old*. Ann Arbor: Survey Research Center, Institute for Social Research, University of Michigan, 1964.

250. Yaillen, Earl. "A Summary of a Survey of Opinions of Jewish Team Members of the Pittsburgh Y-IKC." Pittsburgh: YM-YWHA, Irene Kaufman Centers, November 1967. Mimeographed.

251. Yalom, Irvin, et al. "Preparation of Patients for Group Therapy," *Archives of General Psychiatry*, Vol. 17, No. 4 (October 1967), pp. 416–427.

252. Zalba, Serapio R., and Stein, Herman D. *Assessing Organizational Effectiveness: A Draft Report*. Cleveland, Ohio: School of Applied Social Sciences, Case Western Reserve University, 1969.

253. Zald, Mayer N. "Organizations as Polities: An Analysis of Community Organization Agencies," *Social Work*, Vol. 11, No. 4 (October 1966), pp. 56–65.

254. —— (ed.). *Social Welfare Institutions: A Sociological Reader*. New York: John Wiley & Sons, 1965.

255. Zimbalist, Sidney E. "Major Trends in Social Work Research: An Analysis of the Nature and Development of Research in Social Work, as Seen in the Periodical Literature, 1900–1950." Unpublished doctoral dissertation, George Warren Brown School of Social Work, Washington University, 1955.

PUBLIC WELFARE

By GENEVIEVE W. CARTER

A recent welfare history monograph (13) makes it quite clear that the "welfare mess" has been with us for over a century and a half. Concluding this review of the period 1865–1900, Coll points out how the Charity Organization Society became a model for public welfare agencies and adds:

The COS emphasized personal failure as the major cause of dependency, believed no one would work unless goaded by fear of starvation, investigated every aspect of an applicant's life, reduced relief to the lowest possible level and provided close supervision of any family on its rolls. [13, p. 62]

Throughout the years these basic notions have persisted. Public welfare today is characterized by these values: the "work ethic" must be emphasized for all able-bodied recipients, money payments should be linked with compulsory vocational development of those whose work skills are inadequate, moral surveillance is necessary for recipients of tax-supported welfare benefits, social stigma and subsistence-level existence ensure a punishing situation that increases motivation for self-support, the states and localities must have opportunity for wide variations in treatment of the dependent poor, the cost standard of assistance should be held below the wage level of the working poor.

By incorporating these values into the welfare system, we "serve" a population that can be readily identified and contained. Any other alternative system will cost more tax dollars. The present system offers the cheapest plan for discharging a major national responsibility. What other types of programs could protect these cherished values at minimum cost?

Although obstacles to change are deeply rooted, the current welfare debate has resulted in a broadened concern for action and for a drastic redesign of the present welfare system. There also seem to be changes in public opinion, as manifested in the results of a nationwide 1968 amalgam survey conducted by the National Opinion Research Center (52). (Incidentally, the word welfare is highly charged, and we are learning that the use of other terms to express the same idea produces different responses.) In the NORC survey it was found that well over half the

192

white population believes that people have a right not only to the bare necessities such as housing and medical care, but also to a college education whether they can afford it or not. However, 46 percent of the white population places the blame for poverty on the individual. Sixty percent of all the people in the sample agree that the welfare program should be changed to some kind of guaranteed income, negative income tax, or children's allowance.

These investigators indicate a changing trend in public attitudes with a smaller percentage of the white population believing that people are on relief for dishonest purposes than was found four years previously. They also found some conflict between a segment of the population wanting to help the "needy" and persons believing that those currently being helped may not be appropriate recipients for such help or that program administration may have been faulty.

Surveys of this type tell us that public opinion about the poor and welfare programs is changing but that a number of the value beliefs on which public assistance was founded may impede the implementation of progressive welfare reforms regardless of available national resources.

The Context for Public Welfare

Public welfare does not constitute a field of social work practice; rather, it draws on a variety of disciplines and includes a variety of practices and services. In general the target population groups served are the most poor, although some public welfare agencies in nonurban counties offer the only resources for such community services as adoptions or protective services.

Public welfare is an organizing term that currently brings together for administration a number of public assistance titles, child welfare titles and amendments, and Title XIX of the Social Security Act for medical assistance, as well as supplementary programs in which states and localities utilize local tax funds to augment federally financed programs. With their diverse programs, public welfare agencies operate like an industry, utilizing a number of different types of professional and nonprofessional personnel, and cover a wide range of services. The boundaries of public welfare shift as legislative changes take place and service programs are reorganized.

During the five-year period since Mencher's review of public welfare research appeared in the earlier volume of this series (49), the central public welfare controversies have continued unabated on, for example, inadequacies and inequities of the grant-in-aid standards or illegitimacy and related moral issues. Recent legislation and emphasis on job training and employment have brought new issues to the surface. Rehabilitation and self-support have become guiding policy, and while services to enhance family functioning are not removed from the program, neither are they given strong priority.

The 1962 social security amendments and the separation of the social welfare functions from the insurance functions of the Social Security Administration into a Welfare Administration gave focus and visibility to public welfare functions and, some might add, too much visibility for political acceptance. As a consequence, the merger of the Welfare Administration and the Vocational Rehabilitation Agency took place in August 1967, and a new organizational entity, the Social and Rehabilitation Service (SRS), was created under administrative order. This reorganization at the federal level gave a public emphasis to rehabilitation and vocational development that provided a more acceptable outward symbol for public welfare functions. In addition the Welfare Administration period initiated research and demonstration programs and a research journal, *Welfare in Review*, directed to public welfare and related social welfare issues.

A further increase in social research is expected under SRS as more funds become available for social welfare research and demonstration. The early 1970s will likely bring dramatic changes in what is known as public welfare. What are now called public assistance payments are likely to be viewed primarily as an income maintenance problem to be studied through econometric concepts and measures. The adult categories—Aid to the Blind (AB), Aid to the Permanently and Totally Disabled (APTD), and Old Age Assistance (OAA)—may become so politically acceptable as to be considered income security programs—with money payments as a right.

Income maintenance issues will probably center on the potentially employable, parental responsibility for support of families, and how welfare recipients can maximize income from earnings and money payments. Employment incentives and earnings exemptions are creating a population that is only partially dependent, for which both employment and financial assistance form the family's income. Underlying these and similar issues is the work incentive question, about which there exists meager research and a limited knowledge base but considerable oratory and speculation.

Since research trends will probably follow reorganizational effects, legislative changes, and appropriations, it could be predicted that the organization and reassessment of public social services (and medical care) will be the focus for the next research thrust. Hopefully the major research questions on employment for the poor will shift from attention to personal inadequacies and motivation toward job engineering, job development, and guaranteed jobs, as well as employment training. Increasing knowledge on levels of living and the consequences of poverty and deprivation will continue to open new areas of research concern.

The boundaries of public welfare will change and we may later find the term has lost its former utility. But it may be a long time before the knowledge base about poor people, their problems, or the barriers that separate them from the majority

society will have reached an adequate level for effective guidance of the development and delivery of appropriate service programs.

The Poverty Population

Public welfare programs are generally included in local or national inventories of antipoverty programs. Each administration creates its own nomenclature, and already use of the phrase "the War on Poverty" is diminishing. Estimates of the poverty population (59) provide a basis for establishing public assistance rates that have more meaning than general population rates. In particular, the former show what proportion of the poverty population is reached. Approximately one-third of the poor receive income from public assistance, but this ratio varies greatly among states. The rate for recipients of Aid to Families with Dependent Children (AFDC) will vary as much as eight times between localities. For example, Raleigh, North Carolina, may reach only 24 of 1,000 poor persons, while another large city will reach 201 per 1,000 of its defined poor population (44).

Differences in the AFDC rate are strikingly varied between high- and low-income states or cities. As further explained in the Levinson study (44), New Orleans had 39.7 assistance cases per 1,000 poor persons, while Philadelphia had 84.1 per 1,000. When the new 1970 census figures become available, a more detailed analysis of the impact on poverty of public assistance for all categories can be made. The large differences between cities can be attributed not only to differences in eligibility rules and grant levels—the severer the rules, the smaller the number of eligible poor persons who can gain entrance into the welfare system—but also to the choices and opportunities available to the dependent poor when public assistance is not the only resource (44). For example, when work is available or help from relatives is possible, or when loans or emergency services offer alternatives, the dependent family will have other opportunities to consider.

If public welfare agencies adopt a goal of lifting poor families out of poverty by raising grant levels for all states, then some 10 million people would have their level of living raised to or above the poverty line. (For a nonfarm family of four persons, the revised poverty threshold in 1967 averaged $3,410, compared with $3,335 in earlier definitions. See revisions in poverty standards discussed later in this section.) Such a move, worthy as it seems, would create havoc among the other poor —the some 15 million who could not qualify for public assistance. Perhaps the group most hostile to the welfare population is the working poor—who work full time, pay taxes, but never have sufficient income to support their families adequately. Some states provide grants that are approaching the poverty line and with a state- or locally financed general assistance coverage for some 90 to 95 percent of the poverty population.

Public welfare reaches more of the poor than any other public or private welfare program. It is, however, too circumscribed to claim as its purpose the prevention or reduction of economic dependency, although congressional appropriations frequently attach this purpose to allocation of funds. Realistic strategies for the prevention and reduction of poverty must attend also to other social institutions and practices, for example, education, segregated housing, and discrimination in employment.

Who are the poor? Orshansky has pioneered in defining the poor in her two best-known articles, "Counting the Poor" (59) and "Who's Who Among the Poor" (60). The definition as originally developed by her is based on the minimum food and other needs of families, taking into account family size, number of children, and farm and nonfarm residence. Families that use about the same proportion of their income for a given level of food expenditure are considered to share the same level of living.

For families of three or more persons the poverty level was set at three times the cost of the economy food plan (76).

Orshansky's analysis suggests that when food costs are below suggested essentials (seventy cents per day for a family of four), the likelihood of serious deprivation based on dietary inadequacy is indeed probable. On the basis of 1963 incomes, a poverty cutoff line was developed that allows for analysis of populations subject to greater or lesser risk of poverty. For instance, families headed by a woman are subject to a risk of poverty nearly three times greater than those headed by a man. The majority of the poor, however, are in two-parent families in which at least one parent is employed full time during the year, i.e., the working poor.

Orshansky gives characteristics of the poor by age, race, sex, and employment status for the nearly 35 million individuals below the poverty threshold as defined (60). She reemphasizes the risk of poverty faced by nonwhite families (one out of every two nonwhite persons was considered poor in terms of 1963 income), large families (among the poor are counted 15 million children under 18), aged households, families headed by a woman, and families of nonworkers or chronically low-paid workers.

The unemployment rate in poor families is three times the rate of that in nonpoor families. While a man or woman in a poor family is more likely than a man or woman of the same age in a nonpoor family to be out of the labor force entirely, in more than one-quarter of the white families and nearly one-third of the nonwhite families designated as poor in 1963 (about 2 million), the family head worked full time year-round. Orshansky's work demonstrates the creative use of available demographic statistics in sharpening policy issues.

More recently the U.S. Bureau of the Census has developed descriptions of the changing poverty population and a revision of the poverty threshold. The poverty level trend analysis as prepared by the bureau (74) shows a steady decline in the poverty population. The review of Current Population Reports Series P-23 (1960–68) indicates the following: white residents are continuing to leave the central city; in 1967, 42 percent of all poor city families, as contrasted with only 16 percent of all poor suburban families, were Negro; the proportion of poor families headed by a woman under 65 years of age increased dramatically—and in central cities this increase occurred mainly among Negroes; in the central city the incidence of poverty was three times as great for Negroes; in the suburban ring the incidence for Negroes was five times as great; the number of poor persons declined by one-third between 1959 and 1967; the number of white poor persons dropped by 38 percent, while the number of Negroes declined by 21 percent; the greatest decreases in the poverty population were families with a male head who was white and under 65 years of age. The public welfare and social planning implications of such facts are many, but their explication extends beyond the limits of this chapter.

Revised Poverty Threshold

Modification in the definitions of poverty were adopted in 1969 as a result of deliberations by a federal interagency committee (73). Two changes were made in the original Orshansky definition.

1. A change in the method of adjusting the poverty threshold for annual cost-of-living fluctuation was proposed in order to use the Consumer Price Index (CPI), which is more generally available and which keeps the poverty threshold parallel with change in cost of living. For example, between 1955 and 1966 the CPI went up by 13.7 percent and the poverty threshold increased by 7.9 percent for an average family. The introduction of the CPI cost-of-living adjustment resulted in an increase in the nonfarm poor of 210,000 families or 880,000 persons.

2. The second change in definition resulted in narrowing the gap between farm and nonfarm families. Orshansky had allowed for a 30 percent differential for food grown at home. A change in the differential, based on later studies, resulted in the use of an 85 percent differential, which resulted in an increase of 1.1 million poor farm persons over what had originally been reported.

The published tables show the differences from 1959 to 1968 in the number and percentage of the poor based on both revised and original definitions. The differences become more noticeable over the last three years of the trend. The 1968 figures, under the revised definition, cite 25,389,000 poor persons, or 12 percent of the total population. In 1967 the poor were counted at 27,769,000, or 14 percent of the population; in 1966, 17.3 percent of the population; and in 1959, 22 percent of the population.

Estimating the numbers of the poor for social planning purposes is indeed a complex and difficult job. Income levels appear to be hard data, but those who have labored to reconstruct annual income figures through tedious client interviews are aware of the loopholes. Economists are prone to search for the best available hard data measures. Sociologists and social workers, while not satisfied with annual income measures for differentiating the poor, have offered no better measures. Annual income will therefore continue to serve as a distinguishing measure for the poor, near-poor, comfortable, affluent, and so on.

Research results point toward the irregularity of the annual income of the poor, who not only lack skills and coping capacity to meet the crises that hit them with great frequency, but who also are subject to irregular employment, both of which make them prone to ups and downs not reflected in average annual income figures. A sizable percentage of welfare recipients can be shown to be above the poverty line, but such findings must be interpreted cautiously. For example, a $4,000 average annual income may represent earnings of $4,000 for the first eight months of the year but zero income for the last four months. Regardless of the apparent adequacy of its average annual income, a family may be destitute for a part of the year.

Population at Risk

The notion of population at risk holds promise as a useful construct if dimensions and definitions can be identified in ways that allow for reliable measurement. Although to the writer's knowledge no serious work has been published to date on the subject, references and research proposals have been developed. "Poverty as a system" was presented in a recent report (65) as a model whose boundaries included the states or areas from which the poor migrate to the cities, and poverty centers in which the poor remain in the central city or from which they either return to the rural area from which they migrated or take different routes toward upward mobility. Yardsticks are suggested for program-planning and monitoring. The concepts are interesting, but as discussed by Hoos (32) with respect to the California experience, population data and relevant characteristics are not yet available to enable sorting out what might be termed the population at risk. The 1970 census will offer new data, but maintaining updated information makes the task practically impossible for an ongoing information system.

If risk is defined as the likelihood of "falling into the welfare system and adding to the tax bill," there is growing but fragmented information that past recipients of public assistance are reapplying at a rate of about 50 percent, and about one-third of denied cases do make an entry into the welfare program in six months or so. Past and potential public assistance recipients rates are highest. Vulnerability to risk can be determined to some extent by average annual income, i.e., the cutoff level or the poverty threshold. A female-headed family, especially from a minority group,

creates a higher risk than an intact poor family. Health factors, relatives, and friends as possible resources, coping capacity for handling crises, and client attitudes about the receipt of assistance are some of the intangible and changing factors that influence the risk status. These concepts need further study. But the boundary lines for the large marginal population at risk must be viewed as part of the poverty system that feeds people into the welfare programs. Caseload changes are affected by (1) factors within the poverty population, (2) organizational factors that operate within the welfare programs (eligibility restrictions, agency climate), and (3) community environmental factors (wage levels, job opportunities, social stigma).

Levinson (44) has quantified twelve measures that indicate a rank order placement for eleven major cities across the country. It is this type of data analysis that begins to build knowledge about the interrelationships between the welfare system population and the marginal population that hovers above the active caseload and the differences by cities or regions as to the proportion of the poor population allowed to enter the welfare programs. For example, in rank order New York City, Philadelphia, and Providence rank highest in AFDC caseload per 1,000 poor persons, and Atlanta, Memphis, and Raleigh, North Carolina, rank lowest. New York, Chicago, and Phoenix rank highest in percentage of poor migrants, another factor found to influence the size of the population at risk.

Longitudinal studies of poverty populations are needed to determine what factors lead people in and out of the poverty system. It is becoming clearer that the degree to which the public welfare agencies approach complete coverage of the poor population depends on the kinds of state and local conditions cited in this section. The welfare population is viewed in a position relative to local wage levels and the incomes of the rest of the population. The principle of wage-related benefits and the doctrine of "less eligibility" are deeply rooted in the poverty system.

The AFDC Population

Most of the recent research on public welfare clients has been directed to the AFDC population, since this program is increasingly controversial and has continued to expand. There have been no recent national studies on the AB population. A mail questionnaire survey (11, 18, 23) of the aid to the aged population has disclosed little new information but has demonstrated the use of an economical method of obtaining national data about this group as evidenced by the unexpectedly high response from the self-administered questionnaire.

AFDC Case Mobility

Information about the AFDC population, including unemployed and incapacitated fathers, points to considerable mobility in the caseload. For example, a 1968 interview study of AFDC mothers (6) shows that 20 percent of the AFDC closings took place after less than four months' assistance over a three-year period. About 20 percent of the cases in this nationwide sample were closed with three or more continuous years of welfare assistance. There is only speculation about the changes in conditions or characteristics of these women that moved them from a welfare recipient status. Little is known about reasons for closing cases since usually no agency follow-up is required when the recipient terminates his own case, and this procedure accounts for the majority of closings (as against a jointly planned termination following completion of a case plan).

The Baltimore longitudinal study (67) reveals an unbelievable number of family status changes over a few months' time. Some one-third of denied cases later become eligible, family compensation changes

frequently, and case losses through changes of residence—when efforts are made to follow denied or closed cases—are so high that longitudinal studies of such populations may prove too difficult for research administration.

The New York–New Jersey pilot study (9) provided some interesting leads to researchers. In this study four sample groups were drawn for interviewing: rejected AFDC applicants, accepted applicants, continued cases, and closed cases. By the time the interviewers could reach the respondents, case status had changed so frequently that the four classifications became questionable as categories for analysis. Closed cases involving mothers who had made the greatest use of welfare also had the highest incidence of on-and-off use. Rejected applicants, as expected, used assistance the least and had been denied welfare more frequently than others. Families that received support from intermittent employment of at least one adult member enjoyed a higher level of living than those families that made more nearly continuous use of welfare without supplementation from employment income. By far most of the mothers whose cases are closed are intermittent users of welfare, the kind of persons who find their place again in some type of employment—at least for a while.

Aggregate statistics on the AFDC program give the impression that caseloads are static and involve the same families. Yet one-third of the cases change in a year and another group of families with similar characteristics moves in. In 1961 new recipients accounted for 66.2 percent of the national AFDC caseload. In 1967 new recipients accounted for 59.8 percent of the caseload. There are some indications that the first rise in caseload volume may result from new cases and a second wave from reentries of this expanded base. This pattern, linked with longer case duration, may slow down the present level of case mobility. Also, the current policy of work incentives, which permits both employment and supplementary payments, will affect mobility as recipient families maximize their income potential. People are becoming more self-supporting, but although there will be mobility within the caseload, the caseload volume will appear greater.

Characteristics of AFDC Recipients

In the last two years there has been an increase in younger women among AFDC cases and, because of this, a slight decrease in the number of children per family. This change in composition can be expected because of the population increase for that age segment. There is a higher proportion of reentrees into the welfare system than formerly, running as high as 50 percent in some urban areas. Most important is the improvement in education and occupational levels of AFDC mothers over the past five years. This is especially true of new applicants. Women tend to have attained a higher education than their spouses, and Negro women have had more years of schooling than whites. From health service studies there is evidence that AFDC families are utilizing medical services to a greater extent. In spite of these improvements in general characteristics, the average adults and youths from the AFDC programs are poorly equipped for jobs that pay enough to make the family self-supporting.

In New York City the proportion of high school graduates who were recipients almost doubled from 12.4 percent of the total caseload in 1961 to 23 percent in 1967 (44). At the same time the proportion of women with less than a seventh-grade education was cut in half—from 47.4 percent of the total caseload in 1961 to 22.7 percent in 1967.

About seven in ten AFDC families now live in metropolitan areas. From inspection of preliminary data from the 1967 unpublished characteristics study, the Negro AFDC population is about equal to the white (79). While AFDC mothers are widely distributed, Negro AFDC mothers are concentrated and highly visible in the inner-city areas.

Negative changes in AFDC characteristics over the past several years are reflected in housing conditions (84). Sixty percent of AFDC families are living in substandard, deteriorating, or overcrowded housing. Urban areas report worsening housing conditions in spite of an increase in the size of the grants. In forty-three states the amount a recipient receives for shelter is limited to an arbitrary maximum, regardless of the actual amount that must be paid for shelter. This report shows only 12.2 percent of AFDC families living in public housing, according to 1967 data (84).

One significant negative finding in the New York City study should be examined further when the national 1967 characteristics survey of AFDC families (79) becomes available for trend analysis. The New York City study (44) showed an increase in the number of children age 16–18 who dropped out of school in the period 1961–68. Whereas 12.9 percent of AFDC children age 16–18 dropped out of school in 1961, 19 percent dropped out in 1968.

Two recent studies (36, 43) reinforce our concern regarding the effects of continued deprivation on AFDC children. Levinson (43), in a longitudinal study of a southern city, shows that the longer a family receives assistance, the more likely it will have children with serious problems. External records for early marriages, illegitimacy, school dropouts, mental illness, delinquency, and other problems among the total city youth population were checked to determine the representation of youths by families. Analysis for intergenerational dependency indicates that children whose close relatives receive welfare assistance have more problems than others. Since this study reconstructs the history of welfare recipients identified from a cross-sectional population of a larger educational survey, comparative data about the new welfare population are available. The companion study by Langner (36) covers a small sample but comes to similar conclusions by an intensive clinical approach.

A 1967 mail questionnaire survey (80) directed to a nationally representative sample of 3,659 mothers or female caretakers of AFDC children yielded responses from 81.1 percent of the sample. Additional information on characteristics shows that some 8.4 percent of the women were currently in some type of educational classes or employment training. Thirteen and six-tenths percent said they lived in a bad neighborhood, 24.8 percent said they did not have enough chairs for the family to sit down and eat together, 17.4 percent kept children home from school because they lacked shoes or clothing, 65.4 percent said that people receiving regular welfare checks might need to see a welfare case-worker about their problems not more than every two or three months (21.6 percent of these said "not that often").

Although research aimed at achieving a better understanding of the characteristics of AFDC families still goes on, much of the more recent research is directed toward characteristics of the AFDC population as they relate to welfare organization activities, employment, or training or toward a current issue such as resident participation. A general description of the population, with its rural and urban differences, is now fairly well known. The policy and service implications of this knowledge have still, however, to be detailed and acted on. Regardless of documentation as to levels of deprivation, the implications for improvement and action are more money and higher grant levels. This direction does not, at present, appear to have public support.

Employability of AFDC Mothers

Present national policy still emphasizes the individual opportunity approach to rehabilitate (or habilitate) the incompetent person so he can compete in the nation's social and economic structure. This emphasis on training, educating, and resocializing the economically dependent is likely to continue, although considerable recognition now exists that more than individual opportunity is needed. For example, Rein (63) points to the problem of the resistance of institutions, the uselessness of characterizing the poor as apathetic, and the threat to the opportunity approach to poverty when militancy overturned the image of apathy.

However, there is great reluctance to consider programs of guaranteed employment, although research on work training programs in depressed economic areas (40, 41) indicates clearly that a program of guaranteed jobs is the desirable course of action. Wages for low-skilled women are meager, as is evidenced by median annual earnings of only $1,193 for women who worked in private households full time (90).

The common public stereotype follows the notion that the AFDC adults must be introduced to the "world of work." It requires no sophisticated analysis, however, to compare a family minimum needs budget with average annual income from low-paying jobs. Child care costs for two or three children and other work-related expenses, even with improved wage levels, open the obvious question. What proportion of the female family heads can be vocationally rehabilitated to a wage-earning level that will make the family self-supporting—above the welfare level or above the poverty line?

Rein (64), Carter (10), and others (8, 16, 46) have pointed out the interrelationship of low-paid jobs and the welfare system: Welfare supplements low wage levels and low wages supplement insufficient benefits. Being "on welfare" does not necessarily mean a break with the labor force. The intermittent use of welfare linked with intermittent employment constitutes a pattern of life for a large proportion of AFDC mothers. In essence, the welfare system facilitates the availability of low-skilled labor when needed for seasonal work, part-time employment, and low-paying jobs in general. When the grant level approaches the minimum wage, as Durbin (16) infers, there is a choice between working and welfare. One could hypothesize that the easier the reentry to welfare, the less risk in leaving welfare and the greater use of employment when available.

In a national interview survey (6) of AFDC mothers, a three-year history of work and welfare receipt was reconstructed for each recipient. The work patterns vary markedly by age group. The youngest (under 17) and the oldest (56 and over) have the least work experience; 60 percent of the former and 66 percent of the latter did not work during the three years. Those aged 46–50 have had the longest work records, with 24 percent working twenty-five to thirty-six months out of the three-year period. This older age bracket would likely be eliminated from training programs, but with intermittent supportive services could continue to maintain their labor force connections. Similar work history records were found for the 26–30, 31–35, and 36–40 age groups, of which more than two-thirds have had considerable work experience; 24 percent of the three groups combined worked twenty-five or more months during the three-year period.

In an analysis of months worked by educational level, Negro women worked more months (mean number) for each educational level than did the white AFDC mothers. For all ethnic and racial groups, the higher the education, the more months worked. This relationship is true for working women generally.

When mean self-esteem scores are correlated with welfare status at time of interview, there is a clear association of higher self-esteem with working, with slightly higher scores for closed case and working than for active case but working or denied case and working. Not working was associated with lower self-esteem for all three case-status categories.

There is sufficient evidence to say that the majority of mothers who can work, prefer work to welfare. Program records from Title V work and training projects show clearly the excess of applications for training over the available training slots. Conversely, there was seldom a training project (under Title V) with excess applications from appropriate males waiting for training.

There is little evidence available in a systematic form on assessment of employability of AFDC mothers and fathers (33). Vocational rehabilitation demonstrations and studies have classified disabilities, but the individual case plan is ultimately a clinical judgment based on information about the recipient from several sources. Such a clinical approach is hardly feasible with a large case volume and without intake control based on selective criteria. There is a general lack of knowledge about the potential employability of the persons in any given AFDC caseload. No tested and validated screening techniques are in use, nor is there a means of defining case-status points in a progressive movement toward implementing plans for rehabilitation. For a mass program such as public welfare, it is strange to find this paradox of large-scale management and one-to-one clinical procedures existing side by side. Unfortunately, the computer and the systems approach can contribute little until some of the basic conceptual problems are solved, whereby usable data can be generalized.

For example, a California pilot project (91) first tackled the notion of employability with a series of questions: Is an AFDC recipient employable if there is no demand for his skill in the labor market? Is he employable if his earnings would be less than his public assistance grant? Is he employable if hiring practices discriminate against him? Is a mother employable if she cannot obtain or earn enough to pay for child care? Employability was approached in terms of obstacles, some twenty of which were listed and ranked by a review panel that functioned as the judging, synthesizing medium for the several sources of information on recipients, including personal interviews. The review panel method is, however, too costly for screening large mobile caseloads. Further experimentation and research are needed to assess employability more economically and quickly. Research may tell us at some later date that the answer is as simple as asking the recipient for his own assessment—including full information on employability *for what*.

Data on case closings in public welfare (83) have been collected semiannually on a voluntary basis. (Since collection of such data will now be required, future reports on case closings will be more comprehensive than in the past.) During the period July–December 1968, about half of the states reported on case closings for the AFDC program (California and Pennsylvania were not among these). Of 115,000 reported closings, about a fifth were closed for reasons other than eligibility in respect to need, e.g., refusal to comply, no eligible child in the home, loss of residence, transference to another program. About half of the closings were due to employment or increased earnings of persons in the home, primarily the AFDC father or mother who became employed or increased his earnings beyond the level for eligibility. Most of those clients get their own jobs. With roughly half of all closings the result of employment, there is ample evidence of employability of this population group. As to the duration of the employment, under what conditions it takes place, or what types of recipients soon return to the welfare office, this is not known. Follow-up studies on closed cases over a year or two are not in the literature. Many clients are never heard of again, and the stories of the successes are not known.

Public Welfare Programs

Public welfare can be viewed as a part of the broader social welfare institution. Even in the more remote counties there are re-cipients of social security, veterans' benefits, Bureau of Indian Affairs services, Department of Agriculture services, and other social or economic provisions. One of the functions of public welfare has been income development for the recipient family through organized programs or provision of access to other financial resources such as child-support payments.

Some of the objectives of public welfare programs can be readily identified and defined. Others become controversial because of value conflicts among segments of the tax-paying community, the legislators, professionals, social activists, and clients' groups. Even within the staff of a specific agency there may be sharp value differences.

One image of public welfare is that of a residual agency that doles out money payments at the lowest possible level to the smallest population possible. Another image (held by many professionals) is of an agency that provides cash payments at a decent level of living and, along with issuing money, provides social services to improve family and social functioning—a goal of self-realization for all recipients, present and potential. The third view, which apparently has considerable support judging by recent legislative trends, sees the public welfare agency as a rehabilitation force, changing the skills, habits, and attitudes of recipients. This view usually exempts the aged and older disabled persons, reasoning that the limited service resources of the public welfare agency should be focused on the potentially employable. This is the most direct way to cut program costs and to alleviate public criticism of what appears to be a burden on middle- and lower middle-class workers to support others who do not work. Because of these different sets of expectations and objectives, which at times are in conflict, it is difficult to assess the performance or impact of any public welfare agency. Without clear objectives there can be no research evaluation—and the objectives must be stated as ends or outcomes, not means.

An object of prevention and reduction of dependency is not the same as elimination of poverty, since we are well aware that the standard poverty level includes more working poor than nonworking poor. Without clarification of objectives—ultimate, intermediate, and proximal—it is difficult to pose alternative programs or approaches for achieving similar objectives. Effectiveness and efficiency studies depend on consensus as to objectives whether what is being assessed is a total program's impact or a unit of service delivered to a specific client.

Most of the research reviewed in the following section will, by necessity, be limited to descriptive findings on the nature, distribution, and utilization of services. During the five years of research covered by this review, public agencies have been engaged in four major programs: (1) money payments to needy eligible persons, (2) health care services, (3) work experience and job training, and (4) social welfare services. Since 1968 the public welfare agencies have not conducted work experience or job-training programs, since these functions are now under the auspices of the Department of Labor. It is too early to assess the advantages or disadvantages of this transfer of functions. It is already evident that problems of the coordination between the two government agencies are complex and that raising the skills of the selected trainees is costly and time consuming. This is especially true if successful employment placement means the trainee is working at a wage level above the welfare standard or the poverty line.

It is evident that future program-planning and policy issues will be handled separately for services and cash payments. As this program separation takes place, considerable research effort will undoubtedly be placed on questions about social services. Client choice of services, service priorities, work-load standards, service effectiveness, consumer participation in service planning, and other similar issues will hopefully receive attention in the next few years.

Income Maintenance and Assistance Payments

Money payments to the needy eligible poor have always constituted the major service program in public welfare. Of all persons now classified as poor (25,389,000, or 12 percent of the population), slightly over 10 million received money payments in March 1969—about 116,000 more than the month before (82). The continued upward trend in numbers of people receiving AFDC is reflected in recent changes: 4,906,000 persons in March 1967, 5,587,000 in March 1968, and 6,478,000 in March 1969. OAA has remained fairly stable over the last two years after several years of decline; as of March 1969 this program served 2,030,000 persons. APTD increased slightly, from 597,000 in March 1967 to 728,000 in March 1969. General assistance clients totaled 720,000 in March 1967 and were reported at 827,000 in March 1969.

Maintenance assistance in dollars was reported as $396,482,000 in March 1963 (81), the period covered by Mencher's chapter in the first volume of this series (49). In March 1967 money payments for maintenance were $400,391,000 for the month and by March 1969 were $551,299,000 for the month (82). Thus as of 1969 maintenance assistance payments to eligible recipients were running over $6 billion a year. This is an amount that excludes medical assistance, administration and service, staff development, education, and other costs in public welfare.

Throughout the last decade there have been continuous changes in, liberalizations of, and broadening of the public assistance programs. These minor improvements are called "tinkering with the system" by those who argue for drastic reforms offering entirely new programs based on new sets of income maintenance principles. These incremental changes have taken place at the federal and state levels and are reflected primarily in the 1962 and 1967 social security amendments. At the federal level, earned income exemptions and work incentives have opened the way for important changes. At state levels, for example, New Jersey extended its AFDC program to children whose parents were unemployed or who worked but did not earn enough to maintain their families at the state's assistance standard. Each state has its own pace for improving assistance programs, and in general the inequities among the states have been maintained in the order in which they have existed over the past five years.

Forty-nine states and the District of Columbia, Guam, Puerto Rico, and the Virgin Islands operate federally supported assistance programs for dependent children, the aged, the blind, and the permanently disabled. Nevada has only the first three of these programs. Twenty-four states have extended their dependent children's programs to families in need because a parent is unemployed. Nineteen states are assisting needy adults under a combined program called Aid to the Aged, Blind, and Disabled. Some twenty-five states are operating Medicaid, the new medical assistance for needy persons discussed under health care services.

During 1967 and 1968 there were numerous analytical reports in which models of income maintenance programs have been projected as to cost, population coverage, work-incentive structure, level of payments, and designs for control populations. Interestingly, the social welfare proponents usually favor children's allowance-type models while the economists are clearly in favor of the negative income tax models (53).

Only one field experiment, using a negative income tax model, is actually in progress. This research-based demonstration, commonly called the New Jersey experiment, is jointly funded by the Office of Economic Opportunity and the Ford Foundation. Reported results are not likely to be available before 1971 or 1972. Two other proposed demonstrations are in the planning stages under U.S. Department of

Health, Education, and Welfare auspices, but are not ready for approved demonstration funding.

The problems—technical and political—in designing and implementing an income maintenance experiment are formidable. Also, the more skeptical may question the feasibility of simulating a real income maintenance program for a selected sample when the termination limits of the cash payments are known and when the supportive behavior of the nonsampled neighbors or friends is absent.

There seems to be no question that by the end of the 1960s public interest shifted to reform of the cash transfer system. The debate will continue as to the goals of equalizing individual opportunity and rehabilitation or mechanisms for redistributing income or both. The economists are in the forefront in the analytical analysis of various alternatives (15, 25, 31, 61, 72, 75), while the social work or social welfare researchers are the users and evaluators of the contributions of the economists.

The disciplinary perspectives are different in emphasis, as pointed out by Nicol (55). She explains that the economist does not usually ask, as other social scientists will, whether it is socially desirable for a woman who has small children in a fatherless home to work, even if she could raise her income above her welfare grant. The economist may question the efficiency of such a plan in terms of last-benefit outcomes and be looking toward wages to increase the ratio of benefits to costs. The reduction in public assistance payments to the mother will not, because of her low level of wages, usually cover the public outlay for training or child care services. The economist is looking at payoffs from an investment in human resources and questions the economic benefits from training, employment, and child care programs for low-skilled mothers with several children. Others also are weighing the consequences of training and rehabilitation and an improved cash-transfer system. Both approaches will likely be developed since both directions sustain considerable public support.

Trends and changes in assistance payments. Perhaps the most significant issue in assistance payment programs has been the ever rising caseloads, especially in AFDC. This is a common phenomenon in the majority of states. Since the status of the father determines the dependency of the children, national trends from 1961 to 1967 are significant (78, 79).

In 1961, 8.1 percent of the fathers were absent from the home because of death, but by 1967 the percentage absent for this reason had decreased to 5.8. The proportion of separated fathers had changed only slightly from 14.4 percent in 1961 to 16 percent in 1967. The proportion of fathers absent because of divorce and desertion remained about the same. Unmarried mothers increased from 22.5 to 28.3 percent, indicating the increase in illegitimacy. However, for New York City (44) the proportion of fathers who deserted increased considerably, from 23.7 percent in 1961 to 39.7 percent in 1967 to 46.2 percent in 1968 —indicating an increase in desertion that is much higher in that city than for the nation as a whole. Increased numbers of desertions may be a forerunner to higher AFDC recipient rates and a cause for increased dependency of the children.

National trends also show an increase in the percentage of reentries into the welfare system, from 33.8 percent in 1961 to 40.2 percent in 1967. This trend appears to be one of continuing increase, as noted in more recent statistics.

The Levinson study (44) also revealed another interesting factor associated with rising AFDC caseloads; that is, the larger the amount of funds spent for Community Action Programs under OEO, the higher the AFDC caseload per 1,000 poor persons in eleven cities. In New York City in 1968 the annual expenditures were $169 per 1,000 poor persons and the caseload per 1,000 was 200.7. In Philadelphia the expenditures were $155 per 1,000 and the caseload per 1,000 was 84.1. On the other hand, where CAP expenditures were lower, such as in Atlanta, Memphis, and Raleigh, North Carolina, the caseload ratios per 1,000 poor persons were lower—36.4, 32.0, and 23.7 respectively.

National Welfare Rights Organization memberships by percentage of recipients also showed the same relationship—the higher the membership, the higher the caseload per 1,000 poor persons. However, the number of mothers who reported membership is small. For example, only 4.1 percent of all AFDC women in New York City belonged to the local NWRO chapter at the time of the study.

Undoubtedly more research will be forthcoming on the impact of participation and action of the poor in affairs that greatly affect their lives. These findings, although meager for the total picture, do indicate that there are measurable consequences. A recent review of literature on participation of the poor in policy-making points toward increased research interest in this area (57).

In the analysis of median best wages, grant level, and caseload per 1,000 poor persons for eleven cities (44), it is significant to note that most of the cities with a large differential (some $100) between wages and grants have lower caseloads per 1,000 poor persons, but there are exceptions, such as Rochester, which has a relatively low caseload rate—40.9 per 1,000— and has a grant level of $278 and a wage level of $281.60. An interesting finding from this review shows that the average AFDC woman had never been employed for wages (even the best wages she ever earned) that were as high as the level of the typical wages for unskilled women (44).

If the actual *best* wage-earning potential (discounting training) of AFDC women found in the 11 cities is indicative of the potential of the national caseload, a rising caseload seems inevitable because such women cannot learn enough without the earnings incentives to be economically self sufficient. [44, pp. 43–44]

However, a large percentage of recipients can be expected to maximize their incomes through a combination of welfare and work. This option will tend to increase caseloads.

With recent findings from comparative populations, it is possible to view comparable characteristics and family situations of the welfare population with other poor populations (43, 67). However badly off the denied AFDC cases may be in terms of the multiproblem syndrome associated with poverty, the accepted cases are always on the average worse off. Even a year later in the Baltimore study (67) the accepted cases were still worse off, although about a third of the originally rejected cases found their way into the public assistance caseload after their limited resources were exhausted.

Welfare recipients' greater deprivation was also shown in the southern city study (43), a longitudinal study which revealed that the teen-age offspring of people who had received assistance at any time showed up most poorly on almost every criterion— school achievement, school dropout, delinquency, health, and so on. They showed up more poorly than a poor group of teenagers whose parents had applied for but were denied assistance. This latter group was worse off than a low socioeconomic group of teen-agers who came from families that had never applied for assistance.

One of the aims of the 1968 AFDC interview survey (6) was to test the hypothesis that in states having higher grant levels, recipients would have a higher standard of living. Eligibility restrictiveness and extent of services were also tested against the index comprising level-of-living factors, but differences were not significant. There were indeed measurable differences between higher and lower grant levels as compared to the several dimensions of family living. The smaller the cash grant level by family size, the greater the evidence of deprivation. As would be expected, southern rural deprivation was greatest. It is no wonder that money for survival needs is ranked first by clients as the most important of all the program services provided by the public agencies.

Health Care Services

With the passage of the 1965 amendments to the Social Security Act and the addition of Title XIX to this act, medical care for families with low incomes became one of the major services for which welfare departments are responsible.[1] The amount of federal funds now spent for medical care approaches the amount spent for cash payments. In 1968, $4.1 million were spent by federal and state governments for Medicaid services, and the monthly amount has been increasing rapidly. In most states the program is administered by public welfare departments. Where the program is administered by the department of health or by a combination of the two departments, financial responsibility is still under the welfare department, as is the responsibility for determining the applicant's eligibility.

Title XIX was designed to create a gradual revolution in the financing of health care for people with low incomes. While permitting any state to retain its old medical vendor payment program as late as June 30, 1970, or to initiate a new Title XIX program only slightly more comprehensive in scope and coverage than its old program, Title XIX states clearly that all states are expected to move toward the goal of providing comprehensive medical services to all medically needy individuals by July 1, 1975. The scope of coverage of the program was designed from its inception to provide a more comprehensive range of medical services than was covered by the

---

[1] This section has been drawn primarily from an unpublished paper prepared by Otto Reid, Branch Chief, Intramural Research, Office of Research, Demonstration, and Training, Social and Rehabilitation Service, U.S. Department of Health, Education, and Welfare, Washington, D.C.

preexisting program and to provide medical services to a broader range of individuals. The law required that coverage be extended immediately to all individuals receiving public assistance from any of the four federally supported programs, and it forbade restricting eligibility for medical assistance to otherwise eligible families on the grounds some states formerly used to deny eligibility for public assistance, such as insufficient length of residence in the state or "immoral" behavior of family members. The later 1967 amendments to the Social Security Act called for a cutback in the medical assistance income eligibility level by January 1, 1970, to income levels no higher than 133 percent of AFDC payments.

Rising costs and rising caseloads have aroused considerable public concern. Whereas the initial intent of the law stressed improving the health conditions of the poor, the current questions are about costs and about Medicaid as a financial mechanism, rather than on governmental responsibility for a delivery system of comprehensive services to improve the health of low-income populations.

There are numerous interesting accounts of the development of the Medicaid programs. Perhaps the most colorful is found in *A Sacred Trust* (30), which first appeared as a series of four articles in the *New Yorker*. Another documentary report is a history of the development of California's Medi-Cal program prepared by Greenfield (26).

Several earlier writings on Medicaid's beginnings are available: an analysis by Burns (7) of Medicare and Medicaid, Somers (69) on the potential of Medicaid, a study (48) of state response to Medicaid provisions, and several committee reports (1, 77) on fiscal and administrative issues. The programs not only differ among the states, with some states waiting until the deadline to submit their plans, but also changes in the approved and operating state plans result in a constantly fluctuating national program. Most of the recent changes are cutbacks to hold down the mounting costs.

Health care utilization. A considerable body of research is available on utilization of health care services by the poor and the extent of services obtained through welfare medical programs including Medicaid. One of the first steps in most inquiries on the utilization of health care services is to examine the level of knowledge of low-income families as to the availability of medical care. Public assistance recipients are more knowledgeable about health resources (80 percent) than eligible Medicaid recipients not receiving assistance (60 percent) (92). Only 8 percent of welfare recipients mentioned a Medicaid program as a source of health care. Resources were described as a "county hospital" or a specific clinic.

Poor families are more likely to know about hospital care for the acutely ill than they are about preventive care or free medical examinations (62). In several studies recipients could identify places where medical care was delivered, but few knew about financing sources (34, 35). That is, Medicaid as a special program was not recognized by its name.

In one study (34) 40 percent of non-AFDC recipients interviewed in 1967 did not know of the existence of the Medicaid program, while another 14 percent misunderstood the program. Although 98 percent of AFDC recipients were enrolled in the program and more than 90 percent had received some medical care paid for by the program, public assistance recipients did not distinguish Medicaid as a special program because they appeared to consider it within the context of the welfare department.

In brief, most welfare recipients know where to go if medical care is available but are not aware of the distinctions in financing and program auspices. Those who are eligible but are not welfare recipients are unlikely to get free care unless they are sophisticated about community programs that make such care possible.

Studies that bear on utilization of health services by public assistance recipients indicate that the welfare population makes more use of health care services than do medically indigent individuals (9). For instance, among active cases 86 percent had utilized health services recently while only 74 percent of the denied cases had utilized health services. Persons denied public assistance constitute a comparatively poor group and form part of the continuum—on welfare, denied welfare, never on welfare, and never applied but medically indigent. Similarly, the study of two California cities (92) found visits to physicians and dentists made by 18 percent of welfare recipients during a two-week period as compared to 13 percent of nonrecipients who made such visits during the same period. The New Haven study (34) also found less utilization of health services among poor families not receiving welfare, despite the fact that reported morbidity was equally high for the two groups. Here Medicaid paid for use of health services for 85–90 percent of the welfare families but only 10–20 percent of the nonwelfare medically indigent families.

Although the number of cases was few, in a research demonstration project (58) there was a greater tendency for recipients with higher grants to have seen a physician during the preceding six months for preventive purposes than for the control families receiving the regular financial grant to have done so. This is illustrative of the repeated though fragmentary evidence that better grant levels free the recipient for access to other community resources.

From these available studies and review of the current program statistics of the National Center for Social Statistics, it appears that Medicaid is paying more money for health care for more low-income individuals than was paid under the former medical assistance programs, that the number receiving care is continually increasing, and that medical payments reach twice as many

welfare recipients as nonwelfare medically eligible recipients. Although fewer Medicaid recipients are not on welfare, the total amount spent for the nonwelfare recipients is actually higher. This indicates that nonwelfare medical service recipients use the resource less for small bills, deferring its use until there is a serious or costly illness.

State comparisons in utilization show that usage of medical services is even more likely when a state has a more extensive program. The broader the services offered, the greater use that is likely to be made of them.

Attitudes toward and perceptions of health care services. The research evidence to date does not bear out the claims that the poor health status of low-income families is due to their ignorance about or lack of motivation concerning health or health care services. On the whole they perceive their health status as lower than families with higher income levels perceive theirs to be, they are aware of the consequences of poor health, and they recognize their health problems even if they do not always attend to them. They tend also to be interested in health care services and to use them when possible.

A number of studies have reported on the importance assigned to health matters by low-income families. In a national study of 11,623 AFDC recipients (6), 25 percent of the respondents mentioned poor health as the most adverse factor affecting their lives. (The majority, however, as expected, mentioned lack of a job, money, or income.) Along the same line, a national public opinion survey (29) indicated an even greater value placed on good health. Fifty-nine percent of urban ghetto Negroes and 72 percent of rural Appalachian whites thought health was more important than a good job, compared to 51 percent of the general population.

Poor health, health problems, sickness during the preceding six months, and other indications of health difficulties were reported for from 25 to 40 percent of low-income households, as reflected in a number of studies (19, 22, 34, 58, 67). The local study by Olson (58) suggests the hypothesis that continued improvement of the health of public assistance recipients may depend more on adequate grant levels than on increased health services. As increasing evidence is gained about use of health services by recipients, it becomes clear that insufficient money for food and high rents for ghetto housing may actually retard the gains made by improvements in the delivery of health services. For example, Olson found somewhat fewer days of illness reported for the experimental recipient group, which had higher grants, but the same level of medical service utilization. In at least three local studies (34, 67, 92) in which comparative populations were included in the sample, AFDC mothers were more likely to report health problems in the family than were mothers of low-income families not on welfare.

Income seems to be the key to solution of most of the problems of the poor—translatable into health, proper living arrangements, developmental opportunities for the children, and even life satisfaction.

Factors affecting health care use. The National Center for Social Statistics gathered information from all fifty states for the quarter ending September 30, 1968, on the use of various social services by recipients in the adult categories (86). Health care was by far the service most frequently used by this group of 298,000 cases. Of the cases receiving any service, 55 percent had received health care services. In the AFDC national interview study (6), when asked whether "anyone from welfare helped you in any way," more than half the families (52.5 percent) said they had received help from the welfare department in getting medical or dental care. This was by far the most commonly reported service. (Help with education and training for children was reported by only 21 percent of the group.)

In some of the small-sample local studies the same results are found—health services

are the most commonly used of the various services made available to recipient groups. It was also noted that use of health services is likely to be underreported both by caseworkers, who routinely see that recipients take advantage of health resources, and by recipients, whose recall of events over time is likely to omit some clinic visits.

In cities where medical care is generally available, such as New York City, almost all female family heads checked medical or dental care as a service they felt people on welfare could get from the welfare department. Only some 15–25 percent of the respondents indicated that they would not ask their caseworker about such services if they wanted medical care in the future. About one out of every five respondents said that an appointment for medical care had been made for them by their caseworker. It would appear that public welfare caseworkers are active and alert in getting recipients to medical care resources and that some clients are familiar with available resources and find their own way there without any need for assistance.

When AFDC recipients in the nationwide study (6) were asked if they could get medical care when needed, 84 percent felt that most of the time they could. The most common reason for not getting care was lack of money ("couldn't afford to go"). There was considerable variation associated with urban-rural and welfare statuses and with the characteristics of the particular state's Medicaid program. More urban than rural respondents felt they could get medical care when needed most of the time. Eighty-seven percent of the poor currently on welfare felt they could get medical care, 84 percent of former recipients thought they could, but only 75 percent of applicants denied assistance felt they could. Perceived availability of and access to health service follow the same pattern as the research findings on utilization of health services. This is true even when the Medicaid status of the recipient's state of residence is considered. Perceived availability of medical care was highest for respondents living in states that covered all categories of poor people, intermediate for those living in states covering only public assistance and categorically related recipients, and considerably lower for respondents living in pre-Medicaid states. In the New York–New Jersey AFDC study (9) conducted prior to Medicaid, 21 percent of all respondents stated that during the previous year someone in the family needed medical care but the family did not have the money to meet this need. For dental care the figure was 40 percent and for needed eyeglasses, 29 percent.

The New York City health survey mentioned previously (62) cited the problem of child care for the time required to see a doctor as respondents' most frequent reason for not going to one when there was illness in the family. Twenty-one percent reported waiting periods of less than two hours, but 28 percent reported they had to wait four or more hours. Twenty-five to 30 percent reported doctors and health personnel were rude to them or that they were prejudiced against "welfare people."

Studies reinforce the assumption that poor people continue to use resources similar to those they used before Medicaid (i.e., clinics or county hospitals), even though private resources are supposedly available as alternatives. Findings in various studies are divided as to clients' attitudes about differences in treatment with respect to private physicians and public medical facilities. Results are also unclear as to differences between the treatment given the private patient and the Medicaid patient. Distance as an obstacle to the use of health service turns up in studies only indirectly, since recipients tend to report use primarily of neighborhood clinics.

Health facilities. One of the expectations of the Medicaid provisions was that the poor would have increased choice as to where they could go for health care. A number of studies indicate that the poor continue to select the county clinics or hospitals previously used and have not sought

out private physicians or private hospitals. In the California study of two low-income cities (92) it was found that the majority of respondents had made their contacts with county facilities prior to Medicaid. More than 80 percent of public assistance recipients had prior experience with county or city facilities, compared with 60 percent of the medically indigent nonwelfare poor. However, among the nonindigent nonwelfare poor, only 40 percent had prior contacts with these governmental health facilities.

Kisch and Gartside (35) found that 88 percent of their public assistance recipients considered the county facilities as their usual resource for all medical care. There was some indication that recipients' use of county facilities declined during the first months of Medicaid operation but that the rate of use slowly recovered to 95 percent of the pre-Medicaid level in a short while. Among the few who used other resources, differential quality of medical care was seldom mentioned as a reason.

In a study of 2,179 welfare mothers in New York City conducted in 1966 after the initiation of Medicaid (22), about 76 percent reported usually going to hospitals and clinics—39 percent used emergency room service and 37 percent used clinics. Of another 21 percent who made use of a doctor, only half went to a private physician. When asked what they did when not feeling well, a sizable proportion reported they went to a drugstore and asked the druggist what to take for their illness—40 percent of Negro respondents, 36 percent of Puerto Ricans, and 30 percent of other whites.

Ratings and preferences of the poor regarding sources of medical and physicians' services indicate no strong prejudices. The private specialist is rated highly (29), but the neighborhood doctor is often rated less favorably than the clinic at a major hospital. Most of the poor report they preferred the clinic to a private physician, but their major complaints were long waits for service and the fact that doctors were often not available when needed. All groups are favorably inclined toward the private practitioner, with the more affluent groups giving him the highest preference.

Research in progress. Medicaid is a new and costly program. Research in progress on Medicaid should be mentioned since it suggests questions about all health care delivery systems. A major study is being directed by Edward Suchman and his colleagues at the University of Pittsburgh in collaboration with the Social and Rehabilitation Service of HEW. This research is aimed at examining what, if any, impact has been made by Medicaid on the delivery of health care services to the poor. To what extent and in what way are health facilities being reshaped to do a more effective job? Is the program affecting physical arrangements, health service manpower, availability of requisite supplies and equipment, or organizational arrangements for health service delivery?

The multibillion-dollar annual costs of both Medicare and Medicaid generate considerable concern among administrators as to the possibility of alternative methods of providing health services or reimbursements for them that would permit equal or higher quality of health care at lower cost. Despite the concern of the government—the major source of reimbursement for medical care—little research is available to date on this important question.

Another major nationwide study on utilization of Medicaid services, also sponsored by SRS, is being conducted at the Columbia University School of Public Health. Partial findings are now available and appear to be reinforcing some of the results suggested in this brief review of local studies. In addition, a large poor population not eligible for Medicaid is being identified as greatly in need of medical help but unable to obtain such care. Planning for care of the medically indigent will constitute one of the major problems of the future. Unfortunately, such planning will likely be based on serious considerations of rising medical costs and limitations on expenditures that will direct what care can be made available to indigent groups by some type of categorical restriction.

Employment Programs for Welfare Recipients

During the last five years work experience and training programs for public assistance recipients have assumed major proportions in the United States. The purpose of this section is to review research assessing the impact of such programs.[2] Primarily the focus will be on programs for public assistance recipients and findings of research on program effectiveness and efficiency. Methodology will be discussed only as it influences the nature of the findings. The reader who is interested in methodological considerations will find that this area is well covered in a series of articles that have appeared in *Welfare in Review* (4, 11, 37, 39, 42). Similarly, only passing attention will be given to the issues underlying the employment potential of AFDC women. A good analysis of these matters may be found in an article by Carter (10).

The Economic Opportunity Act of 1964 (EOA) provided for three major employment programs for the culturally and socially disadvantaged: the Job Corps, Neighborhood Youth Corps, and Work Experience and Training. The first two of these programs were targeted on youths; the third was aimed primarily at public assistance recipients, mostly the AFDC mother and father. The first part of this section will be focused on weighing the results of the Work Experience and Training Program (Title V). Consideration will next be given to the more recent and innovative

[2] This portion of the chapter was prepared by Abraham S. Levine, then Acting Chief, Research and Demonstration Division, Office of Research, Demonstration, and Training, Social and Rehabilitation Service, U.S. Department of Health, Education, and Welfare, Washington, D.C.

demonstrations for the disabled public assistance recipient. Finally, the significance of the new Work Incentive program will be considered.

Historical perspective. In 1961 AFDC–Unemployed Parents (AFDC-UP) was enacted to provide federal assistance to states that provided financial assistance to unemployed fathers. The presence of "employable" parents on welfare prompted Congress in 1961 to amend the Social Security Act to permit expenditures for AFDC-UP to be made in the form of payments for work. These amendments also encouraged states to adopt Community Work and Training (CWT) programs designed to offer more meaningful work experience and to help AFDC-UP recipients achieve economic independence. These amendments were the precursors of the greatly expanded federal involvement in work experience and training for disadvantaged groups in the much heralded War on Poverty that was launched with the EOA. AFDC-UP and CWT never achieved anything approaching universality of adoption. Only twenty-two states had AFDC-UP programs and only ten had begun CWT programs by the time the 1964 legislation was enacted.

Although there is little hard data available on CWT, whatever reports exist reflect disappointing results (45). Many reasons exist for this. For example, according to unpublished estimates by the Bureau of the Budget, about 90 percent of the funds were used for work payments (financial assistance), leaving little for such rehabilitative services as vocational training. Also, the provisions of the act favored the traditional social services associated with public assistance. Only 50–50 matching funds with states and localities were allocated for the administrative costs of CWT projects, compared with the three-to-one ratio (75 percent federal–25 percent state) to cover the costs of social services.

In two years the attitude of Congress toward training of and providing employment opportunities for the disadvantaged changed. Title V of EOA provided 100 percent federal financing, and funds many times in excess of those for CWT were made available. The intent was to make as many public assistance recipients and other disadvantaged people as possible economically independent by providing significant work experience and training.

Work experience and training. Several hundred million dollars were expended on the Work Experience and Training Program during the years of its operation. Several hundred thousand people, mostly public assistance recipients, participated. (The average marginal costs per participant ran a little over $1,000.) What were the results?

Perhaps one of the most fruitful ways of assessing Title V program effectiveness was developed by Bateman (4). His objective was not only to determine how effective the overall program was as it operated throughout the United States but also to uncover information that would result in program improvement. Basically his question was: What are the "best practices" to maximize program effectiveness?

First, Bateman reviewed the aggregate impact of about 250 projects throughout the nation on 115,000 trainees who had participated and had left the program for one reason or another. Of these, approximately 36 percent found employment, 13 percent completed training but did not immediately find jobs, and 5 percent went on to advanced training. These percentages account for only slightly more than half the participants. There were many reasons for the program's failure to produce a strikingly successful performance. For example, 10 percent of all trainees terminated because of illness or disability and another 4 percent because of lack of child care facilities. In addition, there were wide variations in outcome. In St. Paul, Minnesota, 70 percent of all trainees who terminated were employed. Along with such apparently highly successful projects there were those that made a poor showing if employment is used as the prime measure of success.

Analyses indicated that the factors that

explained the largest proportion of variation in project effectiveness were these: (1) the unemployment rate in the state in which the project was located, (2) the proportion of male trainees (the higher the better), and (3) the average age of trainees (the younger the better, generally speaking). These three variables were used as a basis for classifying projects in terms of relative effectiveness. Thus a project's effectiveness was judged within the context of these three factors as a basis for ascertaining what the best practices were. An evaluative questionnaire was developed to gather data to identify shortages of critical services and provide some crude indicators of administrative skill in providing such services.

Unfortunately, as a result of certain administrative changes such as the transfer of responsibility for training to the Department of Labor and gradual phasing out of Title V and phasing in of the Work Incentive program (to be discussed later), this methodology received little application. Nevertheless, if Title V is viewed as essentially a series of demonstration projects, much experience has been gained and considerably more information now exists from which to develop more effective programs for the disadvantaged.

In-depth studies. It is not always possible to measure program success in terms of an employment criterion. This point was brought home vividly in a doctoral dissertation by Akbar (2). The cases used in his study comprised 324 male heads of households who were interviewed in 1964 when they were in the AFDC-UP program and then again in 1967, when 275 of them had been in the Title V program for varying periods of time up to thirty-two months, following their transfer from AFDC-UP. These men were white and typically from families who had lived in the region for several generations. About 55 percent were 40 years of age or older. They had an average of 5.5 children, although most expressed a preference for 3 or fewer. About 75 percent of these men had finished less than eight grades of schooling, which was

no more than their own fathers had attained. In the seven-year period prior to 1964, only 12 percent of the original sample had been employed most of the time.

Over 80 percent were assigned to work experience only, mainly in construction work. Even so, the Title V projects in eastern Kentucky had more of a vocational training component than the preceding AFDC-UP program, which was frankly a work relief program. About 84 percent of these men also received either literacy training or high school equivalency education. Half of the grade school graduates had to be placed in adult basic education because they were functionally illiterate.

During the thirty-two months of the program's operation about 65 percent left for various reasons. Of these, 45 percent left for positive reasons—to take a job or to receive more advanced vocational training in another program. There was little relationship between length of time in the program and subsequent employment. The 11 percent of the terminees who went on to other kinds of vocational programs, however, tended to be the better educated ones who were able to avail themselves of high school equivalency training.

For those who eventually found jobs, the program served as an extended unemployment benefit program in the interim. It also served as a preparatory and referral agency for those who went on to more advanced training. For all others it provided a source of necessary income to many impoverished families without keeping the heads of households in forced idleness. The work these men did was useful and did not compete with private industry or displace other people from the labor force. Roads were repaired, rustic bridges were built, dilapidated schools were restored, and the region became more habitable. Moreover, the men liked the program. As a matter of fact, they liked it so much that they preferred it to all of the alternative kinds of employment that only three years before had looked good to them. The findings of this study suggest that a government works program, even if it only provides a sort of sheltered outdoor workshop, makes good sense in rural areas with depressed labor markets—especially for poorly educated older men who are not good candidates for migration.

Even in a good labor market area with a carefully selected group of AFDC mothers there can be serious impediments to employment. The objective of one Title V project in Los Angeles was to train AFDC women as teacher aides in child care centers (11). Although the mothers completed training and were considered qualified by any practical standards, most of them could not obtain such jobs despite labor market shortages because of middle-class biases and state licensing requirements. The result was that the majority of the mothers who completed Title V training went on for further education to qualify as certified nursery school teachers.

Cost-benefit analyses. The foregoing discussion was concerned with program effectiveness—how well a program achieves its objectives. Since the advent of the Planning-Programming-Budgeting System (PPBS), an additional question has been asked: What kind of return on investment is the program producing, or how efficient is it from a cost-benefit vantage point (38)?

In order to begin to answer this kind of question for the Title V program, a special kind of study was undertaken in Albuquerque, New Mexico (71). Two principal objectives of this research were (1) to conduct a comprehensive cost-benefit analysis of a local Title V project and (2) to use this experience to develop a model that could be used to estimate nationwide benefit/cost ratios and a methodology for a careful cost-benefit analysis of the spectrum of projects to be found in the Title V program or similar programs for disadvantaged populations. An important factor in the methodology is the measurement of sociopsychological benefits as well as economic benefits. The economic benefits as well as costs could be expressed in dollar terms and the relatively intangible benefits, in whatever terms were most meaningful.

The specific findings were that the Title V program, as it operated in a slack labor market area such as Albuquerque, would pay for itself in less than five years and even sooner in a tight labor market area. Also, the program resulted in measured improvement in the trainee's self-esteem, family functioning, and motivation or readiness for employment. The occupation the client was trained for made the greatest difference in realized economic benefits. In other words, careful planning was needed to train as many clients as possible for better paying jobs for which there was a community demand.

The Albuquerque Title V project, although it was located in a poor labor market area, had much in its favor: It was well managed and the program had built into it good vocational training components, from job preparatory counseling and instruction in an established technical vocational institute to job development and placement services.

Even as projects vary in effectiveness, so they vary in efficiency as measured in economic cost-benefit terms. This was demonstrated in another study in eight different locales throughout the country (6). Interestingly enough, states that pay less than 100 percent of need show better performance in terms of proportions of former trainees working than do other locales. This phenomenon has been noted before among AFDC mothers who go to work even without the services of a Title V program (14). Dire necessity and survival needs seem to serve as strong prods for those recipients who can possibly go to work. Whether an affluent society should use such methods for its disadvantaged citizens should be seriously questioned, however. Recent legislation attempting to provide the carrot instead of the stick will be discussed later.

Overall, Title V trainees had a higher average monthly income than the comparison group ($14 higher). Persons who benefited most from the training in terms of employment tended to be those who were able to discharge their family responsibilities better, were healthy, had some work experience prior to entrance into the training program, completed the Title V assignment, had more education, and had been employed previously at higher level jobs.

In addition to increased employment and monthly income among Title V trainees, a number of intangible benefits were noted. Title V trainees perceived more improvement in their total family situation than did the comparison group, which they attributed largely to the increase in employment. The training and its consequences also contributed to heightened self-esteem and to a lessening of feelings of alienation among the trainees regardless of whether there was any change in their work or welfare history.

Although the results of this study were consonant with those obtained in Albuquerque in pointing to economic benefits in excess of costs for the Title V program, such benefit/cost ratios were not nearly so impressive as those obtained by Somers (68) in his analysis of a Manpower Development and Training Act (MDTA) project. His study was based on data gathered in interviews with 373 Connecticut workers who were involved in retraining courses. The benefits of retraining were assessed by comparing postretraining employment of blue-collar workers who completed the courses with the experience of workers who did not enter or did not complete the program. The population comprised men who typically had been blue-collar workers with a stable job history and who had been laid off because of technological advances that had made their previously acquired skills obsolete. They were typically better educated than public assistance recipients and did not suffer from the so-called multi-problem syndrome that characterizes the lives of many welfare clients. For the most part, all that the MDTA trainees needed was vocational retraining and jobs.

Rehabilitating disabled recipients.
What happens when an employment-oriented program for welfare clients includes special components such as careful screening and a full battery of services by a team of skilled specialists? This situation is best exemplified by a series of about thirty demonstration projects sponsored by SRS that were designed to demonstrate new ways to rehabilitate disabled welfare recipients. Special attention was given to early identification of those who were disabled, sound criteria for choosing those who could best be served, techniques for motivating them, closer teamwork between rehabilitation and welfare agencies, and development of models to determine costs and benefits of the program.

A comprehensive report (19) was prepared analyzing data on outcomes of fourteen of these projects. Of 7,694 applicants in the fourteen projects, 2,786 (36 percent) were accepted for services and complete data were available on 2,614 of them. Of these, 56 percent were men, 44 percent women; 62 percent were white, 26 percent Negro, and 11 percent Latin American. Their ages ranged from under 20 to over 60, with 90 percent spread rather evenly between 20 and 60. They had an average of eight grades of schooling. Prior work experience had been mostly in the low-skill areas. About 77 percent reported no full-time work during the year before referral, and over half reported none for three or more years. About 44 percent were on AFDC. In all, about 72 percent were receiving some form of public assistance. All of those accepted were disabled in addition to being economically dependent. These disabilities included psychiatric problems and mental retardation as well as physical disabilities.

Of the 2,614 cases for whom complete data were available 44 percent were closed as rehabilitated, 22 percent were closed without having been rehabilitated, and another 34 percent, some of whom would doubtless become rehabilitated, were still being served at the time of the study. Only 6 percent of the 1,146 clients whose cases were closed as rehabilitated indicated that they were unemployed after their case was closed, compared with 78 percent who had been unemployed before entering the program.

The AFDC group, which received more public welfare services than persons in other public assistance categories, had a better rehabilitation rate than any other public assistance group. However, it was not possible to tell from the data whether or how welfare services affect rehabilitation outcome. With regard to rehabilitation services, it was ascertained that those who were rehabilitated received more of these services than those who were not. The data also indicated that in the population studied whites needed more major medical attention and Negroes more job training or retraining.

Average increase in weekly earnings after successful rehabilitation was $46, with men and those with higher educational attainment gaining the most. An average reduction of $48 in monthly welfare payments per client was attained. Using this as a measure of benefit, the average cost of providing services ($561 for each case rehabilitated) would be recouped within a year. Even if the costs of the services for all those who were not rehabilitated were added (an average of $502 per person), the "payback" period in terms of reduced welfare payments would be less than two years. However, the real gain to society and the client came from the $46 increase in weekly earnings, which over the working lifetime of the client would be many times the average cost of services. The authors concluded that a vocational rehabilitation program for disabled public assistance recipients was a worthwhile investment.

A few words should be said about how costs were computed. These costs reflected only the extra items—what the client would not otherwise have received as a public assistance recipient. These included such treatment costs as diagnostic services, surgery, prostheses, hospitalization, training and materials, tools, licenses, and equipment. In many instances some of these services, such as hospitalization, were provided at no cost to the project. There was also wide variation in costs per individual case, which ranged from a few dollars to over $7,000.

It should also be pointed out that a certain amount of "creaming" took place in accordance with a number of criteria used by the vocational rehabilitation specialists to select those clients who were most apt to benefit from the services. Such practices can be defended as making excellent sense from the vantage point of governmental investment, since even in an affluent society there are many programs competing for that scarce commodity, the dollar. Should programs dip deeper and deeper below those most likely to benefit, a progressively smaller economic return can be expected. If legislative policy directs that job-training programs really dip deeply into the hard-core segment, then a more nearly precise measure of economic benefits and an attempt to evaluate human gains (which should include measures of self-esteem and family functioning) become important.

New legislation. Legislation requiring such training has, in fact, been enacted. The social security amendments of 1967 call for a new program to enable AFDC recipients to acquire work skills and to find employment. The Work Incentive (WIN) program for which the legislation provides promises to dip progressively more deeply into the caseload to reach hard-core recipients. Hopefully this new program will incorporate the "best practices" of the more successful projects in the Title V program it is designed to supersede.

An amendment that is in a sense complementary to WIN requires that the states, effective July 1, 1969, disregard all of the earnings of any child receiving AFDC if the child is a full-time student or a part-time student who is not employed full time and also disregard the first $30 a month in the family income earned by persons other than such a dependent child (plus one-third of all additional income earned in the month). The intent of such legislation is to provide a work incentive for public assistance recipients.

Research is currently (in 1969) under way, both in the Department of Labor and in HEW, designed to evaluate the effects of the WIN program and the impact of the earnings exemption provisions on the work response of AFDC recipients under varying conditions of amounts of welfare grants and quality of labor markets.

Social Services in Public Welfare

The 1962 social security amendments provided for the first time legislation and federal funds for social services to public assistance recipients, both past and potential. The 75 percent matching provisions under open-ended appropriations were contingent on the gradual reduction of caseloads to meet a standard of sixty cases per worker. Regardless of the controversy over the objectives to be achieved through this service program, the step represented a dramatic change in the philosophy of administration of cash payments to needy eligible recipients. Service delivery and money payments were companion parts of agency responsibilities, especially for the AFDC program. Some states, especially urbanized ones, had been developing service programs, but for most of the states the introduction of social services was a new venture.

Service provisions were linked to reduction of caseloads for the purpose of providing a range of services defined as prescribed and optional. Consequently an increase could be expected in public welfare personnel—caseworkers as well as program specialists and supervisors—and in the number of persons engaged in staff development and training. Between 1962 and 1966 caseworkers in public welfare agencies across the country increased 40.5 percent, from 37,820 to 53,100. Other professional and administrative employees increased 51.5 percent, from 47,062 to 73,300. The 1962–66 period was considered primarily as a tooling-up phase for expansion of existing programs or introduction of new ones where none had existed.

An understanding of the basis for the development of social services in public welfare is essential to today's research issues, which question the effectiveness of social welfare service programs for low-income and welfare populations. The two basic questions researchers should have answered before an effectiveness or efficiency design could be drafted have never been settled. First, what proportion of the time of the increased numbers of public agency social workers was allocated to social service programs? Second, what objectives were to be achieved?

The first question has been blurred by attempts to classify as services a mixture of activities such as general clerical work, eligibility determination, issuance of special need checks, or obtaining child support payments. Even fraud investigation has been classified as service by some on the basis that client protection is also included in such investigations. The required quarterly home visit has served as the main medium for service. The service objectives on which evaluation should be based were never specified. Is casework supposed to lift recipients out of poverty, off the tax-supported programs? What social service programs have their own specific long-term goals and more immediate objectives? Which are supportive or facilitating for other, perhaps intervening, objectives such as educational gains, employment training, or effective recipient use of medical care? How do such corrective or rehabilitation objectives link with long-range goals?

The intent of providing social services to public assistance recipients was initially described in the 1956 authorization as having an emphasis on strengthening family life, coupled with achieving self-support and self-care. The concept of rehabilitation was incorporated in the 1962 amendments with the phrases "to retain capability" and "attain maximum self-support and personal independence."

In 1969 the federal regulations defined the full range of services in AFDC as follows: services to a family or any member thereof for purposes of preserving, reuniting, or strengthening the family and such other services as will assist members of a family to attain or retain their capability for maximum self-support and personal independence. Child welfare service objectives were defined separately, but provisions require a single organizational unit at state and local levels to provide or supervise all services to families and children.

Presently there are no national research studies or official reports that offer a systematic assessment of the service programs resulting from the 1962 service amendments. Only three data sources of national scope are available: quarterly statistical reports on social services by HEW's National Center for Social Statistics, a report to the Bureau of the Budget (89), and a series of federally sponsored state administrative reviews in 1966 that were quite comprehensive but which have never been brought together in one integrated report (88).

At the national level continued development of PPBS is beginning to yield some gross outlines for analytical evaluation, but the dearth of relevant data for such a broad-scale evaluation will impede progress along that line for some time. The service statistics available are in counts of service cases and frequency of service attention by twelve areas of service, for example, health care, protective service to adults, improving family functioning. Determination of the outputs and outcomes of the total delivery system is further complicated by the fiscal entrapment of the various federal matching formulas, grant-in-aid policies, and state differences in options provided in the non-mandatory services.

A number of nationwide public assistance population surveys have included several items on social services (6, 20, 23). Otherwise, local studies provide most of the available information about services (21). Child welfare as a special field is handled as a separate chapter in this monograph, although the public welfare social services are now referred to as child and family services. Since the development of a new administrative unit on community social services at the federal level, a better integration of public welfare services can be

expected. Also, as new legislation is developed for improved financial assistance to families, attention will undoubtedly be given to new legislative provisions for social services, including new financing and delivery patterns. On the other hand, with the paucity of positive results from the meager investments directed to research on or study of the effectiveness of social services in public welfare, there could be a drastic change in policy whereby service money is shifted to improving money payments as a choice in keeping costs down.

Available research results. Research reports on social services in public welfare would include the following: (1) research-based findings about the nature, need, and characteristics of the various target groups, (2) consumer research and client perceptions about services, (3) research about a conceptual framework for, typology of, and definition of services, (4) research about the nature and effectiveness of services, and (5) research about delivery mechanisms, methods of service provision, and organization of services. The first category has been fairly well covered earlier in this chapter. The fifth, organization and delivery of services, has only recently attracted research attention and there are at this date still no results to report from the studies now in progress—on neighborhood service centers; use of subprofessionals; experiments with the team approach, crisis service units, or self-support service; and similar small-scale innovations. This section will therefore deal briefly with the other three categories.

Consumer reaction to social services in public welfare. The idea of seeking service preferences and reactions from poor people who receive services paid from tax revenues is quite recent. Antipoverty programs emphasized participation of the poor; new regulations in public welfare now require some recipient participation. Model Cities programs represent another kind of social service for which program guidelines require target area resident participation in the planning of programs to serve them.

At present there is no systematic evaluation of the impact of consumer influence on the shape and delivery of services. One of the frequently stated objectives of neighborhood service centers is to achieve involvement of the residents to be served in shaping policy and service delivery to best meet the needs of the neighborhood population (56). What little is known about participation of neighborhood residents in such endeavors indicates that only a small percentage of the more vocal poor are conveying their opinions and desires to the management of these decentralized service centers.

The perception of welfare mothers as service-consumers and of their preferences as to priority, auspices, or type of delivery has hardly been considered in programming. Yet there is ample evidence to indicate that effective utilization of social services depends on the interest and motivation of the recipient.

Society's perception of what services clients want is evidenced in the absolute surprise expressed on the part of the general public by the findings of the New York City survey (93)—that 70 percent of the AFDC mothers studied wanted a job and preferred working to receiving assistance. In the recent evaluation (19) of a joint endeavor to set up decentralized employment counseling centers, the demonstration was found to have bogged down because of the unexpected volume of applicants and a consequent inability to handle the requests for help. Other research has indicated that the first interest expressed by clients is for a source of income and that work is the expected source. In the Baltimore study (67), 40 percent of the mothers said at entry into the welfare system that they expected to be off welfare in six months, meaning that employment would then be their source of income. Reasons for case closings in AFDC statistical reporting also provide evidence that employable women do find jobs on their own, since about half of the closings are due to ineligibility because of income from employment. This percentage of self-determined exits from the welfare system greatly exceeds the percentage routed through training programs. It should be pointed out, however, that research-based information that would compare client-managed employment placements with agency job-training placements as to wage levels and subsequent reentry into the welfare system does not exist.

Consumer preferences for social services must at this time be inferred from the results of a number of studies that were not by purpose designed to investigate consumer services or reactions in any depth. Some inferences about the consumer's point of view can thus be drawn from research findings, but others must be inferred from repeated themes in demonstration project reports and other sources. The priorities given are the following:

1. Money. The need for a job is linked with the money request since employment is considered by the great majority of recipients to be the preferred source of money.

2. Medical services. Serious illness is a major problem in the families of public welfare recipients, according to numerous studies showing the ability of these families to utilize and appreciate good medical care.

3. Housing. The first two consumer priorities are linked with enough money to pay for housing, which is never budgeted by the welfare agency at market costs. Moreover, rental costs must often be taken out of the food allotment (84).

4. Crisis assistance. Clients report being helped when workers give prompt response in a crisis or emergency—e.g., a lost or stolen welfare check or runaway child. Other acts judged to be especially helpful were direct intervention by workers with creditors; help in referrals to other agency resources, training programs, and medical or dental services; school contacts to help a mother with a child's school problems or provision of extra money to meet specific school expenses; help in obtaining better housing; direct intervention with landlords

who refused to make necessary repairs; helping the parents of an arrested youth to plan for his future release on probation (47).

In general survival needs come first in preferred assistance—immediate, concrete help with daily living needs. Food, medical care, shelter, and supportive intervention with landlords, school authorities, police, or bill collectors in regard to eviction, a runaway child, or a lost or stolen welfare check constitute the first-line exigencies for which help is most needed and most appreciated.

Generally the research also indicates that until certain survival needs are met or until the families can operate with better control over crises, more sophisticated services are not likely to be utilized—unless there are broad changes in the total social-economic situation.

Such consumer priorities lead one to question the relevance of practice principles aimed at gradual facilitation of initial service relationships. Serious consideration must be given to the developmental levels at which extremely deprived recipients and other members of their families are able to function. Recognition must be given also to the limitations of agency service as one small resource affecting individual and social change. Under family conditions influenced by continual environmental harassment, maintenance services may constitute the major portion of agency services provided.

Conversely, not all families that are poor and dependent at some time in their life cycle can use *only* concrete, environmental types of help. Excellent casework support has been provided for mothers attending college and carrying out other long-range plans (51). This is also true for the motivated recipients who have a history of employment and are better able to organize their daily living requirements.

The foregoing generalizations about consumer priorities derive from the kinds of studies reported as examples in the remainder of this section. In one such study

it was found that when recipients take the initiative in contacting their caseworker for help, the primary reason for calling is financial matters (28). Eighty-five percent of a sample of 652 AFDC mothers tried to contact their worker at a time other than the regular visit. They wanted various bills paid, needed higher grants for rent, or requested money for purchases or repairs; 25 percent had requests about their checks or basic grants. Thirty-three percent included questions about changing doctors, Medicaid cards, or hospital care. Regarding social service needs, clients called about transportation, baby-sitters, nursery schools, children's camps, special shoes for school, employment, and personal problems, and for general advice. About half the clients in this study, in responding to the question: "What do you think we could do?" expected the caseworker to "grant special need requests more often" or help the respondent "get more money."

Other clues to clients' service expectations were found in the bylaws written by recipients for the council of clubs organized for employment training and placement readiness in the AFDC program in Albuquerque, New Mexico. Here the recipients had written their notions as to the caseworker's function. After several references to the caseworker's responsibility for communicating agency rules and resources, they added: ". . . and when we run into problems which we cannot handle, the caseworker should help us when we request or want her help."

In a nationwide interview study cited previously (6), the respondents (open AFDC cases) listed what help they would like from caseworkers in the following categories (listed here by frequency of response):

1. Food, shelter, clothing, heat, food stamps, or other necessities.

2. Employment.

3. Money or more money for no specific purpose.

4. Furniture, household items, repairs, television, telephone.

5. Health care services.

6. Education for children or aids to children's development—books, encyclopedias, camping opportunities.

7. Advice or counseling in regard to, for example, homemaking, budgeting, behavioral problems of children, marital problems, legal services, divorce.

8. No special kind of help but a desire for caseworkers to be more considerate and understanding—in general, in emergencies, or on special occasions.

Although the fragmented evidence to date appears to show that client preferences are primarily for concrete services or environmental assistance, such evidence derives from research with methodological problems that cannot be disregarded. There are numerous references in these studies to the "friendly chat" or discussions on certain subjects with the caseworker. Even highly verbal middle-class respondents have difficulty in answering such direct questions as: "Did your psychiatrist help you or what help did you expect from your marriage counselor?" A task-oriented service is more easily recalled, identified, and reported than fragments of counseling sandwiched between other activities and offered at several monthly or quarterly intervals by changing casework personnel. Client service preferences or wants can be solicited and stated only in relation to the clients' knowledge of or experience with service and their ability to communicate their problem situations or their aspirations.

Conceptual framework, typology, definition of service. The major problem of research on social services in public welfare is not the lack of standard methodology or research techniques. Rather, it is the depressed level of conceptualization that creates the primary research obstacle. Social service reporting has for decades been based on units identifying media such as the interview, office visit, home visit, telephone call, session, or contact. Such reporting presumably gives some measures of activity. Frequently activity is reported in relation to problems such as illegitimacy,

neglected and abused children, delinquency, or marital conflict.

Little analytical use has been made of the reporting of services in public welfare. One published account of services to the aged as reported by social workers from records indicates that 85 percent of the aged in this national sample received no public welfare social services (23). One cannot tell whether this figure merely reflects omissions in recording, because it appears that workers are likely to underreport specific items such as referrals or routine types of help and may selectively record only what is perceived as a more professional type of counseling such as an attempt to improve family relationships.

Feldman (21), in her report of an intensive service demonstration, also found considerable underreporting of services such as health referrals. Many workers claimed that medical referrals were routine and that they therefore were not reported as service. The confusion as to what constitutes a unit of service prevails throughout the field.

In a comprehensive monograph on rehabilitation of public welfare recipients in fourteen demonstration projects, one group of investigators used available reported service statistics in which fourteen types of services are reported (27). After analyzing rehabilitation outcomes by number of services provided, they suggested that chances of rehabilitation were not materially affected by the number or type of services offered by public welfare. One service that should have surfaced was child care provisions for the mothers in training, but the service-reporting systems did not distinguish among the different types of self-support services used.

Neither case records nor the present statistical reporting system provides adequate service data for the study of effects on special client target groups. Evaluation of social services becomes hazardous speculation without specific data-collection procedures established for the purpose of evaluation. Services reported by objectives or results achieved are absurd in the present approach to service accounting because of lack of clarity in units of activities that can be used for evaluative or accounting purposes.

The preliminary report of *Services for People* (87) has been widely circulated, but to date has not been prepared in final publication form. This report made no attempt to define services, develop categories of services, or clarify objectives that services attempt to achieve, although an illustrative list is offered to show the range and scope of services.

The United Community Funds and Councils of America has developed a glossary of services describing purpose and service elements in each type of service (12). Service categories include overnight camping, shelter care for children in an emergency, vocational counseling, use of visiting nurses, and a broad spectrum of other quite gross categories of service typically offered by United Fund agencies. Some of these categories might have relevance for public welfare studies.

Federal regulations (Title 45, Public Welfare) list mandatory services such as for employment, child care, foster care, prevention or reduction of out-of-wedlock births, family planning, and to meet specific needs of families and children (90). This listing is partially an ordering of objectives and partially a description of types of services. Optional service provisions are also a mixture of objectives and service components. State plans and guidelines vary greatly in the explicitness of the service definitions, and federal regulations on services seem to have generated fifty different sets of state interpretations and definitions of service categories.

One of the more significant contributions to this problem area is a short pamphlet, *A Conceptual Base for Defining Health and Welfare Services* (17). It represents a first step in specifying elements and dimensions of types of services. In this piece Elkin points out the need for improved definitions as essential to long-range planning, priority-setting, cost analyses, statistical systems,

studies of expenditures, definition of workload standards, and measurement of effectiveness, all of which should be viewed as related subsystems. Recently Elkin has further developed his thinking along these lines with a much-needed emphasis on the service delivery system and a refined specification of service objectives. For example, child care services are not viewed as being ends in themselves but rather as part of a program of services that support employment objectives for the mother, lead to broader child development goals, or pursue interim family functioning objectives. Still, much further work is needed in the development of conceptual frameworks that allow for evaluations and other studies of the social services.

There have been a number of attempts to cope with this serious gap in research development, but usually the coding and computers have moved faster than the rationales. There have been waves of popular schemes for collecting service data— e.g., family dysfunctioning and disorders, the service problem orientation of the 1962 amendments, the *Family Unit Register* of St. Paul (20), the target area approach of the antipoverty programs, and, more recently, systems approaches that aim to establish information systems without a full exploration of the state of social service data available. Discussion of the shortcomings in each of these approaches would extend this chapter too far beyond its permissible length. Moreover, the literature has given initial attention to these systems elsewhere.

Finally, other problems hampering progress are the lack of specific funding sources for the research investment needed to finance this kind of developmental work and the absence of a strong demand for improved service reporting. For those who say specification of objectives and measurements of social services are not possible, the inference must be that no research methods are applicable.

Nature and effectiveness of social services in public welfare. There is an interesting linkage between differences in definitions of the social service programs in public welfare and research in such programs. In explanations of the nature of such service and its purposes, research directions are implied. The several examples that follow illustrate the effects on research evaluation of various definitions of public social service.

The California legislative report by Miller (51) on effectiveness of social service defines public welfare service by using a casework model and central concepts in casework practice. Evaluation is based primarily on client perceptions of "being helped." Matched pairs of workers and clients were interviewed some two or three months after the worker's home visit. The conclusions are discouraging about social services in public welfare agencies in at least this particular study in the state of California. Most clients could recall as helpful only services that were concrete or provided additional money or necessities. When home visits average thirty or forty minutes, usually occur but once in three months, and include eligibility redetermination, it would seem rather futile to expect marked behavioral change as a result of casework efforts.

In the Olson study (58), services other than casework were considered in an evaluation using an experimental design. Olson adds an additional dimension to her report—the cost of such services as medical, child, and psychiatric care. Her definition of service is not limited to a casework model in which the worker is the sole provider. All service programs—direct, procured, or purchased—are included in the evaluation.

The Wisconsin social service study (28) also defines public welfare social service within a social work model—direct service activities and interactions with the client that require knowledge and skill in the areas of social casework, social group work, and community organization. The study focuses on topics discussed between worker and client and explores client reactions,

attitudes, and opinions in regard to the service. Three types of social service activities are distinguished: (1) the provision of tangible items clients want, (2) general counseling and advice, and (3) specific advice or guidance regarding particular client behavior. The study points out that dependency and manipulation by the agency arise out of the discretionary distribution of special needs benefits. When clients receive these additional benefits they do not object; they like their benefactors and want to please them.

Thus when the social services are defined to include the procurement of concrete necessities not included in the grant, and when the caseworker is viewed as the sole agent of service delivery, the evaluation is focused on this perception of public welfare social service. In a concluding comment in the report, serious doubt is raised about the argument that services are imposed on clients because of their dependence on the worker for special needs. Evidence from these findings indicates that clients know how to refuse to do (or ignore) the things they do not want to do. Most clients want the service, although there are some who want to be left alone or may find the home visits bothersome.

Another interesting experimental service project, conducted in Mississippi (66), involved four groups of AFDC mothers. One group, with regular agency service and grant level, served as a control. The service variations provided for enriched service program, employment training, and increased grant levels. A final report on this study is not yet available, but progress reports indicate that increased money payments make a distinguishable difference, and there is question as to the value of attempting an enriched social service program or even employment training in locales where welfare recipients are living under seriously deprived conditions and where the community is unsympathetic to opening resources or developing jobs. Although this project includes social work services, it also views agency services in a broader framework that includes such additional services as medical and dental care, basic adult education, job training, and school costs for children (e.g., for meals, extra clothing, school supplies, youth club activities, transportation, homemaking classes, and diagnostic testing).

In a study of nearly 2,000 New York City recipients (93), questions were asked about the recipients' willingness to use service and their reported receipt of service. Service was categorized by topics of discussion between worker and client—e.g., children's education, behavior, or care; advice about marriage and birth control; medical and dental care (where to go for such care and the making of appointments for clients); help in finding a place to live; provision of extra money for clothing or household items; money management or where to shop; job training and job finding.

The most relevant service in terms of clients' perceptions of the welfare department and the caseworker was provision of special grants of money. Discussion about children was a service substantially related to favorable perception of the agency and the worker. Help in finding a place to live and help with medical and dental services were also positively associated with both receipt and use of service. Advice about money management and shopping was associated more with positive feelings about the agency's desire to help than with the receipt of service. Services relevant to return to self-support indicate a more positive association when related to male heads of AFDC families than to the AFDC mothers themselves.

Discussion of the children was linked with a favorable attitude toward the agency as well as with the expressed willingness of clients to ask for service. Birth control information was rated low as a desirable service.

There are a number of earlier studies based on the casework model and on assumptions that place a heavy burden on casework service for bringing about change in economic dependency or deviant behavior among poverty-level populations. For example, the service evaluation in *Girls at Vocational High* (50) depends on a limited counseling input to eliminate delinquency. Such ambitious objectives were no doubt written into the program purposes and accepted by the research investigators. Similar comments could be made about the public welfare service objectives inferred in *The Multi-Problem Dilemma* (5).

As evaluative studies are examined, it becomes clear that it is time to reassess the purposes of casework services offered welfare recipients and other low-income groups for whom problems identified for alleviation are complex and interrelated with other personal, family, and community or societal problems. When families are assaulted by daily living crises and forced to cope with incomes that are inadequate for bare maintenance, there are serious questions as to what behavioral changes can be set in motion without provision first being made for a decent level of living and access being provided to a range of social resources within the agency and the community. The traditional model makes the *worker* the agent for service delivery instead of the *agency*.

More recent approaches place emphasis on the total agency delivery system, a broad range of services and professional disciplines, a broad range of service personnel, and priorities in objectives to be achieved and target groups to be served. These approaches also deemphasize the end objectives of a specific service unit and lead to concerted efforts to achieve agency goals.

Along this line the recent "Guidelines for a Redesigned County Social Service System in Four Pilot Counties" (3) begins with definitions of service objectives and a service delivery system. The total agency inventory of services is so structured that some of the concrete services may be used as social utilities—some only during emergency or crisis periods, others programmed for continued or longer range service objectives. With this view of services, clients are not divided into caseload groups under a specific worker unless referred to the Master Service Unit as described in the guidelines. The study and achievement of service effectiveness in a delivery system approach demand reexamination of the practice of defining objectives for single units of service when the client's service program calls for a mix of service elements and units.

Many service objectives in public welfare are shared by a variety of other public and private institutions. The degree of attainment of defined service objectives is often not studied properly because the research design has been restricted to an evaluation of the public welfare agency's "input and output"—with no attention to objectives and services used by public welfare recipients that are the shared responsibilities of other service systems as well. Employment, housing, health, education, and public safety offer outlets for primary life objectives. Social services support and facilitate the opportunities and options offered through these institutions. The challenge for future research in public service, therefore, is to develop means to classify and observe service interface among institutions so that the levels of attainment of their shared objectives may be measured.

Summary

In preparing this review of research in the public welfare field, the writer has taken liberties in using documents and other materials that would not qualify as producing research-based empirical findings. At this time, however, research in public welfare is not of the same order as in child welfare or family services. The organization of services in any field, their financing, authority, and guiding social policy, all influence the level of the research that can be conducted and, even more basic, the kinds of research questions that can be posed. The current knowledge base for the public welfare arena has roots in guideline materials and program statistics as well as in research findings.

The last five years, since the completion of Mencher's chapter on research in public welfare for *Five Fields of Social Service* (49), have yielded a significant extension of our knowledge about the public welfare field. The next few years may bring about dramatic changes in what is now identified as public welfare. New research questions related to policy development or to policy consequences may be expected. Different federal program arrangements may also change the source and scope of social welfare research financing.

The unsolved social and economic problems of the kinds of people covered by these programs or new ones to follow are likely, however, still to be with us. For their sake the advance of knowledge is essential so that a sounder and more humane social policy may be developed. When this knowledge is missing there is no rational force to counterbalance the emotional influences that shape the political processes and the resultant social policy for social welfare programs in the 1970s and thereafter.

REFERENCES

1. Advisory Committee on Intergovernmental Relations. "Intergovernmental Problems in Medicaid." Washington, D.C.: U.S. Government Printing Office, 1968.
2. Akbar, Mohammad Ali. "The Work Experience and Training Program in Eastern Kentucky: Its Potentials and Limitations." Unpublished Ph.D. thesis, Brandeis University, 1968.
3. "American Public Welfare Association Guidelines for a Redesigned County Social Service System in Four Pilot Counties." Summary of Phase II of the contract between the American Public Welfare Association and the Department of Public Welfare of the Commonwealth of Pennsylvania, Vol. I. Washington, D.C.: American Public Welfare Association, August 28, 1969.
4. Bateman, Worth. "Assessing Program Effectiveness," *Welfare in Review*, Vol. 6, No. 1 (January-February 1968), pp. 1–10.

5. Brown, Gordon E. *The Multi-Problem Dilemma.* Metuchen, N.J.: Scarecrow Press, 1968.

6. Bureau of Social Science Research. "1968 National Interview Study of the AFDC Program." Report to the Social & Rehabilitation Service. Washington, D.C.: U.S. Department of Health, Education & Welfare, 1970.

7. Burns, Eveline. "Policy Decisions Facing the United States in Financing and Organizing Health Care," *Public Health Reports*, Vol. 81, No. 8 (August 1966), pp. 675–683.

8. ———. *Social Security and Public Policy.* New York: McGraw-Hill Book Co., 1956.

9. Burnside, Betty. "Report on Pilot Study of Family Living Conditions, Aid to Families with Dependent Children: Continued and Closed Cases, Denied and Accepted Applicants." Unpublished report to the Welfare Administration, U.S. Department of Health, Education & Welfare, July 1967.

10. Carter, Genevieve W. "Employment Potential of AFDC Mothers," *Welfare in Review*, Vol. 6, No. 4 (July-August 1968), pp. 1–11.

11. ———, and Staff. "Intramural Research in Social and Rehabilitation Service," *Welfare in Review*, Vol. 5, No. 8 (November-December 1967), pp. 10–18.

12. *Catalogue of Functional or Program Services Categories.* New York: United Community Funds and Councils of America, September 1968.

13. Coll, Blanche. "Perspectives in Public Welfare: 1865–1900." Washington, D.C.: Social & Rehabilitation Service, U.S. Department of Health, Education & Welfare, March 1966.

14. Cox, Irene. "Effects of an Earnings Exemption on Employment of AFDC Mothers." Unpublished working paper. Washington, D.C: Rehabilitation Service, U.S. Department of Health, Education & Welfare, 1968.

15. Davis, Martin, and Leuthold, Jane. "Formulas for Income Maintenance: Their Distributional Impact," *National Tax Journal*, Vol. 21, No. 1 (March 1968), pp. 70–93.

16. Durbin, Elizabeth F. "The Effect of Welfare Programs on the Decision to Work." Paper prepared for the Project Labor Market, New York University Graduate School of Business Administration, August 1968.

17. Elkin, Robert. *A Conceptual Base for Defining Health and Welfare Services.* New York: Family Service Association of America, 1967.

18. Eppley, David B. "OAA Recipients in 1965: Data from Recipients' Mail Reports," *Welfare in Review*, Vol. 7, No. 3 (May-June 1969), pp. 21–25.

19. *Evaluation of the Atlanta Employment Evaluation and Service Center and the Los Angeles County Vocational Rehabilitation Project for Community Depressed Areas.* New York: Greenleigh Associates, 1968.

20. *Family Unit Register.* St. Paul, Minn.: Greater St. Paul United Fund & Council, 1969.

21. Feldman, Frances Lomas. "Focus on Service and Setting: Evaluation of the Effectiveness of a Demonstration Project in a Public Welfare Agency." Sacramento: California State Department of Social Welfare, March 1968. Mimeographed.

22. Goodrich, Charles, and Olendzki, Margaret. "Impact of Medicaid and Medicare on Former Welfare Clients." Progress report to the Social & Rehabilitation Service. Washington, D.C.: U.S. Department of Health, Education & Welfare, 1969. Mimeographed.

23. Gray, Shirlene B. "OAA Recipients in 1965: Demographic and Program Characteristics," *Welfare in Review*, Vol. 7, No. 3 (May-June 1969), pp. 11–20.

24. ———. "OAA Recipients in 1965: Financial Circumstances," *Welfare in Review*, Vol. 7, No. 4 (July-August 1969), pp. 13–18.

25. Green, Christopher, and Lampman, Robert. "Schemes for Transfering Income to the Poor," *Industrial Relations*, Vol. 6, No. 2 (February 1967), pp. 121–137.

26. Greenfield, Margaret. "Medi-Cal: The California Medicaid Program." Case Study No. 8 of the Medical Care Administration. Washington, D.C.: U.S. Public Health Service, undated. Mimeographed.

27. Grigg, Charles, Haltmann, Alphonse G., and Martin, Patricia Y. *Vocational Rehabilitation of Disabled Public Assistance Clients.* Tallahassee: Institute of Social Research, Florida State University, 1967.

28. Handler, Joel F., and Hollingsworth, Ellen J. *The Administration of Social Services in AFDC: The Views of Welfare Recipients.* Madison: Institute for Research on Poverty, University of Wisconsin, April 1969.

29. Harris, Louis. "Living Sick: How the Poor View Their Health," *Sources*, Vol. 1, No. 1 (1968), pp. 21–36.

30. Harris, Richard. *A Sacred Trust.* New York: New American Library, 1966.

31. Harris, Robert. "Income Maintenance Systems," *Public Welfare*, Vol. 27, No. 1 (January 1969), pp. 45–51.

32. Hoos, Ida R. *Systems Analysis, Information Handling, and the Research Function: Implications of the California Experience.* Washington, D.C.: U.S. Department of Health, Education & Welfare, 1967.

33. *Impediments to Employment: A Reanalysis of Household Interview Studies.* New York: Greenleigh Associates, November 1969.

34. King, Carol. "Poverty and Medical Care," Vol. I. Master's thesis, Yale University, 1968. Mimeographed.

35. Kisch, Arnold, and Gartside, Foline. "Use of a County Hospital Outpatient Department by Medi-Cal Recipients," *Medical Care*, Vol. 6, No. 6 (November-December 1968), pp. 516–523.

36. Langner, Thomas S., et al. "Psychiatric Impairment in Welfare and Nonwelfare Children," *Welfare in Review*, Vol. 7, No. 2 (March-April 1969), pp. 10–21.

37. Levine, Abraham S. "Cost-Benefit Analysis and Social Welfare," *Welfare in Review*, Vol. 4, No. 2 (February 1966), pp. 1–11.

38. ———. "Cost-Benefit Analysis and Social Welfare Program Evaluation," *Social Service Review*, Vol. 42, No. 2 (June 1968), pp. 173–183.

39. ———. "Evaluating Program Effectiveness and Efficiency," *Welfare in Review*, Vol. 5, No. 2 (February 1967), pp. 1–11.

40. ———. "Research Review of Work Training Programs in Appalachia." Washington, D.C.: Social & Rehabilitation Service, U.S. Department of Health, Education & Welfare, 1968. Mimeographed.

41. ———. "Yesterday's People and Tomorrow's Programs," *Welfare in Review*, Vol. 7, No. 4 (July-August 1969), pp. 8–12.

42. Levinson, Perry. "Evaluation of Social Welfare Programs," *Welfare in Review*, Vol. 4, No. 10 (December 1966), pp. 5–12.

43. ———. "The Next Generation: A Study of Children in AFDC Families," *Welfare in Review*, Vol. 7, No. 2 (March-April 1969), pp. 1–9.

44. ———. "The Social and Economic Conditions Associated with the Rising AFDC Caseload in New York City," in *The Administration of Aid to Families with Dependent Children in New York City*. Report of a Joint Review Council by the U.S. Department of Health, Education & Welfare and the New York State Department of Social Services, September 1969. Mimeographed.

45. Levitan, Sar A. *Antipoverty Work and Training Efforts: Goals and Reality.* Ann Arbor, Mich.: Institute of Labor and Industrial Relations, 1967.

46. Lurie, Irene. *An Economic Evaluation of Aid to Families with Dependent Children.* Washington, D.C.: Brookings Institution, September 1968.

47. McBroom, Elizabeth. "Helping AFDC Families: A Comparative Study," *Social Service Review*, Vol. 39, No. 4 (December 1965), pp. 390–398.

48. *Medicaid: State Programs After Two Years.* New York: Tax Foundation, 1968.

49. Mencher, Samuel. "Public Welfare," in Henry S. Maas, ed., *Five Fields of Social Service: Reviews of Research.* New York: National Association of Social Workers, 1966.

50. Meyer, Henry J., Borgatta, Edgar F., and Jones, Wyatt C. *Girls at Vocational High.* New York: Russell Sage Foundation, 1965.

51. Miller, Dorothy. "Effectiveness of Social Services to AFDC Recipients." San Francisco: Social Psychiatry Research Associates, October 1968. Mimeographed.

52. National Opinion Research Center, "Welfare, Poverty and Racial Prejudice." Unpublished preliminary report, University of Chicago, 1968.

53. Nicol, Helen. "Guaranteed Income Maintenance: Another Look at the Debate," *Welfare in Review*, Vol. 5, No. 6 (June-July 1967), pp. 1–13.

54. ———. "Guaranteed Income Maintenance: Negative Income Tax Plans," *Welfare in Review*, Vol. 4, No. 4 (April 1966), pp. 1–9.

55. ———. "The Role of Economic Research in Public Welfare." Washington, D.C.: Social & Rehabilitation Service, U.S. Department of Health, Education & Welfare, September 1969.

56. O'Donnell, Edward J. "A Nationwide Inventory and Assessment of Neighborhood Service Centers." Washington, D.C.: Social & Rehabilitation Service. U.S. Department of Health, Education & Welfare, in progress.

57. ———, and Chilman, Catherine S. "Poor People on Public Welfare Boards and Committees—Participation in Policy Making?" *Welfare in Review*, Vol. 7, No. 3 (May-June 1969), pp. 1–10.

58. Olson, Irene. "Some Effects of Increased Financial Assistance and Improved Social Services for Families Receiving Aid to Families with Dependent Children Grants." Baltimore, Md.: Baltimore County Department of Social Services, November 1968. Mimeographed.

59. Orshansky, Mollie. "Counting the Poor: Another Look at the Poverty Profile,"

Social Security Bulletin, Vol. 28, No. 1 (January 1965), pp. 3–29.

60. ———. "Who's Who Among the Poor: A Demographic View of Poverty," *Social Security Bulletin,* Vol. 28, No. 7 (July 1965), pp. 3–32.

61. Pechman, Joseph A., Aaron, H. J., and Taussig, M. K. *Social Security Perspectives for Reform.* Washington, D.C.: Brookings Institution, 1968.

62. Podell, Lawrence. "Utilization of Health Services by Welfare Recipients: Basic Cross-Tabulations." Unpublished report to the National Center for Health Services Research and Development, 1969.

63. Rein, Martin. "Choice and Change in the American Cash Transfer System." Paper presented at the Income and Poverty Conference, prepared for the Academy of Arts and Sciences, Brookline, Mass., May 1969.

64. ———, and Miller, S. M. *1968 Manpower Report to the President.* Washington, D.C.: U.S. Government Printing Office, 1968.

65. "Report from the Steering Committee of the Arden House Conference on Public Welfare." Albany, N.Y.: State Board of Social Welfare, Spring 1968.

66. "Report on the Mississippi Project No. 381." University: University of Mississippi, in progress.

67. Shiller, Jeffry, Levinson, Perry, and Levine, Abraham S. "Characteristics of Accepted and Rejected AFDC Applicants in Baltimore, Maryland." Washington, D.C.: Social & Rehabilitation Service, U.S. Department of Health, Education & Welfare, 1966.

68. Somers, Gerald G. (ed.). *Retraining the Unemployed.* Madison: University of Wisconsin Press, 1968.

69. Somers, Herman M. "The Big Sleeper in the Medicare Law," *Medical Economics,* Vol. 43, No. 1 (January 24, 1966), pp. 110–123.

70. Therkildsen, Paul T., and Reno, Philip. "Cost-Benefit Evaluation of the Bernalillo County Work Experience Project," *Welfare in Review,* Vol. 6, No. 2 (March-April 1968), pp. 1–12.

71. ———, and Staff. "Final Report on Cost-Benefit Evaluation of the Bernalillo County, New Mexico, Work Experience Project." Albuquerque: University of New Mexico, Department of Economics, 1969. Mimeographed.

72. Tobin, James. "Raising the Income of the Poor," *Agenda for the Nation.* Washington, D.C.: Brookings Institution, 1968. Pp. 113–114.

73. U.S. Bureau of the Census. "Revision in Poverty Statistics," *Current Population Reports,* Series P-23, Special Studies No. 28. Washington, D.C.: U.S. Government Printing Office, August 1969.

74. ———. "Trends in Social and Economic Conditions in Metropolitan Areas," *Current Population Reports,* Series P-23, Special Studies No. 27. Washington, D.C.: U.S. Government Printing Office, February 1969.

75. U.S. Congress, Joint Economic Committee. *Income Maintenance Programs.* Hearings before the Subcommittee on Fiscal Policy, 90th Cong., 2d Sess., June 1968.

76. U.S. Department of Agriculture. *Food Consumption and Dietary Levels of Households in the United States,* ARS 626. Washington, D.C.: U.S. Government Printing Office, August 1957.

77. U.S. Department of Health, Education & Welfare, Medical Services Administration, Social and Rehabilitation Service. Unpublished report on detailed description of the fluctuating Medicaid programs of the various states as of December 1968. In progress.

78. U.S. Department of Health, Education & Welfare, National Center for Social Statistics, Social and Rehabilitation Service. "1961 AFDC Characteristics Study." Mimeographed.

79. ———. "1967 AFDC Characteristics Study." In progress.

80. ———. "1967 AFDC Study: Preliminary Report of Findings from Mail Questionnaire," Report AFDC-2 (67), January 1969. Mimeographed.

81. ———. "Program and Operating Statistics," *Welfare in Review,* Vol. 2, No. 6 (June 1964), p. 28.

82. ———. "Public Assistance Statistics," *Welfare in Review,* Vol. 7, No. 4 (July-August 1969), pp. 25–54.

83. ———. "Reasons for Opening and Closing Cases," Report A-5, December 1968. Mimeographed.

84. ———. "The Role of Public Welfare in Housing." A report to the House Committee on Ways and Means and the Senate Committee on Finance, January 1969. Mimeographed.

85. ———. "Service Programs for Families and Children," *Federal Register,* Vol. 34, No. 18 (January 28, 1969), pp. 1354–1363.

86. ———. "Statistical Report on Social Services," Report E-1, July 9, 1968.

87. U.S. Department of Health, Education & Welfare, Task Force on Organization of Social Services. *Services for People.* Wash-

ington, D.C.: U.S. Government Printing Office, October 15, 1968.

88. U.S. Department of Health, Education & Welfare, Welfare Administration. "Administrative Review of Social Services," 1966. Mimeographed.

89. ———. "The Implementation and Results of the 1962 Service Amendments to the Public Assistance Titles." Report to the Bureau of the Budget, November 1964. Mimeographed.

90. U.S. Department of Labor, Women's Bureau. *Background Facts on Women Workers in the United States.* Washington, D.C.: U.S. Government Printing Office, May 1967.

91. Warren, Martin, and Berkowitz, Sheldon. "The Employability of AFDC Mothers and Fathers," *Welfare in Review*, Vol. 7, No. 4 (July-August 1969), pp. 1–7.

92. Wood, Ralph, McDuff, Susan, and Dowd, Ronald. *Medical Care Resources and Utilization Among Low Income Families with Dependent Children.* Sacramento: California Medical Care Resources and Utilization Research Project, undated.

93. Yahr, Harold, Pomeroy, Richard, and Podell, Lawrence. *Studies in Public Welfare: Effects of Eligibility Investigations on Welfare Clients.* New York: City University of New York, 1969.

INDEX

Adoption, 15–33; application and selection, 16–17; follow-up studies, 20–40; postplacement contact, 17–18; practice implications, 32–33; "telling," 18–20

AFDC. *See* Aid to Families with Dependent Children

Agency, family service, 109–114; new directions, 112–113; needed research on, 113–114; organizational efficiency of, 110–111; service patterns in, 111–112

Agency, the, 158–162; family service, 109–114; function, 158–160; impact of, 180; program, 161–162; structure 160–161. *See also* Agency, family service

Aid to Families with Dependent Children: case mobility, 198–199; mothers, employability of, 200–202; population, 198–202; recipients, characteristics of, 199–200

Casework. *See* Family services and casework

Child care, institutional, 49–62; child and staff behavior, 54–56; deprivation, effects of, 50–54; follow-up, 56–58; institutional desegregation, 60; practice implications, 61–62; separation, effects of, 50–54; service delivery and staffing, 58–60

Child welfare, 13–69; adoption, 15–33; foster family care, 33–49; institutional child care, 49–62. *See also* Adoption; Foster family care; Child care, institutional

Children: adopted, emotional disturbance in, 24–28; adoption of, 15–33; in foster family care, 33–49; hard-to-place, 28–31; institutional care of, 49–62

Client, the, 133–157; group as, 154–157; identification and belongingness, 140–143; needs and interests of, 137–140; participation of, 134–137; special problems and populations, 140–154. *See also* Client populations; Group, the, as client

Client populations: aging, 149–150; family, 153–154; handicapped, 146–149; hard-to-reach, 143–146; preschool child, 150–152; school deviant, 152–153

Community, the, 162–167; community survey, 163; measuring need, 164–165; neighborhood organization, 165–166; participation of, 75–79; related neighborhood services, 166–167; selected social problems, 163–164

Community organization practice, 70–107; community participation, 75–79; decision-making in, 86–90; interorganizational linkages and relationships, 90–93; planning processes and issues, 71–75; practitioner, roles of, 98–102; research, prospects for, 102–104; social action strategies, 79–86; social services, structure and delivery of, 93–98. *See also* Community participation, Community organization practitioner, Planning, Social action strategies, Social services

Community organization practitioner, roles of 98–102; multiple role orientation, 102; planning styles, 98; process versus task role performance, 101; relationships, 101–102; role definition and practice outcome, 99–100; types of administrators, 98–99

Community participation, 75–79; groups other than the poor, participation of, 78–79; poor, the, participation of, 77–78; relative deprivation, 75–76; status inconsistency, 76–77; structural variables, 79

Decision-making: city council decisions, 88; in community organization practice, 86–90; Congress, the, influencing, 88–89; governor, relevance of, 87–88; group, 157; mayor and city manager, role of, 86–87; political issues, 89–90; setting financial goals, 90

Employment programs: cost-benefit analyses, 214–215; historical perspective on, 212; in-depth studies, 213–214; new legislation, 216–217; rehabilitating the disabled, 215–216; for welfare recipients, 211–217; work experience and training, 212–213

Family, the: black 122–123; cohesion in marriage, 123–124; foster, 33–49; multiproblem, 122; organization and disorganization of, 122–124; social policy and, 124–125

Family services and casework, 108–129; family organization and disorganization, 122–124; family service agency, the, 109–114; social policy and the family, 124–125; social work intervention, 114–122. *See also* Agency, family service; Family, the; Social work intervention

Foster family care, 33–49; coming into care, 34–38; foster care career, 34–38; foster

2M/71
2M/9/72